SHATTERED HOPES

SHATTERED
HOPES

Obama's Failure to Broker Israeli-Palestinian Peace

Josh Ruebner

VERSO
London • New York

First published by Verso 2013
© Josh Ruebner 2013

All rights reserved

The moral rights of the author have been asserted

1 3 5 7 9 10 8 6 4 2

Verso
UK: 6 Meard Street, London W1F 0EG
US: 20 Jay Street, Suite 1010, Brooklyn, NY 11201
www.versobooks.com

Verso is the imprint of New Left Books

ISBN-13: 978-1-78168-120-6

British Library Cataloguing in Publication Data
A catalogue record for this book is available from the British Library

Library of Congress Cataloging-in-Publication Data
A catalog record for this book is available from the Library of Congress

Typeset in Minion by Hewer Text UK, Edinburgh
Printed in the US by Maple Vail

To Mona, with love

Contents

Introduction

On January 22, 2009, the newly inaugurated President Barack Obama, in only the second full day of his term, made the short jaunt from the White House to the State Department to announce the appointment of former Senate Majority Leader George Mitchell as his Special Envoy for Middle East Peace. Flanked by former electoral rivals Vice President Joseph Biden and Secretary of State Hillary Rodham Clinton, Obama boldly asserted to a roomful of State Department employees, "It will be the policy of my administration to actively and aggressively seek a lasting peace between Israel and the Palestinians, as well as Israel and its Arab neighbors."

However, none of the four thought that this would be an easy policy goal to attain. Obama acknowledged "the difficulty of the road ahead." Biden termed the Israeli-Palestinian conflict one of "the most vexing international dilemmas that we face." Clinton admitted that the president's ambitious agenda "puts the pressure on everybody." And Mitchell, the veteran mediator whose marathon efforts helped broker the 1998 Good Friday Agreement, leading to the end of the conflict in Northern Ireland, was under no illusions that brokering Israeli-Palestinian peace would be any easier. "I don't underestimate the difficulty of this assignment," Mitchell remarked. "The situation in the Middle East is volatile, complex, and dangerous."[1]

By wading into the mire of the seemingly intractable Israeli-Palestinian conflict so "actively and aggressively" at the outset of his term, Obama was making good on a campaign pledge to tackle this issue differently than his two immediate predecessors, Presidents

George W. Bush and Bill Clinton. Speaking on the campaign trail in April 2008, the Democratic presidential candidate expressed his disagreement with the "habit of American presidents" who "in their last year, they finally decide, we're going to try to broker a peace deal."[2] This swipe at former presidents referred to the failed attempts of Clinton in 2000 at Camp David and Bush in 2007 at Annapolis to initiate negotiations under US auspices to resolve those "final status" issues—Jerusalem, refugees, settlements, borders, and water—that were deliberatively shelved during the interminable interim phases of the Oslo "peace process," launched in 1993.

Obama's high-profile appointment of Mitchell as his Special Envoy for Middle East Peace not only signaled the president's break from his antecedents' record of making a big push for Israeli-Palestinian peace late in their terms; it also heralded the fact that the Arab-Israeli conflict would hold a pride of place on the foreign policy agenda of an incoming US president in a way not witnessed since the Carter administration. Indeed, by twinning Mitchell's appointment to that of Ambassador Richard Holbrooke as the administration's Special Representative for Afghanistan and Pakistan, Obama was making clear that he placed as much emphasis on resolving the Israeli-Palestinian conflict as he did in managing America's longest-running war, and arguably even more so than on ending the US occupation of Iraq.

According to a leaked summary of an October 2009 White House meeting between General James Jones, Obama's National Security Advisor at the time, and lead Palestinian negotiator Saeb Erekat, the president prioritized Israeli-Palestinian peace above all other foreign policy issues. Jones told Erekat emphatically that "if President Obama could solve only one thing in the world, I'm sure he would choose the Middle East—not Afghanistan, not Iraq—but this. The two state solution will be the one thing he invests the most in to bring about justice and equality, not just for Palestinians, but this is in Israel's strategic interests as well."[3]

Obama's placing of Israeli-Palestinian peace at, or near, the top of his foreign policy agenda was a brave, if not audacious, high-stakes political gamble for a president whose only formal experience with US foreign policy derived from less than one full term in the Senate, where he served on the Foreign Relations Committee and chaired its

Subcommittee on European Affairs. It was especially so given that every president since Harry Truman had tried, to a greater or lesser extent, to resolve the Arab-Israeli conflict in general, and the Israeli-Palestinian conflict in particular, and failed. That Obama was willing to lay so much political capital on the line to prioritize resolving the Israeli-Palestinian conflict was a testament to his boundless optimism and confidence, his personal commitment to the issue, and his "sense of urgency" that in the aftermath of Operation Cast Lead— Israel's devastating three-week land, air, and sea attack against the Palestinian Gaza Strip, which ended just two days prior to his inauguration—the window for a two-state resolution to the Israeli-Palestinian conflict was rapidly shutting.[4]

There is no reason to doubt the sincerity of Obama's intentions. However, after initially exerting pressure on Israel to freeze settlement construction in the Palestinian West Bank and East Jerusalem, as Israel had agreed to do first in the 2003 Roadmap and then again at the 2007 Annapolis Peace Conference, and failing to obtain a meaningful freeze, it became clear that when Obama's political instincts were at loggerheads with his political calculus, the former would lose out to the latter, even when pursuing such a course was to the decided detriment of his agenda. Thus began an inexorable slide from a plausibly coherent and proactive strategy for achieving Israeli-Palestinian peace to a series of reactive and defensive measures that resulted in the United States being even less of an "honest broker" at the end of Obama's term than it was at the beginning.

PART I: US POLICY, 2009–2011

This book endeavors to dissect the anatomy of this painful policy failure by examining when, where, and why US policy toward Israel and the Palestinians went so abysmally wrong during the Obama administration. The first part of the book chronicles and analyzes US policy toward Israel and the Palestinians, preceded in Chapter 1 by an overview of Obama's engagement with this issue prior to his arrival in the White House. This chapter delves into Obama's intimate contacts with both a substantial Palestinian-American constituency while serving as an Illinois state senator, and liberal Jewish-Americans who opposed Israel's military occupation. With this background, the future president undoubtedly came into office with a deeper and more nuanced understanding of the Israeli-Palestinian conflict than any of his predecessors. However, despite his exposure, by the time Obama ran for the US Senate, it became clear that he was willing to sublimate his likely true feelings on this issue in order to advance his political career by taking more mainstream positions, despite revelatory offhand comments to the contrary. This chapter also covers how Obama as a presidential candidate approached the Israeli-Palestinian conflict. It concludes with an overview of how the Obama transition team dealt, or more accurately failed to deal, with Israel's controversial Operation Cast Lead and how congressional support for Israel's attack on the Gaza Strip significantly constrained his room to maneuver in response after his inauguration.

From his inauguration in January 2009 to his maiden speech at the UN General Assembly in September 2009, Obama and his foreign policy team displayed a more or less coherent and proactive strategic approach to resolving the Israeli-Palestinian conflict, a period which is the focus of Chapter 2. During its first nine months, the Obama administration focused on three areas. First, Mitchell and his team met with regional leaders on "listening tours" and reviewed US policy toward the Israeli-Palestinian conflict. Second, the administration wanted to consolidate the fragile cease-fire between Israel and Hamas in the aftermath of Operation Cast Lead by strengthening international efforts to interdict weapons flows to the Gaza Strip, providing significant pledges of foreign assistance to rebuild the devastated area, and urging Israel to loosen its comprehensive and crippling blockade. Third, and most controversially, the administration pressed Israel to fulfill its prior obligations to freeze construction of its illegal settlements in the Israeli-occupied Palestinian West Bank and East Jerusalem, which it persuasively argued would set the correct context for a resumption of Israeli-Palestinian negotiations.

If Obama had dug in his heels and insisted that Israel stop expanding its illegal settlements on Palestinian land, then it is plausible that he would have enabled successful negotiations to take place. However, his unwillingness to put meaningful pressure on Israel to do so doomed the effort, as he failed to even consider integrating sticks into his policy mix alongside the plentiful carrots he proffered to

Israel throughout his administration. On the sidelines of the UN General Assembly, Obama convened a trilateral meeting with Israeli Prime Minister Benjamin Netanyahu and Palestinian Authority President Mahmoud Abbas during which he offered the first of a series of humiliating climbdowns from his initial, public principled position on Israeli settlements. Henceforth, the United States would press the parties to return to the negotiating table immediately, preferably with, but if necessary without, Israel committing to refrain from gobbling up more territory ostensibly designated for the future Palestinian state. This significant volte-face by Obama indicated to Netanyahu that Israel and its supporters in the United States, by pushing back against the White House, could successfully frustrate the president's ambitions without consequence.

Having determined Obama's malleability, Netanyahu declared in November 2010 a unilateral ten-month "moratorium" on settlement expansion, a proposal so shot full of holes as to render its implications on the ground utterly meaningless. Nevertheless, Hillary Clinton erroneously declared Netanyahu's initiative to be "unprecedented,"[5] ushering in an ignominious era of US diplomacy during which the Obama administration twisted the arms of Palestinian negotiators to return to the table, knowing full well that it had failed to obtain the proper conditions for negotiations to stand a chance of succeeding. This pressure on the Palestinians came despite US-Israel relations reaching their nadir since Obama entered office: in March 2010, during an official visit by Biden, Israel announced the expansion of an East Jerusalem settlement, resulting in a furious yet short-lived condemnation by the United States. This period, from the trilateral meeting at the UN in September 2009 until August 2010, when the parties agreed to resume direct negotiations under US auspices, forms the backbone of the narrative in Chapter 3.

In September 2010, Obama convened at the White House a high-profile relaunching of direct Israeli-Palestinian negotiations, the subject of Chapter 4. It was a badly miscalculated, high-stakes gamble to revive the moribund "peace process" that resulted in a spectacular and irretrievable diplomatic defeat. Notwithstanding the goodwill remarks of Obama, Netanyahu, Abbas, Egyptian President Hosni Mubarak and Jordanian King Abdullah II at the opening session of the negotiation, these talks stood little, if any, chance of bearing fruit for several reasons.

First, looming over the talks like an ominous cloud was the impending expiration of Israel's self-declared settlement "moratorium." Israel had made it abundantly clear that it was unwilling to extend this one-time "moratorium," which had provided a barely concealing fig leaf for Palestinians to return to the negotiating table. On the other hand, Palestinian negotiators had made it equally evident that they would not countenance ongoing negotiations with Israel in the absence of even a pretense of a settlement freeze. Thus, when the "moratorium" expired just three weeks after the convocation of negotiations, the resumed talks hit an insuperable obstacle.

Second, the Obama administration failed to offer public terms of reference for these negotiations that would have grounded the talks in international law and UN resolutions. This lack of terms of reference was in contradistinction to the Madrid Peace Conference, convened in 1991 by President George H.W. Bush in the aftermath of the Gulf War to initiate negotiations for a comprehensive Arab-Israeli peace, and even to the much-maligned Oslo Accords of 1993 that initiated direct, bilateral Israeli-Palestinian negotiations. This glaring absence foreordained the negotiations to continue traveling down the fruitless path of nearly two decades of meandering, inconclusive talks, which only served to solidify, rather than end, Israel's military occupation of the Palestinian West Bank, East Jerusalem and Gaza Strip.

Third, the Obama administration deliberately sidelined and snubbed its Quartet partners—the UN, the European Union, and Russia—not to mention the Arab League and Organization of the Islamic Conference, multilateral institutions which had respectively authored and endorsed an Israeli-Palestinian peace plan often commended by the United States. Arrogating to itself sole responsibility for shepherding Israeli-Palestinian negotiations was a marked departure for an administration that touted its multilateral approach to diplomacy, and this move guaranteed a continuation of the biases inherent in the US-monopolized "peace process," favoritisms which had played such a significant role in undermining the chances for successful negotiations in the past.

Having risked it all diplomatically by reconvening Israeli-Palestinian negotiations only to see his effort stunningly shatter, Obama became increasingly desperate to revive the negotiations at whatever cost, in an attempt to salvage the wreckage of his policy. From October to December 2010, the Obama administration shamefully tried to bribe Israel into a one-time, three-month extension of the sham settlement "moratorium" in exchange for exceedingly generous military and diplomatic gifts, in the fading hope that such a deal would be enough to entice Palestinians back to the table. Netanyahu, sensing Obama's political vulnerability, reckoned that he could pocket these promises and cash them in later as necessary. He therefore saw no need to accept this deal, which would force him to renege on his words and unnecessarily provoke a political confrontation with his hardline base of supporters who opposed any limitations on Israel's expropriation of Palestinian land. The Obama administration rather angrily and definitively withdrew its offer in December, thereby marking its last sustained push to negotiate Israeli-Palestinian peace.

From this point forward, the Obama administration flailed about as it unsuccessfully attempted to breathe new life into the corpse of the deceased "peace process" while simultaneously trying to prevent Palestinians from breaking out of the confines of this US-dominated charade. Chapter 5 details how the Palestinian negotiating team, after having given the "peace process" one last shot, belatedly came to the conclusion that it would never get a fair shake out of any negotiating process monopolized by the United States. They should have come to this realization much sooner. In 2005, US "peace process" negotiator Aaron David Miller confessed that "for far too long, many American officials involved in Arab-Israeli peacemaking, myself included, have acted as Israel's attorney, catering and coordinating with the Israelis at the expense of successful peace negotiations."[6]

Instead of continuing to put their misplaced faith in the United States functioning as an "honest broker," Palestinians made a conscious decision to "re-internationalize" the Israeli-Palestinian conflict by taking their demands for redress and justice directly to the UN, an international forum in which they could reasonably expect more sympathy for their long-denied claims to freedom and self-determination. In February 2011, Palestinians floated a trial balloon of this new strategy when they prompted Lebanon, which held at the time a non-permanent seat on the Security Council, to table a resolution mildly condemning Israel's illegal settlement expansion in Occupied Palestinian Territory. The Obama administration then used its first and only veto in the UN to scupper the resolution, which did not even include a threat of sanctions against Israel for violating the Fourth Geneva Convention by constructing these settlements. This veto placed the Obama administration in the untenable situation of attempting to explain how it could veto a resolution based on a policy with which it nevertheless fully agreed. It was a policy incoherence from which the Obama administration never recovered, and it exposed how far Obama was prepared to go to prevent Palestinians from taking the diplomatic initiative.

Having unmasked the pretense of the United States being an "honest broker" through this trial balloon, Palestinians embarked on a much more significant diplomatic initiative, the ramifications of which arguably produced the most dramatic turning point in the diplomatic history of the Israeli-Palestinian conflict since the Oslo Accords were signed in 1993. The repercussions of this initiative, detailed in Chapter 6, are still unfolding today. In September 2011, the Palestine Liberation Organization (PLO) formally submitted an application for Palestine's full membership in the UN, sixty-four years after that international body had recommended, against the wishes of the majority of its inhabitants, to partition the British Mandate of Palestine into a Jewish state and an Arab state. As this initiative gathered momentum, Palestinians also undertook a separate, but related, global campaign to encourage additional countries to extend diplomatic recognition to the State of Palestine. These two moves were conflated by the Obama administration and many members of Congress into one sinister, grand plot by the Palestinians to "unilaterally" declare statehood and permanently abandon negotiations with Israel. However, no membership application in the UN could be granted "unilaterally," and Palestinians made clear that the membership bid was an attempt to level the negotiating field, rather than abandon it. The rhetorical circumlocutions deployed by the United States to rationalize its opposition to these Palestinian initiatives were as unconvincing as those marshaled to explain its veto in the Security Council of the resolution condemning Israel's settlements.

In part to fend off these initiatives and in part to respond to the impulses for freedom and democracy unleashed throughout the region by the Arab Spring, Obama proposed in May 2011 to revitalize Israeli-Palestinian negotiations yet one more time by first tackling the issues of borders and security. However, Obama's reference to Israel's pre-1967 armistice lines as the basis for borders succeeded only in provoking howls of faux indignation from Netanyahu, whose public dressing down of a president in the White House was perhaps unequaled by any foreign leader in the history of the United States. The Obama administration could neither restart negotiations nor prevent Palestinians from taking their case directly to the UN, resulting in the shabby spectacle of Obama serving as Israel's enforcer in determining the timetable for Palestinian freedom.

Although the United States succeeded in burying Palestine's UN membership request in a Security Council committee, the UN Educational, Scientific and Cultural Organization (UNESCO) overwhelmingly voted in October 2011 to admit Palestine as a member. This vote automatically triggered arcane, long-standing provisions in US law, enacted after the PLO declared independence in 1988, which forced the Obama administration to defund the organization. Even though, by slashing UNESCO's budget by nearly one-quarter, the Obama administration was jeopardizing US interests furthered by the organization, it did precious little to convince Congress to change this law. Not that Congress would have been in the mood to oblige the president after many members of Congress had issued a steady stream of often vitriolic denouncements of Palestinians for seeking UN membership and threatened them with sanctions for so doing. In fact, some members of Congress had quietly placed "holds" on US foreign aid to Palestinians even before they submitted a membership application to the UN, effectively sanctioning Palestinians for even thinking about doing something to which Israel and its supporters in the United States objected.

On this despondent note, the chronological narrative of the Obama administration's efforts to achieve Israeli-Palestinian peace ends. After the UNESCO vote, the Obama administration was too preoccupied with preventing an Israeli attack on Iran, or getting dragged into such a conflict by Israel's supporters in the United States (a subject that is unfortunately largely outside the scope of this book), to launch any further initiatives on the Israeli-Palestinian track. Furthermore, shortly after the UNESCO vote, Obama went into full reelection campaign mode. When he was not parrying ridiculous assertions from his Republican challenger Mitt Romney, who had charged that the president had "disrespected" Israel and threw it "under the bus,"[7] Obama was busy deploying himself and others to defend his stalwart support for Israel in a transparent pandering for votes and money that far surpassed his efforts on the campaign trail in 2008.

PART II: THEMES OF US POLICY

However, this linear account and analysis of the Obama administration's failed attempts to achieve Israeli-Palestinian peace paints an incomplete picture of US policy toward Israel and the Palestinians since 2009. That is because certain themes emerge as a pattern in US policy toward Israel and the Palestinians in general, and in the Obama administration's policies in particular, which do not lend themselves to tidy periodization. The second part of this book explores some of those themes, beginning in Chapter 7 with an in-depth examination of how the Obama administration shielded Israel from accountability for its actions at the UN, thereby allowing Israel to act with impunity. As already noted, the Obama administration played a determinative role in scotching a UN resolution condemning Israel's settlements and in shelving Palestine's bid for UN membership. But Obama's protection of Israel at the UN went far beyond these incidents.

During Obama's first term, the UN Human Rights Council commissioned two seminal reports: the UN Fact-Finding Mission on the Gaza Conflict (more commonly referred to as the "Goldstone Report") and an additional fact-finding mission that investigated Israel's 2010 attack on a Gaza-bound flotilla of humanitarian activists. The first report, in painstaking and deeply troubling detail, found that during Operation Cast Lead both Israel and Palestinian militant groups committed violations of human rights and international law, and possible war crimes and crimes against humanity. The second report found that Israel's blockade of the Palestinian Gaza Strip and its attack on the flotilla delivering humanitarian aid were illegal. On both occasions, the Obama administration and Congress marched in lockstep to denounce the entire UN system for its supposed anti-Israel structural bias, condemning the findings of the reports and scuttling their recommendations for the international community to take further action. This shielding of Israel from accountability for its actions at the UN permitted it to get off scot-free, since Israel's own domestic mechanisms predictably failed to substantially hold individuals responsible for violating international law. By literally letting Israel get away with murder, the Obama administration severely strained the credibility of its repeatedly professed commitment to the universality of human rights.

Moreover, while US diplomatic support for Israel subverted the international community's efforts to hold Israel accountable for its human rights abuses, US military support for Israel during the Obama administration continued to make the United States directly responsible for and complicit in those violations. Providing copious amounts of weapons to Israel at US taxpayer expense is a bipartisan tradition that long predates the Obama administration. In the four decades after Israel occupied the Palestinian West Bank, East Jerusalem and Gaza Strip, along with the Syrian Golan Heights in 1967, the United States gave Israel more than $67 billion in military grants and loans. In 2007, the Bush administration signed a memorandum of understanding (MOU) to provide Israel with an additional $30 billion in military aid from 2009 to 2018.

Under the Obama administration, the White House and Congress worked hand in glove to elevate US-Israel military ties to unprecedented levels in at least three ways. First, Obama requested and Congress appropriated the record-breaking levels of military aid to Israel, which have now plateaued at $3.1 billion annually, envisioned in the 2007 MOU. Second, in addition to this munificent military aid, Obama requested and Congress appropriated ever-increasing levels of money for the joint research and development of various anti-missile programs, which amounted to more than $1 billion during Obama's first term. These supposedly "defensive" weapons drastically changed Israel's strategic thinking, making it virtually cost-free for it to go on the offensive against Palestinians while effectively protecting its own civilian populations from retaliatory fire. The deployment of these Iron Dome batteries, designed to knock down short-range projectiles, therefore increases, rather than lessens, the likelihood of another major conflagration on the scale of Operation Cast Lead. Third, joint US-Israel military exercises and US prepositioning of war materiel in Israel also expanded to unprecedented degrees during the Obama administration.

At the same time that these deepening US-Israel military ties further enmeshed the United States in Israel's military occupation and human rights abuses of Palestinians, US assistance to Palestinians perversely entrapped them in a system that perpetuates the injustices inflicted upon them. During the Obama administration, US assistance to Palestinians consisted of four components: direct budgetary transfers to the Palestinian Authority (PA); training for Palestinian security forces in the West Bank, known informally as the "Dayton forces," named after the former US security coordinator Lieutenant General Keith Dayton, who led the mission; economic assistance programs implemented mainly by US nongovernmental organizations; and budgetary support for the UN Relief and Works Agency (UNRWA) for Palestine Refugees.

This US aid to the Palestinians was problematic for several reasons. First, by propping up the PA with cash transfers, the United States colluded with Israel in attempting to construct a Potemkin village. In this illusion, Palestinians in the occupied West Bank, East Jerusalem and Gaza Strip have a nominal, self-governing institution that covers up the reality of being subjected to Israel's harsh and capricious military rule. This situation allows Israel, as the occupying power, to evade its Fourth Geneva Convention obligations to protect and promote the welfare of the protected persons (Palestinians) living in Occupied Territory.

Second, the "Dayton forces" have been accused of human rights violations, including suppressing freedom of expression on behalf of the PA and torturing their political opponents. These "Dayton forces" are widely viewed by Palestinians in the West Bank as a subcontractor for Israel's security, allowing Israel to have an indigenous security force do its dirty work.

Third, although it may be admirable for the United States to provide humanitarian assistance for economic development and for social services to Palestinian refugees, it is the US policy of supporting Israeli occupation and apartheid that necessitates this aid in the first place. Were it not for the United States supplying Israel with the weapons that it misuses to demolish Palestinian infrastructure and hamper economic development by severely constricting Palestinian freedom of movement, and were it not for the US refusal to press Israel to fulfill its international obligation to enable Palestinian refugees to exercise their right of return, it is doubtful that this aid would be needed in the first place.

Thus US foreign assistance to both Israel and the Palestinians under the Obama administration, the focus of Chapter 8, significantly retarded the prospect for establishing a just and lasting Israeli-Palestinian peace.

Given the unprecedented strengthening of US-Israel military ties during the Obama administration, it would be reasonable to expect that this relationship with Israel would provide the United States with significant strategic benefits. Indeed, Israel's supporters in the United States often try to justify this relationship by claiming that Israel is a strategic ally, affording the United States substantial advantages in war-making and intelligence gathering. Undoubtedly some of these claims are true, even if they are difficult to evaluate, as they are based largely on classified information. For example, Israeli military technologies have been deployed by the United States in its wars in Iraq and Afghanistan and many Israeli weapons manufacturers have opened US subsidiaries that directly provide services and weapons to the Pentagon.

However, during the Obama administration, several leading security and intelligence officials openly questioned the canonical wisdom of Israel's actual value as a strategic ally of the United States. Some even went so far as to counter this claim, arguing that Israel is a veritable drag on US strategic interests. This assessment was borne out during the Obama administration by an unlikely duo. Khalid Sheikh Mohammed, the self-described architect of the September 11 terrorist attacks on the United States and his codefendants submitted a pro se filing for their military commission trial in Guantánamo Bay, in which they describe US support for Israel as a motivating factor in their actions. General David Petraeus, former Commander of US Central Command, concurred that "al-Qaeda and other militant groups exploit that anger [over the Palestinian question] to mobilize support."[8]

But the strategic implications of US support for Israel go well beyond the fringe minority of people who act on that anger by engaging in acts of terrorism. Especially in light of the Arab Spring—the most consequential development in the Arab world since the post–World War II decolonization struggles—US support for Israel is becoming much more of a liability than it was when the United States was able to lean on a network of compliant autocrats, monarchs and dictators to adhere to its strategic vision for the region. This anti-democratic thrust was symbolized most clearly by former Egyptian president Hosni Mubarak's willingness to acquiesce and even actively participate in the US-supported Israeli blockade of the Gaza Strip. As truly democratic governments hopefully become firmly implanted throughout the Arab world over the next several years, the United States will find that it is no longer able to so easily manipulate regional governments to line up behind its support for Israel's oppression of the Palestinians, because it is highly unlikely that a responsible, democratic government would be allowed to do so by its people. Thus, by continuing to underwrite Israel's human rights abuses of Palestinians, the United States will only find itself marginalized even further throughout the region. This ledger of Israel's value to the United States as a strategic ally is the focus of Chapter 9.

Perhaps to a greater extent than any other president in US history, Obama's soaring rhetoric about the universality of human rights and the common impulse for freedom and democracy occasioned great hope among the world's oppressed that the pendulum of US foreign policy might finally swing to their side. It was his rhetorical flourishes, along with his future promise to end the US war in Iraq, which garnered Obama, rather prematurely and undeservedly, the Nobel Peace Prize in 2009. During his first term in office, Obama delivered two landmark speeches touching upon US policy toward the Arab and Muslim worlds in general and the Israeli-Palestinian conflict in particular. The first, an address to the Muslim world from Cairo in June 2009, entitled "A New Beginning," won nearly universal accolades from its target audience and touched off frenzied speculation that indeed US foreign policy might undergo a transformational reorientation during the Obama administration. During this speech, Obama expressed a level of empathy for the plight of the

Palestinian people that was unequaled by any previous sitting US president, even President Jimmy Carter.

However, during this speech, Obama also rather paternalistically preached nonviolence to the Palestinians as a surefire method to free themselves from the shackles of Israeli military occupation. But the import of his policies failed to match his empathy for Palestinian suffering, and his administration conspicuously remained mum as courageous acts of Palestinian nonviolence were met with Israeli brutality. Even when US citizens participated with Palestinians in acts of nonviolence and were subjected to severe injury and even death, the Obama administration not only failed to hold Israel accountable, but shamefully threatened those activists with prosecution under US anti-terrorism laws.

In May 2011, Obama delivered a seminal, if not belated, speech on the Arab Spring at the State Department. In this speech Obama expressed admirable support for pro-democracy movements throughout the Arab world but significantly compromised his message by glossing over or omitting completely the authoritarian records of regimes deemed friendly to US strategic interests in the region, thereby signaling that US support for freedom and democracy in the Arab world was inversely proportional to a given regime's toeing of the US line. Moreover, Obama's speech was bifurcated, treating the Israeli-Palestinian conflict as being distinct from regional developments. Rather than viewing Palestinians as fellow human beings who were equally deserving of support for their efforts to achieve freedom and democracy, Obama attempted to shoehorn Palestinian aspirations into sterile negotiating parameters with Israel. (He also ignored the pivotal role played by Palestinian nonviolent struggles against Israeli military occupation in inspiring the tactics of the Arab Spring.) Obama's lack of original ideas for achieving long-denied Palestinian rights via negotiations with Israel only reinforced this double standard. This disconnection between the rhetoric of support for using nonviolent means to advance freedom and democracy, and the reality of the Obama administration's policies toward Palestinians struggling nonviolently to achieve these goals, forms the basis of Chapter 10.

Even as Obama administration officials and members of Congress recited like a mantra that the US-Israel relationship is unbreakable and unshakeable, developments within US civil society during Obama's first term suggest otherwise, as detailed in Chapter 11. From advocates for Palestinian human rights achieving unprecedented access to mainstream US media, to church divestment efforts, to campus boycott campaigns, the pillars of support for US policies that maintain Israeli military occupation and human rights abuses of Palestinians came under greater sustained assault than ever before during Obama's presidency. This phenomenon did not pass unnoticed by the Obama administration and Israel's supporters in the United States. On the contrary, they sounded the alarms bells with increased urgency and alacrity as time passed. Elected officials led the charge in countering what they perceived to be a campaign to isolate and delegitimize Israel, and they even pursued criminal sanctions against individuals for exercising their First Amendment rights to speak and organize in opposition to US governmental policies. The Israel lobby also launched numerous initiatives to try to counter the growing boycott, divestment and sanctions (BDS) movement against Israel. In some cases, the Israel lobby succeeded in intimidating its way into killing such campaigns, but in others it lost the battle and inadvertently drew more attention to it.

Even though elected officials and the Israel lobby pushed back against this phenomenon, their efforts to contain it have been unsuccessful. Simply put, the genie cannot be put back inside the bottle. Discourse in the United States about the Israeli-Palestinian conflict has been fundamentally altered for the better. Thanks in large measure to Israel's brutal assaults on the Gaza Strip in 2008–2009 and on the Gaza Freedom Flotilla in 2010, and also to the diligent efforts of activists to run coherent campaigns challenging US support for Israel's brutality, US public opinion is in the midst of a sea change in its understanding of the Israeli-Palestinian conflict and the role that the United States plays in sustaining it. No outcome is assured, but Israel's supporters in the United States have every reason to be nervous about the long-term sustainability of US support for Israeli military occupation and apartheid toward Palestinians.

Chapter 12 examines the role of the Israeli-Palestinian conflict in the 2012 elections. The rival presidential candidates traded ridiculous accusations about the others' mythical abandonment of US support for Israel. This same dynamic even intruded into several congressional races as well. Ironically, during a period of unmatched, tangible bipartisan support for Israel, this issue devolved into yet another bitter, partisan, mud-slinging debate. Many nonpartisan supporters of Israel in the United States wrung their hands in consternation at this development, fearing that it could undermine actual US support for Israel, whereas transparently partisan advocates of the US-Israel relationship gleefully stoked the fire to improve the odds of their favored side.

While this faux debate over which party loves Israel more has historically been limited to intramural squabbling among Jewish-American supporters of Israel, US policy toward Israel and the Palestinians is increasingly becoming a topic of debate among the general public as well. This is a sorely needed and long-overdue conversation. For far too long, Israel has been treated as a sacred cow in US political discourse, virtually immune to criticism. Americans of all religious and ethnic backgrounds must have an honest conversation in order to reorient our country's policies toward Israel and the Palestinians in a way that supports human rights, international law and equality, rather than Israeli military occupation and human rights abuses. This reconfiguration of US policy will be a prerequisite for Israeli Jews and Palestinians to achieve a just and lasting peace, an incalculable strategic benefit both to them and us.

The book concludes with an overarching analysis of why the Obama administration ran aground in its efforts to broker Israeli-Palestinian peace in its first term. I also provide recommendations for future administrations for how US policy can be fundamentally altered in order to make Israeli-Palestinian peace achievable.

This book is highly unlikely to be the definitive account of US policy toward Israel and the Palestinians during the Obama's first term. That account will only be able to be written once officials have published their memoirs and the archives are open to public inspection. However, the contemporary researcher is aided dramatically in understanding behind-the-scenes US diplomacy toward the Israeli-Palestinian conflict during the Obama administration by two massive leaks of official documents. First, in February 2010, the anti-secrecy group WikiLeaks began to publish more than a quarter million US State Department cables in the largest-ever leak of classified documents, known as "Cablegate." These documents include important correspondence from the US embassy in Tel Aviv and the US Consulate in Jerusalem, which shed important light on the first year of the Obama administration's efforts to freeze Israeli settlements and restart Israeli-Palestinian negotiations. Second, in January 2011, *Al Jazeera* released a trove of more than 1,600 leaked official documents from the Palestinian negotiating team, including meeting minutes, maps, memoranda, and more. Although most of these documents predate the Obama administration, a number of them also reveal important behind-the-scenes developments during this era. Both sets of documents were consulted for this book, in addition to public, non-leaked material.

Despite the acknowledged limitations of writing a contemporaneous account of US policy, this book needed to be written now. The urgency derives from the fact that US policy toward Israel and the Palestinians, especially during the Obama administration, is so morally wrong, so intrinsically opposed to US interests and so inimical to the establishment of a just and lasting Israeli-Palestinian peace as to necessitate an immediate reconsideration. Quite simply put: US policy toward Israel and the Palestinians, by underwriting and undergirding Israel's oppressive policies, makes a just and lasting peace inconceivable. As long US policy remains unchanged, Israel will continue to flout international law and thumb its nose at the UN, knowing full well that it will be backed by the United States in doing so. On the flip side, if the United States were to pull its backing for Israel's oppression of the Palestinians, then Israeli intransigence would melt away in the historical blink of an eye, as it did when President Dwight Eisenhower terminated all US aid programs to Israel after it invaded and occupied the Egyptian Sinai Peninsula in 1956.

As of this writing, Palestinian refugees who were exiled from their homes in a concerted campaign of ethnic cleansing by Israel during its establishment in 1948, along with their descendants, continue to languish in refugee camps sixty-four years later, denied by Israel their fundamental human right of return enshrined in the Universal Declaration of Human Rights and UN General Assembly Resolution 194. Those Palestinians who were not ethnically cleansed from their homes by Israel in 1948 and today comprise approximately 20 percent of Israel's citizenry are suffering under systematic discrimination by their government, which treats them as second-class citizens at best, and unwanted guests at worst. Palestinians living under Israeli occupation in the West Bank, East Jerusalem and Gaza Strip now have been forced to live under unbearable military rule for forty-five years. As long as this condition of apartheid—systematic governmental discrimination and differentiation of law based on one's religion, nationality or ethnicity—obtains, there can be no hope of Palestinians achieving the freedom, justice and equality they deserve, nor of Israeli Jews attaining the security and acceptance they crave.

It is my sincere hope that this book will play a small part in dismantling US support for Israel's apartheid system and human rights abuses against the Palestinians so that a just and lasting Israeli-Palestinian peace is possible. It is up to us as US citizens to challenge and confront those US governmental, institutional and corporate policies that buttress Israel's oppression of the Palestinian people. The time to act is now.

Note on Terminology

The terminology used to describe and analyze the Israeli-Palestinian conflict is every bit as contentious and fought over as the land itself and the competing claims to it. For example, a fierce debate still rages today over whether the presence or absence of the word "the" in French and English translations of UN Security Council Resolution 242 requires a complete or partial withdrawal of Israeli armed forces from Arab territories occupied in the 1967 war.

Keeping this in mind, I have endeavored to be as consistent as possible with the terminology I use throughout the book. While I do not expect readers to necessarily agree with all of the terminology I have chosen to use, the following brief guide will at least hopefully clarify to readers what I intend to convey with my choice of frequently used terms.

"Israel," "Israeli Jews" and "Palestinian citizens of Israel": "Israel" refers to the country established on 78 percent of historic Palestine as determined by the 1949 armistice agreements signed between Israel and Egypt, Jordan, Syria and Lebanon. Recognizing the binational character of this country, its citizens are sometimes termed "Israeli Jews" (approximately 80 percent of the citizenry) and "Palestinian citizens of Israel" (approximately 20 percent of the citizenry), where it makes sense to differentiate their identities.

"Palestine," "historic Palestine," and "State of Palestine": "Palestine" and "historic Palestine" are terms used interchangeably to refer to the totality of this geographic entity as it existed during the British Mandate of Palestine, which spanned the post–World War I era until 1948. The term "State of Palestine" is employed infrequently and only in the context of the PLO's initiative for Palestine to become a member of the UN.

"Occupied Palestinian Territory," and "the West Bank, East Jerusalem and Gaza Strip": These terms are used interchangeably to refer to the 22 percent of historic Palestine subject to Israeli military occupation since 1967. "Occupied Palestinian Territory" is the official UN terminology for the totality of Palestinian land occupied by Israel in 1967, whereas "the West Bank, East Jerusalem and Gaza Strip" refer to its constituent parts.

"Palestine Liberation Organization" (PLO) and "Palestinian Authority" (PA): These are two distinct political entities that should never be referred to interchangeably. The PLO is recognized by the Arab League as "the sole legitimate representative of the Palestinian people" and is responsible for conducting negotiations with Israel and representing Palestinians at the UN. The PA is the entity that was created by the PLO and Israel as part of the Oslo "peace process" in 1994 to administer those fragments of Occupied Palestinian Territory that came under some form of Palestinian security and/or civil responsibility. The confusion stems from the fact that Mahmoud Abbas is currently both the president of the PA and the chair of the PLO. For the sake of brevity, Abbas is usually identified in the text in only one of his capacities.

"Israeli military occupation" and "Israeli apartheid": These terms are frequently used in tandem to refer to the totality of Israel's policies toward the Palestinian people, and also to US support for those policies. These two terms overlap, but they are not used interchangeably. Israel's military occupation of the Palestinian West Bank, East Jerusalem and Gaza Strip includes apartheid policies, such as discrete legal regimes for Israeli settlers and Palestinians, separate license plates and roads, differentiated rights to land, water and other natural resources, etc. However, Israel's apartheid policies toward Palestinians are not confined to Occupied Palestinian Territory. They extend as well to formal laws and institutions, as well as pervasive societal discrimination, which privilege Israeli Jews over Palestinian citizens of Israel. And Israel engages in apartheid by allowing Jews from around the world to freely immigrate and claim citizenship under the "law of return," whereas it forbids Palestinian refugees exiled from their homes from exercising their internationally guaranteed right of return.

Defining Israel's policies toward Palestinians as apartheid is not to say that Israel is exactly like apartheid South Africa. No two historical examples are perfectly analogous, just as Israel's colonization of Occupied Palestinian Territory does and does not have similarities to France's colonization of Algeria.

However, apartheid has a specific legal connotation according to the 1974 International Convention on the Suppression and Punishment of the Crime of Apartheid. This convention defines apartheid, in part, as

> any legislative measures and other measures calculated to prevent a racial group or groups from participation in the political, social, economic and cultural life of the country and the deliberate creation of conditions preventing the full development of such a group or groups, in particular by denying to members of a racial group or groups basic human rights and freedoms, including the right to work, the right to form recognized trade unions, the right to education, the right to leave and to return to their country, the right to a nationality, the right to freedom of movement and residence, the right to freedom of opinion and expression, and the right to freedom of peaceful assembly and association.

While Palestinian citizens of Israel do have some of these rights, they are denied others, whereas Palestinian refugees and Palestinians under Israeli military occupation have few, if any, of these rights. This definition of apartheid is as accurate as any other in encapsulating Israel's policies toward the Palestinians.

"Israel lobby" and "pro-Israel": These terms refer to the constellation of organizations and individuals advocating for Israel in the United States and for strong US-Israel ties. The "Israel lobby" is not a monolithic bloc, as is evidenced by the stresses and strains within this lobby found throughout this book. However, all members of the Israel lobby share the same fundamental policy underpinnings mentioned above, even if its members occupy different places along the political spectrum.

All other, less frequently used terms, including Arabic and Hebrew ones, are defined as they appear throughout the text.

There is, of course, a values-laden judgment behind the choice of most of the above-mentioned terms. However, nothing written above or in subsequent pages of this book should be inferred by the reader to constitute the author's endorsement of or advocacy for any particular resolution to the Israeli-Palestinian conflict. This disclaimer notwithstanding, this book does provide some analysis on the feasibility of a two-state resolution to the Israeli-Palestinian conflict in the wake of the Obama administration's failure to broker such a peace agreement. I also analyze the emerging alternatives to this paradigm.

However the Israeli-Palestinian conflict is eventually resolved, Israel must dismantle its military occupation and apartheid policies toward Palestinians for there to be a just and lasting peace based on human rights, international law and equality. This development is highly unlikely to occur as long as the US continues to provide virtually unconditional military and diplomatic backing for Israel's policies. It is the aim of this book to elucidate how the Obama administration perpetuated and even strengthened these policies. It is the author's hope that by so doing, more Americans will join the growing movement to confront and change these policies for the better.

PART I: US POLICY, 2009–2011

CHAPTER ONE

An Unbelievably Informed President

During a November 2009 congressional delegation to Israel, Israeli Prime Minister Netanyahu expressed to Senator Joseph Lieberman (I-CT) how pleased he was that President Barack Obama was "unbelievably informed" about Israeli-Palestinian issues.[1] In fact, given Obama's intimate engagement with a large and politically active Palestinian-American constituency, which he represented as an Illinois state senator, and given his ties to a coterie of liberal Jewish-American political activists in Chicago who were critical of Israel's policies toward the Palestinians, it is likely the he entered the White House with a deeper and more nuanced understanding of the Israeli-Palestinian conflict than any previous president.

A PRESIDENT EMERGES

As a state senator, Obama developed strong working relations with a politically empowered Palestinian-American constituency in his Hyde Park–based district. He frequently attended community events and relied upon this community to help raise funds for his campaigns. It was through these contacts that Obama likely developed some of his first impressions about the Israeli-Palestinian conflict.

Chicago-based activist and author Ali Abunimah wrote in 2007 that when he first met Obama nearly a decade before, "He impressed me as progressive, intelligent and charismatic. I distinctly remember thinking 'if only a man of this calibre could become president one day.'" Abunimah heard him speak on several occasions to Palestinian- and Arab-American audiences, during which times "Obama was forthright in his criticism of US policy and his call for an even- handed approach to the Palestinian-Israeli conflict." The last time he met with the future president was during Obama's 2004 Democratic primary run for the US Senate. Abunimah recounted: "As he came in from the cold and took off his coat, I went up to greet him. He responded warmly, and volunteered, 'Hey, I'm sorry I haven't said more about Palestine right now, but we are in a tough primary race. I'm hoping when things calm down I can be more up front.' He referred to my activism, including columns I was contributing to the *Chicago Tribune* critical of Israeli and US policy, [by saying] 'Keep up the good work!'"[2]

As Obama's relations with the Palestinian-American community in Chicago become a heated electoral issue during his 2008 presiden- tial campaign, campaign strategist David Axelrod denied that Obama had made those comments to Abunimah, stating, "In no way did he take a position privately that he hasn't taken publicly and consist- ently." According to Axelrod, Obama "always had expressed solici- tude for the Palestinian people, who have been ill-served and have suffered greatly from the refusal of their leaders to renounce violence and recognize Israel's right to exist."[3] Thus began a pattern of Obama shying away from initial remarks he had made that were sympathetic to the plight of the Palestinians, and then instead placing the blame squarely on Palestinian shoulders for their own travails. This type of double-talk raised hopes among those who thought that as president Obama would bring a new US approach to the Israeli-Palestinian conflict, while also stoking suspicion among defenders of the politi- cal status quo that his repeatedly expressed pro-Israel sentiments were insincere and that Obama would undermine the foundations of the US-Israel relationship.

During those early days of his political career, Obama also devel- oped a friendship with his former colleague at the University of Chicago, Professor Rashid Khalidi, an eminent Palestinian-American historian of the Middle East and US foreign policy. At a 2003 farewell tribute to Khalidi, who was leaving for a position at Columbia University, Obama relished the fact that his discussions with Khalidi and his wife Mona had served as "consistent reminders to me of my own blind spots and my own biases . . . It's for that reason that I'm hoping that, for many years to come, we continue that conversation—a conversation that is necessary not just around Mona and Rashid's dinner table," but throughout "this entire world" as well. In turn, Khalidi told the gathering, "You will not have a better senator under any circumstances."[4]

Not only did Obama's connections to Palestinian-Americans early in his political career suggest that he would bring an atypical viewpoint of the Israeli-Palestinian conflict to the White House; his ties to liberal Jewish-American political activists in Chicago did so as well. According to Peter Beinart, "Woven into the life stories of many of the Jews who most influenced the young Barack Obama was a bitter estrangement from the see-no-evil Zionism of the American Jewish establishment. In Chicago, those Jews constituted a geographic and moral community, a community that bred in Obama a specific, and subversive, vision of American Jewish identity and of the Jewish state." Obama's "inner circle of Jewish advisers," which included Axelrod, "whose views of Israel leaned left," according to Beinart, "meant that he was repeatedly reminded, in a way most American politicians are not, that when it comes to Israel, many American Jews disagree with their communal leaders."[5]

Yet despite these relationships and the role they may have played in shaping Obama's early views on the Israeli-Palestinian conflict, it became evident early in his political career that Obama was more than willing to dismiss the knowledge and advice he received from his Palestinian-American and liberal Jewish-American friends if it stood in the way of advancing his career. As early as 2000, when he ran unsuccessfully for the US House of Representatives, Obama crafted policy positions to endear himself to pro-Israel political action committees. In response to a questionnaire by CityPAC, which describes itself as a Chicago-based organization designed "to maintain strong and steadfast Congressional support for Israel," Obama reportedly expressed support for maintaining Jerusalem as Israel's undivided capital,[6] a controversial position repeated during his 2008 presidential run.

When he reached the US Senate in 2005, after a meteoric rise to the national political stage following his electrifying speech to the Democratic National Convention in 2004, Obama developed a fairly routine and undistinguished record on Arab-Israeli issues that synched with the Senate's reflexive and uncritical support for Israel. According to the Congressional Report Cards of the US Campaign to End the Israeli Occupation, during his four years in the Senate Obama did not sponsor any significant resolutions relating to the Israeli-Palestinian conflict.[7] He did, however, cosponsor the notorious "Palestinian Anti-Terrorism Act" (S.2370), a bill passed in the Senate by unanimous consent in June 2006. President George W. Bush later signed a different version of this bill into law. The bill imposed comprehensive and draconian sanctions against Palestinians for freely and fairly voting in 2006 to elect Hamas candidates to a majority of seats in the Palestinian Legislative Council. In July 2006, Obama also cosponsored a blatantly one-sided resolution, S.Res.534, which expressed unabashed support for Israel in the midst of its brutal and punishing wars against Lebanon and the Gaza Strip, which killed more than 1,000 people, most of whom were civilians, and deliberately destroyed billions of dollars of Lebanese and Palestinian civilian infrastructure.

Even though he entered the Senate with little foreign policy experience, Obama received a coveted appointment to the prestigious Senate Foreign Relations Committee, where he served on its Near Eastern and South and Central Asian Affairs Subcommittee. To bolster his firsthand knowledge of the region, Obama made a high-profile, ten-day visit in January 2006 to Qatar, Kuwait, Iraq, Jordan, Israel and Occupied Palestinian Territory. While in Israel, Obama chided the Bush administration and Congress for not being attentive enough to resolving the Israeli-Palestinian conflict. "Because of the distraction of Iraq, and the work we've been having to do there," Obama offered, "we probably haven't been paying as much attention to what is happening here in Israel as we should. We need to be much more actively focused here, and that is one thing I will be focused on when I get back to Washington."[8] After meeting with Israeli Foreign Minister Silvan Shalom, Obama declared, "Violence is not the answer to the long-standing problems that exist in this area and my hope is that US policy will continue to encourage the nonviolent mediation of these issues."[9] These statements presaged his policies as president, when Obama would prioritize Israeli-Palestinian peace and urge nonviolence, although always exclusively to Palestinians and never to Israel.

In March 2007, one month after announcing his candidacy for the Democratic Party nomination for president, Obama addressed a Chicago policy forum of the American Israel Public Affairs Committee (AIPAC), the most powerful and influential of the many groups that comprise the Israel lobby. Obama's views on the Israeli-Palestinian conflict had not been fully articulated up to this point, and a briefing paper by his campaign on his pro-Israel credentials, according to *Chicago Sun Times* columnist Lynn Sweet, "was not widely circulated and clearly not enough. If he was to make a major speech on Israel, there was an interest among Obama's Chicago backers for him to deliver it in the city."[10] The speech did not disappoint its audience. Obama's address contained perfunctory, if not anodyne, references to promoting peace, such as: "We can and we should help Israelis and Palestinians both fulfill their national goals: two states living side by side in peace and security. Both the Israeli and Palestinian people have suffered from the failure to achieve this goal. The United States should leave no stone unturned in working to make that goal a reality." Obama also took the opportunity again to take repeated jabs at the Bush administration for the timing and substance of its Israeli-Palestinian peacemaking efforts. "Our job is to do more than lay out another road map," he said, referencing Bush's stillborn 2003 initiative to restart the "peace process." Obama argued, "For six years, the administration has missed opportunities to increase the United States' influence in the region and help Israel achieve the peace she wants and the security she needs." Instead of seizing these opportunities, Obama belittled Bush's efforts as "trips consisting of little more than photo-ops with little movement in between."

However, expressing his hope for a two-state resolution to the Israeli-Palestinian conflict and taking potshots at the Bush administration for failing to achieving it were not the purposes of this speech. Rather, Obama's intent was to demonstrate his political commitment and personal, emotional attachment to Israel before a skeptical, if not potentially hostile, Israel lobby crowd. In this regard, he succeeded. During his 2006 trip to Israel, he took part in the almost obligatory political ritual for visiting US politicians: taking a helicopter tour arranged by the Israeli military. These aerial briefings were designed to demonstrate Israel's supposed security justifications for why it could not fully withdraw from the Palestinian West Bank. "The helicopter took us over the most troubled and dangerous areas and that narrow strip between the West Bank and the Mediterranean Sea," Obama recounted. "At that height, I could see the hills and the terrain that generations have walked across. I could truly see how close everything is and why peace through security is the only way for Israel." While the term "peace through security" seems banal, to this audience it was a well-understood code to communicate that Obama would not insist on Israel foregoing all of its territorial conquests from the 1967 war.

But even more than proffering veiled policy prescriptions, Obama's speech was designed to tug at the heartstrings of his audience. As Obama told it, the helicopter then deposited him in Kiryat Shmona, a town on the Israeli side of the border with Lebanon that was hard-hit by Hezbollah rocket fire during Israel's 2006 war on Lebanon. "What struck me first about the village was how familiar it looked," Obama marveled. "The houses and streets looked like ones you might find in a suburb in America. I could imagine young children riding their bikes down the streets. I could imagine the sounds of their joyful play just like my own daughters. There were cars in the driveway. The shrubs were trimmed. The families were living their lives." Obama then ventured to a home struck by a Katyusha rocket. "The family who lived in the house was lucky to be alive. They had been asleep in another part when the rocket hit. They described the explosion. They talked about the fire and the shrapnel. They spoke about what might have been if the rocket had come screaming into their home at another time when they weren't asleep but sitting peacefully in the now destroyed part of the house. It is an experience," Obama offered, which "I keep close to my heart."[11] While conjuring great empathy for this Israeli civilian family that suffered during the war, Obama failed to muster one word of sympathy for Lebanese and Palestinians civilians who experienced far greater death and devastation at Israel's hands.

To bolster further his pro-Israel credentials, Obama praised the signing in August 2007 of a US-Israeli agreement for the United States to provide Israel with $30 billion of taxpayer-funded weapons between 2009 and 2018. On that occasion, Obama rather tendentiously hammered the Bush administration's "failed policies in Iraq" for having "emboldened Hamas and Hezbollah." In Obama's view,

"That makes it more important than ever that the United States live up to its commitment to ensure Israel's qualitative military edge in a dangerous region. For that reason, I support the agreement on military assistance reached today."[12] As president, Obama would be responsible for requesting from Congress the record-breaking levels of military aid to Israel envisioned in this agreement.

As Obama segued into full-time presidential campaigning mode, it became clear that the Israeli-Palestinian conflict would take on a central role in his foreign policy platform. And, as the campaign progressed, it also became apparent that Obama's scripted and formal positions on the issue would stay well within the boundaries of acceptable discourse for a presidential candidate, breaking no new ground and offering only hidebound platitudes about the importance he would attach to achieving Israeli-Palestinian peace if elected.

Although the Obama campaign made a pretense of recognizing that the Israeli-Palestinian conflict mattered to various constituencies, the overwhelming preponderance of Obama's campaign material on this issue was consciously and narrowly targeted to Jewish-Americans. Whereas his Arab-American "people" web page contained a fleeting reference to Obama's commitment to "a just peace to the Arab-Israeli conflict," his Jewish-American page contained fulsome praise for Obama's stance on Israel. "Barack, whose name comes from the same root as the Hebrew word *Baruch*, or 'blessed,' has traveled to Israel and witnessed Israelis' determination in the fight against terrorism and their yearning for peace with their neighbors," the campaign gushed. "His commitment to Israel's security, to the US-Israel relationship, and to Israel's right to self-defense has always been unshakable. Demonstrating his personal connection to Zionism and understanding of Israel as the homeland Jews longed for, Senator Barack Obama has stated that it must be preserved as a Jewish state. He will work tirelessly to help Israel in its quest for a lasting peace with its neighbors, while standing with Israel against those who seek its destruction."[13] The campaign tellingly did not realize, or deliberately obfuscated, the fact that the candidate's first name is actually more closely related to and derived from the Arabic word for "blessing," *baraka*.

The Obama campaign also released a position paper, entitled "Barack Obama and Joe Biden: A Strong Record of Supporting the

Security, Peace, and Prosperity of Israel." In the policy paper, Obama and his vice presidential running mate Joe Biden were declared to be "true friends of Israel, stalwart defenders of Israel's security, and effective advocates of strengthening the steadfast US-Israel relationship. They believe that Israel's right to exist as a Jewish state should never be challenged." The campaign asserted that the "first and incontrovertible commitment" of the United States "in the Middle East must be to the security of Israel, America's strongest ally in the Middle East." Lest anyone doubt it, the campaign reminded voters that "Obama delivered the message in 2006 to Palestinian university students in Ramallah that the United States would never distance itself from Israel," thereby rubbing in the noses of these Palestinian students that they could expect no respite from the United States arming Israel to continue occupying and oppressing them under an Obama administration. The campaign's desultory nod toward a two-state resolution to the Israeli-Palestinian conflict was revealingly the sixth of seven issues listed in the paper. However, even that paragraph was devoid of any mention of freedom or self-determination for Palestinians; rather, it focused on the campaign's multifaceted demands of Hamas.[14]

Between May and July 2008, Obama took a number of prominent steps to shore up his pro-Israel credentials. On Israel's sixtieth anniversary, he penned a congratulatory op-ed in the Israeli newspaper *Yediot Ahronot*, in which he maintained that Israel "has lived up to its founders' vision of being a 'light unto the nations.'"[15] Unsurprisingly, his op-ed made no mention of the *Nakba* ("catastrophe" in English), Palestinians' term for the dispossession, ethnic cleansing, and mass killings they suffered during Israel's creation.

Shortly after sewing up the Democratic presidential nomination in June 2008, Obama addressed his first national AIPAC Policy Conference and took the opportunity to elaborate on his personal connections to Zionism and Israel. He related how as an eleven-year-old, his Jewish-American camp counselor who had lived in Israel "told me stories of this extraordinary land and I learned of the long journey and steady determination of the Jewish people to preserve— preserve their identity through faith, family, and culture." According to the presumptive presidential nominee, "The story made a powerful impression on me; I had grown up without a sense of roots." The candidate reminisced that "in many ways I didn't know where I came from, so I was drawn to the belief that you could sustain a spiritual, emotional, and cultural identity and I understood the Zionist idea that there is always a homeland at the center of our story." He also employed humor to disarm an audience that likely had been "receiving provocative emails that have been circulated throughout the Jewish communities across the country," which referred to Obama's alleged Muslim faith and secretly hostile positions toward Israel. Obama stated: "They're filled with tall-tales and dire warnings about a certain candidate for President and all I want to say is let me know if you see this guy named Barack Obama because he sounds pretty scary." But, he reassured the audience, he was "speaking from my heart and as a true friend of Israel."

Beyond these feel-good statements and anecdotes, Obama's speech also contained important declarations and positions, including his inflammatory comment that boycott campaigns against Israel were "bigoted." He also vowed as president to implement the $30 billion agreement for additional US military aid to Israel and pledged that "Jerusalem will remain the capital of Israel and it must remain undivided."[16] Obama slightly backpedaled from this latter comment a day later after being condemned by Palestinian Authority (PA) President Mahmoud Abbas. On CNN, Obama clarified that "obviously, it's going to be up to the parties to negotiate a range of these issues. And Jerusalem will be part of those negotiations."[17]

The next month, Obama visited Israel and the Palestinian West Bank on a two-day leg of a seven-country journey. Although he met with Abbas and PA Prime Minister Salam Fayyad in Ramallah in order to have a semblance of balance, the bulk of this carefully choreographed trip was devoted to meetings with Israeli political leaders from various parties and, perhaps more importantly for his election campaign, to demonstrating to voters back home his commitment to Israel's security. On July 23, 2008, Obama visited the Israeli town of Sderot, a town which on multiple occasions had been hit with rocket fire emanating from the nearby Gaza Strip. "I'm proud to be here today," Obama declared, "and that's why I will work from the moment that I return to America, to tell the story of Sderot and to make sure that the good people who live here are enjoying a future of peace and security and hope." Demonstrating his solidarity with the town's residents, Obama added that "if somebody was sending rockets into my house where my two daughters sleep at night, I'm going to do everything in my power to stop that. And I would expect Israelis to do the same thing."[18] As he did in his 2007 speech to AIPAC, Obama proved facile at empathizing with Israeli civilians while ignoring the far-greater civilian suffering caused by Israel to those in his immediate surroundings.

Yet for all of these and many other clear-cut manifestations of his orthodox pro-Israel campaign orientation, lingering doubts remained as to Obama's true feelings and beliefs on the Israeli-Palestinian conflict. These suspicions were fueled by the inclusion in his campaign of advisers such as Robert Malley, Zbigniew Brzezinski and Samantha Power, advisers whom pro-Israel commentators deemed too willing to criticize Israel.

Moreover, Obama, in less guarded and scripted moments, sometimes appeared willing to revert to the positions he championed earlier in his political career, which were much more sympathetic to the Palestinian narrative. For example, at a Muscatine, Iowa, campaign event in March 2007, Sue Dravis, a member of the Muscatine County Democratic Central Committee and an activist with Concerned Iowans for Middle East Peace, a grassroots organization that bird-dogged the candidates prior to the Iowa caucus, asked the candidate: "What will you do that will be different, that will address the humanitarian as well as the human rights crisis for the Palestinians now?" In Obama's long and nuanced response, he stated that "nobody's suffering more than the Palestinian people from this whole process." In an April 27, 2007 candidate debate, NBC's Brian Williams asked Obama if he stood by that statement. Obama fumbled to explain that "if you have the whole thing, said—what I said is—nobody has suffered more than the Palestinian people from the failure of the Palestinian leadership to recognize Israel, to renounce violence and to get serious about negotiating peace and security for the region." However, a plain reading of the transcript does not indicate that Obama attempted to lay the blame for Palestinians' suffering at the feet of their leadership. Dravis too did not get the impression from Obama "that the onus was only on the Palestinian leadership."[19] Perhaps chastened by this off-the-cuff remark, which may have been indicative of Obama's true feelings toward the Israeli-Palestinian conflict, he later dodged a similar question posed by Pat Minor, another activist with Concerned Iowans for Middle East Peace, at an intimate Iowa City campaign event. According to Minor, the future president "refused to look me in the eye" while he responded in bland terms and in a "disconcerted" manner to her question.[20]

Obama was also willing to push back against narrowly tailored, right-wing visions of what it means to be pro-Israel. In a February 2008 closed-door meeting with Jewish community leaders in Cleveland, Obama staunchly opposed efforts to define the US-Israel relationship monolithically. According to meeting accounts, Obama told the assembled leaders that "there is a strain within the pro-Israel community that says unless you adopt an unwavering pro-Likud approach to Israel that you're anti-Israel and that can't be the measure of our friendship with Israel." In an omen of the distrust and recriminations that would characterize his relations with the pro-Israel community as president, Obama added, "If we cannot have an honest dialogue about how do we achieve these goals, then we're not going to make progress."[21]

However, if Obama harbored deep-seated sympathies for the Palestinians and sought to redefine what it means for a US politician to be a friend of Israel, then following his historic November 2008 presidential campaign victory, there was little, if any, indication that he would populate the senior echelons of his foreign policy team with people similarly committed. In fact, the opposite appeared true, as Obama selected individuals who, for the most part, held long-standing and emotive ties to Israel.

For example, Obama's pick for vice president, Joe Biden, would speak glowingly in front of Jewish and Israeli audiences about his intimate and impassioned identification with Judaism, Zionism and Israel, topics which he often conflated. Even at the apex of the most serious crisis between the United States and Israel during Obama's first term, after the Israeli government had humiliated Biden by announcing the expansion of an East Jerusalem settlement during an official March 2010 visit, Biden was still capable of summoning up his reservoir of good feelings for Israel. He told an audience at Tel Aviv University, "The past few days being back in Israel has been wonderful . . . it's been an honor to be here." Biden continued: "I should probably be used to it by now, but I'm always struck every time I come back by the hospitality of the Israeli people. No matter how long I've been away—and I imagine you've experienced this yourself—the instant I return, I feel like I'm at home. I feel like I never left. I feel like things just picked up where they left off the day that I left being here."[22]

For Biden, any temporary spat between the United States and Israel was eclipsed by the profound lesson, repeatedly instilled by his father, which was that the United States needed to recompense the Jewish people for its inaction during the Nazi Holocaust. "I was not educated in a Jewish school," Biden told a gathering of more than 2,000 rabbis, Jewish educators, and communal leaders in Detroit in November 2011. But "I was educated in the traditions of Judaism. I was educated about the oppression and genocide committed against the Jews, the historic ties between the Jewish people and the land of Israel. I was educated at my dinner table by what my Jewish friends at home refer to—and you would—as a righteous Christian, a man who taught us that without vigilance, the safe haven of Israel, it could happen again without Israel." Consequently, Biden felt no compunction in declaring that "I am a Zionist, for I learned you do not have to be a Jew to be a Zionist. The fact of the matter is that the man who raised me was absolutely committed to the notion that it should never happen again, the man who could not understand why there could even be a debate about the establishment of the state of Israel."[23]

For Obama's newly selected nominee for secretary of state—his former main electoral rival Hillary Rodham Clinton—there was no analogous wellspring of childhood identification with Israel and Judaism. And, among Obama's senior foreign policy team, no member could rightfully hold a candle to Clinton's record of support for Palestinian rights, which included her path-breaking backing of Palestinian statehood, a controversial position she adopted during the Clinton administration long before a two-state resolution to the Israeli-Palestinian conflict became de rigueur among US politicians. As she reminded attendees at a gala hosted by the American Task Force on Palestine in October 2010, "as First Lady, I may have been the first person ever associated with an American administration to call for a Palestinian state and the two-state solution," which, she noted, "is now the official policy of the United States." Clinton was capable of deploying a level of sympathy for the Palestinian people that Biden could not muster. She acknowledged that with a two-state solution, "The indignity of occupation would end and a new era of opportunity, promise, and justice would begin." She recounted how during a September 2010 visit to the West Bank, "as I looked at the faces of the men and women who came out of their shops and homes to watch us go by, it was impossible to forget the painful history of a people who have never had a state of their own. (Applause.) For most Americans, it is hard, if not impossible, to imagine living behind checkpoints and roadblocks, without the comforts of peace or the confidence of self-determination."[24]

Clinton could speak about her personal empathy for and understanding of Israelis as well. For example, in her address to AIPAC's 2008 policy conference, she spoke of how six years earlier she "went to the Sbarro Pizzeria [in Jerusalem] with then President [*sic*] [Ehud] Olmert just a few weeks after that tragic suicide bombing there. I visited with victims of terrorism in the Hadassah Hospital. I've been to Gilo and seen the security fence protecting Israeli families from attacks in their own homes. And I've stood up and spoken out for their right to have that protective fence." Although Clinton averred that her "support for Israel does not come recently or lightly; I know it is right in my head, in my heart, and in my gut,"[25] her fidelity to pro-Israel causes seemed more driven by cold political calculation than by the passion of a politician like Biden.

Obama's pick for US ambassador to the UN, Susan Rice, however, had no such hesitations in wearing her emotions on her sleeve when it came to defending Israel based on her personal experiences. Like Biden, in front of Jewish audiences Rice would feel at ease and would address Israel policy issues from the heart. Rice was fond of throwing in a smattering of Hebrew phrases to endear herself to her audience, as she did when she spoke at a March 2012 AIPAC Synagogue Initiative Lunch. She stated that "being here calls to mind one of my favorite psalms: *Hinei ma'tov uma-nayim, shevet achim gam yachad*— I'll take some lessons afterwards if anybody's willing—but as you know well, that is 'how good it is and how pleasant when we sit together in brotherhood.'" On such occasions, Rice would wax nostalgic about her first encounter with Israel, "when I was just 14 years old. I went with my younger brother and my late father, who was then on the Board of Directors of Trans World Airlines (TWA).

We had the extraordinary experience of flying on one of the very first flights from Tel Aviv to Cairo, just around the time of Camp David. On that same trip, we went to Yad Vashem [Israel's Holocaust museum], we floated in the Dead Sea, we walked the lanes of the Old City, climbed Masada, and picked fruit at a kibbutz. I learned by heart the words of the sacred prayer, the *Sh'ma*. And since that first wonderful visit, my admiration for Israel has grown ever stronger."[26] Undoubtedly, these sentiments would play a significant role in her willing efforts at the UN to shield Israel from accountability for its violations of international law.

OPERATION CAST LEAD

However, even before President-elect Obama had an opportunity to firm his foreign policy team, much less take the oath of office, Israel presented him with a foreign policy challenge of immeasurable proportions, the consequences of which, in many respects, would set the parameters and define the issues for his administration's policies toward the Israeli-Palestinian conflict.

In June 2008, Egypt had brokered a six-month cease-fire between Israel and Hamas that had significantly reduced, but not eliminated, cross-border incidents of violence. Amid mutual recriminations that the other side was not fulfilling its terms, the cease-fire began to break down before its expiration, leaving the possibility of its extension in question. On November 4, 2008, as US citizens went to the polls in a historic election that captivated the attention of the world, Israel launched a major ground incursion into the Gaza Strip that killed six Hamas members and triggered retaliatory rocket fire (no Israelis were injured), shredding whatever slim chance remained of the cease-fire obtaining.[27]

From that point onward, events slid inexorably to their horrifying, cataclysmic conclusion. On December 27, 2008, at a time when people in the United States were in the midst of celebrating the winter holiday season and the US government was virtually incapacitated by the impending departure of the Bush administration and the advent of the Obama administration, Israel launched a massive three-week land, air and sea attack on the occupied and blockaded Gaza Strip, code-named Operation Cast Lead. According to Israeli military sources, Israeli Defense Minister Ehud Barak had ordered plans for this attack six months beforehand, even as Israel was negotiating a truce with Hamas.[28] The results of this attack were devastating. According to the Palestinian human rights organization al-Haq, Israel killed 1,409 Palestinians, of whom 1,172 (or more than 83 percent) were civilians, including 342 children. Israel damaged or destroyed 11,152 Palestinian homes, 211 factories, 703 stores, 100 other commercial and public premises, 6,271 dunams of agricultural land (1 dunam=10,764 square feet) and 396,599 productive trees in a deliberate and systematic assault against civilians and civilian infrastructure in the Gaza Strip.[29] By contrast, according to the Israeli human rights organization B'Tselem, Palestinian rocket fire killed three Israeli civilians during Operation Cast Lead. In addition, ten members of the Israeli military were killed in battle, four of whom were killed in "friendly fire" incidents.[30]

A UN fact-finding mission report, whose recommendations the Obama administration would later attempt to vigorously suppress, concluded that both Israel and Palestinian armed groups committed grave "violations of international human rights and humanitarian law and possible war crimes and crimes against humanity" before, during and after Operation Cast Lead.[31] Innumerable heartrending stories of devastation proliferate from the wreckage of this attack. The full scope of the horror and terror inflicted on Palestinians in the Gaza Strip cannot be adequately addressed in this book, but hopefully a few short vignettes will give a very small insight into them.

For example, Amer Shurrab, a recent graduate of Vermont's Middlebury College and a former camper in the Seeds of Peace conflict resolution program that brings together Arab and Israeli youth, related how his two brothers—Kassab and Ibrahim—were killed and his father, Mohammed, was injured after Israeli troops summarily opened fire on their car after they returned from farming their land during a supposed daily cease-fire. According to Shurrab, "Israeli troops opened fire on them from a house that they occupied in the area. They started firing at them without warning, without saying 'Stop' or 'You can't pass by.' And they fired to kill. They didn't fire at the engine or at the tires. They fired toward the passengers and toward the drivers."[32] The soldiers refused to allow an ambulance access to the wounded civilians until nearly twenty-four hours had passed, by which time Shurrab's two brothers had bled to death under the soldiers' watchful eyes.

On January 4, 2009, Israel fired a white phosphorous shell that hit the Abu Halima household in Sifaya, a village near Beit Lahiya in the Gaza Strip. Sixteen members of the family were taking shelter in the house at the time of the attack. "According to family members who survived," the UN fact-finding report stated, "there was intense fire and white smoke in the room, the walls of which were glowing red. Five members of the family died immediately or within a short period: Muhammad Sa'ad Abu Halima (age 45) and four of his children, sons Abd al-Rahim Sa'ad (age 14), Zaid (age 12) and Hamza (age 8), and daughter Shahid (age 18 months). Muhammad Sa'ad and Abd al-Rahim Sa'ad were decapitated, the others burnt to death. Five members of the family escaped and suffered various degrees of burns: Sabah Abu Halima, her sons Youssef (age 16) and Ali (age 4), daughter-in-law Ghada (age 21), and Ghada's daughter Farah (age 2)." Two other family members—Muhammad Hekmat Abu Halima and Matar Abu Halima—were subsequently shot and killed by Israeli soldiers while trying to transport wounded survivors to a hospital.[33]

These ghastly attacks on civilians and civilian infrastructure, which included strikes against schools, refugee camps, UN installations, hospitals and ambulances, were conducted by Israel with US weapons, including its fleet of 300 F-16 fighter jets, which likely dropped a combination of US-supplied M-82 and M-84 "dumb bombs," along with Paveway II and JDAM guided "smart bombs." Israel also carried out its aerial bombardment of the Gaza Strip with US-supplied AH-64 Apache attack helicopters and AH-IF Cobra helicopter gunships, equipped with AGM-114 Hellfire guided missiles. Israel also made extensive use of its US-provided artillery, which included M433 40mm high-explosive, dual-purpose (HEDP) cartridges, M889A1 81mm high-explosive cartridges, M107 155mm high-explosive artillery rounds, M14 183mm "bunker defeat" munitions, M930 120mm illuminating cartridges and the M971 120mm dual-purpose improved conventional munitions (DPICM), which was jointly developed by the United States and Israel. This latter weapon is described as being "essentially a cluster bomb that separates into 24 submunitions, each containing more than 1,200 fragments, that explode above the target to create a wide and dense area of coverage within a 350-foot radius." Israeli infantry soldiers were also equipped with US-made M16 assault rifles.

Beyond these conventional weapons, Israel deployed a range of special weapons, some of which were provided by the United States, including M825A1 155mm white phosphorous artillery munitions, the same type of weapon that devastated the Abu Halima family. Israel may have also used the tungsten-based, cancer-causing dense inert metal explosives (DIME) munitions created by the US Air Force and bullets and missiles provided by the United States that were coated with depleted uranium (DU), another cancer-causing weapon.[34]

In March 2009, Human Rights Watch (HRW) issued a report entitled "Rain of Fire: Israel's Unlawful Use of White Phosphorus in Gaza," which concluded that Israel's firing of white phosphorus was "neither incidental nor accidental." Rather, its "repeated firing of air-burst white phosphorus shells from 155mm artillery into densely populated areas was indiscriminate and indicates the commission of war crimes." Its researchers noted that all of the white phosphorus shells they found in Gaza were manufactured in the United States, with markings denoting their production in April 1989 by Thiokol Aerospace, which then operated the Louisiana Army Ammunition Plant. Reuters also photographed, on January 4, 2009, an Israeli artillery unit near Gaza handling M825A1 shells with lot numbers indicating they were produced in the United States at Pine Bluff Arsenal in September 1991. HRW recommended that the United States investigate whether Israel's misuse of white phosphorus violated international law and/or US arms transfer agreements and that it halt the transfer of these weapons to Israel until it does so.[35]

Examining the impact not only of white phosphorus, but of the panoply of weapons unleashed by Israel during Operation Cast Lead, Amnesty International, in an earlier February 2009 report entitled "Fuelling Conflict: Foreign Arms Supplies to Israel/Gaza," called upon the UN Security Council to impose a comprehensive arms embargo against Israel and armed Palestinian groups and urged all countries to "act immediately to unilaterally suspend all transfers of military equipment, assistance and munitions." While its recommendation was not specifically directed to the United States, Amnesty

International copiously documented major US arms transfers to Israel in the years preceding Operation Cast Lead and noted that "since early December 2008, the US Military Sealift Command has been organizing three large deliveries by sea of military ammunition and high explosives, including explosives with white phosphorus, from the US base at Sunny Hill, North Carolina, to an Israeli port near Gaza." Tenders issued for these shipments show that they comprised more than 1,300 shipping containers of ammunition totaling more than 7.7 million pounds of net explosive weight, including two shipments initiated four days after Israel embarked on Operation Cast Lead.[36]

Mounting domestic and international outrage over the barbarity of Israel's attack on the Gaza Strip forced the outgoing Bush administration to abstain from voting on UN Security Council Resolution 1860 on January 8, 2009. The adopted resolution demanded, among other things, an "immediate, durable and fully respected cease-fire, leading to the full withdrawal of Israeli forces from Gaza" and "the unimpeded provision and distribution throughout Gaza of humanitarian assistance, including of food, fuel and medical treatment."[37]

However, instead of backing international diplomacy and respecting the Bush administration's decision not to veto this cease-fire resolution, the Senate responded the same day, and the House one day later, by passing resolutions justifying Israel's attacks on the Gaza Strip, thereby providing Israel with a green light to ignore the UN and to continue its carnage for another excruciating ten days.

On January 8, Senate Majority Leader Harry Reid (D-NV) and Senate Minority Leader Mitch McConnell (R-KY) rushed to the floor S.Res.10, a resolution that had been introduced that same day. Neglecting to hold hearings and dispensing with the Senate's infamously slow deliberative process, these senators jammed through by unanimous consent a resolution "recognizing the right of Israel to defend itself against attacks from Gaza and reaffirming the United States' strong support for Israel in its battle with Hamas." Reid asked his colleagues to imagine what they would do if there were "rockets and mortars coming from Toronto and [sic] Canada into Buffalo, NY. How would we as a country react? We would react, and we would react swiftly and quickly." He argued that "Israel has been very patient" by not unleashing this fury against Gaza earlier. McConnell answered Reid's question by asserting that Israelis "are responding exactly the same way we would if rockets were being launched into the United States from Canada or Mexico or some similar situation. The Israelis have every right to defend themselves against these acts of terrorism."

Only Senator Patrick Leahy (D-VT) pointed out the logic of this argument leading only to more bloodshed, noting that "Israel seeks to deal a fatal blow to Hamas militants, to bomb them into submission and moderation. If our country were attacked in a similar way by one of our neighbors we might respond the same way. But there is little if any reason to believe these tactics can work. This latest escalation, with bombs falling and tank artillery striking in heavily populated areas where civilians—more than half of whom are children—have no means of escape, obviously and tangibly is providing ammunition to extremists, inside and outside of Gaza." Leahy also rightfully noted that Israel was far from blameless; its blockade of Gaza, he stated, "has caused extreme hardship for the Palestinian people collectively in Gaza but done nothing to change Hamas's militant policies. The blockade was not coupled with an effective strategy to address the underlying causes of the conflict."[38]

Not to be outdone, the House of Representatives took up debate the next day on a similar resolution, H.Res.34, depicting Israel's actions in even more glorious terms and denouncing Palestinians even more outlandishly. The resolution was adopted overwhelmingly by a vote of 390-5 with twenty-two abstentions. During the debate, dozens of Representatives lined up at the podium to blame Palestinians and praise Israel for its alleged "restraint." Representative Ileana Ros-Lehtinen (R-FL) actively encouraged Israel to disregard the UN cease-fire resolution, arguing that it was "unbalanced" and that "Israel must not abide by it." She declared that "the US and Israel are in this together. We have a saying in Spanish about close alliances that describes the US and Israel friendship perfectly, we are two wings of one bird." Representative Gary Ackerman (D-NY) diminished the significance of the loss of life by likening Operation Cast Lead to an "altercation" that "reminds me of my two boys when they were growing up and they would get in a little hassle with each other." Representative Dana Rohrabacher (R-CA) placed sole responsibility for Operation Cast Lead on Palestinians in a classic blame-the-victim mentality. "The radical Islamists who ruthlessly and without remorse did what they knew would bring retaliation and slaughter on their own people, they are the ones to blame," he argued. "The hatred in their hearts, the hatred of Israel, the irreconcilable hatred of those people obviously outweighs the commitment to the safety of their own women and children in Gaza. They are the ones who are to blame for the carnage that is going on right now." Representative Steny Hoyer (D-MD) took the prize for the most reprehensible statement in defense of Israel's actions. He argued that it would be reasonable for Israel to engage in genocide and full-scale extermination of Palestinians in Gaza, because if the United States faced rocket fire from across its borders, "Mexico would not exist, nor would Canada, quite simply put. We would not tolerate, and no amount of criticism leveled on us would in any way modify our response."

Hoyer's incitement to crimes against humanity notwithstanding, other representatives marshaled surprisingly nuanced and politically brave arguments to counter this congressional grandstanding. Representative Nick Rahall (D-WV) accused Israel of a premeditated attack, reminding the chamber, "This campaign was planned some time ago, not just at the expiration of the cease-fire in December." Representative Betty McCollum (D-MN) rejected hysterical assertions that Israel faced an "existential threat," instead comparing rocket attacks to "a drug gang that uses drive by shootings as a tactic to terrify a neighborhood. When is the solution to this type of terror for authorities to lay waste to the neighborhood?" Representative Jim Moran (D-VA) countered the oft-heard argument that Israel was doing its utmost to avoid civilian casualties by providing advance notice of its attacks. "The citizens of Gaza, most of whom are refugees, have nowhere to go," he commented. "They are prevented from fleeing into Israel or Egypt and are cornered in one of the most populated areas in the world."

A few representatives such as Ron Paul (R-TX) and Dennis Kucinich (D-OH) noted that Israel's use of US weapons during Operation Cast Lead was illegal and harmful to US interests. "I am concerned that the weapons currently being used by Israel against the Palestinians in Gaza are made in America and paid for by American taxpayers," Paul stated. "What will adopting this resolution do to the perception of the United States in the Muslim and Arab world? What kind of blowback might we see from this? What moral responsibility do we have for the violence in Israel and Gaza after having provided so much military support to one side?" For his part, Kucinich noted, "The people of Gaza have no army, no navy, no air force. Israel using F-16 jets and Apache helicopters acquired from the United States is engaged in a military offensive inside Gaza, escalating the conflict in Gaza, and prejudicing the development of peace agreements, contrary to the letter of the stated policies and purposes of US military assistance to Israel."[39]

Despite these contrary opinions, if President-elect Obama needed a reminder that Congress was willing to challenge both presidential prerogatives and the will of the international community when it came to policymaking on the Israeli-Palestinian conflict, then legislative action in the wake of the UN Security Council cease-fire resolution provided ample proof. These congressional histrionics, which reached a crescendo with the overwhelming passage of decidedly one-sided resolutions backing Israel, undoubtedly contributed to, but did not justify, Obama's alarming silence on Operation Cast Lead. On December 31, 2008, Obama's national security spokesperson Brooke Anderson stated that "President-elect Obama is closely monitoring global events, including the situation in Gaza, but there is one president at a time,"[40] relying on a constitutionally correct but politically weak argument to rationalize his unwillingness to take a stand. The fact that "there is one president at a time" did not prevent Obama's transition team from issuing statements about other important foreign policy issues during the interregnum, such as in response to the November 2008 terrorist attacks in Mumbai.

Honolulu-based activist Ann Wright, a retired US army colonel and former US diplomat who resigned in protest in 2003 over the US war against Iraq, organized daily protests in December 2008 and January 2009 outside of Obama's rented Hawaii compound where he was living during parts of Operation Cast Lead. Wright visited Gaza shortly after the cease-fire took hold in late January 2009 and met with representatives of the Palestinian Centre for Human Rights, an organization which had "in their office all sorts of Israeli war materiel and exploded bombs. You could see the US markings on them." She also visited al-Shifa hospital, which had a huge display of damaged ambulances targeted by Israel, along with shrapnel from exploded munitions. Wright said that the hospital had "big photos of many of those killed by this materiel. One felt very ashamed that American bombs and missiles had killed people." It was this knowledge of US complicity in Operation Cast Lead that had impelled Wright to organize daily morning vigils outside of Obama's house, calling on the president-elect to speak out against the atrocities taking place in Gaza. According to Wright, Obama definitely saw the signs as he drove out of his compound for his morning workout at a nearby marine base and was "really was not very friendly about us holding signs condemning the Israeli attack," failing to wave or otherwise acknowledge the protestors' presence. She felt that "surely someone from his team would come out to say something," but no one ever did.[41]

On January 6, 2009, Obama finally broke his silence on the killing taking place in Gaza when he noted that civilian casualties were a "source of deep concern for me." He pledged, "We've got plenty to say about Gaza, and on January 20, you'll hear directly from me."[42] Apparently, the Israeli embassy also had plenty to say to Obama's transition team about Operation Cast Lead. Relying on a confidential source, blogger Richard Silverstein reported that the "Israeli embassy provided regular written briefings for Obama and his staff aimed at presenting Israel's side of the war. An Obama staffer reportedly reassured a top Israeli diplomat, according to my source, that Obama did not wish to intervene in the fighting or the political debate before he became president."[43] However, despite this revelation and Obama's reticence to discuss Operation Cast Lead in public, this lobbying campaign was apparently flowing in both directions. Behind-the-scenes pressure from the transition team reportedly resulted in Israel agreeing to end its assault on January 18, two days before Obama was inaugurated. Investigative journalist Seymour Hersh reported that according to a "former senior intelligence official, who has access to sensitive information, '[Vice President Dick] Cheney began getting messages from the Israelis about pressure from Obama.'" But this pressure from the Obama transition team to end the attack apparently did not extend to a concern about the United States rearming Israel. According to Hersh, the "Obama team let it be known that it would not object to the planned resupply of 'smart bombs' and other high-tech ordnance that was already flowing to Israel."[44]

Whatever the reality was of who pressured whom around extending or ending Operation Cast Lead, it is clear that Israel conveniently timed the entire attack—from the Election Day incursion into the Gaza Strip, to the post-Christmas and pre–New Year holiday launch, to the pre-Inauguration Day cessation of hostilities—to coincide with the US political and holiday calendar. By doing so, Israel presented the incoming administration with a host of immediate policy challenges with which it would have to contend before trying its hand at Israeli-Palestinian peacemaking.

CHAPTER TWO

Settlements Have to Be Stopped

As President Barack Obama entered the White House on January 20, 2009, he made good on his campaign promises to address the Israeli-Palestinian conflict from the outset of his administration. He also upheld his pledge to say something about the situation in the blockaded Palestinian Gaza Strip, which only two days prior to his inauguration had finally received a respite from Israel's devastating Operation Cast Lead. And by appointing former Senate Majority Leader George Mitchell as his Special Envoy for Middle East Peace on only his second full day in office, Obama wasted no time attempting to resolve the nettlesome Israeli-Palestinian conflict.

GEORGE MITCHELL, SPECIAL ENVOY FOR MIDDLE EAST PEACE

Mitchell's appointment signified a possible new dawn in US foreign policymaking toward the Israeli-Palestinian conflict for at least three reasons. First, Mitchell brought to the table a wealth of experience resolving a similarly vexatious conflict in Northern Ireland through sound principles of conflict resolution anchored in concepts of inclusion and reciprocity. Second, Mitchell already had a proven track record of producing a somewhat balanced report on the Israeli-Palestinian conflict—the April 2001 Sharm El-Sheikh Fact-Finding Committee Report, also known as the Mitchell Report—the recommendations of which formed the basis for the 2003 Roadmap, which imposed mutual and simultaneous responsibilities on both

Palestinians and Israelis to take steps toward a peace agreement. Third, Mitchell's ethnic background—part Irish, part Lebanese—and his lack of overt ties to pro-Israel organizations and constituencies made him a much more credible "honest broker" than others responsible for the Israeli-Palestinian "peace process" during the Clinton and Bush administrations. These officials' self-admittedly pro-Israel orientation had played a major role in torpedoing any US-led breakthrough.

In 1995, President Bill Clinton had appointed Mitchell as his Special Envoy for Northern Ireland. In January 1996, Mitchell enunciated six guidelines, known as the Mitchell Principles, which would form the basis for later all-party negotiations that would lead to the 1998 Good Friday Agreement, paving the way to a resolution of the centuries-old struggle for power between Protestants and Catholics. According to Mitchell, these principles included the "total and absolute commitment" of the negotiating parties to "democratic and exclusively peaceful means of resolving political issues"; disarmament of paramilitary groups; independent verification of such disarmament; the renunciation "for themselves, and to oppose any effort by others, to use force, or threaten to use force, to influence the course or the outcome of all-party negotiations"; agreement to "abide by the terms of any agreement" and to "resort to democratic and exclusively peaceful methods in trying to alter any aspect of that outcome"; and an end to retaliatory beatings and killings.[1]

These principles, if extrapolated to the US approach to the Israeli-Palestinian conflict, would presage a dramatic reorientation of its outlook on achieving peace. The Mitchell Principles were fully in keeping with the January 2006 preconditions, issued by the Quartet—the United States, the European Union, Russia and the United Nations—after Hamas won the Palestinian legislative election. These preconditions for Hamas to enter the negotiating process included "nonviolence, recognition of Israel, and acceptance of previous agreements and obligations, including the Roadmap."[2] Khaled Elgindy, a key participant in the Annapolis Peace Conference, noted that although this Quartet "formula has no standing in international law, it has assumed a kind of semi-legal status, particularly among American and Israeli policymakers, many of whom regard it as both immutable and binding."[3] However, during the Bush administration, Israel was allowed to disregard its obligation under the Roadmap to freeze settlements, which are illegal according to international law. The Mitchell Principles, if applied to the Israeli-Palestinian conflict, would rectify this imbalance and hold all sides accountable to their previous commitments. The Mitchell Principles would also demand adherence to principles of nonviolence by all sides, which would compel Israel to renounce concepts such as the "Dahiyeh Doctrine," its policy of terrorizing civilian populations and deliberately targeting civilian infrastructure through massive paroxysms of violence to coerce political change.

Mitchell's experience negotiating an accord to end the Northern Ireland conflict drew the attention of the Negotiations Support Unit (NSU) of the PLO, which attempted to derive lessons learned from Mitchell's negotiating style and anticipate his approach as Special Envoy for Middle East Peace. In an undated, anonymous memorandum most likely written between mid-May and mid-June 2009, the NSU concluded that Mitchell would "undoubtedly rely on" these principles in his new position and predicted incorrectly that "Obama may be close to issuing a set of principles similar to the 'Mitchell Principles' of the Northern Ireland situation by mid-June 2009."[4]

Not only would the Palestinian negotiating team notice parallels between Mitchell's two peacemaking roles; Mitchell himself would often rely on his experiences in Northern Ireland to explain and guide his approach to resolving the Israeli-Palestinian conflict. When he was appointed Special Envoy for Middle East Peace, Mitchell noted that this job, like his previous mediation role, would require patience and perseverance. In negotiating peace in Northern Ireland, Mitchell remarked, "we had 700 days of failure and one day of success. For most of the time, progress was nonexistent or very slow. So I understand the feelings of those who may be discouraged about the Middle East." After having spoken to an audience in Jerusalem about his role in resolving the 800-year conflict in Northern Ireland, Mitchell joked that "an elderly gentleman came up to me and he said, 'Did you say 800 years?' And I said, 'Yes, 800.' He repeated the number again—I repeated it again. He said, 'Uh, such a recent argument. No wonder you settled it.'" But despite the longevity of these two conflicts, from his experience in Northern Ireland Mitchell "formed the conviction that there is no such thing as a conflict that can't be ended. Conflicts are created, conducted, and sustained by human beings. They can be ended by human beings. I saw it happen in Northern Ireland, although, admittedly, it took a very long time. I believe deeply that with committed, persevering, and patient diplomacy, it can happen in the Middle East."[5] His patience and perseverance would be tested to their utmost during his more than two years as Special Envoy for Middle East Peace.

Not only did Mitchell have a track record of successful efforts in resolving the seemingly intractable Northern Ireland conflict; he also had a history of involvement with the Israeli-Palestinian conflict that augured well for his ability to serve as an "honest broker." In 2001, at the height of the second Palestinian intifada, or uprising, Mitchell chaired a distinguished five-person committee that was tasked with investigating the causes of the outbreak of violence and submitting recommendations to restart the "peace process." At this time, the prevailing discourse in the United States placed sole blame for the breakdown of the 2000 Camp David Summit on Palestinian Authority (PA) President Yasser Arafat for rejecting Israeli Prime Minister Ehud Barak's supposed "generous offer" and accused Arafat of supporting, if not orchestrating, Palestinian acts of violence. In this environment, Mitchell's report stood out as a relatively balanced document amid a sea of harsh, anti-Palestinian rhetoric.

The Sharm El-Sheikh Fact-Finding Committee, as it was formally known, which issued its report on April 30, 2001, concluded that both Israel and the PA "should immediately implement an unconditional cessation of violence." In addition to demanding that the PA condemn terrorism, combat anti-Israel incitement, and resume security cooperation with Israel, the report also asserted that Israel must take steps to minimize civilian casualties by adopting and enforcing "policies and procedures encouraging non-lethal responses to unarmed demonstrators." Mitchell also recommended that Israel should "lift closures, transfer to the PA all tax revenues owed, and permit Palestinians who had been employed in Israel to return to their jobs; and should ensure that security forces and settlers refrain from the destruction of homes and roads, as well as trees and other agricultural property in Palestinian areas," in order to significantly reduce the economic impact to Palestinians of Israel's harsh response to the intifada. Most significantly for his appointment as Obama's Special Envoy for Middle East Peace, Mitchell concluded in his 2001 report that Israel "should freeze all settlement activity, including the 'natural growth' of existing settlements."[6] This latter recommendation was reiterated in the first phase of the 2003 Roadmap.[7] Mitchell and the rest of Obama's foreign policy team would rely upon the Roadmap to argue convincingly that its urging of Israel to freeze settlement expansion was not a new demand, but rather represented a fulfillment of prior agreements to which Israel had already committed itself.

The relative evenhandedness of the 2001 Mitchell Report demonstrated that Mitchell could be relied upon not to take an overtly partisan approach to his mediation efforts as Special Envoy for Middle East Peace. In constrast, it was the self-admitted pro-Israel bias demonstrated repeatedly during the Clinton and Bush administrations by "peace process" officials such as Aaron David Miller, Dennis Ross, Martin Indyk and Elliott Abrams that had sunk any hopes of the United States acting as an "honest broker." This predisposition was epitomized best by Dennis Ross, who between government stints cofounded the Washington Institute for Near East Policy, a pro-Israel "think tank" with strong connections to AIPAC. In his self-serving tome that sought to justify his policy failures, Ross admitted to the rigged nature of the "peace process." He wrote that " 'selling' became part of our *modus operandi*—beginning a pattern that would characterize our approach throughout the Bush and Clinton years. We would take Israeli ideas or ideas that the Israelis could live with and work them over—trying to increase their attractiveness to the Arabs while trying to get the Arabs to scale back their expectations."[8] No wonder then that the US-brokered "peace process," guided by officials such as Ross, failed to produce an Israeli-Palestinian peace agreement.

Mitchell entered his position as Special Envoy for Middle East Peace unencumbered by this type of pro-Israel ideological baggage that had bedeviled prior US peacemaking efforts. As Secretary of State Hillary Clinton jested, "George Mitchell's father was Irish and his mother was Lebanese. Well, he solved half of his family's problems. So now he's here working on the second half, and we hope that we will see it come to fruition."[9] This reference to Mitchell's ethnic heritage signaled a break from the Clinton and Bush administrations' record of placing Jewish-American officials in charge of Israeli-Palestinian peacemaking. Although of course there is nothing inherently wrong with appointing Jewish-Americans to these positions, and to suggest otherwise would be to engage in stereotyping, it was nevertheless these individuals' particular pro-Israel orientations that dented the credibility of the United States to act as an "honest broker."

Unfortunately though, the Obama administration was not able to wholly abandon this tradition, as the peripatetic Ross was appointed to ambiguously mandated positions that covered the Middle East, first at the State Department and later in Obama's National Security Council. In these positions, Ross undercut Mitchell, contributing to the latter's frustrations and creating a dynamic "plagued with tension," according to the Israeli newspaper *Haaretz*. At times, "the two refused to speak to one another, partly over Ross' tendency to hold talks with Israeli officials behind Mitchell's back."[10]

However, these tensions were not yet evident at the outset of the Obama administration, and Mitchell's predisposition toward an evenhanded approach to Israeli-Palestinian peacemaking clearly rattled pro-Israel ideologues. Abe Foxman, National Director of the staunchly pro-Israel Anti-Defamation League, condemned Mitchell for his "neutrality," noting that "the Swiss were neutral" during World War II.[11] It would not be the last time that Israel's supporters would traffic in World War II and Nazi analogies in over-the-top, inflammatory attacks on the Obama administration's policies.

THE GAZA STRIP IN THE AFTERMATH OF OPERATION CAST LEAD

But before Mitchell could engage in meaningful, proactive attempts to broker Israeli-Palestinian peace, the Obama administration first had to deal with urgent policy issues stemming from the aftermath of Operation Cast Lead. These efforts included strengthening the international regime to interdict weapons flows to Hamas, monitoring Israel's compliance with demands for greater humanitarian access to the Gaza Strip, helping to coordinate an international donors' conference to pledge reconstruction aid, and responding to (or, more accurately, not responding to) direct Hamas overtures for political dialogue.

Obama had prioritized dealing with the consequences of Operation Cast Lead in his January 22, 2009, speech at the State Department announcing Mitchell's appointment:

> I was deeply concerned by the loss of Palestinian and Israeli life in recent days and by the substantial suffering and humanitarian needs in Gaza. Our hearts go out to Palestinian civilians who are in need of immediate food, clean water, and basic medical care, and who've faced suffocating poverty for far too long ... As part of a lasting cease-fire, Gaza's border crossings should be open to allow the flow of aid and commerce, with an appropriate monitoring regime, with the international [sic] and Palestinian Authority participating. Relief efforts must be able to reach innocent Palestinians who depend on them.[12]

Obama's support for the opening of Gaza's border crossings raised expectations that his administration would pressure Israel to ease, if not end, the devastating and illegal blockade it had imposed in 2007.

Before pressing Israel to loosen its blockade of the Gaza Strip, however, Obama picked up where the Bush administration had left off in strengthening the international regime to interdict weapons flows to Hamas. If the United States helped stanch or eliminate weapons flows to Hamas, then Israel would be deprived of its rationale for maintaining its stranglehold over the Gaza Strip. In the waning days of the Bush administration, the United States and Israel signed a memorandum of understanding, which committed the United States to "work with regional and NATO partners to address the problem of the supply of arms and related materiel and weapons transfers and shipments to Hamas and other terrorist organizations in Gaza, including through the Mediterranean, Gulf of Aden, Red Sea and eastern Africa, through improvements in existing arrangements or the launching of new initiatives to increase the effectiveness of those arrangements as they relate to the prevention of weapons smuggling to Gaza."[13]

Even prior to the signing of this agreement, the Bush administration was already in the process of stanching weapons flows to Gaza by having the US Army Corps of Engineers construct a Border Tunnel Activity and Detection System (BTADS) along the Egypt–Gaza Strip border with US military aid money to Egypt. The Obama administration continued work on this initiative. Even before the project was due to be completed in April 2010, "the process of drilling holes for the seismic acoustic sensors alone has resulted in the daily discovery of 1–3 tunnels per day," according to a December 2009 cable from the US embassy in Egypt. The Obama administration also consulted with Egyptian officials about, but apparently did not fund, Egypt's separate construction of a nineteen-meter-deep steel wall along the border, designed to operate in tandem with the US-funded BTADS to prevent the importation of goods through these tunnels.[14] While these projects undoubtedly reduced the ability of Hamas to smuggle weapons through these tunnels, they also undeniably reduced the capacity of Gaza's civilian population to receive foodstuffs and other needed goods through these same tunnels, products which were often denied to them by Israel's blockade. Thus these efforts to shut down the tunnels to stop weapons transfers to Hamas also exacerbated the humanitarian crisis.

The United States cracked down further on arms flows to the Gaza Strip on March 13, 2009, when it signed a Program of Action with eight other countries—Canada, Denmark, France, Germany, Italy, Netherlands, Norway, and the United Kingdom—to provide "a comprehensive platform for enhanced cooperation and coordination in the areas of information and intelligence sharing; diplomatic engagement; and military and law enforcement activities." According to the State Department, this initiative would provide an unspecified "new mechanism to seek to block arms shipments to Gaza."[15]

While the Obama administration proved eager to implement half of Amnesty International's recommendation to halt arms transfers to both Palestinian armed groups and Israel, it went forward with previously scheduled deliveries of huge caches of weapons to Israel. As noted in Chapter 1, the Obama transition team reportedly did not object to the Bush administration sending large shipments of weapons to Israel immediately before and during Operation Cast Lead. On March 22, 2009, a US-contracted ship unloaded one of these shipments—300 containers of US munitions—at the Israeli port of Ashdod. Although the weapons were supposedly destined for US prepositioned stockpiles of weapons in Israel, under a bilateral agreement, Israel could gain access to and use the US weapons in these stockpiles in an emergency, thereby further increasing the chances that US weapons could be misused again in a future conflagration.[16]

The Obama administration proceeded to deliver these weapons to Israel despite Representative Dennis Kucinich formally requesting from the State Department a report on whether Israel violated the terms of the Arms Export Control Act (AECA) through its use of US weapons during Operation Cast Lead.[17] Although the request was addressed to outgoing Secretary of State Condoleezza Rice on January 5, 2009, Kucinich reportedly did not receive the requested report from the Bush administration, and Obama's State Department shelved it. Had either administration delivered to Congress an honest accounting of Israel's use of US weapons during Operation Cast Lead, it would have concluded that Israel misused them for reasons other than those allowed by the AECA, which are limited to "internal security" and "legitimate self-defense," thus potentially triggering sanctions and making Israel ineligible for future US weapons transfers. This early failure of the Obama administration to hold Israel accountable for its violations of US law would initiate a pattern that encouraged Israel to thwart US laws and policy goals without fearing repercussions.

As the Obama administration forged ahead with new projects to stem the flow of weapons to Gaza while delivering additional arms to Israel, it also progressed along a parallel track of monitoring humanitarian aid access to Gaza and mobilizing the international community to pledge funds for Gaza's reconstruction. However, accomplishing these goals would not be easy. Four days before Obama's inauguration, the Israel Defense Forces (IDF) deputy chief of staff Major General Dan Harel brazenly admitted to US Defense Attaché Office officials from the US embassy in Tel Aviv that the "IDF has destroyed every desk and piece of government infrastructure in Gaza," according to a leaked cable summarizing his remarks. Harel then brashly informed his American interlocutors that "the next stage (i.e. post-conflict reconstruction) would be your problem."[18] The audacity of the Israeli military demanding that the United States clean up the mess that it created, rather than pay reparations to Palestinians for deliberately targeting civilians and civilian infrastructure, was matched only by the obstacles Israel placed in the way of the United States and the rest of the international community when they actually tried to meet this absurd demand.

The Obama administration had ample evidence that Israel was blocking the delivery of humanitarian goods to the Gaza Strip, thereby exacerbating the post-conflict humanitarian crisis there. For example, a February 27, 2009 cable from the US Consulate in Jerusalem noted, "International assistance agency contacts reported that the GOI [Government of Israel] has recently approved a slightly broader variety of goods for entry into Gaza. Overall access for goods into Gaza remains strictly limited, however. ConGen [Consul General] contacts said the GOI continues to reject many everyday items with limited, if any, dual use, e.g., toothpaste, shampoo, children's toys, and clothing."[19] Nor did the situation improve as the cease-fire tenuously held; in fact, the State Department knew that humanitarian access to Gaza was getting worse as time passed. According to a May 6, 2009 cable, "UNRWA [UN Relief and Works Agency] and NGO [nongovernmental organization] contacts report that access to Gaza slightly deteriorated since February. Israel continues to allow entry for only the most basic humanitarian supplies, such as food, medicine, and hygiene materials. The UN Logistics Cluster reported May 2 that roughly 200 MT [metric tons] of humanitarian relief items, including recreation kits, wheelchairs, and baby toys, have either received no response from COGAT [Coordinator of Government Activities in the Territories (an Israeli military position)] or have been denied. NGOs working in Gaza express frustration with repeated delays and rejections."[20]

The State Department also rejected Israeli charges that humanitarian aid to Gaza was being diverted to the benefit of Hamas. On March 11, 2009, the US embassy in Tel Aviv noted, "The highest levels of the GOI [Government of Israel] firmly believe that much of the NIS [New Israeli Shekel] 90 million from February's cash transfer used by [Palestinian Authority] PM [Prime Minister Salam] Fayyad for the UNDP [United Nations Development Program] housing reimbursement program ended up in the hands of Hamas. We have seen no evidence to support that claim despite our requests that the GOI show us the smoking gun." Moreover, the embassy believed that Israel was using this baseless charge as a pretext to propose additional Israeli supervision over international assistance to Gaza. An Israeli draft proposal on humanitarian access to Gaza shared with the United States stipulated that Israel "will maintain the authority to decide the amounts passed to Gaza via the PA [Palestinian Authority]" and "hold the right to veto any transfer of funds pending reports of international inspectors." The embassy summarily rebuffed this proposal, arguing, "Absent proof that there is a problem, we do not see that this mechanism provides either a necessary or sufficient solution. We also do not believe that the USG [US government] should support a mechanism that piles GOI control of donor revenues on top of GOI control of cash transfers between Palestinian banks."[21]

But if the Obama administration knew about the deteriorating humanitarian situation in the Gaza Strip and quashed Israeli efforts to gain additional leverage over international donations, then it largely failed to take the next logical step: to put adequate public or private pressure on Israel to alleviate the dire conditions in Gaza, as a step toward ending Israel's illegal blockade. In fact, at times the Obama administration's public reticence to criticize Israeli actions toward Gaza reached absurd proportions. For example, after Israel held up a Mercy Corps delivery of a Qatari-donated shipment of macaroni, the State Department could not even bring itself to answer reporters' questions about whether the United States considered pasta to be a weapon. On February 25, 2009, acting State Department spokesperson Robert Wood was asked whether pasta, like rice, should be considered by Israel to be a humanitarian item let into to Gaza. He responded, "I, from the podium here, can't tell you whether, you know, pasta should fall into a specific category—into that category of humanitarian assistance or not." An incredulous reporter pushed the issue, asking if Wood could "imagine any circumstance under which pasta could be considered a dual-use item? Or . . . is rigatoni somehow going to be used as a weapon?" Wood repeatedly refused to provide a straight answer. Even after admitting that "food certainly is" a humanitarian supply, he was "not able to tell you from here" whether Israel should allow all kinds of foods into the Gaza Strip.[22]

The ludicrousness of the Obama administration failing to demand that Israel unequivocally assure the delivery of humanitarian goods to the Gaza Strip, as required by the newly passed UN Security Council Resolution 1860, was only partially mitigated by the prominent role it took in convening an international donors' conference for humanitarian aid and reconstruction for the Gaza Strip. At this conference, which took place at Sharm el-Sheikh, Egypt, on March 2, 2009. Clinton stressed the urgency of the situation. "Time is of the essence. We cannot afford more setbacks and delays, or regrets about what might have been had different decisions been made. And now is not the time for recriminations. It is time to look ahead." The international community must do so, she argued, because "human progress depends on the human spirit. That a child growing up in Gaza without shelter, health care, or an education has the same right to go to school, see a doctor, and live with a roof over her head as a child growing up in your country or mine."[23] Notwithstanding Clinton's speech, her concern about the humanitarian situation in Gaza apparently took second fiddle at the conference to holding more than twenty bilateral meetings, during "almost all of" which "Iran was at the top of the agenda," according to the US embassy in Tel Aviv.[24] Nevertheless, the United States pledged a robust $900 million at the conference, including $300 million "to meet urgent humanitarian needs" in the Gaza Strip (the remaining $600 million was earmarked for direct budgetary support of the PA and "economic and institutional reforms in the West Bank").[25] However, this commitment would only scratch the surface of the economic needs in Gaza, which suffered an estimated $2 billion in damage to civilian infrastructure inflicted by Israel, primarily with US weapons.[26]

As these humanitarian efforts were underway, Hamas tried to break out of its political isolation by communicating through and meeting with current and former US elected officials and civil society representatives in an attempt to establish a dialogue with the Obama administration. For example, on a February 2009 trip to Gaza, which he called a "searing" experience, Senator John Kerry (D-MA), chair of the Senate Foreign Relations Committee, was handed a letter to Obama from Hamas.[27] In June 2009, Hamas delivered another letter to Obama via the US peace organization

CODEPINK. The letter, from Dr. Ahmed Yousef, former senior political advisor to Hamas leader Ismail Haniyeh, read, in part:

> We in the Hamas Government are committed to pursuing a just resolution to the conflict not in contradiction with the international community and enlightened opinion as expressed in the International Court of Justice, the United Nations General Assembly, and leading human rights organizations. We are prepared to engage all parties on the basis of mutual respect and without preconditions.
>
> However, our constituency needs to see a comprehensive paradigm shift that not only commences with lifting the siege on Gaza and halts all settlement building and expansion but develops into a policy of evenhandedness based on the very international law and norms we are prodded into adhering to.[28]

Later that month, former president Jimmy Carter traveled to Gaza to survey the wreckage from Operation Cast Lead. During his visit, Carter stated that Palestinians are treated "more like animals than human beings" under Israel's blockade. "Never before in history," he added, "has a large community been savaged by bombs and missiles and then deprived of the means to repair itself." During his trip, Carter met with Haniyeh, after which the latter declared, "If there is a real project that aims to resolve the Palestinian cause on establishing a Palestinian state on 1967 borders, under full Palestinian sovereignty, we will support it."[29]

It is not known whether Obama privately responded to these various Hamas overtures. Despite Hamas's willingness to show flexibility in meeting the Quartet's demands in order to participate in the political process, the Obama administration did not display any public desire to engage with Hamas to achieve such an outcome.

FREEZING ISRAELI SETTLEMENTS

Instead of responding to these Hamas feelers, the Obama administration had embarked on a different course, which included a full-scale review of US policy toward the Israeli-Palestinian "peace process" that was aimed at restarting negotiations between Israel and the PLO. Toward that end, within a week of Mitchell's appointment,

Obama's Special Envoy for Middle East Peace began the first of what were described by the Obama administration as "listening tours" of the Middle East. On one such early trip with Clinton in March 2009, following the Sharm el-Sheikh donors' conference for Gaza, a former senior State Department official traveling with the group recounted that "there was a kind of silence and people were careful," as the entourage drove into the West Bank and passed by Palestinian villages whose roads were blockaded with boulders, "but it was like, my God, you crossed that border and it was apartheid."[30] Interestingly, this anonymous official had no qualms about describing Israeli policies as apartheid, yet the Obama administration would use its bully pulpit repeatedly and vociferously to push back against critics of Israel for trying to "delegitimize" it by describing its policies in such terms. Nevertheless, this hovering disquietude over Israeli policies impelled Obama to admit that the Israeli-Palestinian "status quo is unsustainable" during a March 24, 2009 press conference shortly before Likud politician Benjamin Netanyahu became Israeli prime minister.[31]

To break this "unsustainable" logjam, the Obama administration hit upon a logical and reasonable demand: Israel would have to fulfill its obligations under the 2003 Roadmap to freeze all settlement construction, including the so-called "natural growth" of settlements, in order to create the right conditions and context for a resumption of direct Israeli-Palestinian negotiations. After Obama met with Netanyahu at the White House on May 18, 2009 for the first time in their respective positions as president and prime minister, Obama emphatically declared "that there's a clear understanding that we have to make progress on settlements. Settlements have to be stopped in order for us to move forward. That's a difficult issue. I recognize that, but it's an important one and it has to be addressed."[32] Although Obama never explicitly articulated this step as a precondition for the resumption of negotiations, this statement by Obama would be the most forceful and direct of his administration recognizing that settlement construction would have to cease in order for progress to be made toward Israeli-Palestinian peace.

The next week, after meeting with Egyptian Foreign Minister Ahmed Aboul Gheit, Clinton elaborated on the president's remarks, leaving no doubt as to where the Obama administration stood.

"With respect to settlements, the President was very clear when Prime Minister Netanyahu was here. He wants to see a stop to settlements—not some settlements, not outposts, not natural growth exceptions," Clinton declared. "We think it is in the best interests of the effort that we are engaged in that settlement expansion cease. That is our position. That is what we have communicated very clearly, not only to the Israelis but to the Palestinians and others. And we intend to press that point."[33]

This vehement US insistence on an Israeli settlement freeze was driven home to a somewhat skeptical PA President Mahmoud Abbas when he first met with Obama at the White House on May 28, 2009, the day after Clinton's statement. In their closed-door meeting with only note-takers present, Abbas asked Obama point blank:

> I have one question: are you serious about the two-state solution? If you are, I cannot comprehend that you would allow a single settlement housing unit to be built in the West Bank. If Israel refuses to stop settlements, what is the alternative? A) 1 state or B) chaos, extremism, violence. You have the choice ... If you cannot make Israel stop settlements and resume permanent status negotiations, who can?

Obama reassured Abbas that "the establishment of the Palestinian state is a must for me personally. In an expeditious manner, we will get to the two-state solution." Obama related to Abbas that Israel was hearing the exact same thing in private as he was saying in public. Expressing his frustration with attempts so far by the United States to secure a settlement freeze from Israel, Obama told Abbas: "I cannot report anything to you, what we heard from the Israelis doesn't deserve your time."[34]

In a report back to his staff on the White House meeting, lead Palestinian negotiator Dr. Saeb Erekat marveled at the changed atmosphere in Washington. "Much of what I say to you today is just between us," he told his staff. "The Washington I went to last week isn't the Washington I knew before." This optimism reflected renewed Palestinian hopes that they might get the fair shake from the Obama administration for which they had waited forlornly during the Clinton and Bush administrations.

By taking such a firm position against the expansion of Israel's settlements, it appeared that the Obama administration was standing by a 1979 State Department legal memorandum, prepared for President Carter, which concluded that the establishment of Israeli settlements in Occupied Palestinian Territory "is inconsistent with international law."[35] By building settlements, Israel was violating Article 49 of the Fourth Geneva Convention, which governs Israel's obligations as the occupying power. It states unequivocally that "the Occupying Power shall not deport or transfer parts of its own civilian population into the territory it occupies."[36]

However, during the Clinton and Bush administrations, the United States had virtually disregarded this State Department memorandum and had instead adopted a laissez-faire approach toward the expansion of Israeli settlements, even though under the Bush administration the United States twice got Israel to pledge to abide by documents stipulating an end to settlement growth. Consequently, during the Oslo "peace process," Israel's settler population grew from 281,800 in 1993 to 510,648 in 2009, more than an 80 percent increase.[37] This growing settler population, along with the concomitant expropriation of Palestinian land and natural resources that such expansion entailed, eroded Palestinian aspirations for a contiguous and viable state. More than any other policy, Israeli settlement expansion also contributed to the widespread Palestinian perception that "peace process" negotiations were designed to reinforce, rather than end, Israel's military occupation.

The importance Palestinians attached to this issue was underscored in a leaked March 2009 draft letter from PA Prime Minister Salam Fayyad to Senator John Kerry (D-MA), in which he followed up on their meeting of the previous month. Fayyad reminded Kerry that

As we discussed in our meeting, we, Palestinians, consider Israeli settlements to be *the* [emphasis in original] single greatest threat to the establishment of a viable and sovereign Palestinian state and, by extension, to the two-state solution. Regrettably, US policy opposing settlement expansion has for decades, as you stated, "existed on paper alone." Therefore, as you rightly concluded, "[n]othing will do more to make clear [US] seriousness about turning the page than demonstrating—with actions rather than words—that [you] are serious about Israel freezing settlement activity in the West Bank."[38]

It would remain to be seen whether the Obama administration would demonstrate the depth of its commitment to an Israeli settlement freeze by imposing penalties on Israel for its non-compliance. But, at least for the time being, the Palestinian side appeared convinced that a new page had been turned and that their concerns about Israeli settlement expansion were receiving a sympathetic hearing within the new Obama administration.

Although the Obama administration almost never isolated its demand that Israel freeze settlement expansion from parallel demands that Palestinians beef up security coordination with Israel and crack down on anti-Israel "incitement," and that Arab states take steps to normalize relations with Israel immediately, these latter demands appeared perfunctory and almost tacked on for the semblance of balance. Israel was clearly alarmed by this new tone emanating from Washington, a tone of nearly wall-to-wall and unequivocal opposition to the expansion of Israeli settlements. During Netanyahu's May 2009 visit to Washington, his aides said that the Israeli prime minister was "stunned" after meeting with Jewish members of Congress and hearing from them the exact same opposition to Israeli settlements he heard earlier that day at the White House.[39]

To blunt this demand, Netanyahu embarked on a two-pronged strategy of differentiating between categories of Israeli settlements and types of settlement growth, and signaling for the first time his willingness to allow for the establishment of a Palestinian state. The former line of argumentation proved ineffective, with Israel making distinctions without a difference in the eyes of the United States. For example, Israeli Deputy Foreign Minister Danny Ayalon tried to convince a Congressional delegation in April 2009 that there are actually three types of settlements: settlements that are not settlements, settlements that are legal, and settlements that are illegal. Ayalon maintained that because Israel illegally annexed East Jerusalem in 1980, a move which was not recognized by the United States, "there are no settlements there," according to a US embassy cable summarizing his remarks. Settlements approved by the Israeli government were "legal" in his view and distinguishable from unapproved "illegal" outposts, against which "Israel must take action," he said. Dismantling these "illegal" outposts, Ayalon claimed, was "something 'the left-wing government of [Prime Minister Ehud] Olmert and [Foreign Minister Tzipi] Livni' never did." However, even as staunch a supporter of Israel as Representative Adam Schiff (D-CA) seemed unmoved by this sophistry. Schiff "underlined that no matter how strong or articulate a case Israel makes on settlements, they will not convince the International Community and therefore, settlements will remain a distraction."[40]

Failing to convince with this line of reasoning, Israel then tried deploying mawkishness to explain why it could not countenance a freeze in the so-called "natural growth" of settlements. Netanyahu put it to an Israeli audience that "there is a need to enable the residents to lead normal lives, to allow mothers and fathers to raise their children like families elsewhere. The settlers are neither the enemies of the people nor the enemies of peace. They are an integral part of our people, a principled, pioneering and Zionist community."[41]

After meeting with Clinton at the State Department on June 17, 2009, Israeli Foreign Minister Avigdor Lieberman, himself a settler, tried out this rationale on a US audience. He averred that "we really don't have any intention to change the demographic balance in Judea and Samaria," referring to the occupied Palestinian West Bank by the biblical terms preferred by Israeli settlers. Then, immediately contradicting that statement, he told Clinton "that, you know, as— in every place around the world, baby [sic] are born (inaudible), people get married, some pass away. And we cannot accept—we cannot accept this vision about absolutely completely freezing call [sic] for our settlements. I think that we must keep the natural growth." He added ambiguously that "we had some understandings with the previous administration" about this matter.

But Clinton was having none of it, publicly rebuffing Lieberman's contention. She stated that "in looking at the history of the Bush administration, there were no informal or oral enforceable agreements. That has been verified by the official record of the administration and by the personnel in the positions of responsibility."[42] She then referenced an op-ed by Daniel Kurtzer, US ambassador to Israel during part of the Bush administration, who also authoritatively concluded that "no understandings existed with Israel regarding continued settlement activity" during the Bush administration.[43]

If these arguments did not succeed in reducing US pressure for a complete freeze on the expansion of Israeli settlements, then, perhaps, Netanyahu reasoned, a token nod toward accepting Palestinian statehood—a policy he heretofore opposed—would produce the desired effect. On June 14, 2009, Netanyahu delivered a much ballyhooed speech at Bar-Ilan University, in which he declared his extremely conditional and attenuated support for eventual Palestinian statehood. "If we receive this guarantee," from the United States, he stated, "regarding demilitarization and Israel's security needs, and if the Palestinians recognize Israel as the state of the Jewish people, then we will be ready in a future peace agreement to reach a solution where a demilitarized Palestinian state exists alongside the Jewish state." He affirmed that "if we could agree on the substance, then terminology would not pose a problem."[44]

Yet Netanyahu's terminology did not match the substance of his proposal, which called for a Palestinian "state" devoid of any attributes of sovereignty, such as control of borders and airspace, an independent foreign policy, and the right to raise an army. This was not a state in the sense that Palestinians and the international community understood the term, but represented a warmed-over Israeli vision of a Palestinian Bantustan "state" that had already been presented, and rejected, several times during the Oslo "peace process."

This move was a classic ploy by Netanyahu, who was raised in the United States and therefore believed that "I know what America is . . . America is a thing that can be easily moved . . . moved in the right direction." The once and future Israeli prime minister made this statement in a 2001 video that only surfaced during the Obama administration. In this video, Netanyahu bragged about how he "actually stopped the Oslo Accord" through his stratagems.[45] In this case, Netanyahu would move the United States "in the right direction" by uttering the magic word of Palestinian "statehood" to deflect pressure to freeze Israeli settlements.

Even before nominally accepting the idea of Palestinian statehood, Netanyahu made clear to a congressional delegation in April 2009 that he agreed fully with the previous Israeli government's offers on Palestinian "statehood," but just preferred not to call it a state. He believed that this entity "must be demilitarized, without control over its air space and electro-magnetic field, and without the power to enter into treaties or control its borders," positions which he reasserted in his Bar-Ilan speech. "Netanyahu concluded that he and opposition leader [and Israel's previous Foreign Minister] Tzipi Livni 'only disagree about the name,' i.e. the two-state solution," according to the US Embassy in Tel Aviv.[46]

Thus, by maintaining his strict opposition to Palestinian sovereignty and now simply calling his envisioned outcome of negotiations a "state," Netanyahu succeeded in garnering undeserved plaudits from the Obama administration, which now chose to view him as a flexible statesman capable of advancing Israeli-Palestinian peace, even though he remained intransigent by failing to freeze Israeli settlement expansion. Netanyahu's sleight of hand worked like a charm. "The President welcomes the important step forward in Prime Minister Netanyahu's speech," read a White House statement. "The President is committed to two states, a Jewish state of Israel and an independent Palestine, in the historic homeland of both peoples. He believes this solution can and must ensure both Israel's security and the fulfillment of the Palestinians' legitimate aspirations for a viable state, and he welcomes Prime Minister Netanyahu's endorsement of that goal."[47] Mitchell similarly viewed Netanyahu's speech as a milestone toward resuming negotiations:

> The important thing about the prime minister's speech is that he . . . included in his objective a Palestinian state. So there now is a common objective, which was not the case until that speech was made. And the President rightly noted and welcomed that comment, because now we have both sides moving toward the same objective with different points of view on how best to get there. And what we want is to get into a negotiation on that.[48]

This would not be the last time that Netanyahu outmaneuvered the Obama administration through political theater, but it would be extremely consequential, setting in motion the first of a series of humiliating climbdowns from its initial position that doomed the Obama administration's Israeli-Palestinian peacemaking efforts to an ignominious failure.

CHAPTER THREE

Negotiations Must Begin Soon

SETTLEMENT "MORATORIUM"

If Palestinians had dared to believe that the climate in Washington was changing for the better and that the Obama administration's early advocacy for a full Israeli settlement freeze presaged a more balanced US approach to Israeli-Palestinian peacemaking, then their hopes were abruptly dashed against the unrelenting rocks of US political reality. Between June 2009, when Prime Minister Netanyahu delivered his speech accepting a very truncated form of Palestinian "statehood," and September 2009, when President Barack Obama addressed the UN General Assembly for the first time, the United States conducted a bilateral negotiations with Israel to define the terms for a "package deal" on Israeli settlements that the United States believed would enable a resumption of Israeli-Palestinian negotiations.

The Obama administration undertook this initiative behind the backs of the Palestinian negotiating team, presenting it with a virtual fait accompli just days before Obama planned a trilateral meeting in New York between himself, Netanyahu, and Palestinian Authority (PA) President Mahmoud Abbas on the sidelines of the UN General Assembly. Worse yet, the United States traveled down this path knowing full well that what Israel was prepared to accept in the "package deal" fell short of minimum Palestinian demands and

Israeli obligations under the Roadmap, foreordaining a diplomatic stalemate, if not crisis.

This tactless US initiative rightfully perturbed the Palestinians, who felt demeaned and undermined by the Obama administration. Instead of continuing to insist that Israel uphold its obligations to freeze settlement expansion, the Obama administration suddenly placed Palestinians in the untenable position of either being forced to negotiate with Israel while it continued to colonize Palestinian land, or to rebuff the initiative and be portrayed by Israel and its supporters in the United States as the rejectionist party. For the Palestinian negotiating team, whose senior members were veterans of the Oslo "peace process" negotiations dating back to 1993, this move recalled the very worst of US diplomatic efforts—so cavalierly referred to by "peace process" negotiator Dennis Ross as "selling"— during the Clinton and Bush administrations, when the United States and Israel would collude on their mutually acceptable positions and then publicly blame Palestinians for not adopting them. George Mitchell's potential role as an "honest broker" in his position of Special Envoy for Middle East Peace was fatally compromised from here onward. Obama's Israeli-Palestinian peacemaking agenda was derailed as soon as he climbed down from his initial demand for a full Israeli settlement freeze. Despite launching direct negotiations one year after the trilateral meeting at the UN, Mitchell and his team were never able to put the initiative back on track.

It is unclear exactly why Obama so dramatically reversed course. Several plausible explanations present themselves. First, Obama was definitely feeling the heat from an uneasy and disgruntled Congress, which overwhelmingly preferred to take its foreign policy dictates from AIPAC, rather than reinforce the White House's efforts to freeze Israeli settlements. On May 18, 2009, seventy-six senators sent Obama an AIPAC-initiated letter that signaled their concern over the deterioration in US-Israeli relations. While not specifically mentioning the mounting controversy over the administration's call for a full settlement freeze, the senators noted that "while the United States has an important role to play, the parties themselves are the ones who will need to negotiate and live with whatever agreement is reached. As we work closely with our democratic ally, Israel, we must take into account the risks it will face in any peace agreement." In other words, if Israel did not want to fully freeze Israeli settlements, then the White House should not push it to do so. The senators further wrote that the bilateral relationship "requires that we work closely together as we recommit ourselves to our historic role of a trusted friend and active mediator." As is typically the case, the House version of this letter, signed by 328 representatives and sent to the president on May 28, 2009, was less circumspect. "The proven best way forward," the representatives contended, "is to work closely and privately together both on areas of agreement and especially on areas of disagreement."[1] The rebuke to Obama could not have been more obvious: stop airing dirty laundry in public and settle the disagreement out of the limelight.

Second, on June 25, 2009, Dennis Ross moved from his ambiguous position as Special Advisor for the Gulf and Southwest Asia at the State Department to an even more abstruse spot as Special Assistant to the President and Senior Director for the Central Region at the National Security Council (NSC), a position which was invented for Ross. The increasing proximity to the president of this quintessential "Israel firster" most likely played a role in reigning in Obama's initiative to completely freeze Israeli settlements. Ross's former "peace process" deputy, Aaron David Miller, lauded Obama's transfer of Ross to the NSC as "smart policy, because after we get done with the brouhaha with the Israelis over settlements, we have to deal with them in a very close and intimate way in the event we're going to want to be able to succeed on Israeli-Arab peace and on Iran." In Miller's view, this move constituted Obama providing "the proper adult supervision to keep the policy focused and tough and fair."[2]

Third, Obama's desire to move quickly on resolving the Israeli-Palestinian conflict was being thwarted by Israel's rejection of his initial strategy of freezing Israeli settlements; his impatience and relative lack of foreign policy experience likely contributed to a gnawing sense that a different approach was now required.

Whatever the exact reason for the dramatic shift in US policy during the summer of 2009, its impact on the Palestinian negotiating team was devastating. As media reports broke of bilateral US-Israeli negotiations over the terms of a partial reduction in Israeli settlement activities limited in both time and geographical scope, the Palestinian negotiating team attempted to push back, arguing that a meaningful freeze would have to be comprehensive and unlimited in duration for negotiations to resume and succeed. A draft letter, dated August 10, 2009, from PA Prime Minister Salam Fayyad to Mitchell made this case well. Fayyad argued that

> for a settlement freeze to be effective both on the ground and in the hearts and minds of Palestinians, it must include a cessation of settlement and settlement-related construction (*e.g.*, the Wall, bypass roads, checkpoints, etc.); economic incentives and subsidies for settlements and settlers; confiscation and destruction of Palestinian land and other property, whatever the pretext; planning and authorizations for settlements; and migration to settlements . . . An effective settlement freeze must also remain in effect until a peace agreement is reached and implemented. The reasons for a freeze will be just as compelling and pressing 3 months or 6 months from now as they are today. In fact, I would say, more so: If a deadline for a freeze were set and a peace agreement not reached within that time, the resumption of settlement activity after the deadline would immediately destroy whatever progress might have been made until then.[3]

However, Fayyad's prescient warning, which would come to pass exactly as predicted, fell on deaf ears.

Mitchell, his deputy David Hale and other Obama NSC officials traveled to Israel and the Palestinian West Bank less than one week prior to the scheduled trilateral meeting at the UN. By then it had become swiftly and irrevocably clear to the Palestinian negotiating team that the fix was in: the United States would cut a flawed deal with Israel on settlements and then use that agreement to badger Palestinians back to the negotiating table. In the first of two highly contentious meetings with the Palestinian negotiating team on September 16 and 17, 2009, Hale attempted to assuage Palestinian "misgivings regarding the quality of the package with Israel, but," he noted, "we will not be able to meet all expectations of all parties. In the aggregate, however, it's a good package." Hale omitted any mention of which, if any, Israeli expectations were not being met with this deal. He added that Palestinians should not hold out for a comprehensive freeze on Israeli settlements because, after all, "A freeze is a flexible concept," even though the language in the Roadmap requiring an Israeli settlement freeze is quite unyielding.

Chief Palestinian negotiator Saeb Erekat, after reviewing all of Netanyahu's proposed exclusions from the settlement freeze, informed Hale, "For your information this will mean more settlement construction in 2009 than in 2008. This is the biggest gaem [sic] of deceit since [19]67 . . . If this is the package, it's a no-go. It's about credibility. You had three options: you convince BN [Benjamin Netanyahu], he convinces you, or you maintain a disagreement—it seems he convinced you." Erekat angrily reproached Hale for the Obama administration's lack of a coherent strategy and balanced approach. "You spent 8 months with the Israelis—no time with me. We at least need to spend some time to build a political framework. You don't know what the framework will be. Maybe you don't have a plan. If you do[, then] you have to lay it out." Hale replied, "I understand the freeze possible is a little less than what you wanted, but if there is no [meeting in] New York, we lose everything and you have nothing to show for." Erekat concluded the vexatious meeting with a plea to the United States: "I hope we will not be put in this position: accept, or else—like previous US administrations. It's not that we don't want to—we can't. So please don't put us in this position. To allow us to help you, you need to help us."[4]

Discussions resumed the next day, but the US and Palestinian teams remained far apart in their positions. Erekat accused Hale of naiveté for believing that Netanyahu's proposed package would mean "no new construction." "If you think that," Erekat sardonically noted, "he is putting you on." Hale then backpedaled, adopting the glass-half-full approach: "Restraint on settlements is better than unrestricted growth everywhere," he said. Erekat did not budge: "As far as I'm concerned settlements will continue everywhere" under Netanyahu's plan. "If the US Government now tailors its policy to BN [Benjamin Netanyahu], not just the Palestinians, but the whole region will go down," he warned. The US Consul General in Jerusalem, Daniel Rubinstein, tried to mollify Erekat: "The package includes no new tenders, no new confiscation" for Israeli settlements. Erekat rejected this too as an insufficient reason to accept the deal: "I'm not coming from Mars! 40 percent of the West Bank is already confiscated. They can keep building for years without new tenders!"

Erekat concluded that he was left with three options: "1. we go to NY [New York] to the trilateral under this formula. This is a non-starter. It is not an option for us. 2. We don't go and declare failure—doom and gloom. This will lead to an explosion and strengthen Hamas and others. 3. we have bilateral meetings and continue talking about a package with much more clarity." Dan Shapiro, Obama's senior director for Near East and North Africa on the NSC, then tried to goad the Palestinians back to the table by asking, "so by not going aren't you playing into his [Netanyahu's] hand?" Erekat exploded in rage: "You put me in this position! It's like having a gun to my head—damned if you do and damned if you don't. I thought at the very least you would have a moratorium and not surprise me with this . . . I've been doing this for sixteen years. This is the last shot. I will only go into it with an end game. Preparations must be there."

Hale tried to conclude the meeting by feigning impotence: "We cannot force a sovereign government. We can use persuasion and negotiations and shared interests," he pleaded. Erekat retorted, "Of course you could if you wanted. How do you think this will reflect on the credibility of the US, if you can't get this done?" Shapiro then ended the meeting by making clear to Erekat that his opinion on US credibility was irrelevant. In a statement that encapsulates the Obama administration's myopia on Israeli-Palestinian peace-making, Shapiro declared that only "we make the call on our own credibility."[5]

In the end, none of Erekat's three scenarios was borne out. Instead, because the US and Israel were unable to conclude an agreement on the "package deal" before the UN General Assembly convened, Obama turned the trilateral meeting in New York with Netanyahu and Abbas into an inconsequential photo-op, the exact type of meaningless diplomatic effort for which Obama had excoriated the Bush administration on the campaign trail. On September 22, 2009, in brief comments before the trilateral meeting, Obama declared, "simply put it is past time to talk about starting negotiations—it is time to move forward. It is time to show the flexibility and common sense and sense of compromise that's necessary to achieve our goals. Permanent status negotiations must begin and begin soon. And more importantly, we must give those negotiations the opportunity to succeed." Obama, however, left unanswered the question of how negotiations could convene, much less succeed, with the parties still at loggerheads over the terms of the settlement freeze. Obama could only offer that "all of us know this will not be easy."[6] As if to underscore this point, the United States had forbidden the Israeli and Palestinian leaders from speaking to the media, lest they reveal the insuperable gaps that still needed to be bridged before negotiations could begin.

That same day, Mitchell briefed a skeptical media on the significance of the trilateral meeting and issued an unwarrantedly optimistic, if not Pollyannaish, assessment of where matters stood. "Even nine months ago, such a meeting did not seem possible," Mitchell observed. "Today the atmosphere is different. Both parties share the goal of a two-state solution and of comprehensive peace. And both parties seek the re-launch of negotiations as soon as possible, although there are differences between them on how to proceed." Nevertheless, according to Mitchell, direct negotiations and a peace agreement were now within reach. "We're now going to enter into an intensive, yet brief, period of discussion in an effort to re-launch negotiations. Our aim is clear: to finally succeed in achieving our shared goals and to end the cycle of conflict that has done so much harm." As Mitchell would come to realize, however, direct negotiations, much less a full-blown peace agreement, were nowhere in sight.

The Obama administration was now flailing about for a coherent strategy, something not lost on the members of the media who attended Mitchell's briefing. "I'm sorry," one incredulous journalist began, but "can you start final status negotiations without the settlement issue being resolved? And should that happen?" Mitchell dodged the questions by responding, "We are not identifying any issue as being a precondition or an impediment to negotiation. Neither the President, nor the Secretary, nor I have ever said of any one issue, that or any other, that it is a precondition to negotiations. What we have said is that we want to get into negotiations. We believe the suggestions that we've made and the requests that we've made would, if accepted and acted upon, create the most favorable conditions available to try to achieve success in those negotiations. But we do not believe in preconditions. We do not impose them."[7]

It was true enough that the Obama administration never formally articulated an Israeli settlement freeze as a precondition for resuming talks, but Obama's statement in May 2009 that "settlements have to be stopped in order for us to move forward" gave the distinct impression that this step was the first in a logical progression of actions that were part of an intelligible strategy. Events of the subsequent four months, however, would prove that this was not the case, as the Obama administration lurched from insisting on a full settlement freeze, to discussing an insincere settlement freeze with Israel, to declaring that the time for Israeli-Palestinian negotiations had arrived even in the absence of finalizing the deal with Israel, a bargain which the United States knew the Palestinians would not accept anyway. It was a recipe for a policy disaster.

After the UN General Assembly, US policy on Israel's settlement freeze and resuming negotiations went from bad to worse. As the United States and Israel narrowed the gaps on the "package deal," Clinton lavished inaccurate and undeserved plaudits on Netanyahu. At a press conference with Clinton in Jerusalem on October 31, 2009, Netanyahu publicly reiterated his terms for a deal on Israeli settlements: "I said we would not build new settlements, not expropriate land for addition [sic] for the existing settlements, and that we were prepared to adopt a policy of restraint on the existing settlements, but also one that would still enable normal life for the residents who are living there." Clinton responded warmly to this outline. "What the prime minister has offered in specifics of a restraint on the policy of settlements, which he has just described—no new starts, for example—is unprecedented in the context of the prior two negotiations," she stated.[8]

Clinton dug herself deeper into this hole by trying to square her remarks that Israel's offer only included "restraint" on the growth, rather than a freeze, of settlements with her contention that this overture was "unprecedented." In a press conference with Moroccan Foreign Minister Taieb Fassi-Fihri on November 2, 2009, Clinton faulted others for not understanding what she considered to be the substantial terms of this offer. Referring to widespread international pushback on her statement in Jerusalem, Clinton ventured that "I think a number of my counterparts were not aware that what the Israeli Government is offering would be an end to all new settlement activity in the West Bank, it would be an end to expro-priation, it would mean an end to any permits or approvals." Yet, at the same time, she admitted that "it is not enough. It is not what many people in the region and elsewhere would want to see, but it is fair to characterize it as unprecedented." She added that positive reinforcement was needed, even if Israel continued to fail to meet its international obligations to freeze settlement activity. "When I say that the Israeli Government is making an unprecedented offer, even though it is not what many would hope for, and even though our position remains the same that settlement activity is not legiti-mate, nevertheless, it holds out the promise of moving a step closer to a two-state solution."[9]

In reality though, Netanyahu's offer actually fell far short of previously broken Israeli pledges to not only restrain, but freeze, settlement growth. In fact, since 1978, previous Israeli govern-ments, on at least five occasions, had agreed to as much, if not more, than Netanyahu was offering, thereby making Clinton's assertions historically invalid. As part of the 1978 Camp David Accords negotiating process, President Jimmy Carter stated that "[Israeli] Prime Minister [Menachem] Begin pledged that there would be no establishment of new settlements until after the final peace negotiations were completed."[10] In 1992, Israeli Prime Minister Yitzhak Rabin declared a settlement freeze to resolve an impasse with the United States over extending $10 billion in loan guarantees.[11] This pledge was promptly broken by Rabin and subse-quent Israeli governments during the Oslo "peace process" as they went on settlement building sprees. Israel also formally accepted the 2001 Mitchell Report, the 2003 Roadmap, and the 2007 Annapolis Conference joint understanding, all of which, as noted previously, obligated Israel to freeze all settlement activity, includ-ing the so-called "natural growth" of settlements.

Thus, far from being "unprecedented," Netanyahu's offer on Israeli settlements was a step backward. By lauding Netanyahu, Clinton succeeded only in emboldening the Israeli prime minister to continue defying previous Israeli obligations to freeze settlements and, through loopholes in his offer, to further colonize Palestinian land in violation of international law. When Netanyahu finally announced his self-styled ten-month "moratorium" on West Bank settlement expansion on November 25, 2009, the huge exemptions he carved out rendered the move meaningless in terms of its impact on the ground. Netanyahu declared his initiative to be "far-reaching and painful," yet it completely excluded Israeli settlement building in occupied Palestinian East Jerusalem, where approximately 40 percent of Israeli settlers lived. Defying US and international policy on Jerusalem, Netanyahu asserted that "we do not put any restrictions on building in our sovereign capital." Even in the West Bank, where the "moratorium" supposedly took effect, it only covered new housing starts in Israel's illegal settlements; it did not apply to the thousands of housing units that had already been approved, or to public buildings in the settlements. "We will not halt existing construction and we will continue to build synagogues, schools, kindergartens and public buildings essential for normal life in the settlements,"[12] Netanyahu defiantly stated, thereby further revealing the hollowness of his "moratorium" offer.

Later that day, during a special briefing, Mitchell emphasized that the "moratorium" should be viewed as an exclusively Israeli initiative, thereby underscoring the failure of the United States and Israel to come to terms on a settlement freeze. "The steps announced today are the result of a unilateral decision by the Government of Israel. This is not an agreement with the United States, nor is it an agreement with the Palestinians," Mitchell stressed. "United States policy on settlements remains unaffected and unchanged. As the President has said, America does not accept the legitimacy of continued Israeli settlements."

However, even though the Obama administration continued to view Israeli settlements as illegitimate, and despite the fact that Netanyahu's "moratorium," as Mitchell freely acknowledged, "falls short of a full settlement freeze," the United States nevertheless used the "moratorium" as an opportunity to defuse tensions with Israel and push forward with trying to jumpstart Israeli-Palestinian negotiations. With this new ten-month window of opportunity, Mitchell declared, "We would like very much to begin negotiations on the permanent status issues."

Mitchell also adamantly believed that, despite its limitations and loopholes, Israel's "moratorium" actually would dramatically decrease Israel's colonization of Palestinian land. Without using the discredited word, Mitchell echoed Clinton's theme of this unilateral "moratorium" being an "unprecedented" Israeli step. "Nothing like this occurred during the Bush administration. From 2000 to 2008, there were new housing construction starts on nearly 20,000 new housing units, 9,000 of them between 2004 and 2008. In the moratorium just announced by the Government of Israel, there will be no new housing construction starts during the 10-month period. None. There will be no approval of any housing projects during the 10-month moratorium. None," Mitchell emphatically repeated. "No Israeli Government has ever taken this step," he incorrectly asserted, "and nothing remotely like this occurred during the Bush Administration." Furthermore, "anyone who opposes settlement construction, continued settlement activity, as does the United States, should, of course, take into account that under the moratorium announced today, there will be much less settlement housing construction activity than there would have been if there were no moratorium. That's a fact," Mitchell confidently declared.[13]

But Mitchell's rosy assessments turned out to be wholly unjustified. Instead, lead Palestinian negotiator Saeb Erekat's concerns about Israeli settlements actually expanding under the "moratorium," which he expressed during those contentious meetings with Mitchell's team in September 2009, proved to be far more accurate. The anti-settlement Israeli group Peace Now concluded in July 2010, eight months into the so-called "moratorium," that "settlement construction since November 2009 has by no means been frozen. Indeed, so much construction has been permitted under 'exceptions' that the moratorium would have to be extended, with no new loopholes, for at least a year before construction on the ground would actually stop."[14] The previous month, Peace Now had issued a six-month accounting of the impact of the "moratorium." It noted that during this period, Israel continued construction of approximately 3,000 previously approved units, while also approving construction starts on more than 600 new units, directly contradicting Mitchell's assertion that there would be no new construction starts. Peace Now determined that during the first six months of the "moratorium," Israel was building more housing per 1,000 people for settlers in Occupied Palestinian Territory than was being built for Israelis within Israel's armistice lines. Peace

Now also documented continuing widespread Israeli settlement construction in East Jerusalem, which was never covered by the "moratorium" in the first place.[15]

With this faux settlement "moratorium" in place, the United States pushed hard to resume direct, bilateral Israeli-Palestinian negotiations. On December 30, 2009, the United States presented to the Palestinian negotiating team, and presumably to Israel as well, a "non-paper"—an informal text—on the framework for negotiations. In this "non-paper," the United States maintained that "it is a matter of urgency that Israelis and Palestinians re-launch negotiations, without delay or pre-conditions." The goal of these negotiations would lead to

> an outcome that ends the conflict and reconciles the Palestinian goal of an independent and viable state based on the 1967 lines, with agreed swaps, and the Israeli goal of a Jewish state with secure and recognized borders that reflect subsequent developments and meet Israeli security requirements. This outcome would result in two states for two peoples and end the occupation that began in 1967. It would also ensure true security for all Israelis and Palestinians and ensure a just and agreed solution to the refugee issue.

The negotiations would resolve all outstanding permanent status issues and "should begin as soon as possible and conclude within twenty-four months." For its "terms of reference," the legal bases for the negotiations, the US "non-paper" recommended that the negotiations "fulfill," rather than implement, "United Nations Security Council Resolutions 242 and 338 and the Madrid Letters of Invitation," documents which formed the basis for all "land-for-peace" negotiations.[16]

The Palestinian negotiating team had severe misgivings about resuming negotiations on the basis of this US "non-paper." Its members felt that they could be dragged back into negotiations that were heavy on "process" and light on "peace." They noted that "negotiation alone as a tool is insufficient to reach the objective. Negotiations for the sake of negotiations are not only a waste of time, but they are dangerous as well; they undermine the credibility of the peace process [and] the leadership, and [they] increase cynicism leading towards violence." True as these assertions were, the Palestinian side failed to offer the United States an alternative, or supplement, to direct negotiations at this point. The Palestinian negotiating team also took umbrage at the US definition of the goal of negotiations. "The approach of defining the outcome as a reconciliation of two parties [*sic*] respective goals is problematic, because it implies that there are two equal sides to a dispute, rather than a powerful state imposing an occupation and colonization policy over the other side." Furthermore, "the Palestinian goal is grossly misrepresented," Palestinian negotiators stressed. "What is stated is rather a compromise formula that falls short of minimum Palestinian requirements."[17] They also expressed concerns about the way in which the United States defined the outcome of negotiations on permanent status issues such as Jerusalem and water, and believed the "terms of reference" to be incomplete.

Lead Palestinian negotiator Saeb Erekat raised some of these concerns in a meeting with David Hale on January 15, 2010. Responding to the US "non-paper," Erekat noted, "You got the Israeli goal right: Jewish state, secure borders, security arrangements, and subsequent developments. You said my goal is a viable and independent state based on the [19]67 border with agreed swaps. That is not my goal. Swaps are a Palestinian concession in the interest of peace and reaching an agreement. My goal is a sovereign state on the [19]67 border." Erekat then expressed his exasperation with the US "non-paper," which he viewed as prejudicing the outcome of negotiations against Palestinian interests. "We asked you to give us your position on the end game, not a treaty—give us your position. Countries have positions. Your position is two state solution, Palestinian state, ending the occupation. So we said [19]67 borders with agreed swaps. That's your position, so say it! If you put down such a paper we will call an emergency Arab summit and get it accepted," Erekat challenged Hale. But, instead of laying out parameters for negotiations, the US "non-paper" presented the Palestinian negotiating team with predetermined outcomes on permanent status issues that were unfavorable to Palestinian claims. "What is in that paper gives them the biggest *Yerushalaim* [Jerusalem] in Jewish history, symbolic number of refugees return, demilitarized state . . . What more can I give?" Erekat asked.[18]

However, this "non-paper" quickly became moot. Sometime between the issuance of this "non-paper" in late December 2009 and February 2010, for reasons that are unclear according to available documents, the United States abandoned hope of resuming direct, bilateral negotiations; instead, the Obama administration now pushed the idea of indirect or "proximity" talks, with the United States acting as a go-between, a concept to which both Israel and the Palestinians responded favorably. In their formal February 2010 acceptance of Mitchell's indirect talks proposal, the Palestinian negotiating team argued that the "proximity" talks should last no more than two years and that Mitchell's efforts to tackle border issues first should last no longer than three months. If the parties tackled this subject successfully, then parallel talks on all outstanding permanent status issues would commence. According to the Palestinian negotiating team, the "terms of reference" and the goal of the indirect talks must be clear:

> The objective is to reach a peace treaty between the PLO and Israel on the basis of the resolutions of the UN Security Council and General Assembly, international law, the Road Map and Arab Peace Initiative, guaranteeing the establishment of an independent Palestinian State with East Jerusalem as its capital side by side with Israel on the 4 June 1967 border, with land swaps as agreed between the parties, equal in size and value and not to exceed a percentage (___), along with a just and agreed resolution to the issue of refugees based on UNGA Resolution 194. Once the treaty is signed, all Palestinian detainees/ prisoners will be released.[19]

On this basis, the Arab League reluctantly endorsed these "proximity" talks at a March 3, 2010, meeting. "Despite the lack of conviction in the seriousness of the Israeli side, the [Arab League Peace Initiative Follow-Up] committee sees that it would give the indirect talks the chance as a last attempt and to facilitate the US role," noted a statement read out by Arab League secretary general Amr Moussa. The Arab League imposed a four-month deadline for the talks to bear fruit before reevaluating whether to continue endorsing them. Prime Minister Netanyahu optimistically told the Knesset, Israel's parliament, that "it seems the conditions for proximity talks are ripening."[20] By March 8, 2010, all the pieces had fallen into place. Mitchell was able to announce,

> I'm pleased that the Israeli and Palestinian leadership have accepted indirect talks. We've begun to discuss the structure and scope of these talks and I will return to the region next week to continue our discussions. As we've said many times, we hope that these [indirect talks] will lead to direct negotiations as soon as possible. We also again encourage the parties, and all concerned, to refrain from any statements or actions which may inflame tensions or prejudice the outcome of these talks.[21]

BIDEN'S VISIT

With Mitchell heading to the region, along with Vice President Joe Biden, and with all the parties agreed on commencing indirect talks, the Obama administration, despite the many setbacks it had suffered since taking office more than thirteen months before, felt more confident than ever that its game plan for achieving Israeli-Palestinian peace was now finally back on track.

But Netanyahu had other plans, which "inflamed tensions" between the United States and Israel to such an extent that Israeli ambassador to the United States Michael Oren admitted that "Israel's ties with the US are in the most serious crisis since 1975,"[22] when the Ford administration "re-evaluated" US-Israel ties and delayed weapons deliveries. On March 9, 2010, Biden gave a joint statement to the press with Netanyahu at the Israeli prime minister's residence. At this press conference, the vice president reiterated, "The relationship between Israel and the United States has been, and will continue to be, a centerpiece—a centerpiece of American policy." According to Biden, "the cornerstone of the relationship is our absolute, total, unvarnished commitment to Israel's security." The vice president addressed Netanyahu by his nickname, "Bibi," reminding him that "you heard me say before, progress occurs in the Middle East when everyone knows there is simply no space between the United States and Israel."[23]

After such an effusive display of camaraderie, Biden was livid when, just a few hours later, the Israeli Interior Ministry announced plans to construct 1,600 housing units in the East Jerusalem settlement of Ramat Shlomo.[24] Biden then issued a toughly worded statement in which he "condemn[ed] the decision by the government of Israel to advance planning for new housing units in East Jerusalem. The substance and timing of the announcement, particularly with the launching of proximity talks, is precisely the kind of step that undermines the trust we need right now and runs counter to the constructive discussions that I've had here in Israel. We must build an atmosphere to support negotiations, not complicate them."[25] Biden's statement and subsequent ones by senior officials collectively would stand as the harshest rebuke of Israel by the Obama administration.

The next day, after meeting with Mahmoud Abbas in Ramallah, the still irate vice president pledged, "As we move forward, the United States will hold both sides accountable for any statements or actions that inflame tensions or prejudice the outcome of talks, as this decision did,"referring to Israel's announced settlement expansion of the previous day.[26] It was a humiliating fiasco for the Obama administration, which had spent so much political capital first insisting that Israel honor its obligations to freeze settlement expansion, then acquiescing in a lesser settlement "moratorium" shot full of holes, and then cajoling Palestinians to return to the negotiating table on the basis of this admittedly flimsy "moratorium," only to have Israel then deliberately torpedo the "proximity" talks as Biden traveled to the region to welcome their convocation.

Back in Washington, the Obama administration continued to fume. On March 12, 2010, Clinton delivered a forty-five-minute tongue-lashing to Netanyahu over the phone. According to Assistant Secretary of State P.J. Crowley, Clinton called Netanyahu "to reiterate the United States' strong objections to Tuesday's announcement, not just in terms of timing, but also in its substance; to make clear that the United States considers the announcement a deeply negative signal about Israel's approach to the bilateral relationship—and counter to the spirit of the Vice President's trip; and to reinforce that this action had undermined trust and confidence in the peace process, and in America's interests." The Obama administration's trust that Israel was engaging the "peace process" in good faith reached its nadir. Crowley continued: "The Secretary said she could not understand how this happened, particularly in light of the United States' strong commitment to Israel's security. And she made clear that the Israeli Government needed to demonstrate not just through words but through specific actions that they are committed to this relationship and to the peace process."[27]

But the Obama administration still had not fully vented its spleen. Clinton declared on CNN that Israel's "announcement of the settlements on the very day that the vice president was there was insulting." An anonymous senior US official volunteered that "we think the burden is on the Israelis to do something that could restore confidence in the process and to restore confidence in the relationship with the United States."[28] Another anonymous US official stated, "What happened to the vice president in Israel was unprecedented," ironically using the same word that Clinton had employed to describe Israel's settlement "moratorium."[29]

Obama reportedly exacted his revenge on Netanyahu during a series of bilateral meetings at the White House on March 23, 2010. Netanyahu, who was on a planned visit to Washington for the annual AIPAC conference, held two separate meetings with Obama, which White House Press Secretary Robert Gibbs characterized as "honest and straightforward."[30] However, this placid description of the meetings was belied by the fact that the White House refused to make Obama and Netanyahu available for media availability or even a photo-op. According to one report of the meetings, "After failing to extract a written promise of concessions on settlements, Obama walked out of his meeting with Netanyahu but invited him to stay at the White House, consult with advisers and 'let me know if there is anything new,'" an anonymous member of congress, who described the encounter as "awful," told the *Times* of London.[31] In a subsequent press conference, Gibbs tried to downplay negative accounts of the meetings: "I'm puzzled by the notion that somehow it's a bad deal to get two hours with the President almost entirely alone. That doesn't seem like a lot of punishment to me," he stated. However, Gibbs pointedly declined to reject the reports of Obama having suddenly left the first meeting.[32]

Israel's backers in Congress were clearly perturbed by this very visible quarrel between the Obama administration and Israel. However, they took to the floor of Congress not to defend the president and his foreign policy, but to urge him to sweep the matter under the rug. Representative Eliot Engel (D-NY) did not "think that we should blow the timing of that announcement [of Israeli settlement expansion] out of proportion. We should not have a disproportionate response to Israel. We need to be careful and measured in our response, and I think we all have to take a step back."[33] Senators John McCain (R-AZ) and Joseph Lieberman engaged in a remarkable colloquy on the Senate floor. McCain baited his colleague to answer the following questions: doesn't he think "if we want the Israeli Government to act in a way that would be more in keeping with our objectives, that it does not help them to have public disparagement by the Secretary of State, by the President's political adviser on the Sunday shows? On the contrary, shouldn't we lower the dialog, talk quietly among friends, and work together toward the mutual goals we share?" Lieberman heartily agreed with McCain that "it is time to lower voices and get over the family feud between the United States and Israel. It doesn't serve anybody's interests but our enemies."[34] Representative Jerry Moran (R-KS) called the administration's diplomacy a "misstep." He scolded: "Rather than make demands upon Israel for concession after concession, President Obama should work closely and privately with Israel, recognizing our two Nations' long and trusted alliance."[35] Members of Congress droned on for an entire additional month with their criticisms of Obama's handling of the affair. Senator Ben Cardin (D-MD) took the final jab on April 21, 2010. "President Obama must not place wrongful or unreasonable pressure on Israel," he sniped, "or, worse, to put forward a proposal without Israel's consent."[36]

Thus chastened by members of Congress for daring to publicly confront Israel for its blatant humiliation of the United States, the Obama administration sullenly resumed its efforts to initiate the delayed "proximity" talks, the first round of which ended on May 9, 2010. According to the State Department, Mitchell's "talks were serious and wide-ranging. Both parties are taking some steps to help create an atmosphere that is conducive to successful talks . . . They are both trying to move forward in difficult circumstances and we commend them for that."[37] Shortly before the "proximity" talks convened, however, the trail of documents from inside the Palestinian negotiating team, which were leaked to *Al Jazeera* and published as "The Palestine Papers," ran dry, making it difficult to assess whether the State Department's increasingly bright-eyed depictions of progress and momentum in the indirect talks were accurate.

The Obama administration felt that these "proximity" talks were successful enough, however, to warrant inviting Israel and the Palestinians on August 20, 2010, to direct, bilateral negotiations at the State Department the following month. Clinton proudly and optimistically declared that "I've invited Israeli Prime Minister Netanyahu and Palestinian Authority President Abbas to meet on September 2nd in Washington, D.C. to re-launch direct negotiations to resolve all final status issues, which we believe can be completed within one year." Mitchell sensed that direct negotiations should be relaunched now because of "the cumulative result of the efforts made over that time and the recognition by the parties that this is the right time." However, Mitchell was right to warn "that there remains mistrust between the parties, a residue of hostility developed over many decades of conflict." He recalled the "many previous efforts that have been made to resolve the conflict that had not succeeded, all of which takes a very heavy toll on both societies and their leaders." But, he added: "past efforts at peace that did not succeed cannot deter us from trying again, because the cause is noble and just and right for all concerned."[38]

Mitchell's evaluation of the nobility of Israeli-Palestinian peace was not in doubt. What was uncertain, though, was the Obama administration's political wisdom in convening direct negotiations at this juncture. There was no evidence that the nearly four months of sporadic "proximity" talks had resulted in any breakthrough that indicated the parties were any closer to being able to resolve their core divisions. Furthermore, Israel's self-declared settlement "moratorium" was due to expire just three weeks after the United States convened direct negotiations. Israel had made it abundantly clear that it would not consider extending the "moratorium"; Palestinians had made it equally evident that they would not continue to negotiate while Israel blatantly colonized land supposedly designated for a future Palestinian state. The Obama administration was engaging in a high-stakes, risky gamble that it would succeed in generating enough momentum and goodwill through these direct negotiations to overcome the impending standoff. The next month would determine if its long-shot approach would pay off in spades or devolve into a spectacular policy failure that would doom the Israeli-Palestinian "peace process" for good.

CHAPTER FOUR

Settlements Are Corrosive to Israel's Future

THE RISE AND FALL OF NEGOTIATIONS

As the curtain rose on the stage of the Obama administration's highest-profile and riskiest gambit to achieve Israeli-Palestinian peace—resuming direct, bilateral negotiations under US auspices—President Barack Obama's Special Envoy for Middle East Peace George Mitchell was sanguine about the prospects for success. Speaking the day before Obama would meet at the White House with prime minister Netanyahu, Palestinian Authority president Mahmoud Abbas, Egyptian president Hosni Mubarak, and Jordanian King Abdullah II for a series of bilateral meetings, Mitchell declared, "We believe these negotiations can be completed within one year." Less than four months of inconclusive "proximity" talks between the parties had led to no discernible results in overcoming the stalemate surrounding the impending expiration of Israel's self-declared settlement "moratorium"; nor had these indirect talks occasioned a breakthrough on any of the thorny and elusive permanent status issues. Nevertheless, the United States felt that the parties were on the cusp of a major advance. So strongly did the Obama administration believe that prospects for peace were improving that it shaved off half of the time it anticipated it would take for negotiations to succeed from what was envisioned in its December 2009 "non-paper."

Although Mitchell recognized "that there are many—indeed, many very knowledgeable and experienced people who hold a different view" about the feasibility of negotiating Israeli-Palestinian peace within one year, "we disagree with that. We think it is realistic. We think it can be done." But rather than heed the advice of these experts, the Obama administration confidently believed that it would be able to pound the square peg into the round hole this time around simply by deriving lessons learned from previous failures and by turning over a new leaf. In Mitchell's words, "What we've tried to do is to avoid a slavish adherence to the past while trying to learn what might have been improved in the past, what worked, what didn't work. And so we have avoided deliberately any specific label or identification that this is a continuation of process A or B or C."

But, of course, this was a continuation of a process, and a failed one at that. Seventeen years of negotiating within the framework of the Oslo "peace process" had only soured Palestinian hopes of an independent state resulting from this process, as Israel had implacably and in extremely bad faith continued to colonize the occupied Palestinian West Bank and East Jerusalem throughout this period, rendering a viable and contiguous Palestinian state less and less likely as each year passed without agreement. On the eve of negotiations, Mitchell waxed philosophical about the legacy and meaning of these failed negotiations and pondered "whether the long history of negotiation has been beneficial or harmful. It's actually been both, in some respects," Mitchell reasoned. "Beneficial in the sense that this has been discussed so often that people have a good sense of what the principal issues are and how they might be resolved; harmful in the sense that it's created attitudes among many in the region that it's a never-ending process, that it's gone on for a very long time and will go on forever." Therefore, according to Mitchell, "it's very important to create a sense that this has a definite concluding point," rationalizing his soon-to-be deflated expectation that negotiations could conclude successfully within a year.[1]

If one excerpted the most conciliatory remarks made by Netanyahu and Abbas that September 1, 2010, evening in the White House, then perhaps it was possible to concur with Obama that their "thoughtful statements" led to an "excellent start" to the negotiations that left him "hopeful—cautiously hopeful, but hopeful—that we can achieve the goal" of Israeli-Palestinian peace. The normally bellicose Netanyahu took pains to address Abbas directly as "my partner in peace," stressing that "it is up to us, with the help of our friends, to conclude the agonizing conflict between our peoples and to afford them a new beginning . . . I came here today to find an historic compromise that will enable both our peoples to live in peace and security and in dignity . . . I came here to achieve a peace that will bring a lasting benefit to us all." Abbas, for his part, noted that "the time has come for us to make peace and it is time to end the occupation that started in 1967, and for the Palestinian people to get freedom, justice, and independence. It is time that a [sic] independent Palestinian state be established with sovereignty side by side with the state of Israel. It is time to put an end to the struggle in the Middle East."[2]

After this ceremonial opening of negotiations at the White House, the parties got down to business on September 2. Mitchell characterized this opening round of talks as a "long and productive discussion on a range of issues. President Abbas and Prime Minister Netanyahu expressed their intent to approach these negotiations in good faith and with a seriousness of purpose." Mitchell assessed that the negotiations were held in a "constructive and positive mood, both in terms of their personal interaction and in terms of the nature of the discussion that occurred." He announced the parties' resolve to conclude a framework agreement, whose purpose "will be to establish the fundamental compromises necessary to enable them to flesh out and complete a comprehensive treaty that will end the conflict and establish a lasting peace between Israel and the Palestinians," a statement which lent an air of progress to the initial talks. However, Mitchell cautioned, "I don't want to suggest to you that the meeting was such that there was a detailed and extended discussion or debate on a specific substantive issue."[3] In other words, although the two parties may have agreed to procedural modalities for moving the negotiations forward, the first round of talks in Washington produced no dramatic breakthroughs.

Negotiations resumed for a second, and ultimately final, round in Sharm el-Sheikh, Egypt, and Jerusalem on September 14–15, 2010. At the end of these negotiations, Mitchell remained upbeat and impressed that "the two leaders are not leaving the tough issues to the end of their discussions. They are tackling upfront and did so this evening the issues that are at the center of the Israeli-Palestinian conflict. We take this as a strong indicator of their belief that peace is possible and of their desire to conclude an agreement." Mitchell warned, though, that "I do not want to suggest or imply that discussing issues seriously is the same as agreeing on a resolution to them." But, he added, "it has been extremely impressive to see both leaders engaging in this fashion. They are serious. They mean business. They do have differences. We believe they can be overcome, and we are going to remain and support them with patience, perseverance, and determination."[4] Even at this late hour, Mitchell still expressed confidence that an Israeli-Palestinian agreement could be concluded within a year.

But the confidence exuded by Mitchell, the eternal optimist, was being countered by Obama and Clinton, both of whom were already preparing their talking points in case negotiations broke down over the looming deadline of Israel's settlement "moratorium" expiration. Even before the talks in Sharm el-Sheikh and Jerusalem, Obama was speaking about the negotiations in the conditional tense: "if these talks break down, we're going to keep on trying," the president gamely offered. However, rather than faulting himself for cajoling Palestinians back to the negotiating table just three weeks before Israel's sham settlement "moratorium" expired, or recognizing that it was his unwillingness to exert enough pressure on Israel to freeze settlements completely that had kept Palestinians from returning to the table sooner, Obama did what US presidents did best when their "peace process" efforts broke down: blame the Palestinians.

Like President Bill Clinton, who reneged on his word not to assign blame if the 2000 Camp David Summit ended in failure by promptly censuring PA president Yasser Arafat for his supposed obstinacy at the talks, Obama blasted Palestinians for failing to realize the golden opportunity presented by the hard-won Israeli settlement "moratorium." As if a reminder were needed, Obama warned on September 10, 2010, that "a major bone of contention during the course of this month is going to be the potential lapse of the settlement moratorium. The irony is, is that when Prime Minister Netanyahu put the moratorium in place, the Palestinians were very skeptical" about it, and rightfully so given all of the exemptions Israel stipulated. The president noted that the Palestinians "said this doesn't do anything," a prediction which was amply borne out by Peace Now's analysis of settlement construction during the "moratorium." However, according to Obama, "it turns out, to Prime Minister Netanyahu's credit and to the Israeli government's credit, the settlement moratorium has actually been significant. It has significantly reduced settlement construction in the region," he errantly asserted. "And that's why now the Palestinians say, you know what, even though we weren't that keen on it at first or we thought it was just window dressing, it turns out that this is important to us."[5] But Obama was badly misstating the Palestinian case. Actually, what was important to the Palestinian negotiating team, as articulated clearly to Mitchell and other Obama administration officials, was that Israel comply with international law and its Roadmap obligations to freeze all settlement construction and that the United States understand that Palestinians would no longer agree to negotiate while Israel continued to colonize the land on which they hoped to establish their state.

In the waning days of the negotiations, Clinton too showed great empathy for Israel's supposed magnanimity in offering the settlement "moratorium," and little regard for Palestinians' concerns about its shortcomings. Clinton was asked on Israeli television to comment "on the subject of whether Netanyahu's position—that for 10 months, he did freeze the settlements and nothing happened; Abbas did not make a move. And now, they want him to restart the whole thing and he says, 'Why should I?'" She responded that it was indeed "a fair statement by the prime minister," because, after all, "what he was attempting to do was unprecedented. And I regret, as he does, that we couldn't get into the talks earlier."[6] In Clinton's view too, the impending breakdown of the talks was the fault of the Palestinians because they had not agreed to negotiate on the basis of the sham "moratorium" earlier.

Although both Obama and Clinton publicly called on Israel to extend the settlement "moratorium," due to expire on September 26, 2010, it was done so as a polite request, rather than an unequivocal ultimatum to stabilize the teetering negotiations. These and other last-ditch efforts failed to preclude the inevitable. On September 21, the Quartet released a statement that "noted that the commendable Israeli settlement moratorium instituted last November has had a positive impact and urged its continuation."[7] Obama used his address to the UN General Assembly on September 23 to hope against hope that the "peace process" could still be salvaged. He implored, in words that would come back to haunt him later, that "we should reach for what's best within ourselves. If we do, when we come back here next year, we can have an agreement that will lead to a new member of the United Nations—an independent, sovereign state of Palestine, living in peace with Israel." Despite the upcoming deadline, Obama bravely ventured, "Now is the time to build the trust—and provide the time—for substantial progress to be made. Now is the time for this opportunity to be seized, so that it does not slip away."

But the opportunity was quickly slipping away and Obama's advocacy of continued negotiations was half-hearted at best. He was already testing out the post–"peace process" rhetoric that would characterize his administration's approach to the Israeli-Palestinian conflict in the second half of his first term. With his hopes of rekindling negotiations dashed, Obama began to view the Israeli-Palestinian conflict as a zero-sum game, in which any support for Palestinian rights was viewed as "delegitimizing" Israel. Similarly, any alternative strategy to a US-dominated "peace process" to achieve those long-denied rights was seen by the Obama administration as nothing less than an existential threat to Israel.

Thus, Obama admonished the international community, saying, "Those who long to see an independent Palestine must also stop trying to tear down Israel." He harangued the assembled heads of state: "Efforts to chip away at Israel's legitimacy will only be met by the unshakeable opposition of the United States." And he chided the UN for its allegedly inherent bias against Israel and its ineffectual approach to resolving the Israeli-Palestinian conflict. "The conflict between Israelis and Arabs is as old as this institution," Obama intoned. "And we can come back here next year, as we have for the last sixty years, and make long speeches about it. We can read familiar lists of grievances. We can table the same resolutions. We can further empower the forces of rejectionism and hate. And we can waste more time by carrying forward an argument that will not help a single Israeli or Palestinian child achieve a better life."[8] A frustrated and desperate Obama was unleashing his misplaced anger at the forthcoming ignominious demise of the "peace process" by blaming first the Palestinians and then the UN. No one escaped censure except for Israel and his own failed strategy, or lack thereof, for achieving a two-state resolution to the Israeli-Palestinian conflict.

September 26—the expiration of Israel's bogus settlement "moratorium"—came and went, and both Netanyahu and Abbas proved good on their respective words. Israel would under no circumstance extend the "moratorium," even if doing so would allow for a continuation of negotiations that Mitchell felt were making progress. The Palestinians would under no circumstance return to the negotiating table now that Israel had dropped the fig leaf of a settlement "moratorium" in favor of a more blatant and naked colonization of Palestinian land.

The Oslo "peace process," so hopefully embarked upon in 1993, had finally sputtered its way to an inconclusive death. But before burying it, Obama would engage in one final, frantic and shameful attempt to resuscitate it. Shortly after the UN General Assembly, Obama reportedly sent Netanyahu a letter outlining an extremely attractive package of incentives he would be prepared to provide Israel if only Netanyahu would extend the settlement "moratorium" in its current configuration—excluding East Jerusalem completely and all West Bank settlement construction already underway—for a non-renewable sixty- to ninety-day period.

In exchange for extending the "moratorium," the United States would fund 20 F-35 fighter jets, valued at $3 billion, for Israel.[9] These jets were the first part of a larger deal for the United States to provide Israel with up to 75 F-35 fighter jets, valued at a whopping $15.2 billion if all options were exercised, a potential sale which the Pentagon had previously notified Congress about in September 2008.[10] It was unknown whether Obama was suggesting that the United States pay for these aircraft with part of the $30 billion already pledged in weapons for Israel between 2009 and 2018, or, if as was more likely the case, Obama was proposing an additional $3 billion of military aid for Israel to finance this purchase. Whatever the details of the case actually may have been, this offer for F-35 fighter jets formed the centerpiece of Obama's last-ditch attempt to prevent negotiations from collapsing.

But that was not all. If Netanyahu accepted the deal, the F-35 fighter jets formed just one component of what Israeli journalist Eli

Berdenstein termed "far-reaching commitments" offered by Obama. These commitments included providing Israel with a series of sophisticated weapons systems, frustrating any Palestinian diplomatic initiative at the UN for one year, and promising not to allow Palestinians to raise again the issue of Israeli settlement expansion outside of permanent status negotiations.[11] David Makovsky, a fellow at the pro-Israel Washington Institute for Near East Policy, added rather opaquely that the letter also "pledged to accept the legitimacy of existing Israeli security needs," by agreeing, for example, that Israel could continue to station troops in the Jordan Valley, located in the Palestinian West Bank, even after an Israeli-Palestinian peace treaty.[12]

Obama's new strategy—"to bribe Israel,"[13] in the words of pro-Israel *New York Times* columnist Thomas Friedman, to extend the settlement "moratorium" in the diminishing hope of rescuing the moribund "peace process"—was flawed for several reasons. First, by attempting to extend Israel's faux settlement "moratorium," Obama was merely trying to prolong, rather than correct, the unsound conditions that made the success of these negotiations so unlikely. A true settlement freeze—the only possible Israeli good-faith gesture that would, in Palestinian eyes, justify more negotiations—was not even on the table. With Israel continuing to colonize Palestinian land during an extended settlement "moratorium" period, there would have been absolutely no reason to believe that had the two sides continued negotiations, they would have come any closer to resolving their fundamentally irreconcilable negotiating positions in the short term. By providing incentives to Israel to extend the "moratorium," Obama was only kicking the can down this dead end road. After the extended "moratorium" concluded just two or three months later, with no possibility of being renewed this time, Obama would have found himself in the same deadlocked position.

Second, Netanyahu saw little to be gained and much to lose by accepting Obama's terms. The Obama administration had already provided Israel with unprecedented carrots in the form of increased military aid, expanded funding for joint anti-missile projects, and the largest ever joint US-Israeli military exercises, topics more fully explored in Chapter 8. But, despite all these inducements, Israel had brazenly defied the United States by refusing to adhere to its Roadmap obligation to freeze settlements, provocatively humiliating the Obama administration in the process. Yet the Obama administration steadfastly refused to brandish the proverbial stick, thereby severely limiting the options in its policy toolbox. This created a perverse dynamic to the relationship. Like a spoiled child, Israel received rewards not when it complied with its responsibilities, but when it flouted them. There was no logical reason then for Netanyahu to renege on his words by accepting another settlement "moratorium"—thus appearing meek and deferential to US demands before his hardline constituency—when he knew that he could pocket Obama's chips and cash them in at a later date without having to accept any constraints on his behavior in the present.

Third, there was a certain sense of unseemliness to Obama's proffered package of goodies for Israel, which smacked of desperation and abasement. Here was the spectacle of the president of the United States attempting to pay off Israel to extend a sham settlement "moratorium," which fell far short of what the Bush administration had compelled Israel to accept—a complete settlement freeze—but had not enforced. It was as if the United States were a supplicant, pleading with Israel to do its bidding, instead of the superpower laying down the law and dictating to a client state its demands. If ever there were a case for arguing that the tail wagged the dog in the US-Israel relationship, then Obama's shameful and unsuccessful effort to bribe Israel to extend the settlement "moratorium" illustrated it well.

The various scenarios that could have materialized had Israel accepted the inducements and agreed to a temporary, one-time extension of the settlement "moratorium," however, did not come to pass. Instead, the Arab League, meeting in Sirte, Libya, on October 8, 2010, endorsed Abbas's decision to suspend the talks, but gave the United States one additional month to try to persuade Israel to freeze settlement building before pronouncing the negotiations completely dead.[14] However, the United States was unable to convince Israel to seize the terms of this deal and on December 7, 2010, the United States rather unequivocally and angrily pulled the offer from the table. At the State Department's daily press briefing the next day, Assistant Secretary of State P.J. Crowley explained, "There was considerable thought given to [the] moratorium as being a mechanism by which we could make the kind of progress we're looking for and, at this point after an intensive effort, we've concluded that that particular course is just simply not going to bear fruit at this time and we're going to move in a different direction." Therefore, the incentives package for Israel "is not under discussion at this time."

But instead of admitting defeat and retreating to review its policy options moving forward, the Obama administration proceeded to announce an even more whimsical and chimerical initiative. With direct negotiations stymied, the United States would henceforth revert to the format of indirect discussions between Israel and the Palestinians to "engage with both sides on the core substantive issues at stake in this conflict," according to Crowley. The United States also would consult with "the Arab states and other international partners on creating a firm basis to work toward our shared goal of a framework agreement on all permanent status issues, a goal to which we and the parties remain committed," he added. Crowley remained firmly convinced that a framework agreement was still feasible within the one-year time frame announced when direct negotiations began in September 2010. The Obama administration was now grasping at straws in a misbegotten attempt to convince the world that the Israeli-Palestinian negotiating process was still viable. Crowley unpersuasively argued that "we think we have the right plan. We think we have the right strategy. We are just adapting the tactics in support of that strategy."[15]

Not even senior Obama administration officials, however, could muster enthusiasm over this change in tactics. In trying to explain its new approach to Israeli-Palestinian peacemaking in front of a friendly audience at the annual forum of the Brookings Institution's Saban Center for Middle East Policy on December 10, 2010, Clinton seemed to put the nail in the coffin of a negotiated, two-state solution to the Israeli-Palestinian conflict. Acknowledging the failed state of the "peace process," Clinton lamented that "I understand and indeed I share the deep frustrations of many of you in this room and across the region and the world." She candidly warned that the window of opportunity for a two-state resolution was fast closing. "The long-term population trends that result from the occupation are endangering the Zionist vision of a Jewish and democratic state in the historic homeland of the Jewish people," Clinton cautioned. "Israelis should not have to choose between preserving both elements of their dream. But that day is approaching," she predicted. Clinton also noted, "The lack of peace and the occupation that began in 1967 continue to deprive the Palestinian people of dignity and self-determination. This is unacceptable, and, ultimately, it too is unsustainable."

Although the United States was no longer pursuing an Israeli extension of the settlement "moratorium," Clinton reasserted, "The position of the United States on settlements has not changed and will not change. Like every American administration for decades, we do not accept the legitimacy of continued settlement activity." This was boilerplate language, but her next statement was not. "We believe their continued expansion is corrosive not only to peace efforts and [a] two-state solution, but to Israel's future itself."[16] This statement served as the Obama administration's clearest cautioning to Israel yet that it considered Israel's continued colonization of Palestinian land to be self-defeating of Israel's avowed goal of maintaining a Jewish-majority state living "side by side" in peace with an independent state of Palestine. Without explicitly saying so, Clinton was indicating that absent a fundamental and dramatic change in direction, Israel's own actions were inexorably leading to the eventual dissolution of the two-state resolution to the Israeli-Palestinian conflict, in favor of an inevitable binational or one-state resolution in which Palestinians and Israeli Jews would live as equal citizens under the same governmental structure.

The Obama administration never officially pronounced the Israeli-Palestinian "peace process" dead, and it continued sporadically and lackadaisically to insist that it was engaging in meaningful efforts to restart negotiations. But Clinton's speech marked the end of any sustained and serious attempt by the Obama administration to return the parties to the negotiating table. From this point forward, the Obama administration would no longer promote its proactive, yet deeply flawed, strategy for brokering Israeli-Palestinian peace. Instead, as Palestinians sought to "re-internationalize" the Israeli-Palestinian conflict through the UN, the Obama administration adopted a defensive and reactive policy approach that aimed to defeat these post–"peace process" Palestinian diplomatic initiatives, thereby shielding Israel from the international community's efforts to try its hand where the United States had failed.

WHY NEGOTIATIONS FAILED

At this point in the narrative, with Obama's strategy in tatters, a postmortem examination of the Obama administration's approach to Israeli-Palestinian negotiations is in order. In retrospect, Obama failed in his efforts to generate a credible Israeli-Palestinian negotiating process for at least three reasons. First, Obama pushed for negotiations to resume under unpropitious circumstances. Second, even had Obama convened negotiations under favorable conditions, the lack of publicly identifiable "terms of reference" for the negotiations gave credence to the notion that these negotiations lacked an endgame, despite the aggressive timetable put forward. Third, as in previous Israeli-Palestinian negotiating rounds, the United States deliberately sidelined other parties that had a stake in the outcome of the negotiations, arrogating for itself the role of "peace process" overseer, and thereby ensuring a continuation of the inherent US biases that had sunk previous negotiations.

The Obama administration disregarded its own prescription for convening successful negotiations. As George Mitchell stated in June 2009, "to create the context for the resumption and early conclusion of meaningful negotiations," the United States was "asking all parties to take meaningful steps. Israelis and Palestinians have a responsibility to meet their obligations under the Roadmap, to which they committed in 2003. It's not just their responsibility. We believe it's in their interests as well. For the Israelis, that means a stop to settlements and other actions."[17] Having concluded that same month that Israel would not freeze settlement construction of its own volition and that it was unwilling to apply the necessary political pressure on Israel to compel it do so, the Obama administration should have announced that it had been unsuccessful in creating the conditions for a resumption of negotiations and reevaluated its policy options.

The Obama administration instead engaged in a bilateral negotiating process with Israel, behind Palestinian backs, which whittled down the settlement freeze to a meaningless self-declared "moratorium." Obama then used this "moratorium" to twist the arms of an already skeptical Palestinian negotiation team to return to the negotiating table even though his administration was conscious of having failed "to create the context for the resumption and early conclusion of meaningful negotiations." Having botched the settlement freeze and then tried to resume negotiations under the fig leaf of the settlement "moratorium," it was even less comprehensible that the Obama administration saw fit to convene the negotiations with only three weeks remaining on the settlement "moratorium," which had very little, if any, chance of being extended. Thus, not only did the Obama administration restart negotiations without exacting from Israel the commitment to freeze settlements that it deemed necessary for setting the right conditions for the talks to succeed; it also did so knowing that those disadvantageous conditions would go from bad to worse at the very onset of the negotiating process. It is difficult, therefore, to escape the conclusion that resuming negotiations in September 2010 was a preordained exercise in futility—more negotiations for the sake of negotiations.

Second, having made the mistake of relaunching negotiations under such adverse circumstances, the Obama administration compounded the problem by neglecting to make available public terms of reference for the negotiations. Although it was clear from documents leaked in "The Palestine Papers" that the United States was proposing terms of reference for the negotiations as early as December 2009 and that it was possible that an agreed-upon document was formalized before negotiations recommenced in September 2010, the public was unaware of this development at the time. In fact, the United States appeared to deliberately promote the exact opposite impression. For example, on August 20, 2010, when Mitchell briefed the media on the parties' acceptance of the US invitation to begin negotiations, he responded to a question about the negotiations' terms of reference by curiously declaring, "Only the parties can determine terms of reference and basis for negotiations, and they will do so when they meet and discuss these matters. As you know, both we and the Quartet have previously said that the negotiations should be without preconditions." To make matters worse, in response to a question about whether the parties would be starting their negotiations from scratch, or whether they would pick up the talks from where they last left off, Mitchell declared, "The parties themselves will determine the basis on which they will proceed in the discussions."[18]

These seemingly innocuous statements were anything but. Instead, they represented a radical upending of the traditional role of the United States in convening and shepherding Israeli-Palestinian negotiations, making the United States even less of an "honest broker" for the short-lived September 2010 negotiations than in previous rounds. Ever since the United States convened the post–Gulf War Madrid Peace Conference, establishing the Israeli-Palestinian "peace process," it had set out clear terms of reference for bilateral and multilateral Arab-Israeli negotiations. In the joint US-USSR letters of invitation to the Madrid Peace Conference in October 1991, the United States included unequivocal terms of reference to UN Security Council Resolutions 242 and 338, resolutions which established the principle of "land for peace" as the basis for comprehensive Arab-Israeli negotiations.[19] Thus, before entering into negotiations, all the parties, as well as the public, had a general understanding of the framework in which the negotiations would take place and the parameters of a negotiated outcome. Even the much reviled Oslo Accords, negotiated by Israel and the PLO in September 1993 without the assistance of the United States, stated that the aim of negotiations was "a permanent settlement based on Security Council Resolutions 242 and 338."[20]

Yet here was Mitchell, the supposed paragon of evenhandedness, less than two weeks before negotiations were scheduled to start, unilaterally throwing out these established terms of reference and adopting an attitude of permissiveness to the negotiations that militated against their successful conclusion. After all, it was only by referencing Security Council resolutions that Palestinians had hoped for a modicum of fairness and balance from the previous two decades of negotiations. In the absence of any reference to Security Council resolutions as the framework for these negotiations, Israel, as the incalculably stronger party, would feel free to disregard them and attempt to impose upon the Palestinians treaty terms blatantly at odds with its international obligation to withdraw from territories occupied in the 1967 war, as stipulated in these resolutions. Moreover, by absolving Israel of the requirement to resume negotiations from the point at which they last left off, Mitchell was setting negotiations back to the pre–Oslo Accord era—essentially junking seventeen years of negotiating history—and leaving everything open to being negotiated afresh. This approach suited Netanyahu just fine, as he had never been comfortable accepting or negotiating within the framework of the Oslo "peace process" and had previously bragged about how he had ground that process to a screeching halt in the late 1990s.

It was an inexcusable and unconscionable lapse on Mitchell's part. Had the United States somehow come up with a way to extend the negotiations beyond the expiration of the settlement "moratorium," Mitchell's lack of terms of reference and insistence that the parties were free to disregard their prior positions meant that negotiations would likely have broken down acrimoniously and quickly in any case.

Third, even if the two parties had miraculously negotiated an agreement under these adverse circumstances with no terms of reference to guide them to a fair and equitable resolution, the United States' deliberate exclusion from these negotiations of its Quartet partners, not to mention the Arab League and Organization of the Islamic Conference, meant that no other stakeholders were around the table. These parties would therefore have been unlikely to endorse the process or any finished product that arose from it. Even before negotiations commenced, Robert Serry, the UN Special Coordinator for the Middle East Peace Process, gave voice to this sense of frustration that the United States was excluding the UN from the negotiating process. "Frankly," he told lead Palestinian negotiator Saeb Erekat in October 2009, "I am pissed off that the US is not involving any of us—also Marc Otte [the European Union's Special Representative to the Middle East Peace Process]—in the Quartet."[21] It was true that the Obama administration had invited former British Prime Minister Tony Blair, as the Quartet's representative, to the working dinner at the White House on September 1, 2010. However, the formal exclusion of the European Union, Russia, and the UN from the relaunched negotiations "sparked considerable anger among Quartet members, particularly in Europe," according to Khaled Elgindy, a former member of the Palestinian negotiating team.[22]

Thus did the Obama administration resume Israeli-Palestinian negotiations: under adverse circumstances, with no public terms of reference and in a unilateral fashion that excluded its "peace process" partners. This high-profile gamble turned out to be an ill-conceived disaster. Perhaps then, it was just as well that this round of negotiations broke down after only three weeks, before it did any further lasting damage to the eventual prospects for Israeli-Palestinian peace.

But the breakdown of negotiations in September 2010 did have a silver lining. By going back to the negotiating table to give the "peace process" one final opportunity, Palestinians demonstrated to the world, beyond a shadow of a doubt, that even under a Nobel Peace Prize–winning US president, Palestinians could never hope to attain a fair shake from any US-dominated negotiation. As the sun set on the "peace process," Palestinians finally found themselves freed from the shackles of a US-Israeli agenda that attempted to shoehorn Palestinian human and national rights into Israel's all-encompassing security dictates. Having escaped the straigtjacket of the "peace process," Palestinians, for the first time in more than two decades, embarked on proactive diplomatic initiatives to "re-internationalize" the Israeli-Palestinian conflict. By doing so, they garnered significant international support for their cause. These initiatives put the United States into a highly awkward, defensive posture in which its unvarnished protection of Israel in the international arena stripped away any remaining pretension that the United States was an "honest broker" capable of resolving the Israeli-Palestinian conflict.

CHAPTER FIVE

More than 700 Days of Failure, No Success

TRIAL BALLOON

Even though Palestinians waited until after the irretrievable collapse of the "peace process" in December 2010 to launch their new diplomatic initiative to "re-internationalize" the Israeli-Palestinian conflict by taking their case directly to the UN, it was clear that this idea was percolating even during the initial months of the Obama administration. As the Palestinian negotiating team began to realize in June 2009 that the Obama administration would not lean heavily enough on Israel to compel it to freeze settlements, Palestinians began looking for an alternative strategy to counter Israel's ongoing colonization of Palestinian land. Reflecting on the US reaction to Prime Minister Netanyahu's speech accepting a truncated Palestinian "state," Azem Bishara, a member of the Palestinian negotiating team, noted that "the American response wasn't one we were looking for. Should we give the US a chance to change policy?" he wondered. "For example," he proposed, "we could send a resolution on Jerusalem to the Security Council and see what the American vote will be. We can take similar steps to create change in American actions."[1]

Palestinians would do something similar to this original proposal on February 18, 2011, when they prompted Lebanon, which had at the time a non-permanent seat on the UN Security Council, to table a mildly worded resolution condemning Israel's illegal settlements. The text of the draft resolution reaffirmed "that all Israeli settlement activities in Occupied Palestinian Territory, including East Jerusalem, are illegal and constitute a major obstacle to the achievement of peace on the basis of the two-State solution." The resolution also demanded "that Israel, the occupying Power, immediately and completely ceases all settlement activities in Occupied Palestinian Territory, including East Jerusalem, and that it fully respect all of its legal obligations in this regard."[2] With the one linguistic exception of deeming Israel's settlements to be "illegal"—the Obama administration was always careful to use the less fraught word "illegitimate" in describing Israeli settlement activity—everything in the draft Security Council resolution jibed exactly with the Obama administration's public stance on Israel's settlements.

Yet, by the time the resolution came up for a vote, it was evident that the United States would exercise its first and only Security Council veto during the Obama administration had to prevent the international body from censuring Israel over its ongoing colonization of Palestinian land. Although the Obama administration had steadfastly refused to indicate how it would vote on the resolution, it was obvious that it opposed the initiative. "It is our belief," stated Assistant Secretary of State Crowley, "that New York is the wrong forum to address these complex issues, [and] that the parties should work to find a way back to direct negotiations as the only way to resolve these difficult issues and the conflict once and for all."[3] In this and many similar pre-vote statements, the Obama administration revealed a two-pronged strategy for attempting to deal with the realities of a post–"peace process" Israeli-Palestinian dynamic. First, the United States would pretend that the "peace process" was still salvageable, that heretofore futile direct negotiations would in the future magically bear fruit, that the United States was exerting yeoman efforts to return the parties to the negotiating table, and that the resumption of negotiations was always imminent. Second, following the logic of this argument, because the United States supposedly was so deeply and intensively engaged in attempting to restart the negotiations, any initiative taken outside the framework of these US-dominated talks would be viewed by the United States as an unwelcome thrust into its arena of self-arrogated diplomatic prerogatives.

But the Obama administration's own actions at the UN undercut the logic of these arguments. Rather than sticking to its insistence "that New York is the wrong forum to address these complex issues," the Obama administration proceeded to engage in diplomatic wrangling to scotch the draft Security Council resolution in favor of a diluted and less consequential Security Council presidential statement. According to a US draft of this presidential statement, which was promptly rejected by the Palestinians as inadequate, the Security Council would have reaffirmed "that it does not accept the legitimacy of continued Israeli settlement activity, which is a serious obstacle to the peace process."[4] The Palestinian rebuff of the draft presidential statement caused Ambassador Susan Rice, US Permanent Representative to the UN, to lament that "in recent days, we offered a constructive alternative course forward that we believe would have allowed the Council to act unanimously to support the pursuit of peace," as she cast her veto of the Security Council resolution. However, Rice added, "We regret that this effort was not successful and thus is no longer viable." By admitting to her efforts to pass an alternative presidential statement, Rice was making clear that the Obama administration objected not to the UN taking action per se on the Israeli-Palestinian conflict, but doing so in a way that threatened the hegemony of US discourse about what constituted legitimate criticism of Israel's activities.

This Palestinian diplomatic initiative put the Obama administration in the difficult, if not untenable, position of trying to explain why it would stand against the entirety of the international community to cast its sole veto at the UN to prevent the international body from taking a position with which it essentially agreed. Thus, in her explanation of the US veto, Rice took pains to "underscore our opposition to continued settlements. Our opposition to the resolution before this Council today should therefore not be misunderstood to mean we support settlement activity. On the contrary, we reject in the strongest terms the legitimacy of continued Israeli settlement activity." But the resolution had to be vetoed because every action taken on the Israeli-Palestinian conflict, according to the Obama administration, "must be measured against one overriding standard: will it move the parties closer to negotiations and an agreement?" In Rice's estimation, the answer was no because it "risks hardening the positions of both sides. It could encourage the parties to stay out of negotiations and, if and when they did resume, to return to the Security Council whenever they reach an impasse."[5] Perhaps Rice's rationale would have seemed plausible had a credible negotiating process been underway or even on the horizon. But the fact that there was not, and that the United States was still posturing as if it were able to bring the sides to the negotiating table, made it appear that the United States lacked a sound reason to exercise its veto, exposing the move as one designed to basely shield Israel from the consequences of its actions.

By blocking international action on the Israeli-Palestinian conflict, the Obama administration was, deliberately or not, emulating the worst tendencies of its predecessor, which acted similarly to prevent the international community from taking autonomous action outside of the "peace process" framework. For example, Rice's statement tracked almost exactly with the Bush administration's rationale for opposing the International Court of Justice's (ICJ) ruling in 2004 on the legality of the wall Israel was building in the Palestinian West Bank. Even though President George W. Bush had deemed the wall to be a "problem," making it "very difficult to develop confidence between the Palestinians and . . . Israel—with a wall snaking through the West Bank,"[6] his administration vehemently objected to the ICJ expressing its opinion on this wall. Bush administration lawyers had argued that "the United States believes that the giving of an advisory opinion in this matter risks undermining the peace process and politicizing the Court."[7] Thus, just as Bush was troubled by Israel's wall and Obama was disturbed by Israel's settlement expansion, both presidents would employ similar justifications attempting to prevent the international community from expressing its opinions about these issues.

Israel's backers in Congress were predictably apoplectic that Palestinians would have the temerity to take the initiative and break free from the confines of a US-dominated "peace process." They even chastised the Obama administration for seeking a compromised, watered-down presidential statement as being unduly condemnatory of Israel. Representative Howard Berman (D-CA), ranking Democrat on the House Foreign Affairs Committee, issued a statement reeking of paternalism, especially coming from a member of Congress who would later declare, "My constituents sent me to Washington in large part to fight for a stronger US-Israel relationship," which Berman claimed as "one [of] my top legislative priorities in Congress."[8] Adopting his sternest "father knows best" demeanor, Berman lectured that "the Palestinians are undermining their own best interests in persistently pushing for a UN Security Council vote condemning Israel. Complicated final-status issues like settlements can only be resolved directly between the Israelis and Palestinians, not by the glib declarations of international fora."[9] Representative Ileana Ros-Lehtinen, chair of the House Foreign Affairs Committee, excoriated the Obama administration for even attempting to push through a toothless Security Council presidential statement. According to her, "Offering to criticize our closest ally at the UN isn't leadership, it's unacceptable. Pretending that criticism of Israel is OK if it comes in a 'Presidential Statement' instead of a resolution isn't leadership, it's unacceptable. Twisting and turning and tying yourself in knots to avoid using our veto to defend our allies and interests isn't leadership, it's unacceptable."[10] AIPAC conveniently compiled a dossier running to fifteen pages of these and other similar statements by members of Congress censuring Palestinians for seeking a UN condemnation of Israel's illegal settlements.[11] This pushback from Capitol Hill demonstrated, once again, that even if Obama had been inclined not to veto the Security Council resolution, he would have been shellacked for his stance.

But members of Congress need not have worried. The day before the Security Council vote, Obama called President Mahmoud Abbas to pressure him to withdraw the resolution. According to Abbas, "He said it's better for you and for us and for our relations" to kill the initiative. Having failed to convince Abbas to pull the resolution, "the American president politely made what Abbas describes as a 'list of sanctions' Palestinians would endure if the vote went ahead. Among other things, he warned that Congress would not approve the $475 million in aid America gives the Palestinians," according to an interview Abbas gave to *Newsweek*.[12] Although the threat of US sanctions did not materialize in this instance, despite Palestinians having proceeded with the vote on the Security Council resolution, it set an ominous precedent that would be acted upon when the Palestinians went forward with their bid for UN membership in the fall.

Even though the Palestinians did not succeed in passing a UN

Security Council resolution condemning Israel's colonization of Palestinian land (and, even if the resolution had passed, Israel would have been highly unlikely to cease its settlement expansion anyway), this trial balloon of their new strategy to "re-internationalize" the Israeli-Palestinian conflict was nevertheless a diplomatic triumph for several reasons. First, by forcing the United States to exercise its veto in the Security Council, the Palestinians stripped bare the outrageous claim that the United States was an "honest broker" capable of mediating a just and lasting resolution to the Israeli-Palestinian conflict. Instead, Palestinians made it patently obvious that the United States would continue to act as guarantor and protector of Israel's interests at the UN.

Second, by focusing on an issue—Israel's ongoing settlement expansion—over which the United States had recently clashed with Israel, the Palestinians forced the United States to contort itself into verbal gymnastics to explain unconvincingly how it could veto a resolution in the Security Council with which it nevertheless agreed on substance. By doing so, the Palestinians succeeded in demonstrating that US opposition to Israel's settlements was only rhetorical and that Israel's continued defiance of the United States carried no penalties.

Third, by going forward with the Security Council vote, the Palestinians expanded an emerging rift between the United States and its supposed "peace process" partners in the Quartet, especially member states of the European Union, which were already miffed at having been excluded from the resumption of negotiations in September 2010. During the Security Council debate on the resolution, Sir Mark Lyall Grant, ambassador and Permanent Representative of the United Kingdom Mission to the UN, spoke on behalf of Britain, France and Germany, conveying that these countries "are seriously concerned about the current stalemate in the Middle East Peace Process. We each voted in favour of the draft Security Council Resolution because our views on settlements, including in East Jerusalem, are clear: they are illegal under international law, an obstacle to peace and constitute a threat to a two-state solution. All settlement activity, including in East Jerusalem, should cease immediately."

Not only were EU member states at loggerheads with the Obama administration on this particular resolution; they were already at odds over the next Palestinian initiative at the UN as well. In his statement, Lyall Grant noted, "Our goal remains an agreement on all final status issues and the welcoming of Palestine as a full member of the United Nations by September 2011. We will contribute to achieving this goal in any and every way that we can."[13]

A CONFLUENCE OF EVENTS

Before this drama unfolded at the UN General Assembly in the fall, a remarkable series of events would take place within a two-week span in Washington in May 2011. During this period, George Mitchell would resign as Special Envoy for Middle East Peace; Obama would badly mismanage an attempt to restart Israeli-Palestinian negotiations yet again, this time within the context of the US response to the Arab Spring; Netanyahu would abase Obama at the White House, prompting the president to beg for forgiveness at the AIPAC annual policy conference; and Congress would rapturously applaud Netanyahu for humiliating the president and for defeating the last initiative of the Obama administration to bring about Israeli-Palestinian peace.

On May 13, 2011, the White House released a terse letter to Obama, backdated April 6, from a frustrated and despondent George Mitchell, tendering his resignation. The entirety of the body of the letter read: "When I accepted your request to serve as US Special Envoy for Middle East Peace my intention was to serve for two years. More than two years having passed I hereby resign, effective May 20, 2011. I trust this will provide sufficient time for an effective transition. I strongly support your vision of comprehensive peace in the Middle East and thank you for giving me the opportunity to be part of your administration. It has been an honor for me to again serve our country."[14] Both Obama and Clinton lavished effusive praise on Mitchell and his efforts. Obama called him "a tireless advocate for peace" whose "deep commitment to resolving conflict and advancing democracy has contributed immeasurably to the goal of two states living side by side in peace and security." Obama added, "He is—by any measure—one of the finest public servants that our nation has ever had." Clinton affirmed that Mitchell "represents the best traditions of American diplomacy. Throughout George's distinguished career he has taken on the hardest challenges with determination, talent and old fashioned Maine common sense."[15]

In the end, however, even Mitchell's legendary qualities of resolve and persistence were not enough to produce any breakthroughs toward Israeli-Palestinian peace. As Special Envoy, Mitchell was fond of recalling his experience brokering peace in Northern Ireland to bolster his argument that failure was a necessary component of the negotiating process. "I chaired three separate sets of discussions in Northern Ireland, spanning a period overall of five years," Mitchell reminded the media as he announced in August 2010 the impending resumption of direct Israeli-Palestinian negotiations. He noted that in this case, "The main negotiation lasted for twenty-two months. During that time, the effort was repeatedly branded a failure. I was asked at least dozens, perhaps hundreds, of times when I was leaving because the effort had failed." Mitchell concurred that "if the objective is to achieve a peace agreement, until you do achieve one, you have failed to do so. In a sense, in Northern Ireland, we had about 700 days of failure and one day of success. And we approach this task with the same determination to succeed notwithstanding the difficulties and notwithstanding the inability to get a final result so far, including past efforts."[16]

But as Mitchell passed 700 days on the job as Special Envoy for Middle East Peace, with no prospect of even resuming negotiations anywhere in sight, that one day of hoped-for success seemed as illusory as ever. Mitchell has been extremely tight-lipped about his tenure since his resignation, making it difficult to determine whether the Obama administration's failed paradigm to achieve Israeli-Palestinian peace was the result of an ill-conceived plan designed by Mitchell, or whether Mitchell was simply responsible for implementing a flawed design handed to him by more senior levels of the Obama administration. Whichever of the two scenarios was more accurate, apparently Mitchell finally determined to call it quits after failing to persuade Obama to put forward a new, detailed plan for Israeli-Palestinian peace in his upcoming address on the Arab Spring, according to Bush administration official Elliott Abrams.[17]

On the day before his resignation took effect, Mitchell joined Obama at the State Department on May 19, 2011 to attend one of the president's two most important speeches on the Middle East during his first term, both of which are dealt with more fully in Chapter 10. In this seminal speech on the Arab Spring—the exuberant, spontaneous, and mass protests for freedom and democracy that swept through the Arab world in the early months of 2011—Obama hoped to establish a coherent and systematic US response to this phenomenon, which heretofore had been scattershot and highly selective in its support for anti-regime protests.

As Obama turned his attention toward the Israeli-Palestinian conflict in the closing portions of his speech, Mitchell must have privately sighed as the president perfunctorily re-trod well-traveled US formulations on negotiating an end to the conflict. Lost in the ensuing brouhaha over Obama's speech, however, was the fact that the president took a giant step backward from hoping to negotiate a comprehensive peace deal. The negotiations he convened in September 2010 envisioned simultaneous discussions on all permanent status issues, leading to a comprehensive framework agreement within one year. Duly chastened by the failure of these negotiations, Obama now acknowledged that a comprehensive agreement was no longer a feasible goal during his administration.

Instead, Israelis and Palestinians should focus on negotiating borders of the Palestinian state and security arrangements for Israel. "I know that these steps alone will not resolve this conflict," Obama admitted. He recognized that "two wrenching and emotional issues remain: the future of Jerusalem, and the fate of Palestinian refugees. But moving forward now on the basis of territory and security provides a foundation to resolve those two issues in a way that is just and fair, and that respects the rights and aspirations of Israelis and Palestinians." This new game plan—tackle the supposed "easy" issues up front, save the "hard" ones for an undetermined future—was, however, wishful thinking. Obama could still neither induce Israel to freeze settlement construction nor detour Palestinians from their new strategy to seek UN membership in the fall. Under these circumstances, it was a pipe dream even to suggest that Israel and the Palestinians could resume negotiations, much less achieve agreement on any issue, including the "easy" ones.

The one truly original suggestion in Obama's speech—this new two-phased approach to Israeli-Palestinian peacemaking—was nearly wholly subsumed, however, by the tempest in a teapot that arose over Obama's hidebound formulation regarding where the borders of the future Palestinian state should be. At the State Department, Obama reiterated his administration's long-standing, conventional phrasing: "The United States believes that negotiations should result in two states, with permanent Palestinian borders with Israel, Jordan, and Egypt, and permanent Israeli borders with Palestine. The borders of Israel and Palestine should be based on the 1967 lines with mutually agreed swaps, so that secure and recognized borders are established for both states."[18] This anodyne statement broke no new policy ground and reflected a standard US formulation in use since the Clinton administration. It also reflected the logic of all proposed two-state resolutions to the Israeli-Palestinian conflict under the rubric of UN Security Council Resolution 242.

But Netanyahu, ever the crafty politician with a keen sense for political theater, deemed this an opportune moment to pick a fight with the Obama administration, mobilize Israel's supporters in the United States to back him in this scrum and finally scuttle any remaining hope the president may have had of achieving even minimal progress on Israeli-Palestinian peace during his first term. Word leaked to the *New York Times* that prior to Obama's speech, Netanyahu "held an angry phone conversation" with Secretary of State Hillary Clinton, "in which he demanded that the president's reference to 1967 borders be cut." According to this account, after the White House refused, "Israeli officials continued to lobby the administration until right before Mr. Obama arrived at the State Department for the address. White House officials said he did not alter anything under Israeli pressure, though the president made changes in the text that delayed his appearance by thirty-five minutes."[19]

Netanyahu's feigned indignation over Obama's mention of the pre-1967 armistice lines was risible on two counts. First, Obama never suggested that Israel should fully comply with UN Security Council Resolution 242 and the principle embodied in that resolution of the "inadmissibility of the acquisition of territory by war" by withdrawing to its pre-1967 armistice lines.[20] Instead, he proposed that a two-state resolution should be "based on" those lines "with mutually agreed swaps," which meant, from previous negotiations mediated by the Clinton administration, that the United States would tag-team with Israel to foist an agreement on the Palestinians in which Israel would annex its major settlement blocs and the choicest of Palestinian land. In exchange, Israel would fork over to the Palestinians some barren, uninhabitable sand dunes appended to the Gaza Strip. This was hardly a formulation deleterious to Israel's interests, and Netanyahu knew it.

Second, Israel and its supporters in the United States made truly outlandish assertions about what Obama was allegedly forcing Israel to do, charges that were substantiated neither by the president's actual words nor by an honest analysis of the Arab-Israeli military balance. At the White House the next day, Netanyahu declared Israel's pre-1967 armistice lines to be "indefensible."[21] The Simon Wiesenthal Center, at the time embroiled in a controversy over its macabre and ironic decision to build a "Museum of Tolerance and Human Dignity" by vandalizing and disinterring remains at an ancient Muslim cemetery in Jerusalem, went one step further. The Wiesenthal Center bizarrely and inflammatorily likened Obama's speech to advocacy of genocide against the Jewish people by compelling Israel to return to "Auschwitz" borders.[22]

Of course, as Israel often bragged, its pre-1967 armistice lines were actually so defensible that it was able to steamroll the combined armies of Egypt, Syria, and Jordan from these lines and achieve a crushing victory over them in just six days in June 1967. That was at a time when the Soviet Union was providing advanced weaponry to its Egyptian and Syrian clients, while according to President Lyndon Johnson, to prevent an arms race, "our own military shipments to the area have consequently been severely limited."[23] Neglecting Johnson's concerns about stoking an arms race, over the next four decades, the United States would provide Israel more than $67 billion in loans and grants for US weapons, while pledging an additional $30 billion in military aid over the next decade. If Israel's armistice lines were defensible in 1967, then they were incomparably more so in 2011 thanks to this enormous infusion of US weaponry.

However, Obama's actual words and the realities of the Arab-Israeli military balance were just ancillary and inconvenient facts to be pushed aside. Netanyahu, sensing Obama's political weakness, was out for blood and attacked the president viciously while in Washington for the AIPAC annual policy conference. After meeting with Obama in the White House on May 20, 2011, Netanyahu delivered the most audacious public dressing down of the president that Obama would receive while in office. In his remarks to the press, Obama bent over backward to smooth over any ruffled feathers from his speech the previous day at the State Department. The president noted that the "frequency of these meetings" between the two leaders "is an indication of the extraordinary bonds between our two countries." While he recognized that "obviously there are some differences between us in the precise formulations and language" to achieve Israeli-Palestinian peace, Obama indicated that "that's going to happen between friends."

But Netanyahu was not mollified. He launched into a lecture about Israel's supposed security requirements. "Remember that, before 1967, Israel was all of nine miles wide," Netanyahu scolded. "It was half the width of the Washington Beltway. And these were not the boundaries of peace; they were the boundaries of repeated wars, because the attack on Israel was so attractive. So we can't go back to those indefensible lines," he harrumphed, and for good measure, "we're going to have to have a long-term military presence along the Jordan" as well. Making clear that it was he who spoke for both of them, Netanyahu revealed, "I discussed this with the President and I think that we understand that Israel has certain security requirements that will have to come into place in any deal that we make."

Netanyahu then proceeded to hector Obama on the lessons of Jewish history and on the "ancient nation of Israel. And, you know," he reminded Obama, "we've been around for almost 4,000 years. We've experienced struggle and suffering like no other people. We've gone through expulsions and pogroms and massacres and the murder of millions. But I can say that . . . even at the nadir of the valley of death, we never lost hope and we never lost our dream of reestablishing a sovereign state in our ancient homeland, the land of Israel." He then explained to Obama that "now it falls on my shoulders as the Prime Minister of Israel, at a time of extraordinary instability and uncertainty in the Middle East, to work with you to fashion a peace that will ensure Israel's security and will not jeopardize its survival. I take this responsibility with pride but with great humility, because, as I told you in our conversation, we don't have a lot of margin for error. And because, Mr. President, history will not give the Jewish people another chance."[24]

The Obama administration was rightfully livid at this degrading treatment of the president in the White House. An anonymous US official told Peter Beinart that Obama "felt the office of the presidency, the dignity of the office was insulted" by Netanyahu's performance.[25] But rather than publicly confront Israel and demand an apology, Obama, with his tail between his legs, sauntered over to AIPAC's annual policy conference on May 22, 2011 to try to make amends for daring to suggest that Israel allow for the establishment of a Palestinian state "based on" the pre-1967 armistice line. Referring to his speech the previous week at the State Department, Obama acknowledged "that stating these principles—on the issues of territory and security—generated some controversy over the past few days. (Laughter.) I wasn't surprised. I know very well that the easy thing to do, particularly for a President preparing for reelection, is to avoid any controversy." But the controversy was unwarranted, Obama believed, because as he correctly pointed out: "There was nothing particularly original in my proposal; this basic framework for negotiations has long been the basis for discussions among the parties, including previous US administrations."

Obama then proceeded to address head-on the controversy generated by his statement that the borders of the Palestinian state should be "based on" the pre-1967 armistice lines with mutually agreed territorial swaps. Under this formulation, "the parties themselves—Israelis and Palestinians—will negotiate a border that is different than the one that existed on June 4, 1967. (Applause.) That's what mutually agreed-upon swaps means," the president stressed. "It is a well-known formula to all who have worked on this issue for a generation. It allows the parties themselves to account for the changes that have taken place over the last 44 years . . . including the new demographic realities on the ground."[26] In other words, according to Obama, his administration would continue to work to ensure an agreement that would enable Israel to permanently reap the fruits of its illegal settlement enterprise in the Palestinian West Bank and East Jerusalem by annexing major settlement blocs.

But even this degree of genuflecting to AIPAC's hardline constituency was not considered to be submissive enough by convention attendees. *Washington Post* blogger Jennifer Rubin considered it a triumph of civility that "he was not booed when he entered; most stood and offered brief applause." However, during his speech, the group greeted their president with "long periods of stony silence, and audible boos were heard when he brought up his plan to base an Israeli-Palestinian peace deal on the 1967 border lines."[27] It seemed that the more Obama bent over backward to placate the Israel lobby, the more vitriolic was its reaction to him.

However, Obama's humiliation at the hands of Netanyahu and the Israel lobby had not yet reached its apex, which would occur two days later, when Netanyahu addressed a joint meeting of Congress on May 24, 2011. In his speech, Netanyahu unself-consciously declared that "Israel has always embraced" the path of liberty, on which "human rights cannot be crushed by tribal loyalties." He then continued to explain exactly how his vision of "peace" with the Palestinians would do exactly that: crush Palestinian human and national rights and make them subservient to Jewish national privilege. Netanyahu's address made it crystal clear exactly how rejectionist and unaccommodating was his stance.

First, Netanyahu denied that Israel was even engaged in a belligerent military occupation of the Palestinian West Bank and East Jerusalem. According to him, "In Judea and Samaria [the Biblical terms for these areas employed by pro-colonization Israelis], the Jewish people are not foreign occupiers. We are not the British in India. We are not the Belgians in the Congo." Netanyahu fell back on the Old Testament to justify Israeli military occupation and colonization of Palestinian land, stating, "This is the land of our forefathers, the Land of Israel, to which Abraham brought the idea of one God, where David set out to confront Goliath, and where Isaiah saw a vision of eternal peace. No distortion of history can deny the four thousand year old bond between the Jewish people and the Jewish land." Palestinians, in Netanyahu's estimation, have failed to appreciate that these historical Jewish connections to the land somehow conferred on Israel the "right" to ethnically cleanse, dispossess, and confine them to ever-shrinking reservations within their historic homeland.

Second, Netanyahu disclaimed any responsibility for perpetuating the conflict. Instead, the onus for the continuation of the conflict rested solely upon Palestinians, according to Netanyahu, who asserted that "our conflict has never been about the establishment of a Palestinian state. It has always been about the existence of the Jewish state. This is what this conflict is about." Netanyahu repeated the debunked myth that "the Palestinians twice refused generous offers by Israeli Prime Ministers to establish a Palestinian state on virtually all the territory won by Israel in the Six Day War," proposals which he had nevertheless opposed. This definitively determined, in his racist view, that the undifferentiated "they" were "simply unwilling to end the conflict. And I regret to say this: they continue to educate their children to hate."

Third, the contours of a permanent resolution to the conflict, according to Netanyahu, would be inestimably less favorable to Palestinian rights than those on offer at Camp David in 2000, which themselves were dictated terms of surrender justifiably rejected by the Palestinians. There would not even be a token, much less an actual, implementation of the internationally recognized right of return for Palestinian refugees who were exiled from their homes when Israel was established in 1948. Instead, the best Palestinian refugees could hope for under Netanyahu's plan is "that the Palestinian refugee problem will be resolved outside the borders of Israel."

Unlike at Camp David, there would be no creative formulas for sharing sovereignty in Jerusalem as the capital of two states. Rather, according to Netanyahu, "Jerusalem must never again be divided. Jerusalem must remain the united capital of Israel." Netanyahu realized that it "is a difficult issue for Palestinians" to concede their claims to locate the capital of their state in Jerusalem. "But I believe that with creativity and goodwill a solution can be found," Netanyahu declared, to compel Palestinians to abandon their historical, political, cultural, religious, geographical, and economic rationale for desiring Jerusalem to be their capital.

Finally, Netanyahu promised that "Israel will be generous on the size of the Palestinians [sic] state," as if Israel were being benevolent, rather than dismantling a brutal military occupation to make way for this Palestinian state. However, according to Netanyahu, the borders of the Palestinian state were not up for discussion as they were at Camp David. Instead, it would be left to Israel's sole discretion to determine how much Palestinian land it would annex. He lectured Congress that "we'll be very firm on where we put the border with it. This is an important principle. It shouldn't be lost." Furthermore, the Palestinian "state" that would emerge would be "fully demilitarized" and Israel would "maintain a long-term military presence along the Jordan River."

None of these formulations were new for Netanyahu; they paralleled the terms he set out in his much-applauded June 2009 speech in which he accepted for the first time a Palestinian "state." But what was novel in Netanyahu's address was the bombshell he dropped, revealing the extent to which Israel had now colonized land it had occupied since 1967 and the concomitant irreversibility of this colonization. Netanyahu claimed that 650,000 Israeli settlers now populated these Palestinian lands, the "vast majority" of whom "reside in neighborhoods and suburbs of Jerusalem and Greater Tel Aviv. These areas are densely populated but geographically quite small." Because of this colonization, according to Netanyahu, "Under any realistic peace agreement, these areas, as well as other places of critical strategic and national importance, will be incorporated into the final borders of Israel."[28] Period. No negotiations. Israel's colonization of Palestinian lands was a fait accompli and all major Israeli settlements would be annexed to Israel, leaving Palestinians with tiny, disconnected fragments of land surrounded by these settlements and permanent Israeli walls, checkpoints, bypass roads and military bases. This would be Netanyahu's "generous" Palestinian "state."

One might reasonably expect that in reaction to such bald-faced racism and the trampling of Palestinian human rights, the estimable members of Congress listening to Netanyahu's speech would display polite indifference, or even outright hostility. Instead, however, they repeatedly greeted Netanyahu's remarks with ecstatic and rapturous applause. Members of Congress gave Netanyahu, by one count, twenty-nine standing ovations, more than Obama received during his 2011 State of the Union address.[29] It was difficult to ascertain whether most members of Congress understood the rejectionist nature of the remarks for which they applauded, or whether their exuberance was an affectation which they hoped would be captured on C-SPAN so that the Israel lobby could know to whom to send its campaign donations. In either case, the entire affair was tawdry and unbecoming, as Congress enthusiastically embraced a foreign leader who was publicly undercutting the foreign policy goals of the United States. The carnival-like nature of this political spectacle was confirmed when word leaked that the ovations for Netanyahu were carefully choreographed. "Whenever Republicans rose to applaud Netanyahu's more controversial statements, Democratic Representative Debbie Wasserman Schultz of Florida would turn to her party colleagues and raise her arm, thus signaling them to stand as well," according to Peter Beinart. It was, according to one White House aide, a "cartoon scene."[30]

The only dose of reality in this otherwise surreal paean to Israeli apartheid was provided by Rae Abileah, an activist with CODEPINK: Women for Peace. During Netanyahu's speech, Abileah unfurled a banner from the Capitol gallery, which read "Occupying Land Is Indefensible" and interrupted Netanyahu with chants of "No More Occupation! Stop Israeli War Crimes! Equal Rights for Palestinians!" According to Ablieah, as she was protesting, "Immediately, I was tackled, gagged and violently shoved to the floor by other members of the audience, many of whom were still wearing their badges from the AIPAC conference this past weekend. Police dragged me out of the Capitol gallery, and an ambulance whisked me to the hospital, where I was treated for neck and shoulder injuries and put under arrest for disrupting Congress."[31] Thus did AIPAC demonstrate that it owned Congress, would violently oppose those who dared to dissent and that along with its partner, Prime Minister Netanyahu, would effectively stymie Obama's last diplomatic initiative, thereby boxing him into a corner for the remainder of his term.

Confirmation that this entire clash with the United States was a stage-managed production came soon thereafter. As the United States and Israel were busy patching up their squabble in order to jointly head off the Palestinian bid for UN membership, anonymous Netanyahu aides let it be known that the prime minister, who less than three months earlier had berated Obama in the White House for having suggested it, now quietly accepted that he "would be willing to resume talks with the Palestinians on the basis of the 1967 boundary line."[32] Apparently, these lines were not so indefensible or genocidal after all.

Having already firmly decided to pursue an alternative strategy—applying for UN membership and securing diplomatic recognition from other countries—to advance Israeli-Palestinian peace, Palestinians looked from afar upon these dramatic, if not bizarre, political developments of May 2011. Witnessing the disastrous political defeat of Obama's latest foray into Israeli-Palestinian peacemaking must have only reinforced Palestinian convictions that they would never achieve their rights through any process dominated by the United States. The stage was now set for a dramatic showdown at the UN in September 2011, a confrontation which would pit the United States against the international community in blocking Palestinian hopes of full UN membership and which would demonstrate that the United States would continue to determine its own timetable for Palestinian freedom and self-determination.

CHAPTER SIX

Time for My Courageous and Proud People to Live Free

UN MEMBERSHIP

On November 29, 1947, the UN General Assembly adopted Resolution 181, recommending the partition of Palestine into two states—an Arab state (in 45 percent of Palestine) and a Jewish State (in 55 percent of Palestine)—with a Special International Regime for Jerusalem. At the time the UN voted to partition Palestine, against the wishes of the majority of its inhabitants, Palestinians comprised more than two-thirds of the population, with Jews accounting for less than one-third. In addition, Palestinians owned 93 percent of the land, while Jews owned 7 percent.

This partition of Palestine, which, ironically, would likely never have happened were it not for intensive US diplomatic pressure to sway the vote, was never implemented. Palestinians viewed the dismemberment of their homeland as unjust. The Jewish Agency, the official representative body of Jews in British Mandate–era Palestine, formally accepted the division, but Zionist militias then proceeded to engage in a pre-planned campaign of ethnic cleansing to drive out as many Palestinians from as much of Palestine as possible before, during and after the British evacuated the area on May 14, 1948. After Britain withdrew, Israel declared its independence, and by the time the ensuing war ended with armistice agreements signed between Israel and Egypt, Lebanon, Jordan and Syria in 1949 (establishing those pre-1967 armistice lines that Prime Minister Netanyahu had deemed "indefensible"), Israel had conquered territories beyond those allotted to the Jewish state under the UN partition plan and exercised sovereignty over 78 percent of Palestine.

The remaining 22 percent of Palestine was annexed by Jordan (the West Bank and East Jerusalem) or placed under military administration by Egypt (the Gaza Strip). This situation obtained until June 1967, when Israel conquered the remainder of historic Palestine and placed these Palestinian territories under a military occupation that has now lasted more than forty-six years.

Nearly sixty-four years after the UN had voted to establish two states in Palestine, PA president Mahmoud Abbas would submit Palestine's application for membership in the UN as the General Assembly convened in September 2011. As direct Israeli-Palestinian negotiations broke down almost as soon as they began in September 2010, and as it became evident that Israel would not accept the US package of inducements to extend its sham settlement "moratorium" to breathe a few months of life into the negotiating process, Palestinians finally soured on the prospect of attaining statehood through a US-dominated "peace process." Instead, as noted in the previous chapter, Palestinians began to "re-internationalize" the Israeli-Palestinian conflict by taking their case directly to the UN. Even before they floated their trial balloon of this new strategy by forcing a Security Council vote condemning Israel's illegal settlements in February 2011, the inchoate idea of seeking UN membership began to take shape.

As early as October 25, 2010, Abbas hinted at the possibility that Palestinians would submit an application for UN membership at the next General Assembly meeting. In response to a statement by Prime Minister Netanyahu demanding that Palestinians desist from considering unilateral actions and resume futile negotiations as Israel continued to colonize Palestinian land, Abbas pointed out that "settlements are a unilateral step taken by Israel." By highlighting Israel's unilateral actions, Abbas argued that Israel had no right to dictate to Palestinians a possible alternative path to securing Palestinian rights, "which is to resort to the United Nations."[1] At this early stage, the United States did not appear to be too perturbed by the prospect of Palestinians going to the UN. In response to a question about this verbal sparring between Netanyahu and Abbas over unilateral actions, the State Department merely reminded everyone that "our position has been pretty clear. We continue to encourage the parties to avoid unilateral steps on one side of the ledger or the other."[2]

But this relative indifference on the part of the United States would not last long, especially as Palestinian plans progressed in the waning months of 2010. In order to strengthen their case for UN membership, Palestinians embarked on a global diplomatic campaign to have additional countries recognize Palestinian statehood. Although US policymakers often conflated the Palestinian bid for UN membership with statehood recognition, they were two related, but separate, campaigns with different functions. In international law, statehood recognition is strictly a bilateral matter. It is left to the discretion of one country to recognize another and establish diplomatic relations with it. On the other hand, UN membership is a multilateral affair, requiring both the UN Security Council and the General Assembly to vote to accept the membership application of a state. Obviously though, one diplomatic process affects the other, as the more countries recognize another one as a state, the stronger the prospects are for that state to be admitted as a member of the UN.

On November 15, 1988, the PLO had declared independence, noting that UN General Assembly Resolution 181 "continues to attach conditions to international legitimacy that guarantee the Palestinian Arab people the right to sovereignty and national independence." In a companion document released at the same time by the Palestinian National Council, the legislative branch of the PLO, its goals "in the political field" included "Israel's withdrawal from all the Palestinian and Arab territories which it has occupied since 1967, including Arab Jerusalem."[3] Approximately one hundred countries promptly had recognized this Palestinian state as of early 1989.[4]

Some additional countries recognized the State of Palestine during the 1990s and 2000s—primarily newly independent former Soviet republics—but for the most part, the diplomatic initiative lost steam during these two decades as the Palestinians concentrated their efforts on the "peace process." However, with the UN membership campaign underway, the Palestinians scored important—and to Israel and its supporters in the United States worrisome—diplomatic wins when Argentina, Bolivia, Brazil, Ecuador and Uruguay recognized the State of Palestine in quick succession in December 2010.[5]

As these South American countries began announcing their recognition of Palestinian statehood, the State Department stepped up its criticism of this Palestinian diplomatic initiative. Asked about Brazilian and Argentinian recognition of Palestine, Assistant Secretary of State Crowley viewed it as a sideshow. "We don't think that we should be distracted from the fact that the only way to resolve the core issues within the process is through direct negotiations. That remains our focus. And we do not favor that course of action. As we've said many, many times, any unilateral action, we believe, is counterproductive."[6] Representative Eliot Engel was less circumspect in his denunciation, taking to the floor of Congress to "condemn" Brazil, Argentina, and Uruguay. In a statement reminiscent of nineteenth- and twentieth-century colonialism, in which the superpower dictated if, how, and when the "natives" could have their rights, Engel thundered, "The Palestinians must know that a peace agreement with Israel is the only way they can have their Palestinian state."[7]

Engel's tirade was only the opening salvo in a sustained barrage launched by Israel's supporters in Congress to try to scuttle Palestinian UN membership. On December 15, 2010, the House of Representatives took the highly unusual step of debating and voting on a resolution on this issue through a mechanism known as "suspension of the rules," which limits debate and precludes amendments. This legislative procedure is supposed to be reserved for noncontroversial measures such as naming post offices. In this instance, however, it was used to ram through a substantive resolution whose text was only introduced that same day. In other words, neither members of Congress nor the public had an opportunity to read and consider the resolution before it was approved by voice vote. The resolution, H.Res.1765, introduced by Representative Howard Berman, reaffirmed the House's "strong opposition to any attempt to establish or seek recognition of a Palestinian state outside of an agreement negotiated between Israel and the Palestinians." It urged Palestinians to "cease all efforts at circumventing the negotiation process, including efforts to gain recognition of a Palestinian state from other nations, within the United

Nations, and in other international forums prior to achievement of a final agreement between Israel and the Palestinians, and calls upon foreign governments not to extend such recognition." Finally, it demanded Palestinians to "resume direct negotiations with Israel immediately."[8]

The debate on the resolution provided members of Congress with a platform to engage in one of the most sustained, demagogic and racist attacks against Palestinians in recent history. Berman, the sponsor of the resolution, clearly knew better than Palestinians what was in their best interests. "The Palestinian people don't want a bunch of declarations of statehood. They want a state. And they should have one, through the only means possible for attaining one, negotiations with Israel." Berman reminded his colleagues that "this body has been very generous in its support of their worthy efforts to build institutions and the economy on the West Bank. In fact, I believe we are the most generous nation in the world in that regard." But, he warned, "I think our friends should understand: If they persist in pursuing a unilateralist path, inevitably, and however regrettably, there will be consequences for US-Palestinian relations," hinting at the US sanctions that would follow. Representative Dan Burton (R-IN) was more forthright in calling for sanctions against Palestinians. He believed that "we ought to take a very hard attitude toward the Palestinian Authority. In my opinion, that means cutting off any funding for it until it is willing to seriously sit down and negotiate a peaceful settlement to the problem."

As this talk of sanctioning Palestinians for seeking UN membership commenced in Congress, representatives made alarming, chauvinistic and downright racist claims about Palestinians. Representative Gary Ackerman dictated that Abbas "stop jetting around the [world] looking for alternatives to dealing directly with Prime Minister Netanyahu." He considered Palestinians' concerns that Israel was colonizing their land to be "overwrought." Majority Leader Eric Cantor (R-VA) contended that this Palestinian effort "is a rejection of the very essence of the peace process. It is an unambiguous statement that the Palestinians refuse to honor their obligations in the interest of a lasting peace with Israel," while he simultaneously overlooked Israel's unmet obligations. Engel termed a Palestinian state in the West Bank, East Jerusalem and

Gaza Strip a "preposterous" idea whose proposition was merely "mischief-making" on the part of Palestinians. After nearly two decades of failed negotiations, this Palestinian diplomatic initiative was proof, in Engel's eyes, of "the Palestinian leadership not having the guts to sit down and negotiate a difficult situation" and a "further international attempt to delegitimize Israel." Representative Shelley Berkley (D-NV) accused Palestinians of "stonewalling" negotiations and urged that "all peace-loving nations must reject this Palestinian manipulation." Worse yet, in vicious terms that would be echoed later on the 2012 presidential campaign trail, Berkley flatly denied that Palestinians had an identity or culture, among many other presumed flaws. "While Israel has a strong country and a good education system, a vibrant economy, a national identity, a cultural identity and a strong democracy, the Palestinians, because of their poor leadership, have absolutely none of those," she railed. Even members of Congress who had no geographical grasp of the Israeli-Palestinian conflict felt emboldened to speak on the topic. For example, Representative Ted Poe (R-TX) wondered: "Is this [Palestinian state] going to be a sovereign state within the sovereign State of Israel?"

Only a handful of representatives expressed doubt about the wisdom of Congress passing a resolution to unilaterally condemn Palestinians for taking supposed unilateral action, while eliding Israel's unilateral actions. Representative Gwen Moore (D-WI), alluding to Israel's obligation to freeze settlement construction under the Roadmap, noted that the resolution "conveniently skips around other unilateral actions by the parties that may also harm the atmosphere for peace in the region." Representative Lois Capps (D-CA) wearily criticized "yet another one-sided resolution regarding the Israeli-Palestinian conflict." She argued that "it is truly absurd to argue that serious negotiations can occur when both actors are engaged in activities that threaten the credibility of the peace process. It is likewise unwise to ignore that both Israelis and Palestinians bear responsibility for engaging in these activities." In a blunt statement on the true intention of the resolution, Capps concluded that "resolutions, like the one we are considering today, are clearly done for domestic political consumption much more than for having any positive impact on the conflict. We should not be ignorant of the fact that this Chamber's pattern of passing resolutions that are one-sided can, indeed, undermine our credibility to be serious brokers for peace."[9]

But these small glimpses of rationality were vastly overshadowed by the preceding histrionics. From this debate, it was clear that Palestinians, by breaking free from the confines of the US-dominated "peace process," had touched a raw nerve among Israel's supporters in Congress. Their nightmare of Palestinians taking independent political action to advance their rights and succeeding in mobilizing substantial international support for their initiatives was coming to fruition. Over the months ahead, Congress would pull out all the stops to ensure that the Obama administration would act to derail these efforts.

However, these members of Congress had no cause for concern, as they and Obama clearly were on the same wavelength. In his May 2011 speech on the Arab Spring, which otherwise was devoted to supporting Arab aspirations for freedom and democracy and aligning US policy with the premise that "that every man and woman is endowed with certain inalienable rights," Obama came out vehemently against Palestinian efforts to secure UN membership. The president saw no contradiction between advocating for universal rights while at the same time disabusing Palestinians of the notion that they could achieve their rights absent Israel's assent. "For the Palestinians, efforts to delegitimize Israel will end in failure," Obama pledged. Downplaying the significance of UN membership, Obama lectured that "symbolic actions to isolate Israel at the United Nations in September won't create an independent state." He added, "Palestinians will never realize their independence by denying the right of Israel to exist."[10] Obama's overheated rhetoric failed to explain why, especially within the framework of a two-state resolution to the Israeli-Palestinian conflict, Palestinian efforts to attain UN membership equated to the delegitimization or isolation of Israel, much less a denial of Israel's "right to exist." If any attempt to advance Palestinian rights, in Obama's zero-sum mentality, somehow eroded Israel's very essence, then he also seemed to imply the converse proposition: that Israel's "legitimacy" was premised on and could be maintained only by continuing to deny Palestinians their right to self-determination. This broadside against Palestinian UN membership struck such a discordant note in Obama's address as to make the speech seem bifurcated.

Addressing the AIPAC annual policy conference three days later, Obama upped the ante in countering Palestinian UN membership. "No vote at the United Nations will ever create an independent Palestinian state," Obama declared, conveniently neglecting to mention that the UN had done so already in 1947. Repeating his talking points from the Arab Spring speech, Obama reiterated that "the United States will stand up against efforts to single Israel out at the United Nations or in any international forum. (Applause.) Israel's legitimacy is not a matter for debate. That is my commitment; that is my pledge to all of you."[11]

But Obama's unflinching opposition to Palestinian UN membership and the not-so-veiled threats issued by Congress the previous December did not succeed in deterring Abbas from the initiative; on the contrary, these attacks seemed to strengthen his resolve as the initiative continued to gain momentum. Three days before Obama's speech on the Arab Spring, Abbas penned an op-ed in the *New York Times* laying out the case for UN membership. According to Abbas, the drive for Palestinian UN membership "should not be seen as a stunt." Instead, it was, in Abbas's view, a realistic project to secure Palestinian rights that could not be won at futile negotiations with Israel. "We go to the United Nations now to secure the right to live free in the remaining 22 percent of our historic homeland because we have been negotiating with the State of Israel for twenty years without coming any closer to realizing a state of our own," Abbas explained. "We cannot wait indefinitely while Israel continues to send more settlers to the occupied West Bank and denies Palestinians access to most of our land and holy places, particularly in Jerusalem." Pointing to the inability of the United States to successfully mediate this process, Abbas wrote, "Neither political pressure nor promises of rewards by the United States have stopped Israel's settlement program."

Abbas argued that UN membership for Palestine should be viewed as facilitating, not supplanting, negotiations. "Once admitted to the United Nations, our state stands ready to negotiate all core issues of the conflict with Israel," he stated. Negotiating as a member of the UN, Abbas reasoned, would bring a semblance of balance to the otherwise asymmetrical power dynamic that placed Palestinians at such a disadvantage in these talks. In that case, Abbas stated, "Palestine would be negotiating from the position of one United Nations member whose territory is militarily occupied by another, however, and not as a vanquished people ready to accept whatever terms are put in front of us."[12] Although the Obama administration was unswayed by these arguments, they were resonating with other countries that had grown equally weary of the US-led "peace process." In July 2011, the PLO announced that 122 countries now recognized the State of Palestine.[13]

Clearly, tough talk from Obama and a House resolution bidding Palestinians back to the negotiating table were not enough to dissuade Abbas from his chosen path. Congress would now step up the pressure by overtly threatening Palestinians with sanctions if they proceeded. On June 28, 2011, the Senate passed S.Res.185 by unanimous consent with no debate. Sponsored by Senator Ben Cardin and cosponsored by ninety senators, the resolution noted that "aid to the Palestinians is predicated on a good faith commitment from the Palestinians to the peace process." Their effort to secure UN membership, according to the Senate, "would violate the underlying principles of the Oslo Accords, the Road Map, and other relevant Middle East peace process efforts." Therefore, the Senate would "consider restrictions on aid to the Palestinian Authority should it persist in efforts to circumvent direct negotiations by turning to the United Nations or other international bodies." Furthermore, the Senate resolution called on the president "to lead a diplomatic effort to oppose a unilateral declaration of a Palestinian state and to oppose recognition of a Palestinian state by other nations, within the United Nations, and in other international forums prior to achievement of a final agreement between the Government of Israel and the Palestinians."[14] As if these threats contained in the resolution were not clear enough, Cardin elucidated the next day on the Senate floor that "the Senate is now firmly on record that this kind of action would be directly counterproductive to peace. If the Palestinians pursue this, it may well have implications for the continued US participation with the Palestinians."[15]

Not to be outdone, the House followed suit by passing a similar, but more toughly worded, resolution, H.Res.268, on July 7, 2011, by a vote of 407-6, with thirteen representatives abstaining. The resolution, which was sponsored by Majority Leader Eric Cantor and cosponsored by 356 representatives, stated demonstratively "that Palestinian efforts to circumvent direct negotiations and pursue recognition of statehood prior to agreement with Israel will harm United States–Palestinian relations and will have serious implications for the United States assistance programs for the Palestinians and the Palestinians [sic] Authority."[16]

Israel's supporters in the House were livid that Palestinians refused to fall into line and accept Israel's dictates any longer. Representative Ileana Ros-Lehtinen fumed that the Palestinian initiative amounted to an "international effort to isolate and demonize Israel." Channeling former Israeli ambassador to the UN Abba Eban, she claimed that "Israel does not have a partner for peace and security as the Palestinian leadership continues to never miss an opportunity to miss an opportunity." As punishment, now was the perfect time, in her view, to relocate "our Embassy to Jerusalem, Israel's eternal and undivided capital." Representative Howard Berman noted that he was "deeply disappointed" that Palestinians refused to heed his arguments against seeking UN membership, noting that the initiative would achieve "absolutely nothing." Representative Steve Chabot (R-OH) used the debate to push his resolution calling for the United States "to cut all funding to the UN General Assembly should it vote to recognize a Palestinian state." Representative Chris Smith (R-NJ) called the diplomatic initiative "misguided" and "counterproductive," since the UN is a "haven of anti-Israel and even sometimes anti-Semitic activity." Representative Paul Gosar (R-AZ) spewed, "It is a disgrace and an offense to the U.N [sic] Charter and all acceptable norms of international law to create or recognize a state that itself will not first forsake terrorism, violence, ethnic hatred, and genocide." Representative Eliot Engel lambasted Palestinians for "playing their cute little games."

Few representatives dared to counter this invective. One who did was Representative David Price (D-NC), who lamented that "as usual, the resolution before us today tells only half the story. It says nothing about Israel's responsibility to act as a serious negotiating partner and abide by its previous commitments under the Road Map and other agreements. It says nothing about Israel's refusal to halt settlement construction in order to allow direct negotiations to resume." Instead, Price argued, the resolution "condemns the Palestinian president for his unilateral actions while failing to comprehend that it has been Israel's intransigence that has led him to view the United Nations as his only recourse. And as usual, the resolution has been rushed to the floor without any serious debate or any opportunity for input from the many members of this body who care about this critical issue." Invoking Albert Einstein's definition of insanity, Representative Ron Paul rued that "I do not believe that peace will result if we continue to do the same things while hoping for different results. The US has been involved in this process for decades, spending billions of dollars we do not have, yet we never seem to get much closer to a solution."[17]

However, just because the Obama administration and most members of Congress stood shoulder to shoulder in categorical opposition to Palestinian UN membership, this antagonism did not mean that the rest of the world, including Quartet "peace process" partners, were prepared to back the stance of the United States. In fact, the opposite appeared to be true. As the initiative continued gaining momentum, the fissures that Palestinians opened between the United States and the rest of the Quartet when they forced a US veto in the Security Council in February 2011 now opened up into an unbridgeable chasm as the United States tried unsuccessfully to bully everyone into line. Thus, the United States curtly dismissed a French initiative to convene an international peace conference in a last-ditch effort to stave off the impending imbroglio at the UN. In a June 6, 2011, joint press conference with French Foreign Minister Alain Juppe, Secretary of State Hillary Clinton threw cold water on the French proposal. After spending nearly one year attempting to convince the world that the United States was on the verge of pushing Israelis and Palestinians back to the negotiating table, Clinton now finally admitted to the obvious fact "that there is no agreement that the parties will resume negotiations. And I think the idea of any gathering, a conference or a meeting, has to be linked to a willingness by the parties to resume negotiating." Clinton stressed, "We strongly support a return to negotiations. But we do not think that it would be productive for there to be a conference about returning to negotiations."[18] In other words, if the United States could not succeed in convening Israeli-Palestinian negotiations, then no other country would be allowed to try an alternative approach.

A Quartet meeting convened at the State Department on July 11, 2011 also failed to produce a meeting of the minds between the United States, the United Nations, Russia, and the European Union on the best way forward. Although a senior US administration official speaking on background stated that the Quartet principals "characterized the discussion as excellent and substantive with a full and complete exchange of views," the Quartet's inability to issue a statement at the conclusion of the meeting hinted at deep divisions between the parties. This official did, however, admit "that there are still gaps that are impeding progress. And they concluded that realistically, for the Quartet, more work needs to be done to close those gaps before the Quartet can go forth publicly with the kinds of statements that might allow the parties to actually break through the impasse."[19]

Thus with the prospects for the resumption of negotiations hopelessly deadlocked and the Quartet at an impasse, there was nothing more for the United States to do other than continue to work to defeat Palestinian UN membership. The Obama administration made its opposition official on September 7, 2011, declaring that "if any such resolution" for Palestinian UN membership "were put in front of the Security Council, that we would veto it," according to Wendy Sherman, the Obama administration's nominee for Undersecretary of State for Political Affairs.[20] The following day, in response to a question as to whether Sherman was speaking on behalf of the Obama administration, State Department spokesperson Victoria Nuland confirmed that if "something comes to a vote in the UN Security Council, the US will veto."[21]

At virtually the same time that the Obama administration was formalizing its commitment to veto the Palestinian UN bid, it was also acknowledging what already was widely known in diplomatic circles: that the United States had been engaging in an extensive, global lobbying campaign to combat the Palestinian initiative. On September 6, 2011, Nuland responded, "Yes" when asked: "Would it be fair to say that you've been lobbying other members of the international community not to vote in favor of such a move?" Nuland clarified, "We have been absolutely clear publicly and

privately, first and foremost with all of the states that have traditionally worked actively on this dossier, but also now with states
that could be confronted with a decision in the General Assembly,
and making clear that we think that this is the wrong way to go and
that it could potentially make getting back to the negotiating table
harder."[22] In her nomination hearing before the Senate Foreign
Relations Committee, Sherman went further in describing the scale
of the effort. She stated that "there has been a very broad and very
vigorous démarche [a formal diplomatic demand] of virtually
every capital in the world [and] that this is high on the agenda for
every meeting the secretary has with every world leader."[23] The
scope of the Obama administration's attempts at suasion was so
broad that one State Department official, after pressing 150 diplomats to oppose the initiative, told Peter Beinart that "sometimes I
feel like I work for the Israeli government."[24]

Thus as Palestinians prepared to apply for UN membership nearly
sixty-four years after the UN voted to partition Palestine and create
separate Jewish and Arab states, the United States found itself in the
ironic position of lobbying just as hard, if not more strenuously,
against Palestinian UN membership in 2011 as it did for the partition of Palestine in 1947. With this US lobbying effort acknowledged
and with the United States promising to veto Palestinian UN
membership in the Security Council, as the 66th UN General
Assembly convened on September 13, 2011, only one uncertainty
remained: would Abbas submit an application to the Security
Council for the UN to admit Palestine as a full member, knowing
that a resolution to do so would be vetoed by the United States, or
would Abbas bypass the Security Council and ask the UN General
Assembly, where the United States could not exercise a veto, to
upgrade Palestinian status at the UN? Such an upgrade would elevate
the PLO's standing at the UN from its current "Permanent Observer
Mission of Palestine to the United Nations" to a non-member state
permanent observer, a status at the UN held only by the Vatican at
that time.

As abstruse as these different scenarios may have appeared,
however, the precise formulation for Palestinian status at the UN
was no mere diplomatic rigmarole. In fact, far from being a "symbolic
action," as Obama had derisively dismissed the Palestinian initiative

in May 2011, it turned out that even a seemingly meaningless upgrade to Palestinian status in the General Assembly could have profound political and legal ramifications. Had Obama read Abbas's op-ed in the *New York Times*, he would have been alerted to one of the central reasons for Palestinians undertaking this initiative. As Abbas wrote, "Palestine's admission to the United Nations would pave the way for the internationalization of the conflict as a legal matter, not only a political one. It would also pave the way for us to pursue claims against Israel at the United Nations, human rights treaty bodies and the International Court of Justice."[25]

In this article, Abbas neglected to mention that the PA had submitted a declaration on January 22, 2009 to the International Criminal Court (ICC) voluntarily accepting its jurisdiction as a non-state party to the Rome Statute, which established the ICC.[26] This move triggered an examination, the results of which were still pending at the time of the Palestinian UN membership bid, by the ICC as to whether it had jurisdiction to hear cases of war crimes and crimes against humanity, especially those committed by Israel, which occurred in Occupied Palestinian Territory. If the ICC concluded that this Palestinian declaration did allow it to hear such cases, then Israeli political and military leaders could in the future find themselves hauled before an international court, like Slobodan Milosevic and Charles Taylor, to answer for crimes committed not only during Israel's 2008–2009 assault on the Gaza Strip, but retroactively for any crimes committed since the Rome Statute went into force in 2002. If the Palestinians won even an upgraded status in the General Assembly, then their case for ICC jurisdiction would be strengthened.

Having belatedly caught on to this potentially game-changing implication, Israel's supporters in Congress went berserk. On September 15, 2011, fifty-eight representatives sent an urgent letter to several dozen heads of state in a remarkable display of constitutional excess in which they arrogated responsibility for conducting foreign relations. The letter breathlessly urged foreign countries to oppose the Palestinian UN membership initiative, warning that "one of the major goals of this effort is for the Palestinians to better position themselves to petition the International Criminal Court, very possibly bogging down the court for the foreseeable future."

On September 21, 2011, Israel's supporters in Congress took the unusual step of scheduling a "special order" debate to denounce the Palestinian initiative yet again and sound the alarm bell about the United States potentially no longer being able to shield Israel from the legal consequences of its actions. Representative Shelley Berkley declared,

> We must oppose Abu Mazen's [Abbas's nickname] misguided and dangerous effort to bypass negotiations with Israel and go to the UN with a unilateral resolution in order to create a Palestinian state. The ramifications of that are extraordinary. They could destabilize the entire Middle East, put Israel on the defensive at the International Criminal Court, and create a failed terrorist state right next-door to the State of Israel—controlled by the Iranians, I might add.

Representative Henry Waxman (D-CA) cautioned that "recognition of Palestine by the United Nations will lead to great legal vulnerability to Israel and its government's leaders by giving Palestine standing in several international institutions, such as the International Court of Justice. No settlement of any issues or grievances between the parties can be advanced by legal harassment of Israel in international organizations." After condemning the UN for having served as a "kangaroo court against Israel time and time again," Representative Eliot Engel warned that an upgrade to Palestinians' status at the UN "would allow them to run around and harass Israeli leaders in the different international courts." Therefore, he threatened, "I just think the UN better be careful. It sits in my hometown of New York, and we have always been proud that the UN is in New York. But I think the UN is on the verge of discrediting itself very, very badly."[27]

On that same day, Obama addressed the UN General Assembly, delivering a defensive and unconvincing speech in which he urged more "peace process" negotiations and faulted the international community for the failure of Israeli-Palestinian peace because, in his view, it did not fully accept Israel and its narrative of victimhood. Obama reminded his audience that "one year ago, I stood at this podium and I called for an independent Palestine. I believed then, and I believe now, that the Palestinian people deserve a state of their own." But, he acknowledged, "One year later, despite extensive efforts by America and others, the parties have not bridged their differences." The president continued: "I know that many are frustrated by the lack of progress. I assure you, so am I. But the question isn't the goal that we seek—the question is how do we reach that goal." Obama, however, offered no fresh ideas to attain this objective and once again rejected any alternative Palestinian strategy to achieve their long-denied rights. "Peace will not come through statements and resolutions at the United Nations—if it were that easy, it would have been accomplished by now," the president asserted.

Instead of admitting Palestine as a member of the UN as a step toward achieving Palestinians rights, the international community should rather concede that "each side has legitimate aspirations—and that's part of what makes peace so hard," Obama offered. This "deadlock will only be broken," according to Obama, not when Palestinians are admitted to the community of nations, but "when each side learns to stand in the other's shoes; each side can see the world through the other's eyes. That's what we should be encouraging. That's what we should be promoting." In Obama's view, Israeli-Palestinian peace would emerge "if we can encourage the parties to sit down, to listen to each other, and to understand each other's hopes and each other's fears."[28] Obama's tame calls for dialogue, understanding and negotiation may have been considered path-breaking a generation ago; however, after twenty years of failed negotiations, during which time Palestinians tardily came to the realization that they would never achieve a true state through negotiations with Israel, Obama appeared profoundly anachronistic, out-of-touch and unwilling to admit to the fundamental truth that the "peace process" as the United States and Israel knew it was kaput.

By contrast, on September 23, 2011, Abbas stepped to the podium of the UN, with the eyes of the world upon him, and delivered a masterful, even magisterial, speech reaffirming Palestinian rights. Abbas began his speech by recounting that "a year ago, at this same time, distinguished leaders in this hall addressed the stalled peace efforts in our region. Everyone had high hopes for a new round of final status negotiations, which had begun in early September in Washington under the direct auspices of President Barack Obama." According to Abbas, "We entered those negotiations with open hearts and attentive ears and sincere intentions, and we were ready with our documents, papers and proposals."

But these negotiations broke down, according to Abbas, because "the Israeli government refuses to commit to terms of reference for the negotiations that are based on international law and United Nations resolutions, and that it frantically continues to intensify building of settlements on the territory of the State of Palestine." If left unchecked, then Israel's settlement expansion "will destroy the chances of achieving a two-State solution." When the PLO declared independence in 1988, "in the absence of absolute justice, we decided to adopt the path of relative justice," which entailed creating "the State of Palestine on only 22 per cent of the territory of historical Palestine—on all the Palestinian Territory occupied by Israel in 1967," Abbas reminded the General Assembly. However, since that time, Abbas claimed, "every initiative and every conference and every new round of negotiations and every movement was shattered on the rock of the Israeli settlement expansion project."

Abbas then took aim at US efforts to depict the Palestinian UN membership initiative as anti-Israel. "Our efforts are not aimed at isolating Israel or de-legitimizing it; rather we want to gain legitimacy for the cause of the people of Palestine. We only aim to de-legitimize the settlement activities, the occupation and apartheid and the logic of ruthless force, and we believe that all the countries of the world stand with us in this regard," Abbas predicted. But, continuing the feeble "peace process" was not an option.

> It is no longer possible to redress the issue of the blockage of the horizon of the peace talks with the same means and methods that have been repeatedly tried and proven unsuccessful over the past years . . . It is futile to go into negotiations without clear parameters and in the absence of credibility and a specific timetable. Negotiations will be meaningless as long as the occupation army on the ground continues to entrench its occupation, instead of rolling it back, and continues to change the demography of our country in order to create a new basis on which to alter the borders.

Instead of additional "meaningless" negotiations, Palestinians needed to change their tack. Therefore, Abbas declared, "The time has come for my courageous and proud people, after decades of displacement and colonial occupation and ceaseless suffering, to live like other peoples of the earth, free in a sovereign and independent homeland." He then revealed that earlier that day he had submitted to UN Secretary General Ban Ki-Moon "an application for the admission of Palestine on the basis of the 4 June 1967 borders, with *Al-Quds Al-Sharif* [Jerusalem] as its capital, as a full member of the United Nations." Abbas dramatically held aloft the application to a sustained and boisterous standing ovation from the heads of state and other foreign diplomats gathered at the General Assembly.[29] Abbas's performance revealed the extent to which the position of Israel and the United States—its protector at the UN—was marginalized within the international community.

SANCTIONS

Some members of Congress had not even bothered to wait and see whether Abbas would submit Palestine's application for UN membership before they decided to sanction Palestinians for having the audacity to consider doing something against the wishes of the United States. On October 1, 2011, *The Independent* revealed that since August 18, three congressional committees had blocked the US Agency for International Development (USAID) from spending $192 million of funds already appropriated by Congress in the 2011 budget for Palestinian economic development projects. They did so by placing "holds," or legislative inquiries, on this money. This move imperiled the start of projects, including "teacher-training, large-scale road and water infrastructure developments and an Enterprise Development Programme designed to improve the competitiveness and capacity of the Palestinian private sector." In addition, the freeze of economic aid also threatened the viability of projects underway, including "the purchase of supplies by the UN's World Food Programme for food distribution to impoverished Palestinian families in early 2012, health service reform, training and equipment for the Holy Family hospital in Bethlehem, a pre-school 'Sesame Street' workshop, and a Palestinian Authority political programme for developing the functions of ministers."[30] But this was only half of the story, as Americans for Peace Now revealed on October 3, 2011, that a congressional committee also had placed a "hold" on $150 million in security assistance to the PA.[31]

But the import of these temporary "holds" on Palestinian aid, which the Obama administration eventually persuaded the blocking congressional committees to lift, was soon eclipsed once it became clear that Palestinian membership in subsidiary UN agencies would have even more significant repercussions, requiring the United States to defund them. Two long-forgotten sections of arcane legislation passed two decades before, in response to congressional fears over increased Palestinian participation in the UN system following the PLO's 1988 Declaration of Independence, now came into play as Palestinians applied in October 2011 to become a member of the UN Educational, Scientific and Cultural Organization (UNESCO).

These US laws, enacted as part of Foreign Relations Authorization Acts in the 1990s, stipulated that no US funding "shall be available for the United Nations or any specialized agency thereof which accords the Palestine Liberation Organization the same standing as member states" and that "the United States shall not make any voluntary or assessed contribution . . . to any affiliated organization of the United Nations which grants full membership as a state to any organization or group that does not have the internationally recognized attributes of statehood."[32] This unequivocal language left the Obama administration with no wiggle room, as the prohibition contained no waiver authority the president could invoke on national security grounds to prevent the United States from defunding any UN agency that the Palestinians might join. Despite pleas from both the Obama administration and UNESCO, Congress stubbornly refused to even consider amending the law prior to the UNESCO vote on Palestine's membership application.

On October 31, 2011, UNESCO overwhelmingly and enthusiastically admitted Palestine as its 195th member state by a vote of 107-14 with fifty-two abstentions. In voting against Palestinian admittance to UNESCO, the US permanent representative to UNESCO, Ambassador David T. Killion, argued, "There are no shortcuts, and we believe efforts such as the one we have witnessed today are counterproductive."[33] But the United States was clearly swimming against the historical tide, as the vote occasioned animated applause from UNESCO delegates, one of whom shouted

"Long live Palestine!" PA foreign affairs minister Riad al-Malki hailed the organization, whose vote to admit Palestine as a member "will help erase a tiny part of the injustice done to the Palestinian people."[34] It was a diplomatic triumph for Palestinians and a vindication of their strategy to achieve their rights by "re-internationalizing" the Israeli-Palestinian conflict, and a black eye for the United States and its diplomatic efforts.

The US reaction to the vote was swift and decisive. That same day, State Department spokesperson Victoria Nuland stated, "Today's vote by the member states of UNESCO to admit Palestine as a member is regrettable, premature, and undermines our shared goal of a comprehensive, just, and lasting peace in the Middle East." She announced the United States would not be transferring $60 million in US dues payments to UNESCO previously scheduled for November.[35] Before the funding cutoff, the United States had contributed 22 percent of UNESCO's budget; the US defunding was predicted to result in "immediate cuts in programs and personnel" to a UN agency that "is in the core security interests of the United States," its director-general, Irina Bokova, argued.[36]

The United States was cutting off its nose to spite its face to protect Israel's increasingly untenable denial of Palestinian self-determination. As United Nations Foundation president and former senator Timothy Wirth put it, UNESCO is "good for American business. Through the organization, American companies such as Cisco, Intel and Microsoft have been introduced to expanding Third World markets hungry for high-tech products, and that facilitation by UNESCO has helped to create or retain thousands of American jobs." He also maintained that UNESCO

> protects the lives and safety of US citizens. For example, it was a tsunami warning system coordinated by UNESCO that alerted Californians to a possible tsunami following Japan's devastating earthquake in March. The organization also supports US national security by teaching literacy skills to Afghan citizens who will be taking over security functions when allied forces leave the country.[37]

But the potentially cascading damage to US interests did not end there. Because Congress insisted on denying US funding to any UN organization that admitted Palestine as a member, the United States would no longer be able to protect and promote the patent, copyright and trademark interests of US businesses if Palestinians, now accepted as members of UNESCO, triggered their automatic right to assume membership in the World Intellectual Property Organization (WIPO), an obscure, but important, UN subsidiary agency. The State Department, along with the US Patent and Trademark Office, was so concerned about this eventuality that on the day of the UNESCO vote, they convened a meeting with representatives of the titans of US business and industry. During this meeting, they "underscored US concern that Palestinian membership in WIPO could have serious implications for US leadership in this organization, which supports the global IPR [intellectual property rights] infrastructure and helps US companies protect their intellectual property around the world. The United States is a leading global voice on issues related to patent, copyright, and trademark matters," according to the State Department, but "should the US be unable to provide its contributions to WIPO, the impact of that voice could be significantly diminished," it warned.[38]

Fortunately for the Obama administration, it was not forced to choose between protecting US intellectual property rights and protecting Israeli apartheid. Apparently, enough pressure was exerted on Palestinians to cause them, for the time being, not to pursue membership in WIPO, the World Health Organization (WHO), the International Atomic Energy Agency, or other UN agencies, the defunding of which by the United States would cause further immense damage to US interests and to millions of people whose basic human needs, such as health care, were provided by UN agencies such as the WHO. Luckily too for the Obama administration, the wheels of the UN bureaucracy turn slowly, with the Palestinian application for UN membership conveniently bogging down in the Security Council after its Committee on the Admission of New Members reported on November 11, 2011 "that the Committee was unable to make a unanimous recommendation to the Security Council" on whether to admit Palestine as a member.[39]

Several months later, Ambassador Susan Rice, US Permanent Representative to the UN, crowed to a sympathetic audience from the American Jewish Committee about how the United States had effectively succeeded in checkmating the Palestinian drive for UN membership. "When the Palestinians brought their application in September," she explained, "the Security Council went through the traditional process of considering that application in the membership committee. We went through a sort of an exhaustive legal discussion, debate, analysis. And once that was completed and the committee's report was forwarded to the Security Council, as you mentioned, it's essentially stayed there for the time being." Addressing the deadlocked application, Rice coyly presumed that it was stuck "because the Palestinians decided that given the voting—likely outcome in the Council—it wasn't timely to push it to a vote."[40] After all, if the Palestinians did push for a vote, then their application for membership would be vetoed by the United States.

Thus as 2011 drew to a close, with the United States stymieing Palestinian UN membership, the prospects for renewed Israeli-Palestinian "peace process" negotiations dimmer than ever and Obama well into campaigning mode for the 2012 presidential election, further serious initiatives by the United States to advance Israeli-Palestinian peace during the first term of the Obama administration came to an ignominious halt. Although the Obama administration continued to insist that it was endeavoring to restart negotiations, its halfhearted attempts were mere window dressing on a failed policy. After such an energetic and high-profile beginning to President Obama's quest for Israeli-Palestinian peace, his hopes for achieving it lay shattered.

PART II: THEMES OF US POLICY

CHAPTER SEVEN

Repeated and Unbalanced Criticisms of Israel

THE GOLDSTONE REPORT

During Operation Cast Lead—Israel's brutal assault on the Palestinian Gaza Strip that killed more than 1,400 Palestinians in a three-week span from December 2008 to January 2009—the Israeli army entered the al-Samouni neighborhood of Zeytoun, a rural area of the Gaza Strip south of Gaza City, on January 4, 2009. Early that morning, Israeli soldiers

> entered Ateya al-Samouni's house by force, throwing some explosive device, possibly a grenade. In the midst of the smoke, fire and loud noise, Ateya al-Samouni stepped forward, his arms raised, and declared that he was the owner of the house. The soldiers shot him while he was still holding his ID and an Israeli driving licence in his hands. The soldiers then opened gunfire inside the room in which all the approximately twenty family members were gathered. Several were injured, Ahmad, a boy of four, particularly seriously.

Leaving behind Ateya's body, surviving family members took Ahmad to an uncle's house, but when an ambulance came to evacuate the wounded child later that afternoon, it "was prevented by the Israeli armed forces from rescuing him." He died that night.

That same day, Israeli troops had ordered approximately one hundred members of the extended al-Samouni family into the home of Wa'el al-Samouni. On the morning of January 5, the Israeli military fired unidentified projectiles at the house, killing twenty-one family members and injuring nineteen others. Only after repeated requests by the International Committee of the Red Cross (ICRC) and the Palestine Red Crescent Society (PRCS) to evacuate the wounded and dead had been denied by the Israeli military, were they finally allowed to do so two days later. When the rescue team entered Wa'el al-Samouni's house, they discovered this horrifying sight:

> The ICRC/PRCS team found four small children next to their dead mothers in one of the houses. They were too weak to stand up on their own. One man was also found alive, too weak to stand up. In all there were at least twelve corpses lying on mattresses. In another house, the ICRC/PRCS rescue team found fifteen other survivors of this attack including several wounded. In yet another house, they found an additional three corpses.

In the home of one family member, Talal al-Samouni, Israeli soldiers left graffiti, including some written in blood. Some of the graffiti, written in English, read: "'You can run but you can not hide', 'Die you all', '1 is down, 999,999 to go', 'Arabs need to die' and 'Make war not peace.' " When surviving family members were finally able to return on January 18, 2009,

> They found that Wa'el al-Samouni's house, as most other houses in the neighbourhood and the small mosque, had been demolished. The Israeli armed forces had destroyed the building on top of the bodies of those who died in the attack. Pictures taken on 18 January show feet and legs sticking out from under the rubble and sand, and rescuers pulling out the bodies of women, men and children.

Israel's attacks on the al-Samouni family were documented in an exhaustive 575-page report of the four-person UN Fact-Finding Mission on the Gaza Conflict. These attacks were one of eleven horrific incidents investigated by the fact-finding mission in which Palestinian civilians were killed even though "there appears to have been no justifiable military objective pursued in any of them."[1] The mission, which issued its report in September 2009, was led by South African Judge Richard Goldstone, a self-proclaimed "friend of Israel" who does not "mind being called a Zionist."[2] The report, known informally as the Goldstone Report, concluded that both Israel and Palestinian militant groups committed violations of human rights and international law, war crimes and possible crimes against humanity before, during and after Operation Cast Lead, and recommended both domestic and international judicial procedures to ensure accountability for these actions.

The fact-finding mission owed its existence to a UN Human Rights Council resolution passed on January 12, 2009 by a vote of 33-1 with thirteen abstentions, which authorized the council to

> dispatch an urgent independent international fact-finding mission, to be appointed by the President, to investigate all violations of international human rights law and International Humanitarian Law by the occupying Power, Israel, against the Palestinian people throughout the Occupied Palestinian Territory, particularly in the occupied Gaza Strip, due to the current aggression, and calls upon Israel not to obstruct the process of investigation and to fully cooperate with the mission.

Although the resolution called for an "end to the launching of the crude rockets against Israeli civilians," the original mandate of the fact-finding mission did not call for an investigation of Palestinian actions.[3] The Obama administration and members of Congress would later rely upon this inexcusable omission to discredit the entire mission and its findings, even after Goldstone had successfully lobbied to change the mandate to be inclusive of all parties' actions before he had accepted to head the mission. On April 3, 2009, in announcing the composition of the mission, the president of the Human Rights Council, Nigerian ambassador Martin Ihoeghian Uhomoibhi, clarified that the team's mission would indeed include Palestinian actions as well. He was "confident that the mission will be in a position to assess in an independent and impartial manner all human rights and humanitarian law violations committed" during Operation Cast Lead.[4]

The Bush administration had voted against the establishment of, and then boycotted US participation in, the UN Human Rights Council, underlining its unilateralist approach to foreign policy. The

Bush administration was critical of both the Human Rights Council and its antecedent, the UN Commission on Human Rights, in large measure for these bodies' supposed undue focus on Israel's human rights record. The Obama administration agreed with this critique of the Human Rights Council, noting that "we share the concerns of many that the Council's trajectory is disturbing, that it needs fundamental change to do more to promote and protect the human rights of people around the world, and that it should end its repeated and unbalanced criticisms of Israel." However, the Obama administration, unlike its predecessor, decided that "it furthers our interests and will do more both to achieve these ends and advance human rights if we are part of the conversation and present at the Council's proceedings."[5] In February 2009, the Obama administration sent an observer to the Human Rights Council session, and on March 31, 2009, Secretary of State Hillary Clinton and US Permanent Representative to the UN Ambassador Susan Rice announced that the United States would run for a seat on the forty-seven-nation council during upcoming elections on May 12, 2009.[6]

Although the United States won election to the Human Rights Council, this victory came too late for the Obama administration to try to influence the composition or mandate of the UN Fact-Finding Mission on the Gaza Conflict. However, the United States was still able to collude with Israel to blunt its impact, pressure Palestinians not to advance its recommendations, issue démarches to foreign governments opposing it and vociferously denounce it as it voted against the adoption of the report and the implementation of its recommendations. By actively opposing the Goldstone Report, the Obama administration cast grave doubts on its professed commitment to the universality of human rights. It also demonstrated that beyond its willingness to use or threaten to use its veto in the UN Security Council to protect Israel and frustrate resolutions supporting Palestinian rights, the Obama administration would also work within the UN system to shield Israel from being held accountable for its human rights abuses even when the UN found credible evidence of them. These diplomatic efforts continued to give Israel carte blanche to commit human rights abuses, knowing full well that no matter how egregious its behavior, the United States would ensure Israel's impunity.

Shortly after the UN Fact-Finding Mission on the Gaza Conflict formally commenced its work on May 4, 2009, and just one day before the United States won a seat on the UN Human Rights Council, Israel informed the United States on May 11, 2009, that it would boycott the mission. According to the US embassy in Tel Aviv, the Israeli Foreign Ministry conveyed "that while the GOI [Government of Israel] respects Justice Goldstone personally, and that he has strong personal and professional ties to Israel's legal community, the GOI decided that the mission could not produce a fair result because it originated from a January Human Rights Council resolution on the Gaza operation that put the entire burden on Israel and did not even mention Hamas."[7] This justification for boycotting the mission held no water, however, as the mission was now investigating Palestinian actions as well.

Israel may have come to regret its decision not to cooperate with the mission as it became clear that it would produce a seminal report with important legal and political ramifications. By August 14, 2009, Israel was alerting the United States that it was considering engaging the Human Rights Council to water down any resolution that would ensue from the mission's report. While "Israel welcomes an opportunity to openly and honestly discuss the issue," according to discussions between the US Mission to the UN in Geneva and its Israeli counterparts, "Israel's bottom line is that they do not/not want the issue or discussion of the Goldstone report to move outside the HRC [Human Rights Council] and migrate into other fora, such as UNGA [United Nations General Assembly]."[8] After the Goldstone Report was released one month later, the United States would act in tandem with Israel to bottle up the report in the Human Rights Council, which had no power to implement the report's recommendations for accountability.

Less than one week before the release of the Goldstone Report, the United States was concerned about the report's implications and provided counsel to Israel to blunt its likely impact. In a September 9, 2009, meeting with Israeli Deputy Foreign Minister Danny Ayalon, US ambassador to Israel James Cunningham "warned of the difficulties the Goldstone report could pose, of the possible linkage between it and action in the ICC [International Criminal Court]. The Ambassador noted that Goldstone is credible, has broadened his mandate to include possible Hamas and Palestinian violations, and he would be taken seriously by the international community." Cunningham suggested therefore that Israel engage in "credible investigations" to "help turn aside efforts to engage the ICC." Ayalon was dismissive of Goldstone's motivation, arguing that he "wants a seat on the ICC bench and is hoping to use his report to boost his chances." Nevertheless, he too was "very concerned about the report" and "by the possibility of efforts to indict Israelis. Palestinian involvement in any such efforts will be take [sic] very seriously and badly by the GOI," Ayalon warned.[9]

When the highly anticipated report was released on September 15, 2009, the State Department's public reaction was at first noncommittal. Noting that it was "rather lengthy" and "covers a number of very complex issues and very sensitive issues," State Department spokesperson Ian Kelly said, "We want to take some time to digest it completely and we'll review it very carefully [before commenting on it]."[10] But this phase of digestion did not last long. Even before the United States had completed its review of the Goldstone Report, Rice met with Ayalon at the UN the next day, where the General Assembly had opened. In this meeting, she schemed with him on the "best means to deflect and contain the Goldstone report," which, according to Rice, would be through "demonstrable and early progress on the peace process." Rice asked Ayalon to "help me help you." She noted that "the Goldstone report will not go away but it can be more easily managed if there is positive progress on the peace process."[11] This reasoning explained, in part, the importance the United States attached to the trilateral photo-op meeting between President Obama, Prime Minister Netanyahu and PA president Mahmoud Abbas at the General Assembly the following week. If the United States could not deliver progress on the "peace process," then perhaps the appearance of its momentum would dull the international community's will to follow through with the recommendations of the Goldstone Report.

Over the next few days, the contours of US opposition to the Goldstone Report would publicly emerge. On September 17, 2009, Assistant Secretary of State Crowley expressed concern that the Goldstone Report would set back the prospects for the nonexistent "peace process." He warned that "the report should not be used as a mechanism to add impediments to getting back to the peace process. It would be a sad irony if this report that is designed to protect human rights gets in the way of the process that we believe will benefit all in the region and ultimately lead to greater and deeper human rights in the Middle East."[12] But what was even more sadly ironic about his statement was that the United States viewed international measures to hold human rights abusers accountable as being intrinsically opposed to the goals of peace and reconciliation, rather than a step to promote those objectives.

The State Department issued its official objections to the Goldstone Report on September 18, 2009. These protestations would guide US actions in the months ahead as the Obama administration worked assiduously to prevent the report from being acted upon. According to State Department spokesperson Ian Kelly, the United States would rely on the original "one-sided and unacceptable mandate for this fact-finding investigation," which was superseded by the mission's insistence on investigating the actions of all parties to the conflict, to discredit the entire report. But with the United States forced to acknowledge that "the report addresses all sides of the conflict," it needed a more nuanced critique. Thus the United States would condemn the fact that the Goldstone Report's "overwhelming focus is on the actions of Israel," a true enough assertion which was only logical given that for every Israeli who died during Operation Cast Lead, Israel killed more than one hundred Palestinians. The State Department also asserted, without providing any evidence, that "while the report makes overly sweeping conclusions of fact and law with respect to Israel, its conclusions regarding Hamas's deplorable conduct and its failure to comply with international humanitarian law during the conflict are more general and tentative." This argument was difficult to sustain given the report's conclusion that both Israel and Palestinian armed groups committed violations of human rights and international law, war crimes and possible crimes against humanity.

These spurious claims about the mission's mandate and the contents of its report, however, masked the crux of the Obama administration's rationale for defeating the Goldstone Report; namely, the report opened the door for Israeli political and military leaders to be indicted in foreign courts under principles of universal jurisdiction or, potentially down the road, by the ICC as well. The State Department noted its "very serious concerns about the report's recommendations, including calls that this issue be taken up in international fora outside the Human Rights Council and in national courts of countries not party to the conflict." According to the State Department, there was no need for any outside body to hold Israel accountable for the actions documented in the Goldstone Report because "Israel has the democratic institutions to investigate and prosecute abuses."[13]

This statement reflected grossly undeserved praise for an Israeli judicial system whose military courts convicted an astounding 99.74 percent of Palestinians brought before them.[14] In a further display of the inadequacies of the Israeli judicial system, Israel's Military Advocate General filed indictments against Israeli soldiers in less than 3 percent of more than 300 complaints filed by the Israeli human rights organization B'Tselem from 2000 to 2011 against Israeli security personnel accused of killing Palestinians who did not take part in hostilities.[15] This blatant bias against Palestinians in the Israeli judicial system and the inability of Israel to credibly hold accountable even low-level soldiers for the human rights abuses they inflicted on Palestinians militated for, not against, foreign and international judicial procedures to ensure justice for the crimes documented in the Goldstone Report. This lack of accountability manifested itself again in Israel's domestic judicial proceedings for alleged crimes committed during Operation Cast Lead. Amnesty International concluded that Israel's domestic judicial process rested on a "flawed system of investigations" that has resulted to date in only one Israeli soldier serving jail time—less than one year for credit card theft—for a crime committed during Operation Cast Lead.[16] The ludicrousness of the United States maintaining that Israel was perfectly capable of holding itself accountable was epitomized in May 2012 when Israel closed its investigation into the killings of the al-Samouni family, referred to above, after having "found the accusations groundless" and "that none of the involved soldiers or officers acted in a negligent manner."[17]

The Goldstone Report threatened to end Israel's impunity, and the Obama administration now went into overdrive to maintain it. On September 20, 2009, Palestinian Authority (PA) health minister

Fathi Abu Mughni issued a press release endorsing the Goldstone Report. The United States responded sternly to the PA that it would not tolerate this behavior. A cable from the US Consulate in Jerusalem reported back to Foggy Bottom that "the Consul General has strongly criticized the substance and timing of the press release in a conversation with PLO Chief Negotiator Saeb Erekat." The cable also noted that "the need for PA restraint in public comments about the report had previously been conveyed to both Abu Mazen [Abbas] and Erekat in Ramallah by Special Envoy for Middle East Peace Mitchell and the CG [Consul General] on September 18."[18] Despite these efforts, however, the Israeli Ministry of Foreign Affairs still complained to the United States that its statements designed to sabotage the Goldstone Report "haven't been as clear or focused as Israel had hoped." The report was, after all, in its eyes, an "exceptional delegitimization" of Israel, which called for the United States to pull out all the stops in defeating it.[19]

The United States then redoubled its efforts to kill the Goldstone Report. On September 23, 2009, the State Department sent an urgent cable to US embassies from Abuja to Zagreb instructing its diplomats to deliver US talking points against the Goldstone Report "to host governments at the highest possible appropriate level and to report any substantive response immediately back to the Department." Some of the "key objectives" in this US diplomatic onslaught to derail the Goldstone Report were to "ensure that repercussions from the report do not interfere with our efforts to re-launch Israeli-Palestinian permanent status negotiations," to "avoid an outcome that is one-sided and biased against Israel," and to "contain the handling of the report to Geneva as long as we can, minimize activity in the UN Security Council and the UNGA [United Nations General Assembly], and work to prevent efforts to refer the matter to the International Criminal Court." Henceforth, the United States would not confine its efforts to colluding with Israel and pressuring the Palestinians to kill the Goldstone Report; it would now also deploy its substantial diplomatic power to pressure other countries as well to achieve a "balanced" resolution from the Human Rights Council that would "note the Report, without endorsing it" and thereby essentially defang it.[20]

After Goldstone presented the mission's report to the Human

Rights Council on September 29, 2009, Michael Posner, assistant secretary of state for democracy, human rights and labor, attempted to do just that: eviscerate the report. He urged the council to ignore the calls in the report for further action by additional UN bodies and instead urged the council "to commit with us to pass a consensus resolution that encourages Israel to investigate and address allegations in the Report thoroughly through credible domestic processes."[21]

But an even better outcome than a toothless, consensus resolution would be no resolution at all. For a brief time, it appeared that the United States and Israel would be victorious in this best-case scenario. On October 2, 2009, Abbas, under withering US and Israeli pressure, caved and asked the Human Rights Council to defer consideration of the report until March 2010. He argued unpersuasively for the delay because "the draft resolution did not gather the number of voices that we wanted."[22] In reality, Abbas's decision to delay the vote probably had nothing to do with the anticipated vote count, but had everything to do with the dire threats Israel had been making indirectly and directly to Abbas if he proceeded with the vote. On October 1, 2009, Israel's national security adviser Uzi Arad related to US ambassador to Israel James Cunningham that he had passed on a message to Abbas that he was "playing with fire" by seeking endorsement of the Goldstone Report at the Human Rights Council.[23] Yuval Diskin, head of Israel's internal security service Shin Bet, reportedly told Abbas in an October meeting that if he proceeded with a vote on the Goldstone Report, then Israel would turn the West Bank into a "second Gaza."[24]

Abbas was caught in a political bind. Having succumbed to US and Israeli coercion to defer consideration of the Goldstone Report, Abbas now faced a maelstrom of domestic criticism that proved to be powerful enough to override his concerns of Israeli threats and US pressure. Abbas then reversed course and decided to put the resolution to a vote. In a special session of the Human Rights Council on October 16, 2009, the body voted 25-6 with eleven abstentions to endorse the recommendations of the Goldstone Report. The resolution called "upon all concerned parties including United Nations bodies, to ensure their implementation" and for the General Assembly to consider the report as well.[25]

This vote by the Human Rights Council to endorse the recommendations of the Goldstone Report came despite the United States exerting, once again, last-minute efforts to scotch it. The United States acknowledged that it had failed "to reshape an initial, one-sided Palestinian draft into a balanced resolution on the report" that would have led to a "de-politicized resolution." Therefore, the State Department directed its embassies to "démarche host governments on the US position on the Report of the UN Fact-Finding Mission on the Gaza Conflict" and request them to vote against the resolution. The US strategy conceded defeat but hoped "to maximize the number of 'no' votes." By advocating against the Goldstone Report, the United States realized that it placed itself in a tricky situation that would make it difficult to "balance our efforts by promoting principles of accountability for violations of international law and not being seen as quashing open discussion of a high-profile human rights matter."[76]

In casting a vote against the resolution to endorse the recommendations of the Goldstone Report, the United States, however, failed to achieve this balance through its ham-fisted efforts. The United States accused the Human Rights Council of "precipitous action rather than judicious deliberation" and of intruding on its self-declared exclusive domain of managing the Israeli-Palestinian "peace process" by going "far beyond even the initial scope of the Goldstone Report into a discussion of elements that should be resolved in the context of permanent status negotiations between the Palestinians and the Israelis." Although the United States continued to pay lip service to "the importance of holding all parties to this conflict, and indeed to all conflicts, accountable under international law," it continued to wrongfully assert that Israel had "strong, independent institutions capable of addressing allegations through credible domestic processes." In the view of the United States, international action to ensure accountability for crimes committed during Operation Cast Lead, however, must take a back seat to the "peace process," because the "most important point" was "that the United States continues to focus our attention on our main goal: working with Israel and the Palestinian Authority to re-launch successful permanent status negotiations as soon as possible." The Human Rights Council's endorsement of the Goldstone Report, from the US vantage point, "can only exacerbate polarization and divisiveness," an action which would harm the prospects for restarting negotiations.[27]

As was the case throughout the two-decades-long "peace process," on the Goldstone Report the United States proved itself to be hyper-attuned to crafting its foreign policy position to take into account the report's domestic political ramifications for Israel. Yet, at the same time, the United States was completely tone deaf to the domestic political repercussions for Palestinians that resulted from the pressure that the United States and Israel had exerted to cause the PA to initially request a delay in the consideration of the Goldstone Report in the Human Rights Council.

This imbalance continued even after the Human Rights Council vote to adopt the recommendations of the Goldstone Report. Three days later, PA prime minister Salam Fayyad pleaded with US Consul General Daniel Rubinstein to "tell the Israelis to lay off our backs." Downplaying the possibility of the Palestinians submitting claims to the ICC, Fayyad remarked, "We're not even competent to submit a complaint. But in the wake of Goldstone, we can't not pursue these sorts of claims against Israelis." Fayyad told Rubinstein what the United States already knew: complaints against Israel in the ICC would not be moving forward "and neither is Goldstone." After the PA's October 2, 2009, decision to delay the vote on the Goldstone Report, Fayyad warned, "We don't have political capital to spend." According to the US Consulate in Jerusalem, "Fayyad remained pessimistic about the damage done by the Goldstone issue, which he termed 'completely debasing' of the PA's reputation. 'Goldstone has really damaged us in a very lasting way,' he argued," presumably referring to the PA's waffling on the report, not its content.[28]

But Fayyad's entreaty to the United States—that it allow for the Goldstone Report to play itself out so that the PA could try to recover some of its squandered political capital—proved futile. In fact, at this point, the United States actually ratcheted up the pressure on the Palestinians to desist from taking their case to international bodies. In an October 21, 2009, meeting between Special Envoy for Middle East Peace George Mitchell and lead Palestinian negotiator Saeb Erekat, the two continued to debate a US "non-paper" given to the Palestinians on October 2. This "non-paper" called on the PA to "promote a positive atmosphere conducive to negotiations; in particular during negotiations it will refrain from pursuing or supporting any initiative directly or indirectly in international legal forums that would undermine that atmosphere."[29] Erekat had emphatically rejected that demand prior to the Human Rights Council vote, stating unequivocally that "regarding not taking steps in international forums, I cannot accept this."[30]

Now that the Human Rights Council had endorsed the Goldstone Report, Mitchell tried again, arguing that the statements in the "non-paper" were not "controversial." Erekat disagreed, maintaining that the US imperative of "not going to international bodies" was an extremely divisive demand, especially in light of the PA being roundly criticized for its deferral of the Goldstone Report vote. Mitchell tried to soft-pedal the issue, telling Erekat that this ban was "only during negotiations." However, Mitchell failed to understand that the threat of going to international bodies was the only effective leverage Palestinians could exert on Israel. "This is my only weapon," Erekat attempted to explain to Mitchell. "We have actions by settlers, attacks, provocations, Al Aqsa, home demolitions, families thrown out of their homes. Either we retaliate in a civilized manner or through violence. Which one should we choose? On going to the UN we always coordinate with you. It's our only weapon. Don't take it away from us," Erekat urged. Mitchell was unmoved, and after a few more fruitless exchanges, he suggested, "Let's not get diverted," before changing the subject.[31]

But the US demand that Palestinians abandon the international route would not die. That same language appeared as well in a December 2009 US "non-paper," to which the Palestinian negotiating team responded: "If the United States and the international community consider that such non-violent avenues are not helpful at this time (despite successful precedents such as the case of Apartheid South Africa), then they need to guarantee a credible political process that would provide Palestinians an alternative manner of securing their rights."[32]

However, with a credible political process nowhere on the horizon, the Obama administration could not give Palestinians an adequate reason to desist from taking their case to the international community. The only thing the Obama administration could guarantee to Palestinians at this point was more invective hurled by

pro-Israel members of Congress against international efforts to hold
Israel accountable. The House of Representatives passed a blistering
resolution—H.Res.867—condemning the Goldstone Report on
November 3, 2009. The resolution, which was approved under the
legislative procedure known as "suspension of the rules" that disal-
lowed amendments, easily passed the House by a vote of 344–36
with twenty-two abstentions. The resolution denounced the
Goldstone Report as "irredeemably biased and unworthy of further
consideration or legitimacy," embraced the Obama administration's
contention that the report was "unbalanced, one-sided and basically
unacceptable" and, as if it needed any prodding to do so, urged the
Obama administration "to strongly and unequivocally oppose any
further consideration" of the report at the UN.[33]

Both the debate on the resolution and its text contained a pleth-
ora of inaccuracies, distortions and outright lies about the
Goldstone Report that revealed the depths to which Congress
would sink in order to shield Israel from being held accountable
for its actions. Representative Ron Klein (D-FL) prevaricated that
the report "excuses the actions of terrorist groups" because it was
"motivated by a bias against Israel." Representative Ileana
Ros-Lehtinen dubbed the Goldstone Report a "575-page hatchet
job." Representative Eliot Engel alleged that the report was "part of
an ongoing effort at the UN to single out Israel," even though the
report documented and condemned abuses by Palestinian militant
groups as well. Representative Dan Burton contended that "there
shouldn't be one vote, not one vote in this place against Israel,"
referring to the Human Rights Council, no matter how egregious
were Israel's actions.

However, despite the overwhelming vote in favor of the resolution, something happened on the floor of Congress that day which
was unprecedented in recent memory. Not only did Congress have
an actual debate about a resolution pertaining to the Israeli-
Palestinian conflict; but, even more surprising, opponents of the
resolution actually out-organized, out-classed and out-argued its
proponents. Undoubtedly their courage to attack the resolution in
such harsh terms was stiffened by none other than Judge Richard
Goldstone himself, who had sent members of Congress a point-by-
point refutation of the charges leveled against the Goldstone Report

in the Congressional resolution. Goldstone wrote Representative Howard Berman and Representative Ileana Ros-Lehtinen, the chair and ranking member, respectively, of the House Committee on Foreign Affairs, that he had "strong reservations about the text of the resolution in question—text that includes serious factual inaccuracies and instances where information and statements are taken grossly out of context."[34] Despite Goldstone's willingness to testify before the committee about the report, his offer to appear was snubbed and his "strong reservations" about H.Res.867 were swept under the rug by pro-Israel members of Congress who were intent on rushing through this resolution, with no regard for the truth, to shield Israel from the repercussions of the Goldstone Report as it worked its way through the UN.

Goldstone's opposition to the resolution, the failure of the House Committee on Foreign Affairs to hold a hearing on the resolution that would afford Goldstone the opportunity to testify to Congress about the report, and the bald-faced lies about the report contained in the resolution all combined to push some representatives over the edge and ferociously denounce H.Res.867. This outrage produced a near-mutiny against these types of biased, pro-Israel resolutions, with more than 10 percent of Representatives failing to vote in its favor, a crack in the nearly wall-to-wall unanimity that had characterized votes on previous such resolutions.

Representative Keith Ellison (D-MN), who had visited the Gaza Strip in February 2009, argued that the "resolution should be opposed because it suppresses inquiry" and would "undermine President Obama's commitment that all countries, including our own and our allies, should be accountable for their actions." Representative Jim Moran stated that "rather than deal seriously with the contents and recommendations of the report, rather than ask Judge Goldstone to testify before Congress, so we can debate specifically what sections may be valid or flawed, we are seeking with this resolution to foreclose all discussion and action on the report by our President and our Secretary of State, in every multinational forum." Representative John Dingell (D-MI) argued that the resolution "sets up a set of circumstances where we indicate that we're going to just arbitrarily reject a UN finding and a UN resolution." Doing so "sends a signal to the world that the United States Congress is not serious about pushing the Israelis and the Palestinians toward a peaceful resolution." Dingell maintained that "neither Israel nor Hamas, nor any other country or other non-state political act[or] is exempt from international human rights laws or free of consequence for violations of them."

In perhaps some of the most strongly worded language in recent history employed by a member of Congress to condemn a pro-Israel resolution, Representative Dennis Kucinich stated that the resolution should be called "Down is Up, Night is Day, Wrong is Right" because "today we journey from Operation Cast Lead to Operation Cast Doubt. Almost as serious as committing war crimes is covering up war crimes, pretending that war crimes were never committed and did not exist." Kucinich reasoned that "behind every such deception is the nullification of humanity, the destruction of human dignity, the annihilation of the human spirit, the triumph of Orwellian thinking, the eternal prison of the dark heart of the totalitarian." The former presidential candidate warned that "if this Congress votes to condemn a report it has not read concerning events it has totally ignored about violations of law of which it is unaware, it will have brought shame to this great institution."

While Kucinich demolished the *1984*-like quality of this resolution, Representative Brian Baird (D-WA), who had accompanied Ellison on the February 2009 trip to the Gaza Strip, provided the most poignant and searing moment of the debate. Standing in front of an outsized picture of a Palestinian father grieving over his three small children who were killed by Israel during Operation Cast Lead, Baird stated, "I have twin four-year-old boys at home. When I kiss them goodnight, they look for all the world like these three little Palestinian children. I don't know that father, but I can imagine his grief." Baird demanded of his colleagues, "We must not say that this Congress will unequivocally oppose any consideration of a report by a jurist of this integrity and this reputation. Those children deserve someone to ask why they died, just as these children in Sderot [an Israeli town near the Gaza Strip] deserve someone to say they must not be rocketed." He noted, "Unlike most of my colleagues here, I have been to Gaza and I have read in its entirety the Goldstone Report. And I will tell you he says many things that, though unpleasant, are true and must not be obstructed."[35]

Having lost the debate, but having won the vote, pro-Israel members of Congress had succeeded in adding the imprimatur of Congress to the Obama administration's already considerable efforts to impede the Goldstone Report. The denouement for the US killing of the Goldstone Report was now set. On November 5, 2009, the UN General Assembly, by the lopsided vote of 114-18 with forty-four abstentions, endorsed the report of the Human Rights Council on the Goldstone Report, urged the Security Council to act on its recommendations and called for reconvening a conference of the Fourth Geneva Convention signatories to ensure that Israel abided by the convention in its military occupation of the Palestinian West Bank, East Jerusalem and Gaza Strip.[36] In casting the US vote against the resolution, Alejandro Wolff, Ambassador Rice's deputy, dubbed it "unconstructive," "unnecessary and unproductive" and "unbalanced."[37] With the Goldstone Report having now made its way to the Security Council, whose assent was needed in order to refer cases to the ICC, international efforts to hold Israel accountable for the crimes it committed during Operation Cast Lead came to a standstill. No member of the Security Council tabled a resolution to send cases to the ICC, as it was a foregone conclusion that such a resolution would be met by the implacable and unavoidable US veto.

Even before congressional approval of H.Res.867 and the US vote against the Goldstone Report in the General Assembly, Israeli Foreign Minister Avigdor Lieberman was already grateful for the indispensable role that the United States had played in stymieing efforts by the international community to hold Israel accountable. During an October 21, 2009 meeting with Rice, Lieberman "thanked Ambassador Rice for the US position on the Goldstone report." For her part, Rice beamed about the "positive US engagement with the Israeli Missions in New York and Geneva to blunt the effects of the Goldstone report in those fora." Rice reassured Lieberman that a US veto in the Security Council would not even be necessary because "we had the potential in the Security Council to build a blocking coalition that agrees that the Security Council is not the appropriate forum to consider the report."[38]

GAZA FREEDOM FLOTILLA

Impunity breeds a sense of entitlement that leads to the perpetrator committing additional crimes. In the wake of literally getting away with murder, thanks to successful US efforts to prevent the international community from holding Israel accountable for the crimes documented in the Goldstone Report, Israel felt no compunction in continuing to use deadly force to implement its illegal siege and blockade of the Palestinian Gaza Strip. Israel was now reassured that no matter how outlandish its actions, it would not face any international criminal repercussions as long as US diplomatic support continued to shield it from accountability. Therefore it was shocking, but unsurprising, that on May 31, 2010, Israeli naval commandoes would employ lethal force when they commandeered boats in international waters belonging to an international flotilla of peace activists who were attempting to deliver humanitarian materials to and demonstrate their solidarity with the besieged 1.6 million residents of the Gaza Strip.

According to a UN fact-finding report issued in September 2010, Israeli naval commandoes rappelled from a helicopter onto the main ship of the flotilla, the *Mavi Marmara,* and killed nine Turkish activists, including a US citizen of Turkish descent, Furkan Doğan. "The circumstances of the killing of at least six of the passengers were in a manner consistent with an extra-legal, arbitrary and summary execution," including the killing of Doğan, the report concluded. The report chillingly documented the execution by Israeli soldiers of Doğan, who

was on the central area of the top deck filming with a small video camera when he was first hit with live fire. It appears that he was lying on the deck in a conscious, or semi-conscious, state for some time. In total Furkan received five bullet wounds, to the face, head, back[,] thorax, left leg and foot. All of the entry wounds were on the back of his body, except for the face wound which entered to the right of his nose. According to forensic analysis, tattooing around the wound in his face indicates that the shot was delivered at point blank range. Furthermore, the trajectory of the wound, from bottom to top, together with a vital abrasion to the left shoulder that could be consistent with the bullet exit point, is compatible with the shot being received while he was lying on the ground on his back.

On the *Mavi Marmara*, many survivors of the Israeli attack were injured, including twenty people who were in critical condition inside a makeshift medical cabin, having suffered live gunfire wounds. It took "up to two hours before the Israeli forces took out the wounded persons. However, the wounded were required to leave the cabins themselves, or taken outside in a rough manner, without apparent concern for the nature of their injuries and the discomfort that this would cause." But their ordeal did not end then. "Wounded passengers, including persons seriously injured with live fire wounds, were handcuffed with plastic cord handcuffs, which were often tied very tightly causing some of the injured to lose sensitivity in their hands ... Many were also stripped naked and then had to wait some time, possibly as long as two-three hours, before receiving medical treatment."

Other survivors, both injured and non-injured, on the *Mavi Marmara* and other ships taking part in the flotilla were tightly handcuffed, causing extreme pain and lasting neurological damage, were forced to kneel in inhumane conditions without access to food, water or bathroom facilities for hours, and were physically and verbally abused by Israeli soldiers detaining them. The UN report concluded that Israel's treatment of these survivors "amounted to cruel, inhuman and degrading treatment and, insofar as the treatment was additionally applied as a form of punishment, torture."

The report deemed Israel's blockade to "constitute collective punishment of the people living in the Gaza Strip and thus to be illegal." Since Israel's illegal blockade was "inflicting disproportionate damage upon the civilian population in the Gaza Strip" and, citing evidence from an Israeli investigatory commission, since "it is clear that there was no reasonable suspicion that the Flotilla posed any military risk of itself," the report concluded that "no case can be made for the legality of the interception [of the flotilla] and the Mission therefore finds that the interception was illegal." Unlike the Goldstone Report, however, this UN fact-finding mission did not urge specific domestic and international political and legal steps to hold Israel accountable; instead, it merely noted that victims of

Israel's attack on the flotilla have "a right to an effective remedy which includes judicial remedies as well as the right to reparations which should be proportionate to the gravity of the violations. In cases of torture, victims should in addition be afforded medical and psychological care."[39]

As was the case with the Goldstone Report, the United States engaged in similar efforts to shield Israel from accountability for killing humanitarian activists in international waters. The United States did so by voting first against the establishment of the UN fact-finding mission and then against its report, and by insisting that Israel's domestic investigatory processes were credible and capable of holding Israeli political and military leaders accountable. Although documents leaked in "Cablegate" and the "Palestine Papers" either predate or do not cover Israel's attack on the Gaza Freedom Flotilla, from public statements made by US officials it was clear that the United States was reusing the same diplomatic playbook it had employed to kill the Goldstone Report. Unfortunately, a more detailed and behind-the-scenes accounting of US efforts to prevent the international community from holding Israel accountable for its attack on the flotilla will have to await the opening of official archives.

However, the Obama administration seemed to have derived an important lesson from its heavy-handed attempts to "blunt the effects" of the Goldstone Report, a lesson which would guide its somewhat more subtle strategy in this case. Despite the Obama administration's undeniable success in halting the implementation of the Goldstone Report's recommendations for accountability, the report nevertheless stood as a highly credible, exhaustive and damning indictment of Israel that greatly eroded its standing in the eyes of the international community. Thus a diplomatic victory was still a public relations loss. Undoubtedly, the Obama administration could similarly outmaneuver the UN fact-finding mission on the flotilla by threatening to use or by using its veto power in the UN Security Council if its report progressed that far. But doing so would not, in and of itself, prevent Israel from obtaining another public relations black eye from what would turn out to be another credible, exhaustive, and damning indictment. Therefore, the Obama administration instead supported from the outset a heavily politicized UN Secretary General–led investigation into Israel's attack on the flotilla.

The United States hoped this investigation would overshadow, or at least compete with, a UN Human Rights Council investigation the United States would oppose, but could not prevent.

On May 31, 2010, the day that Israel attacked the Gaza Freedom Flotilla, UN Secretary General Ban Ki-Moon was in Kampala, Uganda for, ironically enough, a review conference on the progress of the ICC. At the conference, he declared that "the old era of impunity is over. In its place, slowly but surely, we are witnessing the birth of a new age of accountability." The secretary general professed himself to be "shocked" at the carnage aboard the flotilla and stated, "It is vital that there is a full investigation to determine exactly how this bloodshed took place. I believe Israel must urgently provide a full explanation."[40] During an emergency, marathon twelve-hour meeting of the Security Council that day, the United States also declared itself to be "deeply disturbed" by Israel's attack on the flotilla. Deputy Permanent US Representative to the UN Alejandro Wolff stated, "We expect a credible and transparent investigation and strongly urge the Israeli government to investigate the incident fully."[41] The United States backed a presidential statement at the end of the session, which read: "The Security Council takes note of the statement of the UN Secretary-General on the need to have a full investigation into the matter and it calls for a prompt, impartial, credible and transparent investigation conforming to international standards."[42]

In the immediate aftermath of Israel's attack on the Gaza Freedom Flotilla, it seemed that the Obama administration was willing to cooperate with, rather than obstruct, an investigation. However, this appearance was fleeting, as the United States straightaway began to unilaterally reinterpret the secretary general's comments and the Security Council presidential statement to argue that an Israeli investigation alone would satisfy these requirements. Indeed, Wolff began to undercut the Security Council action as soon as he left its chambers to speak to the media. When asked whether the just-adopted statement, in calling for an "impartial" investigation, meant that it should be independent and not conducted by Israel, Wolff not only emphatically rejected that claim, but insisted, contrary to the text of the statement, the exact opposite. "No[,] that's not our understanding," Wolff stated. "If you read the text carefully, it makes clear what it means and what it doesn't mean." Although the statement did not explicitly call for an Israeli investigation, Wolff announced, "We are convinced and support an Israeli investigation as I called for in my statement earlier and have every confidence that Israel can conduct a credible and impartial, transparent, prompt investigation internally."[43]

Secretary of State Hillary Clinton hinted at some US flexibility on the crucial question of who would conduct this investigation. She noted on June 1, 2010, "We are open to different ways of assuring a credible investigation, including international participation." But she made clear that this openness to international participation was limited to whatever Israel would accept within the context of its own domestic investigation, since the United States would back any "Israeli investigation that meets those criteria" stipulated by the UN Security Council.[44]

Therefore it came as no surprise that the United States vehemently opposed and voted against a resolution in the UN Human Rights Council the following day "to dispatch an independent, international fact-finding mission to investigate violations of international law, including international humanitarian and human rights law, resulting from the Israeli attacks on the flotilla of ships carrying humanitarian assistance."[45] Although it was difficult to understand how establishing an international fact-finding mission passed judgment on Israel's attack on the flotilla, US ambassador to the Human Rights Council Eileen Chamberlain Donahoe argued that the resolution somehow "rushes to judgment on a set of facts that, as our debate over the last day makes clear, are only beginning to be discovered and understood." Furthermore, the United States opposed the establishment of an international fact-finding mission because it "risks further politicizing a sensitive and volatile situation," according to Donahoe.[46]

But the arguments of the United States failed to impress the member states of the UN Human Rights Council, which voted 32-3 with nine abstentions to establish the fact-finding mission. The United States was even more isolated in its diplomatic protection of Israel when the Human Rights Council voted 30-1 with fifteen abstentions on September 29, 2010, to endorse the recommendations of the international fact-finding mission.[47] In casting the sole vote against the fact-finding mission's report, the United States could find nothing wrong with the substance of the report itself. Instead, it argued that because the mission supposedly had a "flawed mandate" and the Human Rights Council suggested the General Assembly "consider" the report, these flimsy pretexts were sufficient reasons for the United States to oppose it.[48]

The United States felt that it could dispense with substantive arguments against the UN fact-finding mission on the flotilla because, by the time the report was issued, the United States was already heavily invested in promoting an alternative to the UN fact-finding mission report, which it believed would overshadow and neutralize it. On August 2, 2010, UN Secretary General Ban Ki-Moon announced the formation of this separate four-person panel, which was to be chaired by former New Zealand prime minister Geoffrey Palmer, with Colombian president Álvaro Uribe, whose term in office was set to expire in five days, as the committee's vice chair. The establishment of this committee was sui generis; neither the UN Security Council nor any other UN body had mandated it.

In contrast to the US reaction to the UN fact-finding mission, US Permanent Representative to the UN Susan Rice warmly welcomed the establishment of what would be known as the Palmer Panel. From the outset, this panel was designed as a politicized body that was tasked with the impossible mission of squaring the results of irreconcilable national commissions in Turkey and Israel that unsurprisingly would come to diametrically opposed conclusions about Israel's attack on the flotilla. The Palmer Panel would come to no legal conclusions and would definitely not seek to hold Israel accountable for its violations of human rights and international law in attacking the flotilla in international waters. Instead, according to Rice, the Palmer Panel would only "make recommendations as to how to avoid such incidents in the future." In addition, the panel would serve the purpose of being "a vehicle to enable Israel and Turkey to move beyond the recent strains in their relationship and repair their strong historic ties."[49] Here was a UN-sponsored investigation of Israel's actions that the Obama administration could finally accept: one under the thumb of the pliant UN secretary general, with a "flawed mandate" to avoid any legal conclusions or proposals for accountability and with the express purpose not of seeking justice, but of reconciling two US allies at loggerheads.

The Palmer Panel finally released its report in September 2011, following multiple delays as the United States worked feverishly and unsuccessfully to reconcile Turkey and Israel. The Obama administration's failed efforts to conciliate the two countries was unsurprising, giving that Israel stubbornly refused to accept responsibility for the results of its attack on the flotilla or even apologize to Turkey for the killing of its citizens. The results of the panel's report fully substantiated concerns about the composition of the panel and its politicized mandate. The inclusion of Uribe in particular, a notorious human rights abuser who had greatly strengthened Colombia's military connections with Israel during his presidency, had delegitimized the Palmer Panel's impartiality. Although Palmer was considered an expert in international law, his pairing with Uribe made it seem "that 'balance' in this commission involves balance between someone versed in international and human rights law and someone who is adamantly opposed to it,"[50] according to journalists José Antonio Gutiérrez and David Landy.

But, after all, the Palmer Panel was not concerned with the legality of Israel's actions, as it acknowledged in its report. The panel was, it noted, "not a court. It was not asked to make determinations of the legal issues or to adjudicate on liability." Due to severe constraints on its information-gathering capabilities, the panel admitted that it "cannot make definitive findings either of fact or law." Most damning of all, the panel confessed that it "will not add value for the United Nations by attempting to determine contested facts or by arguing endlessly about the applicable law. Too much legal analysis threatens to produce political paralysis." Rather than attempt to establish facts and hold perpetrators accountable for their crimes, the panel instead "searched for solutions that will allow Israel, Turkey and the international community to put the incident behind them."

The panel scrupulously blamed both Israel and the flotilla organizers in equal measure. Although the panel acknowledged that Israel's attacks upon the flotilla "should never have taken place as they did," the panel chided the flotilla participants for having "acted recklessly in attempting to breach the naval blockade." While the force Israel employed in boarding the boats "was excessive and unreasonable" and the loss of life and injuries sustained "was unacceptable," unarmed civilians on the flotilla acting in self-defense to repel Israel's aggression were nevertheless engaged in "significant, organized and violent resistance" that necessitated Israeli soldiers "to use force for their own protection," the panel concluded. This deliberate equivocation was designed to apportion responsibility so that the two countries could get on with the more important task of reconciliation, in the view of the panel. The panel believed that this propitiation could be accomplished merely by Israel making a "statement of regret" and offering "payment for the benefit of the deceased and injured victims and their families." By taking these steps, rather than through apologizing and holding Israeli political and military leaders accountable, the panel envisioned Turkey and Israel reestablishing "full diplomatic relations, repairing their relationship in the interests of stability in the Middle East and international peace and security."[51]

With the UN fact-finding mission having run its course and with the United States instead backing the feckless Palmer Panel that failed in its goal of achieving Turkish-Israeli reconciliation, the Obama administration had again worked effectively to ensure that the UN system would fail to hold Israel accountable for its actions. Whether by vetoing a Security Council resolution condemning Israel's illegal settlements, by blocking Palestinian UN membership, or by stonewalling UN fact-finding missions into Israel's violations of international law during Operation Cast Lead and its attack on the Gaza Freedom Flotilla, the Obama administration repeatedly shielded Israel diplomatically from the consequences of its illegal behavior and its denial of Palestinian self-determination. This diplomatic protection of Israel continued to make the United States indirectly responsible for Israel's human rights abuses of Palestinians; the increased military aid that the Obama administration provided to Israel would make it even more directly complicit in those violations.

CHAPTER EIGHT

A Broader, Deeper, More Intense Military Relationship with Israel than Ever

US-ISRAEL MILITARY TIES

On July 16, 2010, Assistant Secretary of State for Political-Military Affairs Andrew Shapiro stood before a friendly audience at the Brookings Institution Saban Center for Middle East Policy. This think tank was named after its benefactor, Israeli-American media mogul Haim Saban, who once said "I'm a one-issue guy, and my issue is Israel." According to a profile of Saban in *The New Yorker*, his "greatest concern, he says, is to protect Israel, by strengthening the US-Israel relationship."[1] The Saban Center was, therefore, the ideal venue for Shapiro to deliver an address entitled: "The Obama Administration's Approach to US-Israel Security Cooperation: Preserving Israel's Qualitative Military Edge."

In this remarkable speech, Shapiro made an extremely convincing case for how the Obama administration had elevated the US-Israeli military relationship to unprecedented levels. Shapiro stressed President Obama's "enduring commitment to Israel's security" and was "proud to say that as a result of this commitment, our security relationship with Israel is broader, deeper and more intense than ever before." In his position, Shapiro noted that "one of my primary responsibilities is to preserve Israel's Qualitative Military Edge." Under the Obama administration, Shapiro declared, "The US-Israel security relationship is too important to be anything less than a top priority. As surely as the bond between the United States and Israel is unbreakable, our commitment to Israel's qualitative military edge has never been greater."[2]

This unprecedented level of military backing for Israel was a theme to which senior Obama administration officials would turn again and again, especially before pro-Israel and Jewish audiences, in order to bolster their pro-Israel credentials and offset charges that they were being too tough on Israel by requesting it to fulfill its international legal requirement to cease building illegal settlements on occupied Palestinian land. For example, in his March 2012 speech at the AIPAC policy conference, Obama himself reminded the audience that "four years ago, I stood before you and said that, 'Israel's security is sacrosanct. It is non-negotiable.' That belief has guided my actions as president. The fact is, my administration's commitment to Israel's security has been unprecedented. Our military and intelligence cooperation has never been closer. (Applause.) Our joint exercises and training have never been more robust. Despite a tough budget environment, our security assistance has increased every single year. (Applause.)"[3]

In a similar vein, speaking at an anniversary dinner for a Jewish school in Detroit in November 2011, Vice President Biden stated: "With the United States, past Presidents and this President know, that Israel has nowhere else to go. That's why we have done more than any administration on the security front with Israel because we know it has nowhere else to go. To make sure that Israel can stay exactly where she is—a Jewish state, secure and free. And that is why the bond between America and Israel is absolutely unshakeable." But the record-breaking levels of US military aid to Israel under the Obama administration were only part of the picture. "It's not just the technology, but the human relationships that will ensure Israel's qualitative military edge," Biden argued. "Since taking office, we've launched the most comprehensive and meaningful strategic and operational consultations across all levels of our government, unprecedented in their scope, frequency and character."[4]

Even the otherwise obstreperous Prime Minister Netanyahu, who repeatedly clashed with the Obama administration on the Israeli-Palestinian "peace process," was effusive in his praise for the president's leadership in strengthening the US-Israel military relationship. Even at the height of the May 2011 faux crisis between Netanyahu and Obama over the latter's reference to negotiating a

Palestinian state based on Israel's pre-1967 armistice lines, Netanyahu was still capable of summoning up kind words for Obama on this front. As he told the 2011 AIPAC policy conference, "Yesterday President Obama spoke about his ironclad commitment to Israel's security. He rightly said that our security cooperation is unprecedented . . . And he has backed those words with deeds."[5]

Through these and dozens of other similar statements, the consensus opinion of top US and Israeli officials was that the Obama administration had galvanized the US-Israel military relationship and ensured Israel's qualitative military edge (QME) to a heretofore unrivaled degree. Moreover, the Obama administration's commitment to Israel's QME was no mere rhetorical device designed to soothe the Israel lobby's qualms about the president's handling of the "peace process"; rather, inside the acronym-laden Beltway, it referred to the implementation of a recently passed law aimed at ensuring that all US weapons transfers to the Middle East were subordinated to Israel's military superiority.

Although the United States had been negotiating weapons deals for decades while taking into account Israel's QME, the formal responsibility to do so was codified in the 2008 Naval Vessel Transfer Act. Representative Howard Berman had surreptitiously snuck in this non-germane section into the bill and succeeded in passing it by voice vote the same day that the bill was introduced. After the bill similarly sailed through the Senate, President George W. Bush signed into law in October 2008 a provision that would commit the United States to certifying that any "proposed sale or export of defense articles or defense services . . . to any country in the Middle East other than Israel shall include a determination that the sale or export of the defense articles or defense services will not adversely affect Israel's qualitative military edge over military threats to Israel." The law defined Israel's QME as requiring the United States to provide Israel the "ability to counter and defeat any credible conventional military threat from any individual state or possible coalition of states or from non-state actors, while sustaining minimal damages and casualties, through the use of superior military means, possessed in sufficient quantity."[6]

In the continued absence of a formal US-Israel defense treaty, the US commitment to Israel's QME would stand as the next best alternative to guaranteeing Israel's military preeminence in the Middle East. Israeli military leaders recognized the exceptional nature of the US commitment to Israel's QME. According to a State Department cable, in a November 2009 meeting with US Assistant Secretary of Defense for International Security Affairs Alexander Vershbow, the head of Israel's Ministry of Defense Political Military Bureau Amos Gilad "acknowledged the sometimes difficult position the US finds itself in given its global interests, and conceded that Israel's security focus is so narrow that its QME concerns often clash with broader American security interests in the region."[7]

Notwithstanding this Israeli admission that by promoting Israel's QME, the United States often was acting against its own self-defined national interests, the Obama administration nevertheless plunged into the task of assuring Israel's military supremacy with unparalleled vigor and determination. Throughout its first term, the Obama administration advanced Israel's QME in three primary ways. First, the United States would provide Israel with record-breaking amounts of military aid and ensured that Israel received the most sophisticated weapons systems with this money. Second, the Obama administration and Congress worked together to appropriate unprecedented amounts of money for joint US-Israeli research and development of anti-missile systems, which have had significant ramifications for the Israeli-Palestinian military balance. Third, the Obama administration conducted the largest-ever joint US-Israeli military exercises and engaged in the most extensive and high-level military dialogues ever between the two countries.

After Israel commenced its military occupation of the Palestinian West Bank, East Jerusalem and Gaza Strip in 1967, President Lyndon Johnson feared the consequences of Israeli territorial aggrandizement. He warned that Israel should not "permit military success to blind it to the fact that its neighbors have rights and its neighbors have interests of their own." Johnson spoke out against the "waste and futility" and "danger" of the Arab-Israeli arms race that had been taking place since 1948. "We have always opposed this arms race," Johnson stated, "and our own military shipments to the area have consequently been severely limited."[8] Unfortunately, Johnson's successors in the White House dispensed with his restraint. The United States would saturate Israel with $67 billion of US taxpayer-funded military aid grants and loans in the four decades after the war (1968–2008). In 2007, the Bush administration signed an agreement with Israel to provide an additional $30 billion in military aid from 2009 to 2018.

During the 2000s alone, the United States had earmarked more than $24 billion of foreign military financing—the official budgetary term for military aid—to Israel. With these appropriations, the United States licensed, financed and delivered a staggering 670 million weapons, rounds of ammunition and related equipment to the Israeli military through three major weapons transfer programs. These weapons were valued at nearly $19 billion; the remaining approximately $5 billion was presumably spent by the Israeli military on Israel's own domestic weapons industries, a unique legislative exemption for Israel which allowed it to spend up to one quarter of its military aid on non-US weapons manufacturers. In total, US taxpayers financed the transfer of nearly 500 different categories of weapons to the Israeli military during the 2000s. These weapons ranged from the truly mundane—one used food steamer, valued at $2,100—to the most sophisticated US weapons systems—93 F-16D fighter jets, valued at nearly $2.5 billion—and included nearly every conceivable weapon in between these extremes.

This massive arming of the Israeli military made the US taxpayer directly responsible for and complicit in Israel's systematic human rights abuses of Palestinians in the occupied West Bank, East Jerusalem and Gaza Strip. From September 2000 to December 2009, the Israeli military killed at least 2,969 Palestinians who took no part in hostilities, including at least 1,128 Palestinian children younger than eighteen years old, according to the Israeli human rights organization B'Tselem. Israel often killed these Palestinians with weapons provided by the United States.

The disturbing scale of Israel's human rights abuses of Palestinians committed with US weapons should have caused the Obama administration to reevaluate the legality of continuing to provide the Israeli military with this extravagant taxpayer-financed military aid. According to the Foreign Assistance Act, it is the avowed goal of the United States to "promote and encourage increased respect for human rights and fundamental freedoms throughout the world without distinction as to race, sex, language, or religion." To advance this worthy objective, the United States cannot provide any type of "security assistance" to a government that "engages in a consistent pattern of gross violations of internationally recognized human rights." Similarly, the Arms Export Control Act limits the use of US weapons "solely for internal security, for legitimate self-defense," for preventing the proliferation of weapons of mass destruction, for participating in regional security arrangements or for "measures consistent with the Charter of the United Nations." The law stipulates that no credits, guarantees, sales or deliveries of weapons can be extended to a foreign government if it is "in substantial violation" of these narrowly limited uses of US weapons.

But rather than investigate Israel's repeated and blatant violations of these US laws and hold Israel accountable for these violations by ending US weapons transfers, the Obama administration upped US military aid to Israel to unprecedented levels. The US-Israeli 2007 memorandum of understanding called for the United States to provide Israel with $30 billion of military aid from 2009 to 2018, an average annual increase of 25 percent above previous levels. Obama submitted budget requests to Congress that incrementally enlarged US military aid to Israel in accordance with this agreement. During the Obama administration, US military aid to Israel has climbed from $2.55 billion (2009), to $2.775 billion (2010), to $3 billion (2011), to $3.075 billion (2012) and to $3.1 billion (2013), the level at which US military aid is expected to plateau until 2018.[9] Not only has US military aid to Israel reached new heights under the Obama administration; it also comprised the lion's share of overall US military aid. As Assistant Secretary of State for Political-Military Affairs Andrew Shapiro noted, total US military aid "is $5 billion annually and is distributed among some seventy countries. So it is a testament to our special security relationship that each year Israel accounts for just over 50 percent of US security assistance funding."[10]

Unsurprisingly, this increased flow of taxpayer-funded weapons to Israel under the Obama administration continued to exact a devastating toll on Palestinian civilians living under Israeli military occupation and even on US citizens either witnessing or participating in nonviolent Palestinian protests against Israel's human rights abuses. Israel's misuse of US-supplied tear gas canisters served as one particularly egregious example that is illustrative of the phenomenon of Israel severely injuring and killing civilians with US weapons in violation of US law.

Bil'in is a small Palestinian village in the West Bank near the city of Ramallah. Since 2005, villagers, along with Israelis and international activists, have mounted weekly nonviolent protests against Israel's wall and the expansion of Israeli settlements, both of which have expropriated large tracts of the village's land. The Israeli military routinely breaks up these nonviolent protests with deadly force. The Abu Rahmah family of Bil'in has paid a distinctly heavy price for the US decision to supply the Israeli military with tear gas canisters. On April 17, 2009, Israeli soldiers killed twenty-nine-year-old Bassem Abu Rahmah during a weekly protest when he was struck in the chest with a tear gas canister. On January 1, 2011, his thirty-six-year-old sister, Jawaher Abu Rahmah, died of cardiac arrest after inhaling copious amounts of tear gas fired into her village the previous day by Israeli soldiers.

The atrocities Israel has committed with these tear gas canisters were sadly not limited to Bil'in. On March 13, 2009, thirty-seven-year-old US citizen Tristan Anderson was critically injured after an Israeli soldier shot him in the head with a tear gas canister in the nearby West Bank village of Ni'lin while he was observing a nonviolent Palestinian protest. The tear gas canister punctured a large hole in his forehead, causing massive brain damage and leaving him largely paralyzed. A congressional resolution introduced by Representative Barbara Lee (D-CA), who represents Anderson, an Oakland resident, in Congress, called on the United States "to undertake a full, fair, and expeditious investigation of the circumstances that led to the injury of Tristan Anderson" and expressed "sympathy to Tristan Anderson and his family, friends, and loved ones during this trying time."[11] This resolution, calling for a US investigation of a severely injured US citizen shot with a US-supplied weapon, paid for by US taxpayers, by a foreign country that is supposedly a US ally, garnered just four cosponsors and died in committee.

Just as US efforts to scuttle the Goldstone Report provided Israel with impunity for the crimes it committed during Operation Cast Lead and reinforced an Israeli sense of immunity that led directly to Israel's attack on the Gaza Freedom Flotilla, so too did the US failure to investigate, much less hold Israel accountable for, Tristan

Anderson's grave injury breed a sense of entitlement. The United States was signaling to Israel that it could continue to harm US citizens with US weapons or even kill them without consequence, as happened to Rachel Corrie, who died on March 16, 2003 after an Israeli soldier ran over her with a Caterpillar D9 bulldozer as she attempted to protect a Palestinian home in the Gaza Strip from being demolished. This pattern continued when on May 31, 2010, twenty-one-year-old US citizen Emily Henochowicz also was struck in the face by a tear gas canister fired by an Israeli soldier during a demonstration against Israel's attack on the Gaza Freedom Flotilla at the Qalandia checkpoint near Jerusalem. The tear gas canister blinded her left eye.

Similarly, on December 9, 2011, an Israeli soldier fired a tear gas canister from an armored vehicle that was departing the West Bank village of Nabi Saleh, which like nearby Bil'in holds weekly nonviolent protests against Israel's expropriation of the village's land for its illegal settlements. This tear gas canister struck twenty-eight-year-old Mustafa Tamimi in the face. He died of his wounds the next day.

In all five of these cases, there is evidence that these tear gas canisters were supplied to the Israeli military by Combined Systems, Inc. (CSI) of Jamestown, Pennsylvania, a corporation which proudly flew an Israeli flag at its headquarters before protestors drew attention to its profiting from Israel's injuring and killing of civilians with its products. From 2000 to 2009, the State Department licensed the delivery of more than 595,000 tear gas canisters and other "riot control" equipment to the Israeli military, valued at more than $20.5 million.[12] The US provision of these tear gas canisters to Israel represented a small, but nevertheless significant and deadly, percentage of US weapons transfers to Israel, which under the Obama administration increased to new heights.

At a January 2010 town hall meeting with President Obama in Tampa, Florida, a participant referenced Obama's recent State of the Union address during which the president "spoke of America's support for human rights." Given this professed commitment to human rights, the town hall attendee asked, "Why have we not condemned Israel and Egypt's human rights violations against the occupied Palestinian people and yet we continue to support [them] financially with billions of dollars coming from our tax dollars?" A visibly flummoxed Obama blurted out this non sequitur in response: "Look, look, look, the Middle East is obviously an issue that has plagued the region for centuries." After regaining his composure, he pledged, "I will never waver from ensuring Israel's security and helping them secure themselves in what is a very hostile region. (Applause.) So I make no apologies for that."[13] Obama's unwillingness to acknowledge, much less apologize for, the human rights abuses Israel committed against Palestinians with unprecedented levels of US military aid during his administration spoke volumes about his commitment to the universality of human rights. This increased military aid was the most direct way that ensuring Israel's "qualitative military edge" made the United States complicit in Israel's military occupation and apartheid policies toward Palestinians. But it was not the only way.

Under the Obama administration, the United States also appropriated record-breaking levels of funds for joint US-Israeli anti-missile systems. Some of these joint research and development projects had been underway since as far back as 1988, but under the Obama administration they received a considerable boost. When fully completed and deployed, these anti-missile systems will give Israel a multi-tiered capability to shoot down incoming short-, medium- and long-range missiles. During the last four budgets of the Bush administration, the United States appropriated slightly more than $600 million for these anti-missile systems. In the first four budgets approved during the Obama administration, the United States upped its funding for these anti-missile systems to more than $1.3 billion.[14]

The joint research, development and deployment of these anti-missile systems solely benefits Israel at this time. These systems provide no discernible advantage for US strategic interests, unless lining the pockets of war profiteers such as Raytheon and Boeing—two US corporations co-producing these anti-missile systems—at US taxpayer expense is deemed a US strategic interest. Despite the fact that these anti-missile systems are designed to assist Israel, their funding is not technically considered military aid. The money for these projects comes from the Pentagon's budget, rather than through the State Department's budget, under which all official military aid is appropriated. In other words, the Obama administration's record-breaking levels of funding for joint US-Israeli anti-missile systems is in addition to its record-breaking levels of military aid for Israel.

Although the majority of these anti-missile systems are designed to intercept and destroy medium- to long-range missiles in the arsenals of Hezbollah in Lebanon, Syria and Iran, one short-range anti-missile system, dubbed "Iron Dome," is designed to intercept and destroy the crude, short-range missiles and rockets fired from the Gaza Strip by Palestinian militant groups. In the 2011 and 2013 budgets, the United States appropriated $416 million for Israel to purchase Iron Dome batteries, which had been developed by the Israeli weapons manufacturer Rafael Advanced Defense Systems. Israel has deployed three Iron Dome batteries since March 2011 and they have proven their effectiveness. In a March 2012 exchange of fire with Palestinian militant groups in the Gaza Strip, initiated by the Israeli air force, the anti-missile system destroyed more than 90 percent of the incoming missiles it targeted.[15]

The Goldstone Report rightfully noted that the firing of missiles and rockets at Israeli civilians by Palestinian militant groups constitutes a violation of international law and a war crime, and of course both Palestinian and Israeli civilians should be free from the fear, destruction and death caused by missile and rocket fire. However, by providing funding for Iron Dome, the Obama administration and Congress made a deliberate decision to effectively protect Israeli civilians, while leaving Palestinian civilians extremely vulnerable to the infinitely more sophisticated and deadly US-provided arsenal of weapons at Israel's disposal. By doing so, the United States has even further altered the strategic balance in Israel's favor, making it much less costly for Israel to maintain its illegal blockade of the Gaza Strip and enforce it with the application of overwhelming military force with little fear of effective retaliation. This new dynamic unfolded in March 2012, when, according to the Palestinian Centre for Human Rights, the Israeli air force launched thirty-six air strikes, in which at least forty-three missiles were fired, against Palestinians in the Gaza Strip. This attack triggered the retaliatory fire that the Iron Dome batteries successfully intercepted 90 percent of the time. While Israeli civilians were protected by Iron Dome, these Israeli assaults killed twenty-four Palestinians, including four civilians, and injured seventy-nine, including sixty-four civilians. In addition, "dozens of houses, a school, a center of [the] Palestine Red Crescent Society and a grocery shop were damaged, and a car, a greenhouse and a workshop were destroyed."[16]

In addition to providing Israel with unprecedented levels of military aid and appropriations for joint anti-missile systems, during Obama's first term the US military also engaged in the largest-ever joint military exercises with Israel and embarked on the most intimate and extensive military dialogue with its Israeli counterparts in US history. Since 2001, the United States and Israel have held a biannual joint ballistic missile defense exercise, code-named Juniper Cobra, which is designed "to work on integrating interceptors, radars, and other systems."[17] According to the president's special assistant Dennis Ross, the October 2009 Juniper Cobra exercise included 1,300 US military personnel, making it the largest joint military exercise to date. Ross told an AIPAC National Summit in October 2010, "Our military regularly conducts exercises with the IDF [Israel Defense Forces] . . . involving our Navy, Marines, and Air Force. These commitments are real. They are tangible. And they solidify the truly special relationship between the United States and Israel."[18]

More evidence of the "truly special relationship" would be forthcoming in 2012, as the Obama administration planned an even larger joint military exercise, code-named Austere Challenge, which, according to Defense Secretary Leon Panetta, would include more than 3,000 US military personnel.[19] The exercise, originally scheduled for April 2012, was conveniently postponed until October, the month before the US presidential election. The exercise was scheduled to include "the establishment of US command posts in Israel and IDF command posts at EUCOM [European Command] headquarters in Germany—with the ultimate goal of establishing joint task forces in the event of a large-scale conflict in the Middle East." Austere Challenge would also "simulate the interception of missile salvos against Israel."[20] These joint military exercises were just a small component of the deepening US-Israeli military coordination during the Obama administration. As of November 2011, Vice President Biden revealed that the Obama administration had tallied "the most visits by senior high-level Department of Defense officials and their Israeli counterparts—over 200. Such cooperation, as you observed, only exists with the closes[t] allies; cooperation that a friend of mine for 39 years, Benjamin Netanyahu himself, has rightly called unprecedented."[21]

By providing Israel with unparalleled amounts of military aid, funding for joint anti-missile defense systems and joint military exercises, the Obama administration could justifiably term the US-Israel military relationship "broader, deeper and more intense than ever before." Unfortunately for Palestinians living under Israeli military occupation, that burgeoning relationship came at the expense of their human rights.

US AID TO PALESTINIANS

The Obama administration attempted to mitigate the suffering of Palestinians living under Israeli military occupation by increasing bilateral US aid to Palestinians, despite congressional efforts to end US aid to Palestinians as a sanction for their attempt to secure UN membership. In fact, during Obama's first term in office, the United States raised aid to Palestinians by an even greater percentage than it did for Israel, although US aid to Palestinians still paled in comparison to US military aid to Israel. During the four regular budget cycles in President George W. Bush's second term, the United States provided $957.6 million in bilateral aid to the Palestinians. In addition, the United States appropriated $624.9 million of support to the UN Relief and Works Agency (UNRWA) for Palestine Refugees, an agency which provides for the humanitarian needs of some five million registered Palestinian refugees in refugee camps in the Palestinian West Bank, East Jerusalem and Gaza Strip, Jordan, Lebanon and Syria. In total, the United States provided approximately $1.58 billion in aid to Palestinians during these years.

In June 2009, Congress passed a supplemental appropriations bill that included $660 million in US bilateral aid to the Palestinians, plus $119 million to support UNRWA. This total aid package of $779 million represented the vast majority of the $900 million dollars pledged by the Obama administration during a March 2009 international donors' conference in Egypt convened after Operation Cast Lead. In addition, in the four regular budget cycles of Obama's first term, Congress appropriated (2010–12) or is considering appropriating (2013) $1.98 billion in US bilateral aid to the Palestinians. From 2010 to 2012, the Obama administration also provided or plans to provide UNRWA with $713 million (since US funding of UNRWA comes from a portion of the overall funding for worldwide Migration and Refugee Assistance, the State Department does not request specific amounts of money for UNRWA, making the 2013 anticipated expenditure for UNRWA unknown as of this writing). In total, the Obama administration will likely provide more than $3.47 billion in aid to Palestinians in its first term, or more than double the amount of aid during President George W. Bush's second term.[22]

At first, it may appear that this quantifiable rise in US aid to Palestinians under the Obama administration represented an increased commitment by the United States to help prepare Palestinians for the future establishment of an independent Palestinian state. After all, many of the programs funded by the United States are meant to improve socioeconomic indicators, develop infrastructure, professionalize governing and security institutions of the Palestinian Authority (PA), and promote the rule of law and democracy. In their design and impact, however, many US aid programs that supposedly benefit Palestinians actually entrap them into Israel's seemingly never-ending military occupation, thereby perversely reinforcing the Israeli-Palestinian status quo that Obama has deemed to be "unsustainable." By briefly examining each component of US aid to Palestinians, it is possible to outline this admittedly counterintuitive claim.

The largest component of the US bilateral aid package to Palestinians is known as Economic Support Funds (ESF), which during Obama's first term accounted for approximately 80 percent, or $2.1 billion, of bilateral aid. The majority of this money funds projects contracted through the US Agency for International Development (USAID) and largely implemented by US nongovernmental organizations (NGOs). According to USAID, it funds "a wide range of projects that aim to improve the quality of life for Palestinians while also helping the Palestinian Authority strengthen its ability to deliver quality public services." These projects include "programs in the areas of democracy and governance; education; health and humanitarian assistance; private enterprise; and water resources and infrastructure." USAID also provides "continuing assistance for basic human needs in both the West Bank and Gaza, including emergency food, health care, and access to safe water and sanitation systems."[23] While all of these goals may appear laudable, there are nevertheless severe conceptual problems with many of these programs.

Promoting "economic growth" for Palestinians living under Israeli military occupation, while simultaneously flooding Israel with the weapons and providing it with the diplomatic protection it needs to entrench this military occupation, is a nonsensical proposition. At best, these policies reveal that the United States is working at cross-purposes; at worst, they signal that it is trying to reconcile Palestinians to their open-air prison existence by making it slightly more palatable. What USAID fails to understand publicly is that Israel's military occupation is specifically designed to de-develop the Palestinian economy, not to encourage Palestinian economic growth.

Israel's evisceration of the Palestinian economy is integrally woven into the very fabric of its military occupation in innumerable ways. The hundreds of roadblocks, checkpoints and other barriers to movement that Israel maintains in the West Bank and East Jerusalem inhibit the transportation of people and goods, which forces the ever-increasing localization of the economy. Israel's blockade of the Gaza Strip has reduced its population to penury and almost total reliance on international charity for survival. Even before Israel's formal imposition of the blockade on Gaza in 2007, Israel's earlier destruction of the Gaza Strip's only airport and its prevention of the building of a seaport there had greatly constricted Palestinians in the Gaza Strip from engaging in international trade. Similarly, Israel's wall in the West Bank and East Jerusalem, and its control of the West Bank's border crossings with Jordan, greatly reduce trade opportunities as well. Finally, Israel's widespread razing of Palestinian agricultural land and fruit-bearing trees, along with the expropriation of Palestinian land and water resources for its illegal settlements, have devastated the Palestinian agricultural sector. A report published in September 2011 by the Palestinian Ministry of National Economy, in cooperation with the Applied Research Institute—Jerusalem, estimated that these and other policies endured by Palestinians under Israeli military occupation deprived the Palestinian economy of $6.9 billion in 2010, or nearly 85 percent of Palestinian gross domestic product. "In other words," the report concluded, "had the Palestinians not been subject to the Israeli occupation, their economy would have been almost double in size than it is today."[24]

The farcical attempt to promote "economic growth" under these conditions is revealed by USAID's own description of its programs. USAID touts that "with its border improvement projects, the United States is helping ease the movement of Palestinian people and goods, while improving Israel's security."[25] This Orwellian language was eerily reminiscent of the US method of promoting Palestinian "economic growth" during the Bush administration. In 2005, Congress passed a supplemental war appropriations bill that included $200 million in economic aid to the Palestinians. Congress promptly turned over to Israel $50 million of this money "to help improve the movement of people and goods in and out of Israel." As members of Congress rationalized it, they were "aware that infrastructure will be needed on both the Palestinian and Israeli sides of the separation lines and intend that these funds be used to meet the great need in developing this infrastructure."[26] With this money, the Israeli Foreign Ministry announced that it would build high-tech terminals at "crossing points along the revised route of the security fence."[27] In other words, less than one year after the International Court of Justice ruled that "all States are under an obligation not to recognize the illegal situation arising from the construction of the wall [in the West Bank], [and] not to render aid or assistance in maintaining that situation,"[28] the United States was providing Israel money to build high-tech terminals into this wall under the guise of Palestinian "economic growth."

Under the Obama administration, USAID continued this "development of efficient crossing points while addressing legitimate Israeli security concerns" through a more modest $13 million contract with Chemonics International. This contract sought "to ease movement and access restrictions for people and commodities within the West Bank, and between the West Bank and Israel."[29] These restrictions cost the Palestinian economy an estimated $184.5 million dollars in 2010.[30] Rather than eliminate Israel's illegal barriers to Palestinian movement, these USAID projects aimed to acclimate and inure Palestinians to Israel's ever-tightening control of their movement.

The folly of US economic aid to Palestinians is also evident in USAID's water resources and infrastructure projects, which aim to fund "emergency repairs of water, sanitation, and solid waste services to address urgent public health problems." With these projects, the US taxpayer foots the bill for US corporations to rebuild Palestinian infrastructure after already having padded the pockets of US war profiteers whose weapons are misused by Israel to systematically demolish that same Palestinian infrastructure. For example, in 2011, the accomplishments from part of a multi-year $300 million USAID infrastructure project in the Palestinian West Bank included "the rehabilitation of nine well pumping stations; and the construction of five new water wells and three new water reservoirs."[31] Impressive as that may seem, that same year the UN's Office for the Coordination of Humanitarian Affairs reported that Israel destroyed eighty-two Palestinian wells, cisterns and other water infrastructure in the West Bank.[32] As fast as the United States was able to rebuild Palestinian water infrastructure, Israel still demolished it at nearly five times the rate.

In addition to rebuilding what Israel was intent on destroying, USAID infrastructure projects also helped to solidify what Human Rights Watch (HRW) described as a "two-tier system of laws, rules, and services that Israel operates for the two populations in areas in the West Bank under its exclusive control, which provide preferential services, development, and benefits for Jewish settlers while imposing harsh conditions on Palestinians." One conspicuous example of this Israeli apartheid in the Palestinian West Bank is the segregated road infrastructure that Israel has built. According to HRW, Israeli "settlers enjoy virtually unfettered freedom of moment, with easy access to roads, built for them at considerable expense, that bypass Palestinian populated areas and connect settlements to the Israeli road network, other settlements, and major metropolitan areas inside Israel. In some cases, Palestinians are not only barred from these roads, but are effectively cut off from their lands and other villages and cities."[33] Research conducted by the Applied Research Institute–Jerusalem "reveals some damning facts" about how USAID is funding this apartheid road network in the West Bank, according to Nadia Hijab and Jesse Rosenfeld. They concluded that "32 percent of the PA roads funded and implemented by USAID neatly fall into a proposal the Israeli Civil Administration (the military occupation authority) presented to donors in 2004. Israel wanted donors to fund some 500 kilometers of alternative roads to serve the Palestinians it was blocking from the main road network." Wisely, Hijab and Rosenfeld wrote, "The donors rejected the proposal at that time, but it now turns out that PA-USAID efforts have effectively implemented 22 percent of Israel's plan."[34]

When these Economic Support Funds (ESF) were not handsomely profiting US corporations to entrench Israeli military occupation and apartheid toward Palestinians, they were earmarked for the direct budgetary support of the Palestinian Authority. Of the $2.1 billion in ESF allocated for Palestinians during the Obama administration, the president has, as of this writing, directed $750 million, or approximately 35 percent of the total, to the coffers of the PA. According to USAID, this budgetary support is used "to service debt to commercial suppliers and commercial banks" or "to pay for upcoming purchases from commercial suppliers or reimbursements of recent purchases from suppliers."[35] In announcing the transfer of $200 million to the PA in July 2009, Secretary of State Hillary Clinton told PA prime minister Salam Fayyad, "The ability of the United States to provide support directly to the Palestinian Authority is an indication of the bipartisan support for the effort to secure the peace in the Middle East, as well as for the fundamental reforms that the Palestinian Authority has undertaken."[36] What she neglected to mention was that by propping up the PA financially, the United States was also engaging in an elaborate charade that benefited Israel and the perpetuation of its military occupation of Palestinian land.

Israel and the PLO established the PA during the Oslo "peace process" as an interim, administrative structure for Palestinians to manage areas of the West Bank and Gaza Strip that devolved to full- or semi-Palestinian autonomy during the five-year time frame envisioned in these accords. The PA was never designed to be a permanent governing institution, much less one that exercised sovereignty. In fact, the legal mandate of the PA expired in May 1999, but by this time, with successful permanent status negotiations in grave doubt, it served the interests of all actors to maintain the façade that the PA continued to have legal relevance. This development served Israel's interests especially well. By maintaining the

PA in this indefinite interim state with severely circumscribed powers, Israel could effectively pawn off the PA as a ward of the international community, absolve itself of its responsibilities under the Fourth Geneva Convention to provide for the daily needs of the population under its military occupation, while at the same extending its colonization of the West Bank and East Jerusalem. Plus, the existence of the PA always provided Israel with a convenient bogeyman against whom it could perpetually gin up charges to argue that it did not have a "partner for peace" in order to justify its continued stranglehold over Palestinian territories occupied in 1967. By funding the PA, the United States was perpetuating this "peace process" shell game.

The other $529 million, or 20 percent, of bilateral US aid to Palestinians during the Obama administration was allocated through the innocuously sounding program entitled International Narcotics Control and Law Enforcement (INCLE). However, this aid was anything but harmless. Although some of this aid went to the PA Ministry of the Interior to support rule of law programs, the vast bulk of this money went to training, equipping and constructing bases for elite PA Presidential Guard units and special battalions of the National Security Forces (NSF). These US-trained and equipped Palestinian security forces are known informally as the "Dayton forces," named after Lieutenant General Keith Dayton, the US Security Coordinator (USSC) who led this mission from 2005 to 2010.

Two audits published in 2011 by the State Department's Office of Inspector General revealed important details about the scope of this US program. One component of this program involves "constructing nine operations camps, refurbishing and expanding a training center and the Presidential Guard College, and building five police stations." As of March 2011, significant progress had been made, with construction having begun of six of the nine operations camps. "In the next three to five years," according to the State Department, "these camps will train and accommodate an estimated 3,500 of the approximate 5,000 PASF [Palestinian Authority Security Forces] troops." The construction of the first six bases, a training center and the Jericho Presidential Guard College, which was partially "built by Palestinian military personnel with no construction background," necessitating its immediate repair, were all expected to be completed by early 2012 at a cost of $77 million. The remaining construction is expected to be completed by early 2013 at an additional cost of $51 million.[37]

A separate, but related, component of this program is the US training and equipping of these Palestinian security forces through a contract awarded to the US mercenary corporation DynCorp, which is overseen by the USSC mission from its offices in the US Consulate in Jerusalem. From 2007 to 2010, the United States spent $395 million on this project, including $157 million for training and $72 million for equipping these forces. According to the State Department, however, the project management was problematic. DynCorp failed to provide an "overall performance accountability plan" or a "contract implementation plan" as required by this contract. As a result, the State Department "could not fully determine whether DynCorp's training of the PASF is effective."

While the US-funded construction of training and operations centers in the West Bank is underway, a considerable portion of this training of Palestinian security forces has taken place at the Jordan International Police Training Center (JIPTC), located outside of Amman, a facility which was originally built by the United States in 2003 to train the Iraqi police during its war on and occupation of Iraq. As of July 2011, the facility at "JIPTC has provided specialized battalion training to 3,100 PASF troops" and DynCorp mobile training teams have trained an additional 3,942 military personnel in the West Bank. In addition to this training, the program has provided "tens of thousands of pieces of equipment" to these security forces, "including vehicles, armored vests, communication equipment, and other non-lethal items."[38]

The State Department's sanitized mission of the USSC is "to transform and professionalize its [the PA's] security sector" and "support other US rule of law programs that assist the Palestinians [to] improve the performance of the Justice and Corrections Sectors."[39] Such anodyne goals belie, however, the true intentions of these "Dayton forces," as revealed by Dayton's own candid admissions and by documents leaked to *Al Jazeera* in "The Palestine Papers." These actual objectives included creating Palestinian security forces that would collaborate with Israel, thereby effectively subcontracting Israel's military occupation to indigenous forces, crushing Hamas's infrastructure in the West Bank and quelling internal dissent to the PA. Along the way, Dayton acknowledged that these forces engaged in human rights violations, including torture.

In May 2009, Dayton delivered a controversial speech at the pro-Israel Washington Institute for Near East Policy (WINEP), a partisan "think tank" with strong connections to AIPAC. By admitting to his reliance upon WINEP, Dayton immediately dispelled any notion that the Palestinian security forces he was training and equipping were for the benefit of the Palestinians. He stated that WINEP is "the foremost think tank on Middle East issues, not only in Washington, but in the world . . . I read the Institute's reports, I talk with the Institute fellows and staff about key matters. The people here at The Washington Institute give analytical and unbiased advice. I depend on it, and sometimes I feel I would be lost without it." He acknowledged that the "knowledge and wisdom" of Lieutenant Colonel Michael Eisenstadt, a senior fellow at WINEP, "has contributed much toward our future plans and strategy."

This pro-Israel contribution was evident in Dayton's remarks. The main purpose of creating these forces, according to Dayton, was "to allay Israeli fears about the nature and capabilities of the Palestinian security forces." Thus, Dayton noted, no training or equipment was provided to these Palestinian forces "unless it has been thoroughly coordinated with the state of Israel and they agree to it." Dayton explained that these forces were trained in Jordan so as to be far "away from clan, family, and political influences," or, in other words, not to expose them to charges of collaboration by having them trained by US mercenaries nearer home. Despite its initial hesitation about the United States creating these professionalized Palestinian security forces, Israel quickly came to realize their utility. According to Dayton, "the performance of these Jordan-trained graduates in Jenin, which was their first deployment, was so impressive that six months later, the IDF not only allowed the reinforcement in Hebron, but led it, facilitated it, and extended it."

Most damning of all, Dayton revealed that his forces had performed so well in the West Bank that the Israeli military was pleased to slough off security responsibilities to them to better concentrate its efforts on devastating the Gaza Strip during Operation Cast Lead. According to Dayton, "before the ground invasion, my IDF colleagues warned in confidence that massive civil unrest in the West Bank was coming. Some even predicted a third intifada—something they dreaded but were willing to risk to stop the rocket fire against southern Israel. Yet as it turned out, none of these predictions were true." Dayton attributed this lack of "massive civil unrest" during Israel's onslaught to the "new professionalism and competency of the new Palestinian security forces." The Israeli military, Dayton argued, felt that "they could trust them. As a matter of fact, a good portion of the Israeli army went off to Gaza from the West Bank—think about that for a minute—and the commander was absent for eight straight days. That shows the kind of trust they were putting in these people now." Thus, as the "Dayton forces" held down the fort in the West Bank, the Israeli military was able to more easily kill more than 1,400 Palestinians in the Gaza Strip.

Toward the end of his speech, Dayton cited an Israeli military official who was formerly skeptical of his efforts. This official now believed that "the USSC is doing a great job, and as the Palestinians do more, we [the Israelis] will do less." Dayton maintained that "those are words to live by and to make a reality." Dayton concluded that "peace through security is no longer an impossible dream," citing Theodore Herzl, the founder of the modern Zionist movement, as his inspiration for this motto. Herzl, Dayton reminded the audience, had similarly stated: "If you will it, it is not a dream."[40]

The irony of Dayton quoting Herzl to describe his mission was not lost on the Pentagon. Afterward, an officer on the Joint Chiefs of Staff told author Mark Perry, "We [in the United States] have reached new heights of supplication." A US Army colonel weighed in that the "Dayton forces" are "just a stupid idea—it makes us look like we're an extension of the Israeli occupation."[41] But if the Pentagon was dismissive about this program, which was run by the State Department, then its trainers and boosters were myopic about it, viewing the "Dayton forces" as a virtual panacea for resolving the Israeli-Palestinian conflict. For example, Steven White, a former senior advisor to the USSC, and P.J. Dermer, a former Army attaché to Israel, argued that the "Dayton forces" have been an "unalloyed success." They outlandishly claimed that the accomplishments of the USSC and the Palestinian security forces "have formed the foundation of every claim of progress made by successive US administrations in the Israeli-Palestinian conflict." Were it not for the fact that "Obama's Middle East team to date has sought to diminish Dayton's role rather than build on the USSC's successes in the field," then peace would be at hand, according to them. They denounced "Palestinian politicians, as well as many within the State Department" who "overly concerned themselves with the USSC's close relationship with Israel's security apparatus." They criticized those pesky Palestinian politicians and those bleeding hearts at the State Department for "behaving as though Israel's presence in the West Bank was solely something to decry rather than something to be mitigated through intense work with both sides."[42] If only the USSC could convince Palestinians and the rest of the US government that "mitigating" Israel's military occupation was the path toward peace, then US policy would be righted, in their view.

Even Dayton's knowledge that Palestinian security forces were torturing Palestinians was not sufficient reason to pull the plug on this ill-conceived program. "By the way, the intelligence guys are good," Dayton told lead Palestinian negotiator Saeb Erekat in a June 24, 2009 meeting. "The Israelis like them. They say they are giving as much as they are taking from them—but they are causing some problems for international donors because they are torturing people." Thus, in Dayton's eyes, the fact that Palestinian security forces were torturing Palestinians was not problematic; his only concern was that international donors were finding out about this torture. But, he started to explain, "Hamas does it . . .," at which point Erekat cut him off by stating, "That is not an excuse."[43]

Despite all of these obvious benefits to Israel of US bilateral aid to Palestinians, some over-zealous pro-Israel members of Congress continually railed against and worked to end this aid program, to the great consternation of Israel and its less rabid US supporters. At the height of the congressional frenzy that threatened Palestinians with sanctions and a cutoff of aid for pursuing UN membership, Representative Ileana Ros-Lehtinen, chair of the House Foreign Affairs Committee, called a transparently biased hearing in September 2011, which was composed solely of pro-Israel witnesses. However, the hearing, whose purpose was to lay the groundwork for legislation to ban US aid to Palestinians, backfired on Ros-Lehtinen. David Makovsky of the Washington Institute for Near East Policy testified at the hearing that "I am not convinced that a decision to cut off assistance to the PA is the best response, since I fear it would lead to the collapse of the Palestinian Authority." If this occurred, Makovsky fretted that the "previously unimaginable levels of Israeli-Palestinian security cooperation that have benefitted Palestinians and Israelis alike," made possible by US funding of the "Dayton forces," would fall by the wayside.[44] This sentiment was shared by the Israeli military. As the UN Educational, Scientific and Cultural Organization (UNESCO) prepared to vote on Palestinian membership in October 2011, Israeli brigadier general Nitzan Alon, "reflecting a consensus among Israeli defense officials," warned Congress against cutting off, or even decreasing, US aid to the Palestinians. "Stability in the region includes the ability of the Palestinian Authority to pay its salaries," he maintained. Therefore, "Reducing the Palestinians' ability to pay decreases security. American aid is relevant to this issue."[45]

These warnings scared off Congress from taking drastic action in the aftermath of Palestinians securing membership in UNESCO. However, this admittance of Palestinians to a UN agency did serve as a pretext for Congress to intensify its efforts to limit US aid to Palestinians, which, even before the Obama administration, was already the most conditioned, restricted, scrutinized, audited and vetted of any US foreign assistance program. In the 2012 budget, Congress reaffirmed the five perennial sections of the budget restricting US aid to Palestinians; these sections prohibit US funding to a future Palestinian state that does not meet stringent requirements, ban US funding for conducting business with the PA in Jerusalem, bar US funding to the Palestinian Broadcasting Corporation, vet all recipients of US aid to the West Bank and Gaza Strip for links to "terrorist activity" and prohibit US funding of the PA without the exercise of a presidential waiver. For good measure, Congress also added the banning of US aid to the PA if Palestinians obtained membership in the UN or one of its specialized agencies unless the secretary of state certified that it was in the "national security interest" of the United States to do so.[46]

If a large portion of US bilateral aid to Palestinians during the

Obama administration went to these nefarious purposes of inuring Palestinians to a model of "economic growth" within the confines of Israeli military occupation, building "separate and unequal" apartheid infrastructure for Palestinians in the West Bank and propping up Palestinian security forces to do Israel's dirty work, then at least the remainder of US aid to Palestinians was devoted to the better aim of providing for the humanitarian needs of Palestinian refugees. Pro-Israel members of Congress unleashed a deluge of attacks against UNRWA, recklessly accusing the UN agency of everything from promoting anti-Semitism, to supporting terrorism, to deliberately perpetuating the status of Palestinian refugees (who remain refugees only because Israel denies them their right of return). Nevertheless, under the Obama administration, the United States provided UNRWA with at least $713 million for food, health, and education of Palestinian refugees.

Perhaps the most of many sinister efforts by members of Congress to restrict or eliminate US aid to UNRWA during the Obama administration was undertaken by Senator Mark Kirk (R-IL). He proposed an amendment to the 2013 State Department and Foreign Operations appropriations bill that would narrowly define for US policy purposes a Palestinian refugee "as a person whose place of residence was Palestine between June 1946 and May 1948, who was personally displaced as a result of the 1948 or 1967 Arab-Israeli conflicts, who currently does not reside in the West Bank or Gaza and who is not a citizen of any other state."[47] By attempting to define Palestinian refugees in this narrow way, Kirk sought to strip refugee status from millions of Palestinians in the hope of eventually having the United States defund UNRWA. But the gambit backfired. The State Department urged the Senate to reject the amendment on the grounds that "the status of Palestinian refugees is one of the most sensitive final status issues confronting Israel and the Palestinians; it strikes a deep, emotional, chord among Palestinians." Therefore, the State Department "cannot support legislation which would force the United States to make a public judgment on the number and status of Palestinian refugees."[48] The resulting compromise amendment only called on the State Department to report on how many refugees were born prior to 1948, but not to judge whether their descendants are also entitled to refugee status.

The saga of attempts to further restrict or end US aid to the Palestinians during Obama's first term concluded on this unscrupulous note, with pro-Israel members of Congress attempting to chip away at US funding of UNRWA and only grudgingly accepting ongoing US bilateral aid to the Palestinians after the Palestinians had defied their threats and sought UN membership. Meanwhile, with Congress and the Obama administration working hand in glove to elevate the US-Israeli military relationship to unprecedented levels, it would be logical to assume that Israel's value as a strategic ally of the United States remained unquestioned. However, interestingly enough, even as US-Israel military ties deepened during the Obama administration, Israel's strategic value to the United States came under question to a greater extent than ever before.

CHAPTER NINE

Anti-American Sentiment Fomented by US Favoritism for Israel

ISRAEL'S STRATEGIC VALUE TO THE UNITED STATES

B uried in Section 227 of the report filed by the House Armed Services Committee on the 2013 National Defense Authorization Act, there is a remarkable admission from members of Congress that some US largesse to Israel has had no strategic benefit to the United States. In its report, the committee mandated that the US Missile Defense Agency establish "a program office for cooperative missile defense efforts on the Iron Dome system to ensure long-term cooperation on this program." Evidently this collaboration from Israel had not been forthcoming voluntarily. The committee noted that "the total US taxpayer investment in this [Iron Dome] system will amount to nearly $900.0 million since fiscal year 2011, yet," quite remarkably, "the United States has no rights to the technology involved." In other words, rather than being a jointly researched and developed short-range anti-missile system that would benefit both the United States and Israel as advertised, Iron Dome was instead a nearly $1 billion cash cow for the Israeli weapons manufacturer Rafael, which was milking the US taxpayer for its handout. Before disbursing more money for Iron Dome, the House Armed Services Committee called on the Pentagon to ensure "that the United States has appropriate rights to this technology for United States defense purposes." The committee also urged the Pentagon to "explore any opportunity to enter into co-production of the Iron Dome system with Israel, in light of the significant US investment in this system," so that US weapons manufacturers could get a slice of the pie too.[1]

But if one listened to members of Congress on May 19, 2010, debating H.R.5327, the US-Israel Rocket and Missile Defense Cooperation and Support Act, a bill which would later inspire Congress to begin appropriating money for Israel to purchase Iron Dome batteries, then one could be forgiven for assuming that the strategic value to the United States of its military relationship with Israel was unquestionable. That day, members of Congress waxed fondly about the manifold benefits to the United States of the US-Israel military relationship, despite their candid admission two years later that the United States was gaining nothing from its investment in Iron Dome.

During this debate, which took place a little more than one year after Israel's Operation Cast Lead had killed more than 1,400 Palestinians in the Gaza Strip and less than two weeks before Israel would attack the Gaza Freedom Flotilla in international waters, killing nine humanitarian activists, Representative Ted Poe argued that "Israel is a stabilizing force" in the Middle East. Poe maintained that the massive US arming of Israel served as a way for the United States to project its power, because "our alliance with Israel is a force multiplier in a region of great strategic importance to not only Israel but the United States."

Representative Glenn Nye (D-VA), the sponsor of the bill, took this line of reasoning one step further, holding that Israel's actions actually promoted US security. "A safe homeland begins abroad," Nye contended, "and Israel has long been central to that security." Just as US funding for the "Dayton forces" of the Palestinian Authority Security Forces allowed Israel to subcontract its security so that it could better concentrate its military forces, Israel served a similar function in US strategic thinking, according to Nye. He reasoned that "it is because of Israel's strength and cooperation that the US no longer has to constantly keep a carrier strike group in the Mediterranean, allowing us to use our forces more judiciously."

Israel is, after all, strategically located in a region replete with avowed enemies of the US, members of Congress reasoned. In the words of Representative Steve Rothman (D-NJ), Israel is situated in "a bad neighborhood. A lot of the actors who would want to hurt Americans around the world and on US soil are inspired, if not financed, from that region." This geographical fact means that "the national security of the State of Israel is critically important to the national security of the United States of America," Rothman contended.[2] Members of Congress overwhelmingly agreed with these sentiments, voting 410-4 the next day to authorize the United States to approve funding for Iron Dome.[3]

It is understandable that members of Congress would regurgitate these types of often tautological arguments praising the supposed value to the United States of the US-Israel military relationship, since senior Obama administration officials responsible for security and military affairs often argued along similar, but more sophisticated, lines. For example, James Jones, who served at the time as Obama's National Security Advisor, told the Washington Institute for Near East Policy in April 2010 that joint US-Israeli military exercises constitute "essential elements of our regional security approach, because many of the same forces that threaten Israel also threaten the United States." Beyond these joint threats, Jones related to this pro-Israel audience that "from long experience" he knew "that our security relationship with Israel is important for America." This relationship was important, Jones argued, because "our military benefits from Israeli innovations in technology, from shared intelligence, from exercises that help our readiness and joint training that enhances our capabilities and from lessons learned in Israel's own battles against terrorism and asymmetric threats," not to mention Israel's field testing of new US weapons systems against Palestinian civilians. In this partnership, Jones stated, the United States and Israel are "working together for our shared security and prosperity."[4]

Andrew Shapiro, assistant secretary of state for political-military affairs, maintained that the US-Israel military relationship was a win-win. "We are fully committed to Israel's security because it enhances our own national security," he claimed. Beyond those reasons articulated by Jones, the relationship directly benefited US war-making capabilities, according to Shapiro. "Israeli-origin equipment deployed on Iraqi and Afghan battlefields are [sic] protecting American troops every day. This includes armor plating technology for US military vehicles and unique medical solutions such as the 'Israeli bandage'—a specially designed antibiotic-treated dressing that has been used widely by our men and women in Iraq and Afghanistan." He also noted that Israeli weaponry employed by the US military in Iraq and Afghanistan "includes sensors, surveillance equipment, unmanned aerial vehicle technology, and detection devices to seek out IED's [improvised explosive devices]." Although it is highly debatable whether the US wars against Iraq and Afghanistan have made people in the United States more secure, Shapiro concluded that "many such partnerships and investments between our two governments and US and Israeli defense firms have yielded important groundbreaking innovations that ultimately make us all safer."[5]

But if Israeli military technology undeniably benefited US war-making capabilities, especially through the development of drones, and if Israel provided the United States with important intelligence and counter-terrorism coordination, a claim whose benefits are difficult to assess given the classified nature of this information, then it was also true that a number of different factors led to a widespread reassessment of Israel's strategic value to the United States during the Obama administration. These factors included a new evaluation from within the upper ranks of the US military and political establishment that Israel's unwillingness to engage in credible negotiations to end its military occupation of Palestinian land made it a strategic burden on, rather than an asset for, US objectives in the Middle East, especially in relation to the fight against al-Qaeda and the wars in Iraq and Afghanistan. In addition, the interests and policy preferences of the United States toward Turkey, Arab countries and Iran visibly clashed with the actions and hoped-for policy outcomes of Israel and its cadre of supporters in the United States, a confrontation which led to increasingly diverging strategic trajectories between the two countries.

The first sign of this reassessment came on January 16, 2010. On that day, General David Petraeus, commander of Central Command (CENTCOM)—one of ten US combatant commands within the US military, with an area of responsibility (AOR) that covers twenty countries, including all Arab countries (minus North Africa), Iran, Afghanistan, Pakistan and Central Asia[6]—sent senior military officials from his staff to brief Joint Chiefs of Staff Chairman Admiral Michael Mullen on the strategic implications for the United States of the ongoing Israeli-Palestinian conflict. According to author Mark Perry, this "unprecedented" briefing "stunned" Mullen. "The briefers reported that there was a growing perception among Arab leaders that the US was incapable of standing up to Israel, that CENTCOM's mostly Arab constituency was losing faith in American promises, [and] that Israeli intransigence on the Israeli-Palestinian conflict was jeopardizing US standing in the region." To gain greater control over the situation, Petraeus proposed to Mullen that Occupied Palestinian Territory, which, along with Israel, was attached to the military's European Command, now be given over to CENTCOM.[7] Although Mullen rejected this suggested change, a former diplomat who favored attaching both Israel and Occupied Palestinian Territory to CENTCOM confirmed that Mullen's reaction was one of "astonishment" when briefed "on the effects of our slavish policy of doing everything the Israelis say and giving them everything they want."[8]

An even harsher message was allegedly carried directly to Prime Minister Netanyahu by Vice President Biden during his March 2010 visit to Israel. After Biden was publicly humiliated by Netanyahu, whose government announced the expansion of an East Jerusalem settlement during Biden's trip, Biden reportedly told Netanyahu behind closed doors, "This is starting to get dangerous for us." Referring to Israeli settlement expansion and the absence of a credible negotiating process with the Palestinians, the vice president claimed, "What you're doing here undermines the security of our troops who are fighting in Iraq, Afghanistan and Pakistan. That endangers us and it endangers regional peace." Although an Obama administration official would claim on March 16, 2010 that this account of the meeting, published in the Israeli newspaper *Yediot Ahronot*, was "absolutely not accurate," that very same day Petraeus would testify to similar, but more diplomatically expressed, sentiments before Congress.[9]

In his written statement submitted to the Senate Armed Services Committee on "The Posture of US Central Command," Petraeus warned, "The enduring hostilities between Israel and some of its neighbors present distinct challenges to our ability to advance our interests in the AOR." He noted that "Israeli-Palestinian tensions often flare into violence and large-scale armed confrontations." Petraeus saw the Israeli-Palestinian conflict as negatively affecting

US interests in four ways. First, "The conflict foments anti-American sentiment, due to" what he delicately referred to as "a perception of US favoritism for Israel." Second, "Arab anger over the Palestinian question limits the strength and depth of US partnerships with governments and peoples in the AOR and weakens the legitimacy of moderate regimes in the Arab world." Little did Petraeus know at the time how prophetic his words would become. Less than one year later, the Arab Spring would undermine and eventually overthrow "moderate regimes in the Arab world," a US euphemism for dictatorial regimes like Hosni Mubarak's in Egypt that acquiesced in or actively advanced US and Israeli agendas, such as the blockade of the Gaza Strip. Third, Petraeus argued that "al-Qaeda and other militant groups exploit that anger [over Palestinian suffering at the hands of Israel] to mobilize support." Fourth, he contended, "The conflict also gives Iran influence in the Arab world through its clients, Lebanese Hizballah and Hamas," thereby strengthening the hand of this long-standing US nemesis.[10]

According to a former US diplomat, Petraeus's testimony on Capitol Hill highlighted that "obviously there is a lot of daylight between us. The interests of Israel and the United States do not overlap, and sometimes they clash." This testimony sent "shock effects through AIPAC because they know that they can control everything" in the political system, "but they cannot control" the military, the former diplomat added. "It really scared them, because if there is a wedge between American and Israeli interests that is perceived and accepted by the American public, then all the work of AIPAC goes down the drain." The former diplomat continued: "CENTCOM, when I worked there, seemed to get that Israeli and American interests were divergent, and that when they diverge, that sometimes for political reasons, Israel's interests would trump American interests. This is what Petraeus was trying to say in the gentlest way he could without setting off more fireworks than he did."[11]

But more fireworks would go off one month later during a press conference following a forty-nine-nation Nuclear Security Summit convened in Washington by the Obama administration. There the president asserted, "It is a vital national security interest of the United States to reduce," but not eliminate, struggles such as the Israeli-Palestinian conflict, "because whether we like it or not, we remain a dominant military superpower, and when conflicts break out, one way or another we get pulled into them. And that ends up costing us significantly in terms of both blood and treasure."[12] This seemingly impromptu remark by Obama was anything but off-the-cuff, reflecting a carefully calibrated and deliberate policy shift that had "resulted from a lengthy debate among his top officials over how best to balance support for Israel against other American interests,"[13] according to the *New York Times*.

This growing US discomfiture with Israel's policies negatively affecting US strategic interests even seeped into a December 2011 speech delivered by Defense Secretary Leon Panetta before a largely pro-Israel crowd at the high-profile annual forum of the Brookings Institution's Saban Center for Middle East Policy. In an address otherwise devoted to highlighting the advances in the US-Israeli military relationship during the Obama administration and reaffirming "the determination of the United States to safeguard Israel's security," Panetta nevertheless issued a stark warning to Israel. He noted that "in every strong relationship built on trust, built on friendship, built on mutual security, it demands that both sides work towards the same common goals. And Israel, too, has responsibility to pursue our shared goals to build regional support for Israel and the United States' security objectives." But Panetta lamented that "over the past year we have seen Israel's isolation from its traditional security partners in the region grow, and the pursuit of a comprehensive Middle East peace has effectively been put on hold." Although Panetta did not place sole blame on Israel for its growing isolation from US allies such as Turkey, Egypt and Jordan, he did call on Israel to do more to "reach out and mend fences with those who share an interest in regional stability." When asked about "Israel's responsibility towards peace" and the steps it should take now to achieve it, Panetta bluntly replied: "Just get to the damn [negotiating] table," an assertion he repeated to surprising applause from the audience.[14]

These remarks by Panetta, Petraeus, Biden and Obama, taken as a whole, represented a veritable sea change in thinking at the most senior political and military levels of the Obama administration about the supposed benefits accrued to the United States from the US-Israel relationship. By publicly noting that Israel's actions placed the United States in the uncomfortable position of having to choose sides between its different allies in the Middle East, by contending that US policies toward Israel hampered US war objectives in the region, and by implicating Israel's policies as being detrimental to the safety of US soldiers and civilians, the Obama administration took a position diametrically opposed to the often facile claims made by members of Congress that Israel was an unadulterated boon to US strategic interests. However, the Obama administration's correct diagnosis of the problem did not prompt it to reevaluate its policies toward Israel. On the contrary, by continuing to strengthen the US-Israel military relationship even while acknowledging the ever-increasing divergence between Israel's policies and US strategic interests, the Obama administration reinforced a dynamic that perversely rewarded Israel for often working at cross-purposes with the United States. The Obama administration's unwillingness to use its extensive leverage with Israel to force it to fall into line with larger US regional interests was a primary reason that it failed to achieve its goal of Israeli-Palestinian peace.

A military commission trial at Guantánamo Bay, Cuba drove home the point that US support for Israel had a deleterious impact on the safety of people in the United States. In a March 2009 pro se filing, Khalid Sheikh Mohammed, the self-professed mastermind of the September 11, 2001, terrorist attacks against the United States, and his fellow al-Qaeda defendants, explained that their desire to strike the United States was inspired, in part, by US aid to Israel. In attempting, but failing, to justify their attacks against US civilians, they accused the United States of "attacking us in Palestine and Lebanon by providing political, military, and economic support to the terrorist state of Israel, which in turn, is attacking unarmed inno-cent civilians." The defendants also accused Israel of "causing grave bodily harm by using weapons that are forbidden internationally, such as: cluster bombs in Lebanon and the rubber and live ammuni-tions in Palestine and breaking bones of Palestinian children." They also claimed that the United States has "violated the law of war by supporting the Israeli occupation of Arab land in Palestine and Lebanon, and for displacing five million Palestinians outside their land. You have supported the oppressor over the oppressed and the butcher over the victim."[15] While deliberately attacking civilians is never justifiable under international law, these statements would be the clearest indication during Obama's first term that the United States had paid a devastating price on September 11 in part for its backing of Israel.

There is no public evidence that the Obama administration's reassessment of the strategic value of Israel to the United States resulted from the proceedings of the military commissions at Guantánamo Bay. Instead, it appears that the timing of the spate of public and private utterances cited above, clustered between January and April 2010, was linked more to the administration's frustration with Israel's lack of a meaningful settlement freeze and the humiliation it suffered during Biden's March 2010 trip. Although the Obama administration's public questioning of Israel's strategic value largely died down thereafter, there was no doubt that as Obama's first term in office progressed, both Israel's actions and regional developments beyond its control caused US and Israeli strategic interests to diverge further.

CONFLICTING INTERESTS

Even before Israel's assault on the Gaza Freedom Flotilla, Turkey's displeasure over Israel's attack on the Gaza Strip during Operation Cast Lead and its mounting frustration with Israel's intransigence in continuing to colonize Palestinian land impinged upon US strategic interests in the Middle East. For example, the United States indefinitely postponed a planned multinational military exercise scheduled to take place in Turkey in October 2009 following "a decision made by the government of Turkey to change the concept of the scenario in a way that would not enable the US to participate," stated Defense Department Secretary Geoff Morrell. In other words, he explained, "frankly speaking, Israel was removed from the exercise, from the list of participating nations, and the US government believes it is inappropriate for any nation to be removed at the last minute."[16] Turkey's disinviting of Israel from this multinational exercise reflected the degree to which the Turkish-Israeli military relationship had already sunk during the Obama administration, after having reached its pinnacle in the 1990s and 2000s, when Turkey awarded Israeli weapons manufacturers major contracts and the Israeli air force used Turkish airspace for training purposes.

Israel's attack on the Gaza Freedom Flotilla on May 31, 2010, which resulted in Israeli naval commandoes killing eight Turkish citizens and one US citizen of Turkish heritage, exacerbated this already strained relationship, especially after Israel repeatedly refused to apologize for its actions. As noted in Chapter 7, the United States responded to this assault by attempting to scuttle a UN Human Rights Council investigation that sought accountability for Israel's attack on the flotilla. Instead, it favored the establishment of the admittedly politicized Palmer Panel, whose mandate from the UN secretary general was not to promote international legal mechanisms to hold Israel accountable, but rather to prevent similar occurrences in the future and reconcile the findings and recommendations of separate Turkish and Israeli domestic investigations.

However, after Turkey and Israel released the results of their internal investigations and predictably came to polar opposite conclusions about Israel's attack on the flotilla, the United States found itself in the unenviable position of trying to explain how both of its allies' reports could be credible if they were diametrically conflicting. On January 26, 2011, Assistant Secretary of State Crowley termed Israel's domestic investigation "transparent and independent." When asked if he would "use the same adjectives to describe the Turkish report," Crowley demurred, stating "that Turkey has put forward its own good-faith effort." Pressed further as to why Turkey's report was "directly at odds with the Israeli report," Crowley tried to square the circle by reasoning that "given the incident and the circumstances, I don't think that we're surprised that there are differing views of what transpired. That is expressly why we support the UN panel so that we can take the Turkish perspective, and it has a valid perspective; we can take the Israeli perspective, it has a valid perspective; and together, try to fully understand what happened." But if both countries had a "valid perspective," then why would the United States "not use the same words to describe the Turkish report as the Israelis'?" Finally, Crowley conceded that Turkey also had "an independent, credible report. I'm not challenging either one."[17]

If the United States cringed at the prospect of refereeing the competing legal and political claims stemming from the Turkish and Israeli domestic investigations, then Turkey's dissatisfaction with the Palmer Panel, whose results were published in September 2011, threatened to place the United States in an even more hazardous strategic situation. On September 8, 2011, Turkish Prime Minister Recep Tayyip Erdoğan noted that Turkey still had humanitarian aid to deliver to the Gaza Strip. He vowed that "our humanitarian aid will not be attacked anymore, as happened to the *Mavi Marmara*." He was prepared to back up this promise by stating that, in the future, "Turkish warships will be tasked with protecting the Turkish boats bringing humanitarian aid to the Gaza Strip."[18] Although this scenario failed to materialize, the mere possibility of the Turkish and Israeli navies colliding in the Mediterranean Sea provoked grave consternation at the State Department.

Were Israel to attack Turkish naval ships, Turkey, which has been a member of the North Atlantic Treaty Organization (NATO) since 1951, could conceivably invoke Article 5 of the treaty. This treaty article states that an attack upon a NATO member "shall be considered an attack against them all" and obligates NATO members to "assist the Party or Parties so attacked by taking forthwith, individually and in concert with the other Parties, such action as it deems necessary, including the use of armed force" against the non-NATO member.[19] Thus if tensions between Turkey and Israel continued to mount and culminated in an exchange of fire, then the United States eventually could find itself torn between breaking its NATO obligations or attacking Israel. To avoid these nightmarish "hypothetical places that we don't want this situation to get to," State Department spokesperson Victoria Nuland noted the next day that the United States was working actively with the hope of seeing "both sides cool it and get back to a place where they can have a productive relationship."[20]

Even if the Israeli-Turkish relationship did not deteriorate to the point of war, Turkey still had opportunities to block Israel's participation in NATO and other multinational forums, against the wishes of the United States. For example, the consensus-based decision-making process of NATO allowed Turkey in April 2012 to block Israel's participation in NATO's summit in Chicago the following month, "unless they issue a formal apology and pay compensation for the Turkish citizens their commandos killed in international waters," according to a senior Turkish official. "Those countries," including the United States, "who wish to see normalization in ties between Turkey and Israel should advise Israel" to fulfill these Turkish demands.[21] But since the United States was not willing to pressure Israel to apologize and pay compensation, there was little leverage it could exert on Turkey to lift its veto. Asked if it were important to the United States for Israel to participate in the NATO summit, State Department spokesperson Victoria Nuland balked at directly responding. Instead, she only would insist that "it's important that we come to a consensus agreement at NATO about a strong partnership aspect of this summit."[22]

Similarly, in June 2012, upon Turkey's request, the United States barred Israel from participating in the first meeting in Istanbul of the recently created Global Counterterrorism Forum (GCTF), a multinational body of twenty-nine states and the European Union organized by the State Department and co-chaired by Turkey. According to one account in the Israeli newspaper *Globes*, "Israel tried hard to obtain an invitation to the meeting, and its exclusion, despite the tight US-Israeli intelligence ties, has greatly disappointed officials in Jerusalem."[23] On July 10, 2012, Patrick Ventrell, director of the State Department's press office, reiterated, "We've discussed the GCTF and ways to involve Israel and its activities on a number of occasions, and we're committed to making this happen." However, he repeatedly refused to divulge what, if any, concrete steps the United States was taking to overcome Turkey's objection to Israel's participation.[24] In the end, Israel participated neither in the NATO summit nor in the GCTF.

Esther Brimmer, assistant secretary of state for international organization affairs, could rightfully claim credit for the Obama administration's "far-reaching efforts to normalize Israel's status in and across the UN and broader multilateral system, and to counter head-on efforts of" what she termed the "de-legitimization" of Israel.[25] Nevertheless, it was also true, as evidenced by these cases, that the Obama administration was unwilling to go the mat to prevent Israel's isolation from these multilateral forums when a US strategic ally opposed its participation. Apparently, the Obama administration feared risking the wrath of Turkey, which by providing the United States with important military and humanitarian support in its efforts to overthrow regimes in Iraq, Libya and Syria, arguably proved of much greater strategic benefit to the United States than did Israel, whose own strategic value to the United

States appeared increasingly ephemeral, especially in light of the Arab Spring.

On December 17, 2010, a young Tunisian street vendor, Mohammed Bouazizi, enraged at the petty corruption and tyranny of the local police force, which had earlier impounded his cart after he failed to pay the requisite bribe, lit himself on fire in a desperate act of protest. As he doused his body in gasoline, little could he have foreseen that his death would literally provide the spark that would ignite the Arab world in protest against its sclerotic and dictatorial regimes, as millions of Arabs from Marrakesh to Manama took to the streets to demand freedom and democracy.

The Obama administration, like many long-standing Arab regimes that now found themselves the objects of mass protest and revolt, was caught flat-footed, resulting in a chaotic, disjointed, inconsistent and unprincipled policy response. The United States abandoned or helped to ease out of power rulers traditionally aligned with US foreign policy interests (Tunisia, Egypt and Yemen), armed other friendly rulers to crack down on dissent (Bahrain), ignored altogether the authoritarian records of other allies (Saudi Arabia and Oman), while providing overt and behind-the-scenes support to armed insurrections (Libya and Syria). As events unfolded, Obama tried unconvincingly to plaster a veneer of universal rights onto this haphazard US policy toward the Arab Spring. Speaking at the State Department five months after the outbreak of the protests, Obama stated categorically that the United States "opposes the use of violence and repression against the people of the region. We support a set of universal rights. Those rights include free speech; the freedom of peaceful assembly; freedom of religion; equality for men and women under the rule of law; and the right to choose your own leaders." Moreover, US "support for these principles is not a secondary interest—today I am making it clear that it is a top priority that must be translated into concrete actions, and supported by all of the diplomatic, economic and strategic tools at our disposal."[26]

Although Obama immediately airbrushed Palestinians out of this regional picture and absolved the United States from following these supposed "universal rights" as its policy guidepost for its stance toward Israel's human rights abuses of Palestinians, the president did not shy away from warning Israel and its supporters that a new era had emerged. For example, just three days following his speech on the Arab Spring at the State Department, Obama told AIPAC that one of "the facts we all must confront," rather than celebrate, was that "a new generation of Arabs is reshaping the region. A just and lasting peace can no longer be forged with one or two Arab leaders. Going forward, millions of Arab citizens have to see that peace is possible for that peace to be sustained."[27] In other words, the era of the United States and Israel, in the words of "peace process" negotiator Dennis Ross, "selling" their policy agenda to pliant, corrupt dictators was now officially over.

This stark realization accounted for the tepid, if not nervous, response of Israel and its supporters in the United States to the Arab Spring. Suddenly, the anti-democratic regional system of governments from which it benefited was being upended by popular protest. This revolution carried with it both profound practical ramifications for Israel's policies toward the Palestinians and philosophical challenges to Israel's strategic relationship with the United States.

On the operative level, the most immediate challenge of the Arab Spring to Israel's policies toward the Palestinians stemmed from the US abandonment and subsequent ouster of Egyptian president Hosni Mubarak. This stunning development called into question the viability of Israel maintaining its nearly hermetically sealed blockade of the Gaza Strip at its previous level. Without the Mubarak regime's acquiescence, and even active participation, in enforcing Israel's blockade, as was revealed by Wikileaks and documented in Chapter 1, it would have been impossible for Israel to control the flow of people and goods between the Gaza Strip and Egypt to the extent that it did.

After Mubarak's overthrow, bowing to popular opinion that seethed with the knowledge that Egypt had been complicit in the Israeli blockade of the Gaza Strip, the Egyptian Supreme Council of the Armed Forces (SCAF) announced in May 2011 the liberalization of the Rafah border crossing to now allow for the exit of Palestinian women and children, as well as men above the age of forty.[28] Although this move did nothing to ease the Israeli blockade on products entering or exiting the Gaza Strip, as the Rafah border crossing does not have a commercial terminal, it nevertheless symbolized a break from past Egyptian policies. Beyond such workaday Israeli preoccupations with the ramifications of the overthrow of the ancien régime in the Arab world, the onset of the Arab Spring presented Israel and its supporters in the United States with a conceptual quandary in its attempts to continue to justify the US-Israel "special relationship." To squarely align US policy with Israel's interests against those of Arab countries, Israel's supporters in the United States have relied on a hodgepodge of shifting rationales throughout the decades. Until the Soviet Union collapsed in 1991, the argument that Israel served US interests as a beachhead against the expansion of Communism in the Middle East did the trick quite well for a public that generally viewed US foreign policy through a simplistic Cold War prism. The tragedy of the September 11 attacks against the United States presented a new opportunity for Israel and its supporters to replace this anachronistic line of reasoning. As Israeli prime minister Ariel Sharon told Secretary of State Colin Powell two days after the terrorist attacks, Palestinian Authority president Yasser "Arafat is our Bin Laden."[29] In other words, the "special relationship" was vindicated because the United States and Israel supposedly shared a common enemy in international terrorism. But with General David Petraeus and Khalid Sheikh Mohammed separately maintaining that US support for Israel was actually a windfall for the recruiting efforts of al-Qaeda and a motivating factor to attack the United States, this argument lost its salience.

Therefore, during the Obama administration, the argument that the United States and Israel shared a set of values, the most important of which was democracy, took on additional prominence as a justification for the US-Israel strategic relationship. But the Arab Spring threatened to eviscerate the specious claim that "Israel is the only democracy in the Middle East." Of course, Israel is a democracy only in the sense that apartheid South Africa was a democracy for its privileged white voting populace. Since its establishment in 1948, Israel has ruled over Palestinians through a similar apartheid system, in which those of the "wrong" nationality or religion have received lesser or no political rights. Despite this fact, Israel and its supporters had largely convinced public opinion in the United States that this plucky little island of democracy thrives amidst a sea of barbaric totalitarianism. As the Arab Spring presented US audiences with the entirely different spectacle of millions of Arabs demanding, and tens of thousands dying for, the values of freedom and democracy that the United States claims to hold dear, not only were Israel's pretensions to uniqueness in the region becoming precarious, but its apartheid policies toward Palestinians were also coming into bolder relief.

If the Arab Spring presented Israel and its supporters in the United States with the new challenge of maintaining the special US-Israeli strategic relationship based on supposed "shared values," then competing US and Israeli approaches toward Iran's program of nuclear enrichment also widened the gap between the strategic interests of the two countries. It was true that the Obama administration and Israel agreed that Iran obtaining a nuclear weapon was an outcome that both states would not countenance. In addition, both countries actively pressed for the implementation of comprehensive US and international sanctions against the Iranian economy to pressure Iran's government to abandon its nuclear enrichment program. Also, Obama did continue a Bush-era joint covert operation, code-named Olympic Games, between the National Security Agency, the Central Intelligence Agency and Israel that successfully sabotaged Iran's centrifuges through malware dubbed Stuxnet.[30] However, it was also evident that the United States and Israel drew vastly different conclusions about whether Iran would attempt to weaponize its enriched uranium, how quickly it could succeed at doing so if the decision were made to pursue nuclear weapons, how much time and effort should be devoted to finding a diplomatic resolution to the conflict and whether employing force, either by the United States, Israel or in tandem, should be considered an immediate policy option or a last resort.

Within these parameters and tightly constrained options, the Obama administration generally tended to favor a combination of grinding sanctions—specifically targeting Iranian energy, banking and transportation sectors, exacting a heavy toll on the Iranian economy—limited rounds of multinational diplomacy and repeated threats that "all options are on the table," with the ultimate option being the "military component."[31] Meanwhile, Israel tended to play down the prospects of success stemming from sanctions or diplomacy and warned that time was running out for Israel to launch an offensive to attack Iran's nuclear enrichment facilities. Israeli defense minister Ehud Barak cautioned that Iran "is steadily approaching maturation and is verging on a 'zone of immunity'—a position from which the Iranian regime could complete its program without effective disruption, at its convenience."[32]

These contrasting policy positions on Iran's nuclear enrichment program came to a head at the 2012 AIPAC policy conference. There Obama stated that "I firmly believe that an opportunity still remains for diplomacy—backed by pressure—to succeed." He abhorred that there was "too much loose talk of war. Over the last few weeks, such talk has only benefited the Iranian government, by driving up the price of oil, which they depend on to fund their nuclear program. For the sake of Israel's security, America's security, and the peace and security of the world, now is not the time for bluster. Now is the time to let our increased pressure sink in, and to sustain the broad international coalition we have built" in favor of sanctions and diplomacy.[33] Netanyahu, however, adopted a more bellicose approach, maintaining, "For the last decade, the international community has tried diplomacy. It hasn't worked. For six years, the international community has applied sanctions. That hasn't worked either. I appreciate President Obama's recent efforts to impose even tougher sanctions against Iran." Netanyahu conceded, "Those sanctions are hurting Iran's economy. But unfortunately, Iran's nuclear march goes on. Israel has waited patiently for the international community to resolve this issue . . . None of us can afford to wait much longer."[34]

But if the Obama administration appeared in no hurry to attack Iran, then members of Congress would pressure the president to provide Israel with the weapons that military experts deemed necessary for Israel to have a chance to successfully strike Iran on its own and disrupt its nuclear enrichment program. In June and July 2012, the Senate and House respectively passed the AIPAC-inspired resolution S.2165, the United States–Israel Enhanced Security Cooperation Act of 2012. This resolution found that "a nuclear-weapons capable Iran would fundamentally threaten vital United States interests" and called upon the United States to furnish Israel with "air refueling tankers" and "specialized munitions," such as "bunker buster" bombs, to penetrate reinforced concrete structures located underground.[35] As of this writing, the United States and

Israel were unable to reconcile their competing strategic approaches to Iran's nuclear enrichment program.

The reassessment of Israel's strategic benefit to the United States begun during the Obama administration was impelled by multiple factors. These included a growing US impatience toward Israel's military occupation and colonization of Palestinian territory, a realization that Israel's policies toward the Palestinians endangered US counter-terrorism efforts and set back US war-making objectives, and a recognition of the divergent US and Israeli perceptions of regional developments such as the Arab Spring. It would be tempting to attribute this reassessment of the US-Israeli strategic relationship to a clash of personalities between the two countries' leaders. There certainly was no love lost between them, as evidenced by the embarrassing "hot mic" incident in November 2011 during which Obama was overheard telling French president Nicolas Sarkozy, "You're sick of him [Netanyahu]—but I have to deal with him every day!"[36]

But crediting this widening gap solely to two individual policy-makers' penchant for confrontation with one another is an overly simplistic and reductionist argument. It neglects a more fundamental and systematic reorientation that is underway. This reorientation did not escape notice in a landmark policy paper on the subject published in 2011 by Haim Malka, senior fellow and deputy director of the Middle East Program at the Center for Strategic and International Studies (CSIS), an inside-the-Beltway, mainstream think tank. In his paper, entitled "Crossroads: The Future of the US-Israel Strategic Partnership," Malka bemoaned the fact that "uncertainty is growing about how the United States and Israel can and should cooperate to secure their interests and confront common challenges in a region undergoing dramatic shifts. Even more profoundly, Americans and Israelis increasingly see each other's policy choices as undermining their interests." He warned that this "trend deepens US doubts of Israel's strategic value and reinforces Israeli fears about US commitments and guarantees to its security."[37]

Thus, as the Obama administration's first term came to a close, it had paradoxically strengthened the US-Israeli military relationship to unprecedented levels while at the same time questioning the strategic rationale for this relationship. This irony was testament to the fact that the deepening of the US-Israeli military relationship during Obama's first term was more of a political sop to Israel and its supporters—intended to counter charges that the president was too tough on Israeli settlements—than a component of a coherent strategic foreign policy vision for the Middle East.

CHAPTER TEN

We Don't Do Gandhi Very Well

On February 4, 2010, US officials met with Israeli Major General Avi Mizrachi, general officer commanding of the Israeli army's Central Command, its branch which was responsible for Israeli military units in the occupied Palestinian West Bank. According to US officials, Mizrachi "expressed frustration with on-going demonstrations in the West Bank." He warned that the Israeli military "will start to be more assertive in how it deals with these demonstrations, even demonstrations that appear peaceful." After viewing two of what Mizrachi dubbed "so-called peaceful demonstrations," he was dumbfounded by these protests, stating that "he did not know what they were about; the villages were not near the barrier [Israel's illegal West Bank wall] and they had no problems with movement or settlers." Why in the world would these Palestinians have any cause to protest after living under Israeli military occupation for forty-three years, he seemed to wonder. Regardless, in Mizrachi's view they must not be allowed to proceed. He warned his US interlocutors "that he will start sending his trucks with 'dirty water' to break up these protests, even if they are not violent, because they serve no purpose other than creating friction." As the US embassy in Tel Aviv noted, "dirty water" was the Israeli military's "chemically treated water that duplicates the effects of skunk spray." This exchange was a perfectly candid example of what Israeli Defense Ministry official Amos Gilad meant when he had earlier told US officials that "we don't do Gandhi very well."[1]

OBAMA ON NONVIOLENCE

Exactly eight months prior to this meeting of US officials with Mizrachi, President Barack Obama, still riding high on a wave of international popularity, and just four months shy of his controversial nomination for the Nobel Peace Prize, stood before a packed theater at Cairo University on June 4, 2009 to deliver a speech that he hoped would reset US relations with the Muslim world, which had sunk to their calamitous nadir under his predecessor's watch. "I've come here to Cairo," the president asserted, "to seek a new beginning between the United States and Muslims around the world, one based on mutual interest and mutual respect, and one based upon the truth that America and Islam are not exclusive and need not be in competition. Instead, they overlap, and share common principles—principles of justice and progress; tolerance and the dignity of all human beings."

As part of his commitment "to seek a new beginning," Obama expressed unprecedented sympathy on the part of a sitting US president for the plight of the Palestinian people. The president affirmed that it was "undeniable that the Palestinian people—Muslims and Christians—have suffered in pursuit of a homeland. For more than sixty years they've endured the pain of dislocation. Many wait in refugee camps in the West Bank, Gaza, and neighboring lands for a life of peace and security that they have never been able to lead. They endure the daily humiliations—large and small—that come with occupation." He characterized "the situation for the Palestinian people" as being "intolerable," vowing that "America will not turn our backs on the legitimate Palestinian aspiration for dignity, opportunity, and a state of their own." It was noteworthy that Obama mentioned not only the suffering of Palestinians under Israeli military occupation, but that he alluded also to their "displacement brought about by Israel's founding." Here was a US president who, with the possible exception of President Jimmy Carter, appeared most capable of empathizing with the Palestinian narrative as much as with the Israeli narrative, thereby dramatically raising global expectations for a more evenhanded US policy.

In a portion of the speech dedicated to the implications of an interconnected, globalized world, Obama held that "human history has often been a record of nations and tribes—and, yes, religions—subjugating one another in pursuit of their own interests. Yet in this new age, such attitudes are self-defeating. Given our interdependence, any world order that elevates one nation or group of people over another will inevitably fail." Although he did not directly reference the Israeli-Palestinian conflict in these statements, Obama's call for equality of peoples to take the place of national and religious superiority carried with it a profound moral obligation for the United States to finally act to dismantle Israel's apartheid policies toward Palestinians.

However, despite Obama recognizing both Palestinian suffering and the preeminence of equality as a guiding principle for international relations in an era of globalization, the president, in a topsy-turvy fashion, stressed that for Israeli-Palestinian "peace to come," the onus was first and foremost on Palestinian shoulders. He paternalistically lectured Palestinians that they "must abandon violence. Resistance through violence and killing is wrong and it does not succeed." Obama was mum, however, about Israel abandoning the state-sponsored, systematic and incomparably more devastating violence it inflicted against Palestinians with US-supplied weapons. Instead, Obama harkened back to successful examples of nonviolent struggles to assure Palestinians that this was the correct path to follow to achieve their human and national rights. He noted that "for centuries, black people in America suffered the lash of the whip as slaves and the humiliation of segregation. But it was not violence that won full and equal rights. It was a peaceful and determined insistence upon the ideals at the center of America's founding. This same story can be told by people from South Africa to South Asia; from Eastern Europe to Indonesia." For Obama, these examples illustrated "a story with a simple truth: that violence is a dead end." He concluded by haranguing Palestinians that "it is a sign neither of courage nor power to shoot rockets at sleeping children, or to blow up old women on a bus. That's not how moral authority is claimed; that's how it is surrendered."[2]

Undoubtedly, Obama was correct in his assessment that Palestinian violence deliberately targeted at Israeli civilians not only violated international law, but greatly eroded potential support for Palestinian human rights and self-determination. However, by subsuming all

Palestinian resistance to the category of terrorism, Obama was grossly mischaracterizing the overwhelmingly nonviolent nature of Palestinian resistance. This omission recalled the question asked repeatedly and snidely by Israel's supporters: "Where is the Palestinian Gandhi?" This crude taunt, which conveniently overlooks the fact that many Palestinian practitioners of nonviolence have been jailed, exiled or killed by Israel over the decades, is designed to reinforce a racist stereotype of Palestinians perpetuated by Israel's supporters. This stereotype suggests that Palestinians are inherently violent, genetically incapable of sublime acts of nonviolence, and therefore subhuman and undeserving of the universal rights to which all others are entitled. Deliberately or not, Obama was obfuscating more than a century of Palestinian nonviolent resistance, first to Zionism's and later to the State of Israel's encroachments upon their human and national rights.[3] Had Obama chosen to do so, he could have cited the recent widespread use of nonviolent strategies—from protests, to consumer boycotts, to tax strikes, to non-cooperation—that defined the first Palestinian intifada against Israeli military occupation from 1987 to 1991.[4]

Similarly, in his May 2011 encomium to the Arab Spring, Obama lauded the fact that "shouts of human dignity are being heard across the region. And through the moral force of non-violence, the people of the region have achieved more change in six months than terrorists have accomplished in decades." Noting that "we face an historic opportunity," Obama fully pledged to support the "moral force of non-violence" sweeping the Arab world. "We have embraced the chance to show that America values the dignity of the street vendor in Tunisia more than the raw power of the dictator," he claimed. "There must be no doubt that the United States of America welcomes change that advances self-determination and opportunity ... after decades of accepting the world as it is in the region, we have a chance to pursue the world as it should be."

In this speech, however, Obama again would completely ignore Palestinian efforts to nonviolently struggle against Israeli military occupation, instead blaming them for their woes after having "walked away from talks." Not only did Obama reject nonviolent Palestinian efforts to advance their self-determination by seeking UN membership; he also denigrated the initiative as a "symbolic action" designed "to delegitimize Israel" that "will end in failure." While the president lent rhetorical backing to those "shouts of human dignity" reverberating across the Middle East, tangible US support for Palestinian dignity, self-determination and opportunity would have to wait for a more propitious time—a time that would never materialize during Obama's first term. No matter how relentlessly Israel continued to colonize Palestinian land, no matter how much it entrenched its military occupation of Palestinian territory and no matter how intensified its apartheid policies toward Palestinians became, Obama remained trapped in the "peace process" paradigm. Within this framework, Obama stubbornly, and against all evidence to the contrary, presumed that Israel would negotiate in good faith to end its military occupation and agree to a Palestinian state with a semblance of actual sovereignty. Freedom, justice and equality for Palestinians, unlike Obama's rhetorical support for the universality of these principles in relation to the Arab Spring, were, in his view, equivocal and subject to Israel's veto. As he reminded his audience at the State Department: "it is up to Israelis and Palestinians to take action" to achieve a peace agreement. "No peace can be imposed upon them," even though one side, through more than six decades of repression, systematically attempted to strip away the human and national rights of the other.[5] Thus, ironically, did Obama, who had summoned Palestinians to nonviolence in Cairo, citing the historical example of African-Americans, two years later in his speech on the Arab Spring now do something that Dr. Martin Luther King, Jr., found odious: "set the timetable for another" person's "freedom."[6]

Huwaida Arraf, a Palestinian-American lawyer and human rights activist who has organized and participated in innumerable acts of Palestinian nonviolent resistance since the outbreak of the second Palestinian intifada against Israeli military occupation in 2000, found Obama's rhetoric on Palestinian nonviolence to be "extremely frustrating and hypocritical." Arraf stated that "morally, in principle," she agreed with the president that she did not want "to see violence or people hurt, and that if there is a nonviolent path that could be just as, if not more, effective, then that is the way to go." However, she found it infuriating that Obama would "preach nonviolence to oppressed people who are struggling for their basic human rights, without recognizing the violence of the oppressor," while at the same time failing to "recognize the long history of Palestinian nonviolence that has been going on for decades and that still goes on today with no support from the United States." When Palestinians do engage in nonviolent acts, Arraf asserted, "they get attacked by Israel with weapons supplied by the United States." However, when these attacks occur, the Obama administration does not "even come out with words of condemnation," much less "cut off the US support for Israel that allows it to use violence against unarmed resisters." Obama's rhetoric on Palestinian nonviolence was not only ahistorical and insincere, but counterproductive as well, according to Arraf. "This kind of US duplicity lends credence to the argument made by many that nonviolent resistance is ineffective, because when Palestinians resist nonviolently, they get quashed, and the United States, Israel's biggest political and financial supporter, lectures the victim, while continuing to provide the oppressor with unconditional support."[7]

US POLICY TOWARD PALESTINIAN NONVIOLENCE

In a sense, Israeli Major General Avi Mizrachi's threats to break up nonviolent Palestinian demonstrations with force were only natural. After all, the Israeli military had been accustomed to suppressing any nonviolent form of Palestinian political expression ever since it began its military occupation of the West Bank, East Jerusalem and Gaza Strip. According to the Palestinian human rights organization Addameer: Prisoner Support and Human Rights Association, Israel's Military Order Number 101, issued in August 1967, "criminalizes civic activities including: organizing and participating in protests; taking part in assemblies or vigils; waving flags and other political symbols; [and] printing and distributing political material. In addition, the order deems any acts of influencing public opinion as prohibited 'political incitement'."[8] This military order flagrantly violates Articles 19 and 20 of the Universal Declaration of Human Rights, which protect the "right to freedom of opinion and expression" and the "right to freedom of peaceful assembly and association."[9]

Yet despite these severe constraints put on Palestinian nonviolent action by Israel, and despite the risks of imprisonment, injury and death faced by Palestinian nonviolent protestors and their international supporters, throughout the Obama administration Palestinians and their international allies continued to engage in regular, vibrant and creative forms of nonviolent resistance to Israeli occupation and apartheid. These protests have included regular demonstrations against Israel's expropriation of Palestinian land and resources to construct Israel's illegal West Bank wall and settlements, nonviolent challenges to Israel's apartheid public transportation system in the West Bank, and mass hunger strikes by Palestinian political prisoners opposing the conditions under which they were being held.

Given Obama's beckoning of Palestinians to nonviolence in his speech in Cairo, and his reaffirmation of the power of nonviolent action to achieve basic rights in his speech on the Arab Spring, when confronted with Palestinians taking nonviolent action to counter Israel's oppression, the Obama administration should have enthusiastically backed these efforts. However, the Obama administration's response was woefully inadequate. Time and again, the Obama administration offered only the bare minimum acknowledgement that it was following the cases of Palestinian nonviolent practitioners jailed by Israel. It backed Palestinians' right to peaceful protest in only the most abstract sense. It also failed to take any action to sanction Israel for injuring or killing nonviolent Palestinian protestors or even US citizens who acted in solidarity with them. Worse yet, in one instance, the Obama administration even threatened its own citizens with prosecution under US anti-terrorism laws for attempting to engage in nonviolent action.

The US diplomatic response to Israel's May 2010 attack on the Gaza Freedom Flotilla, during which Israeli naval commandoes killed nine peace activists aboard the Turkish ship *Mavi Marmara*, has already been detailed in Chapter 7. However, the Obama administration's response to Israel's execution of US citizen Furkan Doğan aboard the *Mavi Marmara* has not yet been explored fully. When he was executed, as so chillingly documented in the UN Human Rights Council's investigation of Israel's attack on the flotilla, Doğan, who was born in Troy, New York, was just nineteen years old. His father, Ahmet Doğan, who was studying at Rensselaer

Polytechnic Institute in Troy at the time of his son's birth, recalled him as "a humanistic and conscientious child and a fine young man. I remember Furkan as unfailingly polite, helpful and generous. He disliked violence his entire life." According to Ahmet Doğan, his son, "deeply concerned by the plight of Palestinians suffering under the Israeli siege" of the Gaza Strip decided to participate in the flotilla because "he was determined to take humanitarian aid there with his own hands and give it to the children of Gaza . . . He wanted to breathe the same air as these children, commiserate and make life a bit more bearable for them."[10]

When it became evident that Israel had killed a US citizen on the flotilla, Secretary of State Hillary Clinton remarked on June 3, 2010, "We've offered not only our heartfelt condolences" to the Doğan family, "but any kind of consular assistance that the family might need at this time." She affirmed, "Protecting the welfare of American citizens is a fundamental responsibility of our government and one that we take very seriously. We are in constant contact with the Israeli Government, attempting to obtain more information about our citizens." Clinton added, "We have made no decisions at this point on any additional specific actions that our government should take with respect to our own citizens."[11]

However, despite the State Department pledging that same day to "carefully evaluate all the information that we can gather about the circumstances of his death" and promising that "those facts will lead us wherever they lead to," the Obama administration apparently failed to even initiate an investigation into Doğan's death.[12] Nearly nine months later, on February 23, 2011, Ahmet Doğan met with the State Department for the first time to receive an update on what the United States was doing to hold Israel accountable for the death of his son. Nothing tangible resulted from this meeting, since on the first anniversary of his son's killing, after again having pressed the US government to open an investigation, Doğan reported that still "no action has [been] taken by the US authorities."[13]

Based on the track record of the United States failing to hold Israel accountable for severely injuring and killing other US citizens, some of whose cases were discussed in earlier chapters, it is highly unlikely that such action will be taken in the future with respect to Doğan's killing. To date, the only step taken by Congress to hold Israel accountable for incidents in which US citizens were injured or killed occurred in July 2010, when the Senate published a report accompanying the 2011 State Department appropriations bill. This report directed the Secretary of State to submit a report "detailing actions being taken by the Government of Israel, the Palestinian Authority, and the Department of State to conduct thorough, credible, and transparent investigations of each case involving the death or serious injury of an American citizen in the West Bank and Gaza since 2001."[14] However, as Congress failed to pass separate appropriations bills that year, opting instead for a catch-all, omnibus budget bill that did not include this reporting requirement, this modest effort to begin to hold Israel accountable for injuring and killing US civilians quietly died.

If US citizens could be gravely injured or even killed by Israel while witnessing or participating in nonviolent actions in solidarity with Palestinians without the United States investigating, much less holding Israel accountable for, its actions, then Palestinian practitioners of nonviolence stood even less of a chance of receiving support from the United States. Take, for example, the Obama administration's fecklessness regarding the case of Abdallah Abu Rahmah, the coordinator of the Popular Committee against the Wall and the Settlements in Bil'in, a small West Bank village that has held weekly nonviolent protests against Israel's expropriation of the village's land since 2005. The Abu Rahmah family had already paid a heavy price for engaging in nonviolent protest against Israel's policies. Abdallah's cousin Bassem was killed by an Israeli soldier when he was struck in the chest with a tear gas canister, and Bassem's older sister Jawaher also died after inhaling tear gas fired into her village by Israeli soldiers, cases which were highlighted in Chapter 8.

On December 10, 2009, Abdallah Abu Rahmah was arrested, ironically enough on International Human Rights Day, and later indicted on the most Orwellian charge imaginable: assembling into the international symbol for peace used M-16 bullet casings and spent tear gas canisters the Israeli military fired at nonviolent protestors in Bil'in.[15] Israel sentenced Abu Rahmah to one year in prison, a sentence which was later arbitrarily extended. Abu Rahmah wrote a letter from Israel's Ofer Prison in which he stated:

I know that Israel's military campaign to imprison the leadership of the Palestinian popular struggle shows that our non-violent struggle is effective. The occupation is threatened by our growing movement and is therefore trying to shut us down. What Israel's leaders do not understand is that popular struggle cannot be stopped by our imprisonment . . . Unlike Israel, we have no nuclear weapons or army, but we do not need them. The justness of our cause earns us your support. No army, no prison and no wall can stop us.[16]

Amnesty International deemed Abu Rahmah "a prisoner of conscience, jailed solely for the peaceful exercise of his right to freedom of expression and assembly" and called "for his immediate and unconditional release."[17]

In another ironic twist, Israel arrested Abu Rahmah the same day that Obama received his Nobel Peace Prize. His wife, Majida Abu Rahmah, wrote, "Twelve hours after Abdallah was taken to a military jail from our home, I listened as President Obama received the Nobel Peace Prize and spoke of 'the men and women around the world who have been jailed and beaten in the pursuit of justice.'" Recalling the price paid by her husband and many other villagers for nonviolently protesting against Israel's illegal wall that cut off the villagers' access to much of their land, she "wondered if President Obama will take action to support our struggle for freedom."[18]

Unfortunately, the answer was no. One year after Abu Rahmah's arrest, on December 10, 2010, the State Department held a town hall meeting to mark International Human Rights Day. In response to a question I asked at this event, Michael Posner, assistant secretary of state for democracy, human rights and Labor affirmed that "there is a single universal standard" of human rights "that applies to every country, including our own. We apply it to the Israelis, and we also view . . . Palestinians as being human beings under the Universal Declaration [of Human Rights] and entitled to those rights."[19] But that very same day, the State Department deferred answering a question from Matthew Lee of the Associated Press as to whether it had "anything to say about the case of this Palestinian activist, nonviolent leader, Abdallah Abu Rahmah, who was—has been imprisoned by the Israelis."[20] After repeated questioning, the State Department only later lackadaisically offered "that this is a case that they continue to monitor" at the US embassy in Tel Aviv. "So the United States doesn't feel any—or the administration doesn't feel any compunction to speak out about this, as . . . other members of the Quartet have done?" Lee asked indignantly. Assistant Secretary of State Crowley responded meekly, "I can just provide you what I was provided by post. They are watching the case closely. And that beyond that, I'll probably direct questions to the Embassy in Tel Aviv." Lee sardonically retorted that "you monitor the weather in Beijing closely. What does this mean? Why is it beneath the United States to come out and say something about this person . . . who is a practitioner of nonviolence?" Summing up the Obama administration's approach to providing political support for Palestinian practitioners of nonviolence jailed by Israel, Crowley could only respond: "Again, I'll defer the question to the Embassy in Tel Aviv."[21]

Even Israel's mass killing of unarmed Palestinian protestors who attempted to symbolically assert their rights provoked the Obama administration's condemnation of Israel's neighbors, rather than Israel. Each year, Palestinians commemorate May 15, the day after Israel's establishment, as Nakba Day ("catastrophe," in Arabic) to recall the massacres, expulsions and ethnic cleansing that Israel committed against Palestinians in 1948 and to reaffirm Palestinian refugees' right of return to their homes. On May 15, 2011, Palestinians marched toward Israel's 1949 armistice lines from the Palestinian West Bank, East Jerusalem and the Gaza Strip, and from Lebanon, as well as toward the Israeli-occupied Syrian Golan Heights. In response to these Palestinians marching to affirm symbolically their right of return, and to the Syrians expelled from their homes on the Golan Heights who joined them, Israeli soldiers opened live fire, killing thirteen demonstrators.[22]

Rather than censure Israel for these killings and uphold the fact that Palestinian refugees' right of return is consistent with the Universal Declaration of Human Rights, which states that "everyone has the right to leave any country, including his own, and to return to his country," the United States defended Israel's actions.[23] Asked whether the United States condemned Israel's killing of unarmed protestors, State Department spokesperson Mark Toner testily brushed aside the question. "I was pretty clear in saying that we regret these deaths and injuries and express our sympathies and condolences, but just to make clear that Israel does have the right to defend its borders." In attempting to absolve Israel of culpability for these killings, Toner dismissed the Nakba Day protests as an "effort by the Syrian Government to play a destabilizing role." Apparently, even when Palestinians engaged in mass nonviolent action to secure their rights as demanded by the president, the Obama administration was nevertheless prepared to strip away their agency in organizing these protests. Thus, the Nakba Day demonstrations were not an indication of Palestinians' ability to successfully organize internationally coordinated acts of nonviolence, in the State Department's view. Instead, these demonstrations were "clearly an effort by them [Syrian government officials] to take focus off the situation that's happening right now in Syria, and it's a cynical use of the Palestinian cause to encourage violence along its border as it continues to repress its own people within Syria," Toner stated. Asked later if Israel had used excessive force to quell the protests, Toner noted instead that the US-trained Palestinian security forces in the West Bank "did play a constructive role, and that was an encouraging sign. But we call on all sides, I think, to show restraint moving forward."[24]

However, in the Obama administration's lexicon, "showing restraint" meant that Palestinians and their international supporters should refrain from engaging in "provocative" acts of nonviolence, not that Israel should cease injuring and killing nonviolent protestors. This warped approach to Palestinian nonviolent resistance and Israel's lethal response to it reached the height of absurdity in June 2011, when the Obama administration threatened US participants in the Gaza Freedom Flotilla II with prosecution under US laws. More than one year after Israel's attack on the first Gaza Freedom Flotilla had resulted in Israel's killing of nine humanitarian activists, including US citizen Furkan Doğan, with the United States failing to hold Israel accountable for its actions, the United States now warned participants in this flotilla against "taking irresponsible and provocative actions that risk the safety of their passengers." Rather than demand that Israel allow for the freedom of navigation on the high seas, including for US-flagged ships, refrain from attacking US and other nonviolent humanitarian activists and dismantle its illegal blockade of the Palestinian Gaza Strip—a step which would obviate the need for these flotillas—the Obama administration left US citizens to their own devices. Even worse than doing nothing to protect its citizens on these flotillas, the State Department crudely threatened participants with prosecution to deter their nonviolent efforts. According to the State Department, "delivering or attempting or conspiring to deliver material support or other resources to or for the benefit of a designated foreign terrorist organization, such as Hamas, could violate US civil and criminal statutes and could lead to fines and incarceration."[25]

US citizen Huwaida Arraf, who played a leading role in organizing many ships to sail to the Gaza Strip to break Israel's blockade, scoffed at the notion that the activists involved in the flotillas were providing "material support" for terrorism. "We were not working with the government in the Gaza Strip. Our partners in the Gaza Freedom Flotillas were Palestinian civil society organizations," she categorically stated. Ever since she began organizing boats to Gaza in 2008, Arraf was in communication with the US Consulate in Jerusalem, which knew the names of the US citizens participating and the materials on the ships. These items were "mainly symbolic because our aim was not just to deliver humanitarian aid, but to challenge a policy that was leaving Palestinians in need of this aid, a policy which has devastated Gaza." Arraf dismissed the State Department's warning of prosecution as "an attempt to try to scare people, but an ineffective one, because no one paid it any attention. We knew we had international law on our side. No one even gave it a second thought." She found it "frustrating that our government would make ridiculous and unfounded claims in order to intimidate US citizens who are doing something that the US government should be doing, which is to uphold human rights and humanitarian law." Above all else, Arraf viewed the State Department's declaration as an "indication that they were not going to do anything to protect US citizens" on the flotilla.[26]

With the State Department threatening US citizens with prosecution for participating in the flotilla and with Israel effectively bottling up the ships in Greek ports through a reported combination of political pressure against the Greek government and sabotage of the ships, international solidarity activists who wished to engage in nonviolent actions with Palestinians living under Israeli military occupation turned to a new strategy. In July 2011, hundreds of international activists would converge on Israel's Ben Gurion Airport in a "flytilla" to assert their rights to visit with and partici-pate in nonviolent resistance in coordination with Palestinian civil society organizations.

On this occasion, the State Department badly contradicted itself in asserting a universal right to nonviolent protest, while simultane-ously backing Israel in preventing these protests. Asked if the United States had "any problem with them [international activists] . . . stag-ing a protest," State Department spokesperson Victoria Nuland defended Israel in preventing these activists from entering Occupied Palestinian Territory. She declared that "it's any government's sover-eign right to decide who comes into their country and who doesn't." But by leaving the decision to Israel's sovereign discretion, the State Department ignored the fact that Israel controlled all ingress to and egress from the Palestinian West Bank and East Jerusalem, territories which were, even under the US government's definition, emphati-cally not "their country." Nuland added noncommittally that "with regard to protests, you know where we are: Peaceful protests are peaceful protests." But even if the right of people to "protest anywhere in the world, also applies to Israel," then the United States would not leverage pressure against Israel to actuate this right.[27]

However, US citizens did not need to travel to Ben Gurion Airport with the explicit intention of participating in Palestinian nonviolent protest in order to be denied entry by Israel and to have the United States fail in its obligation to advocate for the right of US nationals "to pass without delay or hindrance," a duty which is printed inside the passport of every US citizen. In fact, during the Obama adminis-tration, US citizens traveling to Israel and Occupied Palestinian Territory could be subjected to discriminatory treatment by Israel and the United States merely for planning to meet with Palestinian and Israeli nonviolent activists to learn more about their struggles for peace and justice. This discrimination was applied to Sandra Tamari, a US citizen and Palestinian Quaker, when she tried to enter Ben Gurion Airport in May 2012 as part of an interfaith delegation. As Tamari described her ordeal: "'Are you Jewish?' is the first ques-tion the US embassy staffer asked me on the phone while I sat in Israeli detention at the airport in Tel Aviv. When I responded that I was a Palestinian born in the United States, he said he could do nothing for me." As a result, Tamari endured "eight hours of interrogation by Israeli authorities. When I would not grant them access to my email account, I was accused of being a terrorist." Tamari wryly noted, "The heavy-handed treatment resulted from my participation in an interfaith delegation to listen to Palestinians and Israelis working for peace. Israel decided to deport me and deny my participation in this project, deeming me a 'security risk.' I spent the night in prison and then was put on a flight home the next day."[28]

Instead of protesting Israel's pattern of ethnically and religiously profiling US citizens trying to enter the country and invading their privacy, and apologizing for the US embassy's blatantly discriminatory treatment, the State Department tried to sweep Tamari's case under the rug. State Department deputy spokesperson Mark Toner called Tamari's case "a little bit of a—he said, she said" scenario.[29] Finally, after repeated questioning, the State Department issued a carefully worded statement on June 6, 2012, in which it claimed, "The State Department's number one priority is the protection of US citizens overseas." The State Department did not deny that a US embassy employee had asked Tamari her religion and then refused to provide assistance based on her answer. Rather, the State Department only promised that, in the future, "we will provide assistance to any US citizen who requests it, regardless of the citizen's religious or ethnic background." However, the State Department noted, "Decisions about entry are up to the Government of Israel" no matter how discriminatory those decisions may be.[30]

Even when Palestinian nonviolent action literally rose to the level of life and death, as it did during one of the largest mass hunger strikes in history, the Obama administration remained silent. In its 2011 Country Reports on Human Rights Practices, the State Department remarked that Israel's "1979 Emergency Powers Law allows the [Israeli] Defense Ministry to detain persons administratively without charge for up to six months, renewable indefinitely." Furthermore, the State Department acknowledged, "The military courts may rely on classified evidence denied to detainees and their lawyers when determining whether to prolong administrative detention." As of December 14, 2011, the State Department noted that Israel was imprisoning 307 Palestinians under this practice of "administrative detention."[31] This policy flagrantly violated the

Universal Declaration of Human Rights provision that "everyone is entitled in full equality to a fair and public hearing by an independent and impartial tribunal, in the determination of his rights and obligations and of any criminal charge against him."[32]

In protest of Israel's illegal policy of "administrative detention," Khader Adnan endured a sixty-six-day hunger strike between December 2011 and February 2012. Facing imminent death, Adnan wrote, "The Israeli occupation has gone to extremes against our people, especially prisoners. I have been humiliated, beaten, and harassed by interrogators for no reason, and thus I swore to God I would fight the policy of administrative detention to which I and hundreds of my fellow prisoners fell prey."[33] Adnan's hunger strike, which ended successfully after Israel agreed to release him from "administrative detention" after his initial four-month sentence, served as an inspiring triumph for Palestinian political prisoners struggling against Israel's unjust detention policies.

Adnan's hunger strike led to other individual Palestinian political prisoners beginning hunger strikes of their own. They were joined in an open-ended hunger strike on April 17, 2012, Palestinian Prisoners' Day, by an estimated 1,200 prisoners, along with 2,300 prisoners who engaged in other forms of disobedience. According to Addameer: Prisoner Support and Human Rights Association, the prisoners' modest demands included an end to the isolation of prisoners, an end to "administrative detention," an end to the denial of family visits for prisoners from Gaza and an end to the denial of a university education.[34] The mass hunger strike concluded on May 14, 2012, with Israel conceding many of the Palestinian prisoners' demands, but later reneging on their implementation. However, individual hunger strikers continued their fasts, with prisoners forsaking food for as much as 102 days, as in the case of Akram Rikhawi, who won a pledge for early release from his prison sentence in July 2012.[35]

Throughout the hunger strike, as many Palestinian political prisoners were on the cusp of death—as they struggled nonviolently for their fundamental human rights whose denial was even acknowledged by the State Department—the Obama administration did not utter one word of encouragement for the hunger strikers, nor place any public pressure on Israel to accede to their modest demands. For example, on May 11, 2012, shortly before the agreement concluding the mass hunger strike, Thaer Halahleh, who had "exceedingly low blood pressure," a body temperature "fluctuating at dangerous levels," and was "vomiting blood" and "bleeding from his gums and lips," began his seventy-fourth consecutive day without food.[36] That same day, State Department spokesperson Victoria Nuland flippantly responded to a question on the hunger strike: "I don't know if we have a comment on it." Although she pledged to "take the question," which in State Department parlance signifies that a formal, written response will be issued later, the State Department never released a statement.[37]

Palestinians and their international supporters, including US citizens, certainly did not require Obama's admonishment in Cairo to continue their nonviolent resistance to Israeli occupation and apartheid, even as these campaigns nevertheless intensified and scored important victories during the Obama administration. However, having boldly challenged Palestinians to adopt nonviolence, while ignoring historical and contemporary examples of Palestinian nonviolence, and then failing to provide any tangible support for Palestinian nonviolence throughout his first term, Obama exposed the shallowness of his commitment to the "moral force of nonviolence." Even worse, Obama's duplicitous summoning of Palestinians to nonviolence placed them in a catch-22 scenario: pick up weapons to defend themselves against Israel's overwhelming and systematic violence and face condemnation, isolation and sanctions for doing so, or hew to the path of nonviolence, as the United States looked on while Israel, with its arsenal of US weapons, continued to jail, injure and kill nonviolent activists with impunity.

Even though Palestinians engaging in nonviolent resistance to Israeli occupation and apartheid were abandoned by the Obama administration, their effective actions have nonetheless helped spark a reevaluation of the Israeli-Palestinian conflict in US public discourse. By successfully dramatizing to US audiences that Palestinians were the underdog David confronting the overwhelming power of Goliath, these examples of nonviolent resistance have compelled Americans to rethink the role that their government has played in perpetuating the Israeli-Palestinian conflict. These acts of Palestinian nonviolence, and the increasing brutality of Israel's violence, combined with effective Palestinian civil society–led international campaigns for boycott, divestment and sanctions (BDS) against Israel and corporations profiting from its human rights abuses of Palestinians, have laid the groundwork for the beginning of a fundamental shift in US civil society attitudes and actions toward the Israeli-Palestinian conflict. The president recognized that the Israeli-Palestinian status quo was "unsustainable," but failed to find a way out of the rut. US civil society would not wait until the politicians figured it out.

CHAPTER ELEVEN

An Ordinary Political Discourse

BOYCOTT, DIVESTMENT AND SANCTIONS (BDS)

Early in the Obama administration, on May 3, 2009, Howard Kohr, the Executive Director of AIPAC, the largest and most influential of the many groups of the Israel lobby, stepped to the podium of AIPAC's annual policy conference in a somber mood and with a dire warning for those in attendance. "We all know Israel is a target. No nation—none—is the target of so many lies, so much contempt, smear, and double standard," Kohr began his address. "But this is different," he warned. "What we are experiencing today, the rhetorical war of words, is a concerted effort, a campaign, part of a larger strategy."

This campaign was not limited to the Middle East, Europe or the UN, in Kohr's estimation. "It is coming home right here to the United States. We see it already on our college campuses, America's elite institutions of higher learning, the places we've entrusted with the education of our children." Nor was this campaign a fringe political phenomenon, "confined to the ravings of the political far left or far right, but increasingly it is entering the American mainstream: an ordinary political discourse on our T.V. and radio talk shows; in the pages of our major newspapers and in countless blogs, in town hall meetings, on campuses and city squares." This campaign must be taken seriously, Kohr argued, because "this is a conscious campaign to shift policy, to transform the way Israel is treated by its friends to a state that deserves not our support, but our contempt; not our protection, but pressured to change its essential nature."[1]

What was this ominous campaign of which Kohr spoke so grimly? It was a campaign of boycott, divestment and sanctions (BDS) against Israel and corporations that profited from its human rights abuses of and apartheid policies toward Palestinians. On July 9, 2005, the one-year anniversary of the International Court of Justice's landmark advisory opinion ruling Israel's wall in the Palestinian West Bank to be illegal, more than 170 Palestinian civil society organizations issued a historic call to action for BDS campaigns. This initiative was self-consciously "inspired by the struggle of South Africans against apartheid and in the spirit of international solidarity, moral consistency and resistance to injustice and oppression." This call for BDS urged "international civil society organizations and people of conscience all over the world to impose broad boycotts and implement divestment initiatives against Israel similar to those applied to South Africa in the apartheid era. We appeal to you to pressure your respective states to impose embargoes and sanctions against Israel. We also invite conscientious Israelis to support this Call, for the sake of justice and genuine peace." The call continued: "These non-violent punitive measures should be maintained until Israel meets its obligation to recognize the Palestinian people's inalienable right to self-determination and fully complies with the precepts of international law." Israel must do this by "ending its occupation and colonization of all Arab lands and dismantling the Wall," by "recognizing the fundamental rights of the Arab-Palestinian citizens of Israel to full equality" and by "respecting, protecting and promoting the rights of Palestinian refugees to return to their homes and properties as stipulated in UN [General Assembly] resolution 194."[2]

Kohr was undoubtedly correct in his analysis that these BDS campaigns sought to "shift policy" and "transform the way Israel is treated." This strategy followed the same game plan of the international movement of solidarity against apartheid in South Africa. In that case, these types of campaigns raised awareness about the human rights abuses that were taking place against black South Africans, highlighted how governments supported and corporations profited from these policies, created vehicles for civil society to take action against these policies and ultimately succeeded in transforming apartheid South Africa from an accepted member of the international community into a pariah. This process, combined with effective, nonviolent actions by South Africans, ultimately toppled the apartheid regime. In the sense that BDS campaigns "pressured [Israel] to change its essential nature" of being an apartheid state that through laws, semi-official institutions, military orders and widespread societal discrimination privileged Israeli Jews at the expense of Palestinians, who exercised circumscribed political rights or had no political rights whatsoever under Israeli rule, Kohr was again spot-on.

Omar Barghouti, a founding member of the Palestinian Campaign for the Academic and Cultural Boycott of Israel (PACBI) and the Palestinian Civil Society Boycott, Divestment and Sanctions (BDS) campaign against Israel, maintained that the BDS movement arose out of a need for "the entire Palestinian conceptual framework and strategies of resistance" to be "thoroughly and critically reassessed and transformed into a progressive action program capable of connecting the Palestinian struggle for self-determination and justice with the international social movement." Barghouti argued, "The most effective and morally sound strategy for achieving these objectives is one based on gradual, diverse, context-sensitive, and sustainable campaigns of BDS ... and other forms of popular resistance, all aimed at bringing about Israel's comprehensive and unequivocal compliance with international law and universal human rights."

Although various fragmented and diverse boycott, divestment and sanctions initiatives against Israel had been taking place in the United States and throughout the world beforehand, this 2005 Palestinian civil society call provided these campaigns with a much needed Palestinian-led set of principles and source of inspiration on which to base and expand these efforts. The establishment in 2008 of the Palestinian BDS National Committee (BNC) further strengthened this movement, by creating, according to Barghouti, the "reference and guiding force for the global BDS movement, which was all along based on the Palestinian-initiated and -anchored BDS Call." [3]

As Kohr mentioned in his speech to AIPAC, it was not just the ability of this movement to connect with other progressive social movements that worried the Israel lobby. It also was the increasing effectiveness of BDS activists in influencing the decisions of mainstream institutions such as churches and universities that provoked great concern. This phenomenon led the Jewish Federations of North America and the Jewish Council for Public Affairs to launch in October 2010 a new $6 million initiative, dubbed the "Israel Action Network," to "enlist the help of key leaders at churches, labor unions and cultural institutions to fight anti-Israel boycott, divestment and sanctions campaigns."[4] However, simply throwing money into combating this phenomenon would not silence or defeat the largely grassroots and underfunded movement propelling BDS campaigns, nor would it make Israel's increasing image problems vanish.

In fact, BDS campaigns became so prominent during the Obama administration that policymakers began to express concern about them and pledge their support to counter them. For example, in the aftermath of Israel's attack on the Gaza Freedom Flotilla in May 2010, as US BDS campaigns gathered momentum, Representative Adam Schiff took to the floor of Congress to bemoan the many perils that faced Israel, which, he asserted, ranged from increasingly sophisticated arsenals possessed by Hezbollah and Hamas, to its frayed relationship with Turkey, to Iran's uranium enrichment program. However, "Most worrisome in the long term" for Israel was "the broad-based international campaign to delegitimize Israel." Schiff fretted that "university campuses have been divided by divestment campaigns" and "there have been academic and economic boycotts of Israel."[5] This concern about the BDS movement reached as high as the president, who told AIPAC in March 2012 that "when there are efforts to boycott or divest from Israel, we will stand against them. (Applause.) And whenever an effort is made to de-legitimize the state of Israel, my administration has opposed them. (Applause.) So there should not be a shred of doubt by now—when the chips are down, I have Israel's back."[6]

Although the president pledged to "have Israel's back," BDS campaigns in the United States not only proliferated during the Obama administration, but racked up significant victories as well. These advances have signified the beginnings of a new US civil society approach toward its government's role in perpetuating the Israeli-Palestinian conflict. These BDS campaigns have succeeded in getting endorsers of and investors in problematic corporations to drop their relationships with and holdings in these companies, have convinced artists and other performers to cancel scheduled appearances in Israel, and have pressed dockworkers not to unload Israeli products from ships. They have forced universities to divest from US corporations profiting from Israeli occupation, have achieved boycott and sanctions victories in mainstream church denominations and have delisted from socially responsible investment funds US corporations that profit from Israeli occupation. For every BDS campaign that achieved a victory—despite intensive opposition from the Israel lobby—there were even more BDS campaigns that did not attain the requisite support needed to formally win, but nevertheless succeeded in raising awareness about US complicity in Israeli military occupation and apartheid policies toward Palestinians. The following examples, while not exhaustive, are illustrative of the growing strength and prominence of BDS campaigning in the United States during the Obama administration.

In November 2007, Adalah-NY: The New York Campaign for the Boycott of Israel began an energetic and creative BDS campaign against Israeli diamond tycoon Lev Leviev. His multinational holdings and investment corporation—Africa Israel Investments, Ltd.—was constructing the Israeli settlement of Matityahu East on the land of Bil'in, the West Bank village profiled in earlier chapters, along with several other illegal Israeli settlements. Activists from Adalah-NY frequently picketed the high-end Madison Avenue Leviev jewelry store, including on Valentine's Day, Mother's Day, and during the Christmas shopping season. They performed skits and parodies of songs that highlighted Leviev's profiting from Israel's dispossession of Palestinians from their land.

As the campaign generated increasing amounts of negative publicity for Leviev and his Africa Israel corporation, celebrities stopped wearing Leviev jewelry, charities such as Oxfam refused contributions from Leviev, and big investors—such as the financial services company TIAA-CREF and European governments—divested their holdings in the corporation. The *Jewish Daily Forward* termed activists in the Adalah-NY BDS campaign against Leviev "effective gadflies."[7] Just three years after initiating its campaign, Adalah-NY was able to claim a "major boycott movement success." In November 2010, Africa Israel announced, "Neither the company nor any of its subsidiaries and/or other companies controlled by the company are presently involved in or has any plans for future involvement in development, construction or building of real estate in settlements in the West Bank." According to Ethan Heitner, an activist with Adalah-NY, this victory was "clearly a result of pressure from the growing Boycott, Divestment and Sanctions movement. This provides concrete evidence of the way in which the BDS movement can change companies' behavior."[8]

Other Israeli corporations that profit from expropriating Palestinian natural resources also found themselves to be the targets of increasingly effective BDS campaigns in the United States. Take, for example, the "Stolen Beauty" BDS campaign, run by CODEPINK: Women for Peace, which targets Israeli cosmetics manufacturer Ahava Dead Sea Laboratories. Ahava produces its cosmetics from mud illegally extracted from the Palestinian portion of the Dead Sea that is under Israeli military occupation and manufacturers them in the illegal Israeli West Bank settlement Mitzpe Shalem. CODEPINK formally launched its boycott campaign of Ahava in July 2009 and scored an early, important victory in August 2009 when Oxfam suspended *Sex and the City* star Kristin Davis as its goodwill ambassador for the duration of her contract as a spokesperson for Ahava. Davis's contract with Ahava lapsed shortly thereafter and was not renewed.[9] In January 2010, in response to a social media campaign asking it to de-shelve Ahava products, retail giant Costco announced that once remaining stocks of Ahava products "have sold they are no longer available."[10] After protests against Ahava spread throughout the United States and worldwide, Abigail Disney, a principal investor in Shamrock Holdings Incorporated, which owns 18.5 percent of Ahava, announced in July 2012 that "I cannot in good conscience profit from what is technically the 'plunder' or 'pillage' of occupied natural resources and the company's situating its factory in an Israeli settlement in the Occupied West Bank." Although legal and financial arrangements prevented her from divesting her stock, Disney promised to "donate the corpus of the investment as well as the profits accrued to me during the term of my involvement to organizations working to end this illegal exploitation."[11]

In addition to Israeli corporations that profit from Palestinian human rights abuses losing spokespeople and investors in recent years, several famous cultural, artistic and athletic icons also refused to perform in Israel, as doing so would validate and normalize Israel's oppression of the Palestinians. By boycotting Israel, these figures were responding to a global call launched in 2004 by the Palestinian Campaign for the Academic and Cultural Boycott of Israel. Its guidelines stated that "international artists and cultural workers are urged not to exhibit, present, or showcase their work (e.g. films, installations, literary works) or lecture at complicit Israeli cultural institutions or events, or to grant permission for the publication or exhibition of such work by such institutions."[12] US musicians who either cancelled or refused to play concerts in Israel included Snoop Dogg, Gil Scott Heron, The Pixies, Cat Power, Carlos Santana, and Cassandra Wilson, who often picketed Israel in response to campaigns by US activists. US authors such as Judith Butler, Angela Davis, Sarah Schulman and Alice Walker publicly spoke out in favor of BDS, and the legendary US basketball player, civil rights activist and author Kareem Abdul-Jabbar cancelled a scheduled visit to Israel.[13] In the aftermath of Israel's attack on the Gaza Freedom Flotilla in May 2010, Walker, the Pulitzer Prize-winning author of *The Color Purple*, encapsulated this growing support for BDS among cultural figures by writing that BDS campaigns would "begin to soothe the pain and attend the sorrows of a people wrongly treated for generations." She encouraged people to "disengage, avoid, and withhold support from whatever abuses, degrades and humiliates humanity" by partaking in BDS campaigns against Israel.[14]

Israel's attack on the Gaza Freedom Flotilla also prompted dockworkers in Oakland to take the unprecedented action in the United States of refusing to unload Israeli cargo from a ship. On June 20, 2010, more than 500 demonstrators picketed before dawn at Berth 58 at the Port of Oakland. They were protesting the impending arrival of a ship owned by Israel's Zim shipping line. According to the *San Francisco Chronicle*, "Two shifts of longshoremen agreed not to cross the picket line, leaving nobody to unload the vessel." This action achieved the protestors' goal of preventing the Israeli cargo from being unloaded for one day.[15]

In July 2010, the Olympia Food Co-Op in Olympia, Washington, became the first US grocery store to institute a boycott of Israeli products. The location of this boycott was symbolically important, as Olympia was the hometown of Rachel Corrie, the US citizen who was run over and killed with a Caterpillar D9 bulldozer by the Israeli military as she nonviolently protected a Palestinian home from demolition in the Gaza Strip in March 2003. Rob Richards, a board member of the co-op, explained that in voting for the boycott, "there is a moral imperative that goes beyond any financial concern" about refusing to stock Israeli products. He acknowledged that "the Olympia Food Co-Op boycott is not going to change the Israeli policy, but I believe that these small drops will eventually have an effect."[16] But Richards underestimated just how seriously Israel and its supporters viewed the boycott and the drastic financial ramifications they sought to impose on the co-op for voting to de-shelve Israeli products. He would soon find out, however, as lawyers affiliated with the pro-Israel organization Stand With Us filed a lawsuit against the co-op.[17]

But the plaintiffs had made a serious legal mistake, having previously sent a threatening letter to the co-op promising a "complicated, burdensome, and expensive" lawsuit if the co-op did not overturn its decision. As a result of this letter, a judge dismissed the case in February 2012, ruling that it was a strategic lawsuit against public participation (SLAPP). According to the Center for Constitutional Rights (CCR), which defended the co-op in the suit, SLAPP cases

> target the constitutional rights of free speech and petition in connection with an issue of public concern. Although many cases that qualify as SLAPPs are without legal merit, they can nonetheless effectively achieve their primary purpose: to chill public debate on specific issues. Defending against a SLAPP requires substantial money, time, and legal resources, and can divert attention away from the public issue and intimidate and silence other speakers.

By dismissing the Stand With Us–inspired lawsuit, the judge refused to countenance these attempts at intimidation and sent "a message to those trying to silence support of Palestinian human rights to think twice before they bring a lawsuit," stated Maria LaHood, a senior staff attorney with CCR.[18] In further vindication of the co-op's right to boycott Israeli products, the judge ruled in July 2012 that the plaintiffs must pay the named defendants $160,000 in damages.[19]

Not only did Israeli companies, especially those that profited from

Israel's military occupation of Palestinian land, become the targets of concerted boycott campaigns during the Obama administration; US corporations that profited from Israel's human rights abuses of Palestinians also suffered financial losses as divestment campaigns against them succeeded. In February 2009, Hampshire College, in Amherst, Massachusetts, became the first US college to divest its holdings from corporations that are complicit in maintaining Israel's military occupation of the Palestinian West Bank, East Jerusalem and Gaza Strip. Students for Justice in Palestine (SJP) at Hampshire College had organized a multi-year campaign to press the college's board of trustees to divest from six corporations—Caterpillar, United Technologies, General Electric, ITT Corporation, Motorola and Terex—that profited from Israeli occupation. The trustees agreed that the college should not invest in these corporations. The college's president "acknowledged that it was the good work of SJP that brought this issue to the attention of the committee." It was only fitting that Hampshire College was the first US college or university to divest from US corporations supporting Israeli occupation; it was also the first US campus to divest from apartheid South Africa. "SJP has proven that student groups can organize, rally and pressure their schools to divest from the illegal occupation," it modestly noted. "The group hopes that this decision will pave the way for other institutions of higher learning in the US to take similar stands."[20]

Students for Justice in Palestine at Hampshire College held a BDS conference later that year to facilitate this goal and to build on their monumental victory, which had inspired additional campus divestment campaigns to persevere in their efforts and also sparked a new generation of campaigns at US universities to divest from corporations profiting from Israeli human rights abuses of Palestinians. This burst of momentum led to the first National Students for Justice in Palestine Conference at Columbia University in October 2011, which was attended by more than 350 students from more than one hundred US universities. This conference laid the groundwork for a nationally coordinated campus effort to promote BDS campaigns, signifying "the beginning of a new era in Palestine solidarity organizing in the United States."[21]

Long-standing BDS campaigns also made significant headway in mainstream churches in recent years. In May 2012, the United Methodist Church's General Conference, meeting in Tampa, Florida, voted to approve boycott and sanctions resolutions. These resolutions called on the US government to "end all military aid to the region," urged "all nations to prohibit . . . any financial support by individuals or organizations for the construction and maintenance of settlements" and counseled "all nations to prohibit . . . the import of products made by companies in Israeli settlements on Palestinian land."

But, paradoxically, the church voted against a resolution to divest from three US corporations—Caterpillar, Motorola and Hewlett Packard—profiting from Israel's military occupation. The divestment resolution was backed by United Methodist Kairos Response (UMKR), an organization that supported the 2009 Kairos Palestine document, which was issued by Palestinian Christians calling on their coreligionists around the world to engage in BDS campaigns. Even though the United Methodist Church did not divest from these corporations profiting from Israeli occupation, Anna Baltzer, the National Organizer of the US Campaign to End the Israeli Occupation, noted, "Broad media coverage of and grassroots contributions to UMKR's divestment campaign, however, have caught the attention of the world and amplified criticism of the Israeli occupation and complicit US corporations . . . BDS has entered the very highest levels of mainstream US institutions."[22]

Although the United Methodist Church did not divest in 2012, it left the door open for doing so at the international level in the future. Meanwhile, in May 2012, the Friends Fiduciary Committee (FFC), which manages $200 million in Quaker assets, decided to divest all $900,000 of its stock in Caterpillar. This corporation, which has been a long-running target of BDS campaigns, profits from Israeli military occupation through the demolition of Palestinian homes, agriculture, and infrastructure, as well as through the construction of Israeli settlements and Israel's wall in the West Bank. In announcing its decision to divest, FFC declared, "We are uncomfortable defending our position on this stock" and have "zero tolerance for weapons and weapons components," underscoring the fact that Israel repeatedly misused these US taxpayer-funded Caterpillar bulldozers as weapons. The Ann Arbor Friends, which had requested the FFC to divest from Caterpillar, noted that by divesting, the committee was "truly upholding the core commitment of the Society of Friends to peace."[23]

Caterpillar, along with Motorola and Hewlett Packard, faced an additional potential loss of investment as the Presbyterian Church USA (PCUSA) met in Pittsburgh, Pennsylvania, in July 2012 to consider divesting their holdings from these corporations. In a historic vote, the church's Middle East and Peacemaking Issues Committee overwhelmingly endorsed divestment by a margin of more than three to one. The church plenary, however, by the narrowest of margins—333 to 331—voted to substitute a resolution calling for investment in the Palestinian economy rather than divestment from corporations that were aiding Israel in debilitating the Palestinian economy. By voting to invest, rather than divest, PCUSA was ignoring Palestinian calls for justice, not charity, including calls from Palestinian Presbyterians such as Moufid Khoury, a lay pastor from Lehigh, Pennsylvania, who testified that a Caterpillar bulldozer demolished his home and termed the Israeli military occupation "the worst form of terrorism."[24] Despite this setback for divestment, the church nevertheless took the significant step of voting to boycott all Israeli settlement products. According to Jeff DeYoe, Advocacy Chair of the Israel Palestine Mission Network of the PCUSA, which backed these BDS campaigns, the boycott vote was a watershed moment because "as recent as two years ago, the word 'boycott' could not even be uttered in the Church."[25]

Although Caterpillar only narrowly missed losing investments from the PCUSA, it suffered a huge loss shortly before. MSCI, which describes itself as "a leading provider of investment decision support tools to around 6,200 clients worldwide, ranging from large pension plans to boutique hedge funds," decided in February 2012 to downgrade Caterpillar and remove it from several socially responsible investment indices.[26] MSCI noted that one of the "key factors" in the decision was "an on-going controversy associated with use of the company's equipment in the occupied Palestinian territories."[27] Following MSCI's downgrading of Caterpillar, between May and June 2012, TIAA-CREF—the largest pension fund in the United States—sold off from its socially responsible investment fund all of its nearly $73 million in Caterpillar stock, which made this divestment decision by far the most financially consequential yet taken in the United States. This move was a major victory for the "We Divest Campaign," which calls on TIAA-CREF to divest from five corporations that profit from Israeli occupation. "By selling weaponized bulldozers to Israel, Caterpillar is complicit in Israel's systematic violations of Palestinian human rights," reasoned Rabbi Alissa Wise, director of campaigns at Jewish Voice for Peace and national coordinator of the We Divest Campaign. "We're glad to see that the socially responsible investment community appears to be recognizing this and is starting to take appropriate action."[28]

This effective BDS campaign clearly riled the Israel lobby, including its stalwart backers in Congress. Representative Gary Ackerman blasted what he termed an "ill-conceived and dangerous effort" by professors and staff at New York University to encourage TIAA-CREF to divest from corporations profiteering from what he referred to as Israel's "so-called" military occupation. Ackerman obliquely threatened the university with cutting off federal funds if they persisted in their campaign. He asked goadingly: "Would they like federal dollars to be 'divested' from universities whose research or policy preferences don't accord with the administration's view?"[29]

MEDIA AND POPULAR CULTURE

If the increasing visibility and successes of BDS campaigns in the United States during the Obama administration perturbed Israel and its US cheerleaders, then changes in popular culture and media coverage of the Israeli-Palestinian conflict similarly undermined the long-standing dominant narrative of Israel as the victim. This reshaped public discourse now began to take into account Palestinian suffering and the role that US policy plays in perpetuating these injustices.

As recently as 2006, Patrick O'Connor of Palestine Media Watch was able to state authoritatively after analyzing the op-ed pages of the five US newspapers with the largest circulation—the *Wall Street Journal*, the *New York Times*, the *Los Angeles Times*, *USA Today*, and the *Washington Post*—that "in the US media, Palestinians generally aren't allowed to speak for themselves or to articulate their historical narrative. Israelis, however, are permitted to speak, to explain the Israeli experience and even to explain about Palestinians. As a result, the Israeli story is known in the US while Palestinians are dehumanized." O'Connor reviewed 680 op-eds from these newspapers between September 2000 and December 2005, an era which spanned the outbreak of the second Palestinian intifada and Israel's brutal response to it, the death of Palestinian Authority President Yasser Arafat and Israel's unilateral withdrawal from the Gaza Strip. He discovered that for every op-ed from a Palestinian writer, these newspapers printed 2.5 op-eds from Israelis. O'Connor additionally found that "even Israelis who challenge the narrow mainstream discourse on Israel/Palestine that is accepted in the US are rarely published, despite the general propensity to publish Israelis." This analysis of op-ed pages led O'Connor to conclude that "a consistent reliance on establishment voices explains which writers are published and what issues are addressed on Israel/Palestine in the US op-ed pages, not journalistic standards of balance or a concern to represent a variety of views."[30]

During the Obama administration, US mainstream media coverage of the Israeli-Palestinian conflict has continued to exhibit disturbing biases and conflicts of interest. For example, former *New York Times* Jerusalem Bureau Chief Ethan Bronner was largely absolved by his paper after investigative reporter Max Blumenthal revealed that the journalist was being paid speaking fees as a client of a right-wing Israeli public relations firm that simultaneously pitched him stories as the paper's bureau chief. This conflict of interest came to light after it had become public earlier that Bronner's son was serving in the Israeli military.[31]

Nevertheless, despite some continued problematic US media coverage of the Israeli-Palestinian conflict, a twenty-five-year veteran advocate for Palestinian human rights, who has focused intensively on improving US media coverage for the last seven years, noted that during this time she has seen "a palpable shift" in coverage. She noted, "There has been a sea change in the space for and interest in including Palestinian voices among mainstream US media." In years past, "there did not seem to be an acceptance or understanding that this voice had a right to be included whether or not it was included in response to or alongside a 'balancing' piece from the other side." Although she noted that "it is still a battle" to get fair coverage and that "the playing field is still very uneven," it is "now nevertheless a very different situation" than before. In the past, "Palestinian voices were never allowed to stand by themselves; now they are to an unprecedented extent."[32]

This newfound receptivity to including more articles on the op-ed pages of the largest-circulation US newspapers from Palestinians, Palestinian-Americans, and people from a variety of backgrounds who support Palestinian human rights can be illustrated by a few examples. In September 2010, as fruitless Israeli-Palestinian direct negotiations were resuming, the *Washington Post* published an op-ed by University of California Hastings College of the Law professor George Bisharat, entitled "Israel and Palestine: A True One-state Solution." Bisharat argued that Israel's colonization of Occupied Palestinian Territory made the establishment of an independent, negotiated Palestinian state unfeasible. Instead, he maintained, "A de facto one-state reality has emerged, with Israel effectively ruling virtually all of the former Palestine." Rather than maintaining Israel's apartheid rule over Palestinians, Bisharat wrote, "The answer is for Israelis and Palestinians to formalize their de facto one-state reality but on principles of equal rights rather than ethnic privilege ... Israel/Palestine should have a secular, bilingual government elected on the basis of one person, one vote as well as strong constitutional guarantees of equality and protection of minorities, bolstered by international guarantees."[33]

US newspapers provided Palestinians with op-ed space to critique not only Israeli policies, but also US policies. After Obama witheringly dismissed the Palestinian bid for UN membership in September 2011, Columbia University Professor Rashid Khalidi blasted the US-led "peace process" in *USA Today*. Khalidi stated that two decades of failed negotiations "may have made a two-state solution to the conflict impossible. The process has made peace more distant." He blamed this bipartisan "debacle" on four US presidents who "all cared more about the dictates of domestic politics than Middle East peace." Rather than being an honest broker, "the United States is Israel's patron," Khalidi argued. "The US needs only to tie our massive support for Israel to a simple requirement—to abide by international law and previous agreements—for peace to be within reach. But the United States is highly partisan. And Palestinians suffer the consequences."[34]

In a May 2012 op-ed in the *New York Times* commemorating the *Nakba*, Yousef Munayyer, executive director of the Jerusalem Fund, noted that "many of Palestine's native inhabitants were turned into refugees" during Israel's establishment in 1948, including 95 percent of the residents who were expelled by Israel from his hometown of Lydda. Munayyer wrote that Palestinian refugees are not allowed to exercise their right of return because

> Zionism requires the state to empower and maintain a Jewish majority even at the expense of its non-Jewish citizens, and the occupation of the West Bank is only one part of it. What exists today between the Jordan River and the Mediterranean Sea is therefore essentially one state, under Israeli control, where Palestinians have varying degrees of limited rights: 1.5 million are second-class citizens, and four million more are not citizens at all. If this is not apartheid, then whatever it is, it's certainly not democracy.

Munayyer faulted US and Israeli leaders for failing to "grapple with this nondemocratic reality." He concluded, "For all the talk about shared values between Israel and the United States, democracy is sadly not one of them right now, and it will not be until Israel's leaders are willing to recognize Palestinians as equals, not just in name, but in law."[35]

While it is difficult to quantify the impact that this changing media landscape has had on public discourse in the United States, it undoubtedly has exposed millions of Americans to perspectives on the Israeli-Palestinian conflict from which they had largely been shielded before.

Beyond the op-ed pages of the leading US newspapers, it has also become clear that other segments of the US media are no longer so willing to treat Israel with kid gloves. For example, in October 2011, the *Washington Post*'s "Fine Print" columnist Walter Pincus argued that "it is time to examine the funding the United States provides to Israel." He noted that Israel cut its military expenditures in response to domestic protests for greater social services. "If Israel can reduce its defense spending because of its domestic economic problems," he asked, "shouldn't the United States—which must cut military costs because of its major budget deficit—consider reducing its aid to Israel?"[36] As Congress considered providing Israel with nearly $1 billion for additional anti-missile programs, on top of $3.1 billion in regular military aid, in the 2013 budget, Pincus asked: "Should the United States put solving Israel's budget problems ahead of its own?" As US citizens faced impending, across-the-board budget cuts, which could adversely impact tens of millions of Americans, he provocatively answered, "When it comes to defense spending, it appears that the United States already is."[37] Such a straightforward admission that US politicians were prioritizing Israel's needs over those of their constituents showed that the media could no longer be counted upon for automatic approval of US policies toward Israel.

Some media even went so far as to publicly rebel against and expose Israel's attempts to suppress stories it deemed to be hostile. For example, in April 2012, *60 Minutes*, the most-watched television news program in the United States, aired a segment entitled "Christians of the Holy Land," which examined the declining numbers of Palestinian Christians and cited Israel's oppression of Palestinians as a reason for the community's decline. The episode also highlighted how Palestinian Christians were calling on their coreligionists around the world to end Israel's occupation and apartheid policies toward Palestinians by organizing BDS campaigns in their churches. The fact that CBS News broadcast this segment at all was noteworthy in and of itself. However, the episode turned into a truly watershed moment in the media's coverage of the Israeli-Palestinian conflict when correspondent Bob Simon revealed on the program that Michael Oren, Israel's ambassador to the United States, had "phoned Jeff Fager, the head of CBS News and executive producer of *60 Minutes*, while we were still reporting the story, long before tonight's broadcast. He said he had information our story was, quote 'a hatchet job.'" A visibly discomfited Oren appeared on the program, sputtering, "I do that very, very infrequently as ambassador," admitting, nevertheless, that he had attempted to influence US media coverage before. Oren stammered, "When I heard that you were going to do a story about Christians in the Holy Land and my assum—and—and had, I believe, information about the nature of it, and it's been confirmed by this interview today." But Simon was having none of it. "Nothing's been confirmed by the interview, Mr. Ambassador, because you don't know what's going to be put on air," Simon countered. "Okay. I don't. True," Oren was forced to admit.

Simon then told the Israeli ambassador, "I've been doing this a long time. And I've received lots of reactions from just about everyone I've done stories about. But I've never gotten a reaction before from a story that hasn't been broadcast yet." Oren arrogantly retorted, "Well, there's a first time for everything, Bob."[38] The episode gave Israeli propaganda an inglorious black eye, leaving millions of Americans with the distinct impression that Israel had good reason to try to hide its treatment of Palestinians from their television screens.

In recent years, criticism of US policy toward Israel, in the form of sarcastic and biting humor, has even invaded popular culture. In the run-up to the 2008 presidential election, *Saturday Night Live* comedian Tina Fey played, to great acclaim, Republican vice presidential candidate Sarah Palin. In an October 2008 episode spoofing the vice presidential candidate debate, singer and actress Queen Latifah, playing PBS news anchor Gwen Ifill, asked Fey, "What is your position on health-care regulation?" Fey responded, "I'm gonna ignore that question and instead talk about Israel. I love Israel so much. Bless its heart. There's a special place for Israel in heaven. And I know some people are going to say I'm only saying that to pander to Florida voters, but from a very young age, my two greatest loves were always Jews and Cuban food."[39]

In March 2010, an episode of the cartoon comedy *The Simpsons*, entitled "The Greatest Episode Ever D'ohed," featured the Simpson family and other Springfield residents traveling to the Holy Land on a religious tour. As they waited for their baggage at Israel's Ben Gurion Airport, a sign above the conveyor belt read: "Welcome to Israel: Your American Tax Dollars at Work."[40]

In March 2012, Comedy Central's *The Daily Show with Jon Stewart* ran a two-part piece entitled "America's Problem with UNESCO," which the United States defunded after UNESCO voted to admit Palestine as a member in October 2011. In the first segment, correspondent John Oliver interviewed former Representative Robert Wexler (D-FL), who admitted that the defunding of UNESCO harmed US interests. "But we're sending a point, and the point is we have interests, we set up a law, we warned you," Wexler argued. Oliver retorted in mocking agreement, "Right, and when you physically cut off your nose to spite your face, you're sending a message. And that message is don't fuck with me. Because if I'm willing to do this to myself, what am I willing to do to you?" In the second segment, Oliver traveled to Gabon, the West African nation which contributed $2 million to help plug UNESCO's funding gap in the wake of the United States pulling its funding. Oliver went there, in his words, to "confront these tyrannical philanthropists face to face." Oliver explained to Gabonese schoolchildren that "once upon a time, twenty years ago, there was a US congressional law that outlawed funding to any UN organization that allowed Palestine to be a member. And that is why you can't have books anymore," he declared, as he pounced on a table to try to confiscate the schoolbooks.[41]

Although these mockeries of US policy toward Israel and the Palestinians did not change the actual absurdities of the policy itself, they demonstrated that Israel was no longer the sacred cow it once was in US popular culture. These humorous sendups, along with the profound changes in mainstream media coverage of the Israeli-Palestinian conflict and significant BDS campaign victories, combined to produce a newfound willingness among the US public to question its government's policies toward Israel and the Palestinians and to take action to alter them for the better. However, if US politicians were cognizant of these changes, they betrayed no hint of it in the run-up to the 2012 elections. In several congressional races, as well as in the presidential campaign, candidates took pandering to Israel's backers to a new level of abject abasement, as partisan bickering over which party loved Israel the most became a prominent campaign issue.

CHAPTER TWELVE

Throwing Israel Under the Bus

GROWING PARTISANSHIP OVER ISRAEL

Representative Anthony Weiner's (D-NY) June 2011 resignation from Congress served as a most unexpected and unusual prelude to one of, if not the most, heated and partisan electoral campaign cycles in which the two major US political parties competed for the mantle of being most advantageous to the interests of Israel. The disgraced member of Congress, who lied about sending lewd photos to women through social media, was one of Israel's most brash supporters on Capitol Hill.

When it came to the Israeli-Palestinian conflict, Weiner's guileless mendacity and sheer disconnection from reality were on full display during a March 2011 debate with former representative Brian Baird (D-WA). While still in Congress, Baird had visited the Gaza Strip after Operation Cast Lead and skewered his congressional colleagues for voting in favor of a resolution to condemn the Goldstone Report without even bothering to read it. Among other absurdities, Weiner held forth that there is "no occupation in the West Bank" and that Israeli troops are not regularly based there. "There are people who believe that settlement activity is going on in Palestinian territories," Weiner continued to pontificate, but "I don't believe that." Baird and *New York Times* columnist Roger Cohen, who moderated the debated, gazed at Weiner with incredulity. "Where do you think the settlement growth is happening right now if it's not in Palestinian territories?" Cohen wondered. "Right now the settlement that is going on is going on in Israel," Weiner declared, asserting that his earth-is-flat statement was "not a controversial thing to say." Weiner capped off this bravura performance by agreeing with a heckler from the audience that Israel's borders extended to "the Jordan River," as if Israel already had formally annexed the Palestinian West Bank and this illegal expropriation of Palestinian land had been recognized by the international community.[1]

Weiner's unhinged comments typified, albeit to an extreme degree, the inanities that characterize congressional policy toward Israel and the Palestinians. His departure from Congress a few months after this debate would leave a gaping hole among the relatively small cadre of zealot members of Congress whose incessant championing of Israel, backed by the unremitting lobbying of AIPAC, held the rest of Congress in thrall to a policy that a few intrepid members of Congress publicly recognized to be flawed, biased and self-defeating. Thus it came as little surprise that the candidates who sought to replace Weiner in a September 2011 special election bickered over which of the two could better fill this hole.

David Weprin, the New York State Assembly member who ran as the Democratic Party candidate to replace Weiner in the special election, made perhaps the most unlikely candidate ever to serve as a lightning rod of criticism for the perceived inadequacies of US support for Israel. Weprin is an Orthodox Jew who has Israeli cousins, had visited Israel at least eight times, including during Israel's 2006 war against Lebanon, a trip with colleagues which he claimed "put our lives in danger." Furthermore, he had sponsored, over the course of ten years in the New York City Council and New York State Assembly, according to his recollection, "many, many pro-Israel resolutions" and had served as a backer of Manhattan's annual Salute to Israel Day Parade.

In fact, Weprin viewed himself as the logical heir apparent to Weiner and saw himself building on Weiner's extensive track record of shucking for Israel in Congress. In an interview with *Politicker*, a website of the weekly *New York Observer*, Weprin described the fallen member of Congress as a "strong supporter" of Israel, but argued that he himself "certainly would be just as strong if not stronger in my support of Israel." During his campaign, Weprin even went so far as to condemn the president for paying back Prime Minister

Netanyahu for his humiliation of Vice President Joe Biden during his March 2010 trip. Weprin indignantly spewed, in reference to Obama having forced Netanyahu to cool his heels at a subsequent White House meeting, that "I thought it was outrageous the way he treated Prime Minister Netanyahu." The candidate appeared bewildered, and rightfully so, that people would "question my support of the state of Israel and my outspokenness, regardless of party affiliation."[2]

It was not, however, Weprin's policy positions or credentials that animated the most stringent and heated opposition to his candidacy, even from within the ranks of his own party. This opposition arose instead out a fervent desire on the part of Israel's staunchest backers to deliberately punish Obama and the Democratic Party for its perceived anti-Israel bias by electing a Republican to fill Weiner's vacated position. Thus prominent New York City Democratic politicians would snub Weprin in favor of his Republican rival Bob Turner—a Catholic who had never visited Israel and who had never shown any fealty to it—in order to hobble the Democratic Party in the House of Representatives.

The most significant example of this phenomenon occurred in July 2011, when former Democratic New York City mayor Ed Koch, speaking at a podium next to an Israeli flag, endorsed Turner, claiming that Obama displayed "open hostility to the State of Israel." According to Koch, "many believe," presumably including the former mayor himself, "that he [Obama] is willing to throw it [Israel] under the bus and end the special relationship which has existed between the US and Israel." Koch made clear that although he considered Weprin to be "a major supporter of Israel and highly critical of President Obama's hostile actions to that state," he nevertheless argued that the Democratic candidate "could not be an effective messenger." Koch reasoned that even with another Democrat in Congress slamming the president's policies toward Israel and the Palestinians, Weprin's "election would be viewed by President Obama as simply that of another Democrat elected to office in what is one of the largest Jewish constituencies in the nation and acceptive [sic] of the president, notwithstanding criticism of his positions." Therefore, Koch concluded, it would be better to cross party lines to help elect a Republican to Congress and "send a message" to the president.[3]

Koch's endorsement of Turner left Weprin flabbergasted. Upon hearing the news, "My first thought is to quote one of Mayor Koch's famous lines: 'That's ridiculous!' It's just absurd," Weprin stated.[4] Although Koch's endorsement of Turner was not necessarily the decisive factor in the race, it undoubtedly contributed to Turner's stunning upset victory, which placed New York's 9th Congressional district in the hands of the Republican Party for the first time since President Warren Harding occupied the White House.

What accounted for this bizarre political phenomenon of a prominent Democratic politician bucking his party's own candidate, whose stalwart and undoubtedly heartfelt record of advocating for Israel was second to none, for the sake of electing a Republican with only a transparently political and newfound interest in promoting Israel's cause, just to "send a message" to the Democratic president? It was an extreme example of the intensifying battle over which of the two major political parties was, or should be, more supportive of Israel. This brouhaha was largely a faux debate, as very few members of Congress from either party actively and consistently spoke out against US policy toward Israel and the Palestinians. However, these types of partisan accusations were nevertheless tending to break down the former carefully constructed bipartisan consensus on this issue, rendering the question of US support for Israel into yet another bitter, mudslinging partisan issue that was added into the toxic sludge of political discourse in which the US political system had become mired.

While this phenomenon was not entirely new, it intensified dramatically during Obama's first term, as Republicans increasingly used Israel as a wedge issue with which to hurt the administration and the president's party. In previous Congresses, Democrats and Republicans alike vied for the dubious distinction of having the legislative record most supportive of Israeli occupation and apartheid. In the 107th to 109th Congresses (2001–2006), Republicans only slightly outnumbered Democrats in the "Hall of Shame" Congressional Report Cards of the US Campaign to End the Israeli Occupation. The trend toward partisanship began in the 110th Congress (2007–2008), as Republicans accounted for approximately 60 percent of Members of Congress making the "Hall of Shame." However, this trend accelerated markedly in the 111th Congress

(2009–2010), with Republicans accounting for 90 percent of the "Hall of Shame." As of June 2012, of the fifty members of Congress with the worst legislative records on Israeli-Palestinian issues during the 112th Congress (2011–2012), forty-seven were Republicans, with only Representative Steven Rothman (NJ), Senator Ron Wyden (OR), and Representative Jan Schakowsky (IL) cracking the list for the Democrats.[5]

This trend certainly did not mean that Democrats had seen the light and embraced a new evenhanded approach to the Israeli-Palestinian conflict. Indeed, as documented throughout this book, Democrats have wholeheartedly joined Republicans in overwhelmingly passing all major pro-Israel, anti-Palestinian resolutions during Obama's presidency. Fundamental critiques of US policy toward Israel and the Palestinians in Congress have remained confined to the small, progressive wing of the Democratic Party and the even more politically inconsequential isolationist wing of the Republican Party. This tendency has demonstrated, however, that during the Bush administration, Democrats gladly crossed the aisle to frequently join with their Republican counterparts to serve as a backstop to the president's undisputed pro-Israel, anti-Palestinian policies. Obama's actual policies have been just as, if not more, tilted toward Israel than were those of Bush. However, because Obama sometimes disguised these policies with rhetorical flourishes more sympathetic to Palestinian rights, this discourse has permitted the Republicans to exploit for their own political gain the perception that Obama is hostile to Israel. As a result, Republicans have unleashed a barrage of anti-Palestinian resolutions that are designed to frustrate, constrain and undermine the president's policymaking. For the most part, Democrats in Congress, unlike Ed Koch, have refrained from jumping onto the bandwagon to undercut a Democratic president.

As the 2012 congressional and presidential election campaigns got underway, pro-Israel members of Congress, the Obama administration and proponents of the existing US-Israel relationship were disconcerted by this increasing partisan polarization around Israel. For example, Representative Gary Ackerman, one of Israel's staunchest supporters in Congress, was greatly perturbed by the implications of the administration's policies on Israel and the Palestinians being dragged into the special election to fill Weiner's vacated seat.

He urged "extreme caution to anyone proposing to make Israel into a partisan truncheon in our domestic politics." Ackerman deemed this squabble to be "deeply irresponsible," saying that it does Israel a considerable disservice."[6]

Anthony Blinken, deputy assistant to the president and national security advisor to the vice president, elaborated on these concerns before the liberal pro-Israel advocacy group J Street in March 2012, as the campaign season was well underway. Although "we welcome the debate" over the Obama administration's policies toward Israel and the Palestinians, Blinken warned, "what could actually harm US-Israeli relations, and the security of the Jewish state, is subjecting either to the vagaries of partisan politics or turning them into election-year talking points." However, he wanted to be clear that "this is not about stifling discussion, disagreement or dissent." Rather, Blinken urged, "It is about a simple proposition: when it comes to discussing US policy toward Israel in our political arena, by all means we should question each other's judgments—but not each other's motives." He concluded by correctly noting, "For generations, there has been a broad bipartisan consensus in America on those ideas." Blinken warned, "The stakes are too high—for us, and for Israel—to let that change now."[7]

Many individuals and organizations promoting a strong US-Israeli relationship felt the exact same way as Blinken, but found that they were ineffectual in preventing this partisan sniping over Israel from gaining momentum. Haim Malka, the Israeli-American senior fellow and deputy director of the Middle East Program at the Center for Strategic and International Studies, whose report on the diverging strategic interests of the United States and Israel was cited in Chapter 9, lamented that the "partisan wedge" over support for Israel "is likely to deepen, posing considerable challenges to Israel and the US-Israeli partnership." He warned, "Growing partisanship in the United States not only alienates Democratic Party supporters but also does little to guarantee consistent Republican Party support."[8] In an attempt to check this burgeoning trend, two stalwarts of the Israel lobby—the Anti-Defamation League (ADL) and the American Jewish Committee (AJC)—issued a National Pledge for Unity on Israel in October 2011, which beseeched "national organizations, elected officials, religious leaders, community groups and individuals to rally around bipartisan support for Israel while preventing the Jewish State from becoming a wedge issue in the upcoming campaign season."[9]

However, instead of calming the waters, this pledge only served to roil them more. William Kristol, the founder of the Emergency Committee for Israel, a right-wing political advocacy organization, which had probably done more than any other organization to drive this wedge by running ads against the supposed anti-Israel records of Democratic candidates for office, excoriated the joint ADL/AJC campaign. "You must be kidding," Kristol stated in response to the pledge. These organizations "need a refresher course on the virtues of free speech and robust debate in a democracy," he scolded. "Their effort to stifle discussion and debate is unworthy of the best traditions of America, and of Israel." Matt Brooks, executive director of the Republican Jewish Coalition, was similarly appalled by the pledge, which he viewed as an "effort to stifle debate on US policy toward Israel" that "runs counter to this American tradition" of free speech. Brooks vowed that his organization "will not be silenced on this or any issue."[10]

Meanwhile, on the liberal end of the pro-Israel advocacy spectrum, Jeremy Ben-Ami, the founder of J Street, whose political action committee funneled campaign contributions to Democratic candidates who it deemed to be supportive of Obama's agenda for a two-state resolution to the Israeli-Palestinian conflict, also fretted about this polarization. "Pushed by a vibrant echo chamber of pundits and activists," Republican candidates "are seeking to claim the term 'pro-Israel' as the exclusive property of the political right," Ben-Ami claimed. As his organization attempted to shift the definition of "pro-Israel" to the political left, in a true partisan fashion he rather disingenuously argued, "Their agenda is not to ensure bipartisan support for aid to Israel or nurturing US-Israeli ties based on shared interests and values."[11]

It was hard to ignore that the vast majority of the consternation and hand-wringing over the politicization of US policy toward Israel was an intramural affair, confined to the Jewish-American community's self-defined "pro-Israel" advocacy crowd. In this back-and-forth struggle, long-established organizations sought to uphold the traditional bipartisan amicability on US policy toward Israel, while overtly partisan newcomers struggled to shift the demarcation of what constituted being "pro-Israel" to their own political bent. However, if this struggle played out within the limited boundaries of the various "pro-Israel" advocacy organizations, its consequences would reverberate throughout the US political arena, as partisanship over Israel became a prominent feature of the 2012 presidential election.

ISRAEL, PALESTINIANS AND THE 2012 ELECTION

In their attempts to distinguish themselves both from other candidates within their own political party and from the opposing party, the candidates for the 2012 presidential election deployed an unprecedented degree of falsehood and vitriol to denigrate their competitors' allegedly deficient support for Israel and to puff up their own credentials by disparaging the Palestinians. With the possible exception of former Pennsylvania senator Rick Santorum, whose adherence to the precepts of Christian Zionism appeared genuine, the presidential candidates seemed motivated by crass political gain in their ever-greater pledges of fidelity to Israel. In both the cases of Obama and his Republican challengers, there were two perceived political benefits to kowtowing to Israel and presenting their opponents as saboteurs of Israel's security: campaign contributions motivated primarily, if not exclusively, by the candidates' professed commitments to Israel; and Jewish-American votes. In the case of Republican candidates, an added motivation for staking out these positions was to capture and mobilize the Christian Zionist voting bloc, a constituency which was largely written off by the Democratic Party as being unreachable.

As of August 2012, the total campaign contributions given to congressional and presidential candidates during the 2012 election cycle by individuals and political action committees (PACs) described as being "pro-Israel" amounted to $7.7 million, according to the Center for Responsive Politics. Surprisingly, given the extent to which large segments of the "pro-Israel" advocacy community had upbraided Obama during his first term for his supposedly hostile positions toward Israel, the president, with $359,000, was the largest recipient of these funds. Former Massachusetts governor Mitt Romney, Obama's Republican challenger, was the fourth-leading recipient with $249,000.[12] However, given that federal campaign finance laws still restricted the amount that both individuals and PACs could contribute to federal candidates, this relatively small pot of money was not the one for which candidates fought in their pandering for "pro-Israel" campaign financing.

In January 2010, the Supreme Court issued a landmark and highly controversial ruling in *Citizens United v. Federal Election Commission*, which stipulated that independent political expenditures by corporations and unions constituted protected free speech under the First Amendment and could not be limited by the government. This decision paved the way for the establishment of "super PACs," which allowed individuals and the aforementioned entities to make unrestricted contributions to organizations that ran ads for and against particular candidates, as long as those ads, with a wink and a nudge, were not officially coordinated with the candidate's campaign. More than any other recent development in US campaign financing, the emergence of "super PACs" demonstrated how the fabulously wealthy gamed the US political system to their advantage. As of August 2012, a total of only 6,448 individuals had contributed approximately $215 million to these "super PACs" in the 2012 election cycle, according to the Center for Responsive Politics. Even within this aristocracy, there was an even further tier of hierarchy and elitism, as the top one hundred individual donors gave nearly three-quarters of this sum.[13]

"Pro-Israel" individual donors were quick to take advantage of the opening provided by these "super PACs" to push their agenda of ever-increasing US support for Israel. By calibrating their positions on Israel to appeal to the mega-donors of these new "super PACs," the candidates hoped to strike gold. At least three of the top one hundred donors to "super PACs" in the 2012 election cycle made no secret of the fact that their political donations were motivated primarily, if not exclusively, by their desire to ensure the continued domination of Israel over the Palestinians. These donors included casino tycoon Sheldon Adelson, who, along with his Israeli-born wife Miriam, had donated $36 million as of August 2012 to "super PACs" supporting the candidacies first of Republican presidential hopeful

Newt Gingrich and later Romney, making the Adelsons by far the largest "super PAC" donors.[14] Before Gingrich dropped out of the Republican primary race in May 2012, *Forbes* reported that Adelson, whose personal wealth is reputed to be $25 billion, pledged up to $100 million to defeat Obama; further donations beyond that could be "limitless," according to an aide.[15]

Adelson's views on the Israeli-Palestinian conflict placed him on the far-right wing of the Israeli political spectrum. His 2007 establishment of the free Israeli newspaper *Yisrael Hayom*, which toes the line of his close friend Prime Minister Netanyahu, reflected perhaps the mildest of Adelson's political opinions. Speaking at a December 2011 event hosted by Birthright Israel, an organization to which he has donated more than $100 million and which provides young Jews who have not visited Israel with an all-expenses-paid, highly selective, propagandistic tour of the country, Adelson denied the existence of the Palestinian people. "Read the history of those who call themselves Palestinians," he thundered, "and you will hear why Gingrich said recently that the Palestinians are an invented people."[16] Adelson held Israel blameless for failing to make peace with Palestinians because the Palestinians' "sole mission is to destroy you [Israel]." Palestinians must not be permitted an independent state since it would lead to genocide against Jews, according to Adelson, who maintained that "the two-state solution is a stepping stone for the destruction of Israel and the Jewish people." These types of incendiary comments against Palestinians even extended to Adelson's critique of Obama's policy toward Israel. He preposterously accused the president of taking measures "against the state of Israel" that "are liable to bring about the destruction of the state."[17] Adelson even apparently held Israel more dearly in his heart than his own country, revealingly stating in July 2010, "The uniform that I wore in the military, unfortunately, was not an Israeli uniform." The fact that Adelson's political contributions were, in large measure, designed to draw US politicians closer to his extremist views helped explain the grotesque pandering of politicians to Israel during the 2012 elections.[18]

Adelson was joined on the list of top one hundred donors to "super PACs" by other "pro-Israel" political donors such as Haim Saban, the Israeli-American entertainment mogul whose donations on behalf of strengthening the US-Israel relationship were cited in Chapter 8. Saban and his wife Cheryl's nearly $2 million in contributions, as of August 2012, made them the sixteenth largest "super PAC" donors, while Irving and Cherna Moscowitz donated slightly more than $1 million to "super PACs," placing them thirty-first in the ranking.[19] Moscowitz owned a bingo hall in the destitute city of Hawaiian Gardens, near Los Angeles, taking the profits from his working-class clientele to funnel tens of millions of dollars to organizations that supported Israel's colonization of Palestinian land, including some of the Israeli settlements populated by the most extremist settlers in the Old City of Jerusalem and Hebron.[20]

The political donations of people such as Adelson, Saban, Moscowitz and numerous others who contributed in less eye-popping amounts were certainly a compelling reason for candidates to moderate or alter their positions on Israel, or simply to say what they thought the contributors wanted to hear. Another factor that propelled this phenomenon was the perceived need to pander to the Jewish-American community on Israel to win its vote. This pandering, hardly a new development, was problematic on two fronts. First, it stereotyped Jewish-Americans as maintaining Israel as their overriding political concern. An April 2012 Public Religion Research Institute opinion survey found this prioritization was true for only a small section of the Jewish-American community. Only 4 percent of respondents rated Israel as their top political concern in the 2012 elections and only 6 percent noted it as their secondary concern. Moreover, despite widespread analysis that Obama would lose Jewish-American support due to his insistence on an Israeli settlement freeze early in his administration, the survey found that "current levels of support for Obama among Jewish voters are nearly identical to levels of support for Obama among Jewish registered voters at a comparable point in the 2008 campaign," an election in which Obama won 78 percent of the Jewish-American vote.[21]

Second, the tendency of politicians to pander to the Jewish-American community on Israel demonstrated a profound disregard for the opinions of Palestinian-, Arab- and Muslim-American voting constituencies, whose national, ethnic and religious ties to the Holy Land were just as important as those of Jewish-Americans, and who tended to be profoundly concerned about the plight of

Palestinians. For example, an April 2012 Institute for Social Policy and Understanding opinion survey found that 87 percent of Muslim-Americans backed the United States supporting the establishment of an independent Palestinian state, and 80 percent agreed that the United States should reduce its level of support to Israel to attain this goal.[22] If these voting constituencies become larger and more politically engaged, and if the Jewish-American community continues to splinter over its attitudes toward the Israeli-Palestinian conflict, then politicians in future elections are likely to find that this type of unqualified pandering to Israel works to the detriment of their vote count.

But if the presidential campaigns had any understanding of these electoral nuances and subtleties, then they certainly did not let on. Instead, the electorate was treated to one over-the-top statement after another, as the candidates engaged in risible rhetoric that treated the Israeli-Palestinian conflict as inane political theater rather than an important foreign policy issue in need of serious scrutiny and reevaluation. Republican challengers leveled absurd charges against Obama, such as when Romney accused the president in May 2011 of having "thrown Israel under the bus."[23]

Republican presidential candidates, with the exception of Representative Ron Paul, whose support for ending US aid to Israel made him persona non grata at the event, used the Republican Jewish Coalition's December 2011 presidential candidate forum to ratchet up their condemnations of Obama's policy toward Israel. Texas governor Rick Perry maintained that Obama had "undermined our historic friendship with Israel." He claimed that Obama's demand that Israel cease settlement activity was one of the "unheard-of preconditions" Obama was attempting to impose on Israel, conveniently neglecting the fact that Perry's predecessor as Texas governor—George W. Bush—insisted on the same stipulation when his administration issued the 2003 Roadmap. All of these "preconditions" and other specious claims amounted to the Obama administration having unleashed a "torrent of hostility towards Israel," according to Perry.[24]

Representative Michele Bachmann (R-MN), referencing Israeli settlement expansion, chided Obama for being "concerned about Israel building homes on its own land," thereby denying Palestinian national claims to the West Bank and East Jerusalem. She accused the president of displaying "weakness in the Middle East that has emboldened the Palestinians," and invoked the ghost of Neville Chamberlain to assert that Obama "has confused engagement with appeasement and has inspired Israel's enemies." Obama had, in her view, engaged in a campaign of "delegitimization" and "defaming" of Israel. A Bachmann administration, the candidate claimed, would move the US embassy to Jerusalem, recognize Israel's illegal annexation of the Syrian Golan Heights and back Israel's incorporation of whichever settlement blocs it chose to annex.[25]

These types of outlandish policy statements characterized the entire presidential forum. Perhaps fearing that his own speech at the Republican Jewish Coalition was not hard-core enough in its support for Israel, former Speaker of the House Newt Gingrich claimed later that week in an interview with the *Jewish Channel* that Palestinians were an "invented" people. Gingrich's comments were not a bad garbling of Benedict Anderson's classic study of modern nationalism, in which Anderson argued that nationhood is a modern construct of an "imagined political community."[26] Rather, this was part of a conscious campaign to denigrate and deny Palestinian identity and political rights, which undoubtedly pleased his main booster Sheldon Adelson. Instead of backing down from this incendiary comment, Gingrich further prevaricated that "'Palestinian' did not become a common term until after 1977. This is a propaganda war in which our side refuses to engage and we refuse to tell the truth when the other side lies."[27] During this December 11, 2011, primary debate, Gingrich further upped the ante by stating, "Somebody oughta have the courage to tell the truth." That somebody was him. "These people," Gingrich added, referring to Palestinians, "are terrorists."[28]

The Obama reelection campaign was also guilty of indulging in cant regarding its opponents' supposed lack of devotion to Israel in order to boost its campaign coffers. For example, a prominent Facebook ad sponsored by Obama's campaign provocatively asked: "No Aid to Israel?" The ad claimed, "Mitt Romney, Rick Perry, and Newt Gingrich say they would start foreign aid to Israel at zero." The ad breathlessly implored voters to "reject their extreme plan now!" After signing a petition to this effect on Obama's reelection website, one was greeted by a beaming photo of the president with a caption underneath declaring, "Any plan to cut foreign aid to zero across the board is dangerous and ignorant. It's up to us to get the word out about it. Donate now to help us spread the facts about the Romney-Perry-Gingrich plan to wipe out foreign aid to allies like Israel."[29] The problem was that Obama's ad did not jibe with reality. Although some Republican presidential candidates did favor beginning the discussion on foreign aid to all countries at zero and then deciding the actual amounts each country would receive from that starting point, all of them, with the exception of Paul, unabashedly supported fully funding military aid for Israel. The Obama campaign's transparent ploy to secure "pro-Israel" donations by distorting his opponents' statements was yet one more manifestation of the growing electoral partisanship over Israel.

As Romney secured enough delegates to become the presumptive Republican nominee for president, a trifecta of inane statements by the candidate cast grave doubt on his knowledge of the Israeli-Palestinian conflict and his ability to manage this major foreign policy issue if elected. In the same December 2011 Republican primary debate in which Gingrich called Palestinians "terrorists" and dated their national identity to 1977, Romney stated that before making such incendiary remarks, as president he would "get on the phone to my friend Bibi Netanyahu and say, 'Would it help if I said this? What would you like me to do? Let's work together, because we're partners.'"[30] In other words, making hateful and racist statements about Palestinians was only inappropriate, in Romney's eyes, if Israel had not first blessed the initiative. Thus under a Romney administration, the United States would not be able to conduct an independent foreign policy toward Israel and the Palestinians, but instead would have to take their cues from the Israeli government.

In addition, when asked on the campaign trail in June 2012 how his administration would conduct its policy toward Israel and the Palestinians, Romney summed up his approach this way: "You could just look at the things the president (Barack Obama) has done and do the opposite."[31] For a candidate who tried to portray himself as being more "pro-Israel" than the incumbent, it was a monumental mistake by Romney, who revealed his stunning ignorance of the extent to which the Obama administration had ramped up US military and diplomatic support for Israel to new levels. Representative Debbie Wasserman Schultz (D-FL), chair of the Democratic National Committee, gleefully took Romney to task for "playing politics with America's bipartisan support for Israel." Responding to Romney's pledge to do the opposite of Obama, she rightfully noted "that means a Romney administration would slash security assistance funding, abandon Israel at the UN, de-fund the Iron Dome system protecting Israelis from terrorist rockets, and dismantle the hardest hitting sanctions Iran has ever faced."[32]

Finally, during a widely panned July 2012 political pilgrimage to Israel, Romney termed it "a deeply moving experience to be in Jerusalem, the capital of Israel," parroting a similar controversial statement made by Obama on the 2008 campaign trail.[33] However, these remarks were overshadowed by Romney's observation at a Jerusalem fundraiser that there existed a "dramatic, stark difference in economic vitality" between Israelis and Palestinians. This "stark difference," in Romney's opinion, had nothing to do with the fact that Israel's military occupation of Palestinian land was intentionally designed to eviscerate the Palestinian economy and render it completely dependent on Israel. Rather, Romney held that "culture makes all the difference. And as I come here and I look out over this city and consider the accomplishments of the people of this nation, I recognize the power of at least culture and a few other things." One wonders if the hand-selected Jewish-American donors at the fundraiser squirmed uncomfortably in their chairs as Romney played up this anti-Semitic trope of Jewish business acumen, while relegating Palestinians to being their cultural inferiors. But it was not just "culture" that explained Israel's success; the preternaturally disposed presidential candidate also saw "the hand of providence in selecting this place." He vaguely mused, "There's also something very unusual about the people of this place," which explained their success.[34]

While US support for Israel became a mud-slinging, partisan issue during Obama's first term and the 2012 elections—much to the chagrin of Jewish-Americans supporters of Israel, who were worried that this hyperbole would undermine the traditional bipartisan comity that had previously existed—the faux debate over which candidate or party was most supportive of Israel was devoid of substance. Despite the bitterness of the political rhetoric, during

Obama's first term the president and a huge bipartisan majority in Congress worked hand-in-glove to provide Israel with unrivaled diplomatic and military support, making the United States even less of an "honest broker" to the Israeli-Palestinian conflict than it had been beforehand.

If there was a silver lining to this gross display of political buffoonery, then it lay in the possibility of Israel becoming normalized as a political issue, rather than treated as an untouchable political sacred cow. Ironically, by fighting over which candidate and party love Israel most, politicians may inadvertently be opening up the political space that is needed to eventually have a more honest discussion over whether current US policy toward Israel and the Palestinians is on the right track. This is a serious, national political debate that is long overdue. Unconditional US diplomatic and military support for Israeli military occupation and apartheid policies toward Palestinians is morally wrong, economically unsustainable and undermines US foreign policy objectives and strategic interests. When the history is written of future administrations' policies toward Israel and the Palestinians, it will hopefully document how the United States changed its long-standing policies toward Israel and the Palestinians to support human rights, international law and equality, leading to the establishment of a just and lasting Israeli-Palestinian peace.

Conclusion

W hy did the Obama administration so spectacularly fail in its high-profile gambit to negotiate an Israeli-Palestinian peace accord in its first term? According to senior administration officials, the United States was not really at fault. After all, the United States could not want Israeli-Palestinian peace more than the players involved in the conflict, they argued. Addressing the US-Islamic World Forum in Doha, Qatar, in February 2010, after having spent more than a year fruitlessly attempting to get Israeli and Palestinian negotiators back to the table, Secretary of State Hillary Clinton acknowledged the frustration that many felt at the inability of the United States to reconvene talks, much less shepherd them to a successful conclusion. "I know people are disappointed that we have not yet achieved a breakthrough. The President, Senator Mitchell, and I are also disappointed," she stated. "But we must remember that neither the United States nor any country can force a solution. The parties themselves must resolve their differences through negotiations."[1]

This explanation, or lack thereof, for the supposed powerlessness of the United States to broker Israeli-Palestinian peace served as a convenient catchall for the Obama administration. Not only did Clinton deploy this reasoning to account for why the United States struggled to reconvene Israeli-Palestinian negotiations; President Barack Obama also fell back on this same theme to exculpate his administration after the short-lived resumption of negotiations, held under US auspices, ingloriously fizzled out in September 2010. Speaking at the UN General Assembly one year later, as the Obama administration furiously beat back the Palestinian bid for UN membership, the president told the assembled body of world leaders that "a genuine peace can only be realized between the Israelis and the Palestinians themselves." Obama greatly regretted that "despite extensive efforts by America and others, the parties have not bridged their differences." Like Clinton in Doha, Obama recognized "that many are frustrated by the lack of progress. I assure you, so am I." But, again, neither the United States nor the international community could want a peace agreement more than the Israelis and Palestinians, Obama argued. More direct negotiations were the only conceivable path, since "ultimately, it is the Israelis and the Palestinians—not us—who must reach agreement on the issues that divide them: on borders and on security, on refugees and Jerusalem."[2]

If Obama were President Theodore Roosevelt, and Israel and the Palestinians were Russia and Japan—countries which actively sought out the impartial mediation of the US president to end their 1905 war (a successful effort for which Roosevelt won the Nobel Peace Prize)—then perhaps the Obama administration's attitude would have seemed plausible. However, Israel and the Palestinians were not two sovereign nations at war asking the United States to resolve an international conflict. Rather, Israel had dispossessed the majority of Palestinians from their homes and lands through a deliberate campaign of ethnic cleansing in 1948. These Palestinians and their descendants remain refugees to this day because Israel denies them their internationally guaranteed right of return. Those Palestinians not driven from their homeland in 1948 became second-class citizens of Israel. And Palestinians in the West Bank, East Jerusalem and the Gaza Strip have lived under Israel's brutal military occupation for more than forty-five years.

Under these apartheid conditions, it was disingenuous, to say the least, for Obama to fail to recognize this asymmetry, to treat the parties as equals in power and responsibility and to shrug his shoulders when he determined that the parties just were not ready to resolve their conflict. This stance was problematic in several respects. First, how could Israel and the Palestinians resolve their conflict through negotiation when the oppressor sought to use these negotiations to consolidate its apartheid rule, while the oppressed attempted to undo at least part of this injustice through those same negotiations? After two decades of failed "peace process" negotiations, the lesson learned should not have been that the parties needed more time to talk; rather, the lesson learned should have been that these direct negotiations came about too soon because Israel remained throughout the process as committed as ever to perpetual domination over the Palestinians. As was the case in ending apartheid rule in South Africa, an Israeli-Palestinian peace agreement could come about only after the oppressor had agreed to the principle of living in equality and coexistence with the oppressed, not beforehand.

Second, the Obama administration's self-exoneration for its failure to broker Israeli-Palestinian peace elided the fact that its policies of providing Israel with unconditional military and diplomatic support solidified the very conditions that made peace impossible. The United States was giving Israel the war materiel that it needed to sustain, deepen and entrench its military occupation of the Palestinian West Bank, East Jerusalem and Gaza Strip, and to further Israel's illegal colonization of Palestinian land. Any attempt by the Obama administration to blame the lack of credible negotiations on Israelis and Palestinians not wanting peace badly enough, while simultaneously ignoring the fact that the United States was violating the rule of non-maleficence by larding Israel with weapons, was a gross distortion of political reality.

Third, the Obama administration's lack of introspection on the crucial role it played in sinking the prospects for Israeli-Palestinian peace was compounded by a chauvinistic, heavy-handed approach to international diplomacy that belittled and quashed any alternative efforts outside of the US-dominated "peace process" framework to resolve the Israeli-Palestinian conflict. Speaking at the same UN General Assembly meeting in 2011, Obama assured his fellow heads of state that "the question isn't the goal that we seek—the question is how do we reach that goal." However, it was obvious that Obama had run out of ideas to attain that objective, as the president had nothing to offer other than platitudes: "I am convinced that there is no short cut to the end of a conflict that has endured for decades. Peace is hard work." But if Obama had no sense of how to reach Israeli-Palestinian peace, then he was also cocksure that the UN did not have an answer either. "Peace will not come through statements and resolutions at the United Nations," he sanctimoniously intoned, because "if it were that easy, it would have been accomplished by now."[3]

However, Obama was being extremely dishonest by deprecating the UN for adopting so many resolutions in its attempts to end the Israeli-Palestinian conflict. The fact that the UN returned so often to the Israeli-Palestinian conflict was evidence not of its incompetence or supposed systemic anti-Israel bias, but of the fact that US diplomatic protection of Israel at the UN enabled Israel to thumb its nose at the world body with impunity. If it were not for the US veto in the Security Council, or the threat thereof, then perhaps it is true that peace still would not have been attained. But had the international community been able to hold Israel accountable for the crimes it committed during Operation Cast Lead and its attack on the Gaza Freedom Flotilla, had Palestine been admitted to the UN as a member state, had the UN imposed sanctions on Israel for repeatedly failing in its obligations to implement UN resolutions, then perhaps peace would be at hand, if not yet realized. But Obama's claim that UN statements and resolutions on the Israeli-Palestinian conflict were ineffectual would have to remain an untested hypothesis, as the actions of the United States prevented them from being implemented.

The Obama administration's efforts to attribute the lack of Israeli-Palestinian peace to the parties themselves were unconvincing, as it mischaracterized the nature of the conflict and whitewashed US culpability in providing Israel with the military and diplomatic support that perpetuated it. Besides, with the United States arrogating to itself the role of mediating the Israeli-Palestinian conflict, while simultaneously relegating other interested actors to the role of cheer-leaders for, or even bystanders to, US diplomatic efforts, the success or failure of the Israeli-Palestinian "peace process" lay just as much, if not more, with the United States than with the primary players. In this respect, the Obama administration deserves just as much opprobrium as its three immediate predecessors for leading a failed "peace process," even if it pursued the issue at the outset of its tenure with more energy and determination than the Bush administration it followed.

In assessing the Obama administration's approach to achieving Israeli-Palestinian peace, kudos, however, must be given to the president for insisting early in his first term on a full Israeli settlement freeze. For nearly two decades of the Israeli-Palestinian "peace process," Palestinians had looked on in consternation as Israel continued and even accelerated its colonization of Palestinian land that was supposedly intended for a future Palestinian state. This colonization, perhaps more than any other single factor, symbolized for Palestinians the sham nature of the "peace process" and Israel's demonstrable lack of good faith in negotiations. At the outset, the Obama administration intuitively understood that in order to salvage the receding prospects for a two-state resolution of the Israeli-Palestinian conflict, Israel would first and foremost have to comply with international law and its commitments under the 2003 Roadmap to freeze all settlement activity. As the president viewed it, his unequivocal policy on Israeli settlements was both a continuation of and improvement upon the stance of the Bush administration. In May 2010, Obama met with a delegation of thirty-seven Jewish members of Congress to discuss their concerns about the crisis in US-Israeli relations that had resulted from Vice President Biden's ruinous trip to Israel in March 2010. As the president explained to the members of Congress, "My policy on settlements is no different than George Bush's policy towards settlements." However, Obama believed that his policy was more consistent, telling the members of Congress that unlike Bush, "I won't wink and nod" at Israel's settlement expansion.[4]

However, by the time of this meeting, the Obama administration had, for nearly one year, been doing exactly what the president had accused Bush of doing: offering desultory and ineffectual statements opposing Israel's settlement expansion, while tolerating it nonetheless. As early as June 2009, the Obama administration concluded that it could not secure a complete freeze on Israeli settlement expansion. Rather than reevaluating its policy options, the Obama administration began to engage in an unseemly and unprincipled bazaar-style haggling with Israel over the terms of a limited settlement "moratorium" that the administration privately and publicly acknowledged fell short of Israel's requirement to freeze settlements. Worse yet, the Obama administration did so behind the backs of the Palestinian negotiating team and, once the parameters of the "moratorium" became clear, Secretary of State Hillary Clinton and Special Envoy for Middle East Peace George Mitchell lavished unearned praise on it and attempted to foist the unilateral Israeli measure upon the Palestinians as a flawed basis for the resumption of negotiations.

In retrospect, it is fairly evident that the Obama administration was rather naively unprepared for the intensity of the pushback from Israel and its supporters in the United States to its demand that Israel freeze settlements. In a defining fight-or-flight moment for his administration's policy on the Israeli-Palestinian conflict, Obama decided to bow to this pressure, rather than openly confront it. Had Obama appealed to the public for support in his position, he would have found overwhelming receptivity. A public opinion survey released in April 2009 by World Public Opinion, a project of the Program on International Policy Attitudes at the University of Maryland, found that three-quarters of Americans opposed Israel's building of settlements in Occupied Palestinian Territory, with a whopping 83 percent of Democrats registering their opposition to Israeli settlement expansion.[5]

Obama's decision to override this clear majoritarian sentiment and accede to the demands of the Israel lobby was a dramatic manifestation of Mancur Olson's classical hypothesis that the US political system is geared to favor well-organized special interest groups, even when their agendas are opposed to common sense and public opinion. In his book *The Logic of Collective Action: Public Goods and the Theory of Groups*, Olson had argued, "In small groups with common interests there is accordingly *a surprising tendency for the 'exploitation' of the great by the small* [italics in original]."[6] Facing the wrath of AIPAC in May 2009, as this premier Israel lobby organization mobilized three-quarters of Congress to send Obama "cease and desist" letters, the president capitulated. Later that month he told the quintessential "Israel-firster" policymaker Dennis Ross that Ross would now "quarterback" all Middle East issues. Although Ross's formal move from the State Department to the National Security Council, the perch from which he would now direct Israeli-Palestinian policy, was not announced publicly until one month after this conversation, this shift had the almost immediate effect of undercutting and undermining the public statements of Obama, Clinton and Mitchell declaring that a complete Israeli settlement freeze was in order. In Ross's view, "the problem" with the Obama administration's policy on freezing Israeli settlements "was that it put the emphasis on one issue when it wasn't the only, or even most important, issue and, in any case, needed to be put into context."

By the time Obama first met with approximately one dozen

Jewish-American organizational leaders in mid-July 2009, the climb-down from his initial insistence on an Israeli settlement freeze was already well underway. During this meeting, Abe Foxman, the National Director of the Anti-Defamation League, expressed concern that the Obama administration was not being "evenhanded" in its approach to the Israeli-Palestinian conflict, an extraordinarily hypo-critical assertion given that Foxman had just recently condemned Mitchell for his supposed "neutrality." Instead of defending his posi-tion on Israeli settlements, Obama responded: "Abe, you are abso-lutely right and we are going to fix that," noting that "the sense of evenhandedness has to be restored."

From this point forward, Obama's goal of achieving Israeli-Palestinian peace stood no chance of succeeding, as the Obama administration defined "evenhandedness" as reverting to the default stance of the Clinton and Bush administrations, which had coordi-nated their positions with Israel and then tag-teamed to try to bend Palestinians to their will. But in its disheveled effort to broker Israeli-Palestinian peace with this discredited approach, the Obama admin-istration lurched from one initiative to the next as it failed to develop a coherent strategy. After jettisoning his insistence on Israel freezing settlements and compromising instead on an insincere "morato-rium," Obama repeatedly asked his advisors, "What's the strategy here?" Obama wanted to know how a "moratorium" on settlements would "get us where we want to be? Tell me the relationship between what we are doing and our objective," the president demanded.[7]

The rapidity with which the Obama administration changed courses was evidence of his advisers' inability to answer this ques-tion. In quick succession from May 2009 to December 2010, the Obama administration called for a freeze on Israeli settlements, urged negotiations to resume with or without a settlement freeze, cheered on a faulty settlement "moratorium," arm-twisted the Palestinians back to the negotiating table on the basis of this "mora-torium," convened negotiations which were doomed to failure and then tried to bribe Israel back to the negotiating table before giving up the effort. These abrupt changes in approach gave the Obama administration's Israeli-Palestinian policymaking an incoherent feel.

After December 2010, the Obama administration was wholly concerned with fighting rearguard actions to protect Israel from diplomatic initiatives of the Palestinians, who had belatedly realized that they would never get a fair shake from any US-dominated "peace process." Obama fought tooth and nail to scupper these initiatives, which included the February 2011 UN settlement resolution and the fall 2011 drive for membership in the UN and its subsidiary agencies. With the one feeble exception of suggesting in May 2011 that Israel and the Palestinians confine a new round of negotiations to borders and security, deferring all other permanent status issues to an undetermined future date, the Obama administration made no further effort to restart the "peace process" during the second half of its first term.

Obama's failure to achieve Israeli-Palestinian peace resulted not only from his unwillingness to go to the mat with the Israel lobby over the issue of fully freezing Israeli settlements, nor only from the scattershot, frenetic lurching of his policy initiatives thereafter. Obama also foundered because his approach relied solely on providing Israel with carrots. With the trivial exceptions of denying Israeli Prime Minister Benjamin Netanyahu photo-ops at the White House on a few occasions and reportedly forcing him to wait for several hours before a meeting, Obama never brandished the proverbial stick. But these personal insults did nothing to create incentives for Israel to cease openly and brazenly defying US policy objectives.

In fact, it seemed that the more Israel deliberately frustrated and humiliated US efforts to broker Israeli-Palestinian peace, the more rewards it was offered by the United States as a result. Like parents who try to purchase the good behavior of their child with an extravagant toy and wind up with a spoiled child who always demands more, the Obama administration actually incentivized Israel's refusal to stop colonizing Palestinian lands. The most egregious example of this attempt to buy Israel's love occurred in the immediate aftermath of the all-too-predictable collapse of the relaunched Israeli-Palestinian negotiations in September 2010. The Obama administration begged and pleaded with Israel to agree to a meaningless, one-time, sixty- to ninety-day extension of its sham settlement "moratorium," which would only have delayed the inevitable collapse of the "peace process" by a few months. To sweeten the deal for Israel, Obama was prepared to throw in $3 billion worth of F-35 fighter jets and diplomatic pledges of inestimable greater value.

Israel rightly reasoned that it made no sense to accept any limitation whatsoever on its behavior knowing that it could defy the president and still get ever-greater amounts of military aid and diplomatic protection from the Obama administration.

The transparent absurdity of this all-carrots, no-sticks policy was noted repeatedly by members of the media who grew weary of listening to State Department spokespersons repeat ad nauseam that the United States had expressed to Israel that it was "concerned about continuing Israeli action with respect to housing construction" in Occupied Palestinian Territory. Take, for example, a small portion of an extended exchange between several media members and State Department spokesperson Victoria Nuland on August 11, 2011. Israel had just given its final approval for the construction of 1,600 settlement housing units in East Jerusalem, the same project whose initial announcement during Biden's March 2010 trip to Israel led to the gravest crisis in US-Israel relations during the Obama administration. After the project's final approval, the United States had registered its perfunctory disapproval. An exasperated Matthew Lee of the Associated Press pleaded with the State Department to change "this monotonous drone" because "it obviously doesn't do any good. It was just two days ago that you said you were deeply—or whatever it was—gravely concerned about settlement activity, and then two days later, the Israelis just go in and do it again. So your words of concern fall, obviously, on deaf ears." Nuland responded: "I apologize if you don't like our phraseology."

But it was not just the phrasing that perturbed attendees of the State Department press briefing. Rather, it seemed to Lee that the United States expressing concern about Israeli settlement expansion was an "exercise in futility. It's kind of like this bizarre kabuki dance where you express concern about something and the Israelis go ahead and do exactly what you're concerned about. And it happens over and over again." He wondered if "there might actually be a consequence for their action." Israel's actions did have consequences, in the view of the State Department. Israeli settlement expansion "undercuts trust" and "makes it harder to get folks back to the table," Nuland stated. However, "that's hardly a negative consequence from the Israeli point of view if they're not interested in getting back to the table," Arshad Mohammed of Reuters reasoned. "I mean, it's not like you're withholding loan guarantees, for example. It's not a tangible consequence that might actually cause the Israelis some financial or other discomfort." Imposing actual costs on Israel for defying the United States was not the point, though, Nuland argued. "The focus of our diplomacy," she stated, was "to get these parties back to the table."[8]

This circular logic epitomized the Obama administration's unwillingness to even consider using all of the policy tools at its disposal to compel a change in Israel's behavior. In this respect, Obama could have learned a lesson from President Dwight Eisenhower's deft handling of Israeli belligerence in the aftermath of the British-French-Israeli war against Egypt in 1956. Having already suspended US governmental aid to Israel after it had invaded Egypt's Sinai Peninsula in October, Eisenhower spoke before 18,000 people at a Philadelphia auditorium on November 1, 1956—less than one week before the presidential election that would return him to office for a second term—to reiterate US condemnation of Israel's aggression against Egypt. The United States "cannot and will not condone armed aggression—no matter who the attacker, and no matter who the victim," Eisenhower stated. "We cannot—in the world any more than in our own nation—subscribe to one law for the weak, another law for the strong; one law for those opposing us, another for those allied with us. There can be only one law or there will be no peace."[9] This forceful rhetoric was backed up with compelling action. One day after the presidential election, with Israel still dragging its feet on agreeing to vacate the Sinai Peninsula, the Eisenhower administration warned Israel that it would end all US governmental and private assistance forthwith if Israel continued its obstinacy. Israel announced the next day that it would withdraw from Egyptian territory.[10]

Would the end result of the Obama administration's efforts to achieve Israeli-Palestinian peace have looked different if Obama had emulated Eisenhower's tough response and matched his rhetoric in support of Palestinian self-determination with actions, including the threat of or actual implementation of sanctions against Israel? Unfortunately, this hypothetical scenario must be relegated to the "what if" bin of historical conjecture, as the Obama administration made clear that the option of sanctions, no matter how mild, was not on the table.

For example, in January 2010, on *The Charlie Rose Show*, Special

Envoy for Middle East Peace George Mitchell acknowledged that "the United States has both carrots and sticks." But, he cautioned, "you have to be very careful about how and when you use them and apply them." Rose wanted to know when the last time was that the United States used the stick with Israel. "I'm serious about this," Rose insisted. "You sit there and you say to Israel, look, if you don't do this—what?" Mitchell then referenced a US law first enacted during the George H.W. Bush administration that mandated deductions, which were equivalent to the amount spent by Israel on its settlements, in money made available to Israel for loan guarantees. "That's one mechanism that's been publicly discussed. There are others, and you have to keep open whatever options," Mitchell vaguely hinted. However, Mitchell immediately backed away from this nebulous threat of sanctions. "But our view is that we think the way to approach this is to try to persuade the parties what is in their self-interest. And we think that we are making some progress in that regard and we're going to continue in that effort, and we think the way to do it is to get them into negotiations."[11] Although the Obama administration and Congress had no qualms about threatening and later imposing sanctions on Palestinians for seeking membership in the UN and its subsidiary agencies, when it came to Israel, Mitchell's oblique reference to loan guarantee deductions would be the closest the Obama administration ever came during its first term to reminding Israel of the possible consequences of its actions.

Just as the Obama administration deserved credit for its initial, though short-lived, insistence that Israel freeze all settlement building, it also deserved credit for its clear-eyed understanding that the window for a negotiated two-state resolution to the Israeli-Palestinian conflict was quickly closing. Senior administration officials repeatedly attempted to convey this warning to Israel and its US supporters, as Obama himself did at the 2011 AIPAC policy conference. The president asserted that "no matter how hard it may be to start meaningful negotiations under current circumstances, we must acknowledge that a failure to try is not an option. The status quo is unsustainable." Maintaining that "real friends talk openly and honestly with one another," Obama cautioned that "the number of Palestinians living west of the Jordan River is growing rapidly and fundamentally reshaping the demographic realities of both Israel and the Palestinian Territories. This will make it harder and harder—without a peace deal—to maintain Israel as both a Jewish state and a democratic state."[12] This statement was an extremely delicate way of phrasing what was acknowledged more bluntly by former Israeli prime ministers such as Ehud Olmert and Ehud Barak: if Israel did not succeed soon in establishing a Bantustan-style Palestinian "state" devoid of sovereignty, then the two-state paradigm for resolving the Israeli-Palestinian conflict would collapse, leading to a struggle by Palestinians to attain equal rights with Israeli Jews within the context of a unitary or binational state.

The Obama administration's warnings about the imminent collapse of the two-state framework, however, went unheeded. In fact, toward the end of the Obama administration's first term, long after the Israeli-Palestinian conflict had been relegated to the backburner of US foreign policy priorities as the 2012 elections neared, Israel ostentatiously hammered another, possibly conclusive, nail into the coffin of the two-state resolution to the Israeli-Palestinian conflict and the charade of the "peace process." July 9, 2012, was the eighth anniversary of the International Court of Justice's landmark advisory opinion, which ruled Israel's wall in the West Bank to be illegal. In this ruling, the judges also reiterated that Israel's settlements in Occupied Palestinian Territory violate the Fourth Geneva Convention's prohibition on a state transferring its civilian population into territory that it occupies.

However, not coincidentally, that same day a committee appointed by the Israeli government to investigate the status of Israeli settlements released its diametrically opposed conclusion. The Levy Commission, named after its chair Edmund Levy, a former Israeli Supreme Court judge, determined in its report that Israel was not engaged in a military occupation of the Palestinian West Bank, East Jerusalem and Gaza Strip. According to the commission, "the classical laws of 'occupation' as set out in the relevant international conventions cannot be considered applicable to the unique and sui generis historic and legal circumstances of Israel's presence in Judea and Samaria [Israel's Biblical terms for the West Bank] spanning over decades." Furthermore,

the provisions of the 1949 Fourth Geneva Convention, regarding transfer of populations, cannot be considered to be applicable and were never intended to apply to the type of settlement activity carried out by Israel in Judea and Samaria. Therefore, according to International law, Israelis have the legal right to settle in Judea and Samaria and the establishment of settlements cannot, in and of itself, be considered to be illegal.[13]

It is difficult to imagine the Israeli government more brazenly thumbing its nose at the international community and the Obama administration on the issue of Israeli settlements. Perhaps even Netanyahu realized these conclusions were just too galling for the world to see; a promised "translation of the principal recommendations into the English language" found on page ninety of the report is nowhere to be found on the Israeli prime minister's website.[14] Could there be any more blatant proof than the Levy Commission that Israeli professions of wanting to return to the negotiating table were nothing more than a cover for its ironclad determination to continue colonizing Palestinian land?

With Netanyahu enjoying a solid and stable parliamentary coalition behind this pro-colonization agenda, the pertinent question at the end of the Obama administration's first term was not "where is the Palestinian Gandhi?" but, rather, "where is the Israeli de Gaulle?," the French premier who charted "a new course" and unequivocally committed France to the decolonization of Algeria. Where was the Israeli politician who would echo de Gaulle's comments to the French nation in November 1960, when he called for a transition "from government of Algeria by metropolitan France to an Algerian Algeria. That means an emancipated Algeria . . . an Algeria which, if the Algerians so wish—and I believe this to be the case—will have its own government, its own institutions, its own laws"?[15]

With no such Israeli political leader on the horizon and the Israeli government steadily moving more to the right, Israel's decolonization of Occupied Palestinian Territory—a step which could set the table for a credible two-state resolution to the Israeli-Palestinian conflict— seemed as dim a prospect as ever as the Obama administration ended its first term. As a result, in its second term the Obama administration will likely be confronted with several or all of the following challenges to US policy to establish a Palestinian state. First, without a drastic change of course, when Obama's term ends in January 2017, Israel's military occupation of the Palestinian West Bank, East Jerusalem and Gaza Strip will be entering its fiftieth year. There will likely be close to one million Israeli settlers living illegally on expropriated Palestinian land in the West Bank and East Jerusalem. Construction of Israel's wall encircling Palestinians into an open-air prison in the West Bank will likely be finalized, with Palestinians there as completely blockaded as their fellow Palestinians in the Gaza Strip are today. In short, Israel's de facto illegal annexation of the West Bank and East Jerusalem will be complete and its reversal unlikely.

Second, as a result of Israel's continuing colonization of Occupied Palestinian Territory, growing numbers of Palestinians, both principled and pragmatic Israeli Jews and people around the world will reject the feasibility and even the desirability of a two-state resolution to the Israeli-Palestinian conflict. It is worth recalling that the acceptance of a two-state resolution to the conflict by mainstream Israeli and Palestinian actors was only a recent development and is not set in stone. This plan of action was not adopted by the PLO until its 1988 Declaration of Independence. The first time that an Israeli leader put forward a formal proposal in negotiations with Palestinians for a truncated "state" was during the 2000 Camp David summit. The longer the two-decades-long "peace process" dragged on, with Israel choosing settlements over Palestinian sovereignty, the more people came to the realization that achieving a two-state resolution to the Israeli-Palestinian conflict was like trying to hammer the proverbial square peg into the round hole. As growing numbers of Palestinians sour on the prospects for a genuine two-state resolution, pressure is likely to grow from Palestinian civil society to disband the Palestinian Authority—which, as of this writing, is being propped up by Israeli loans—to democratize the decision-making of the PLO and to formally abandon the political program for a Palestinian state on the West Bank, East Jerusalem and Gaza Strip.

Third, if this scenario were to materialize during Obama's second term, then there would likely commence a long and difficult struggle for Palestinians to achieve equal rights with Israeli Jews under the same political entity, whether that government was a unitary democratic state (one person, one vote) or a bi-national state that would reflect two different national identities—Palestinians and Israeli

Jews—in its governing institutions. At present, US policy is totally unprepared for this possibility, with the United States insisting that a negotiated, two-state resolution to the Israeli-Palestinian conflict is the only conceivable outcome that can be pursued.

Perhaps the Obama administration will embark on one final, desperate initiative to somehow miraculously salvage a two-state resolution during its second term. Perhaps the United States will continue to muddle through its policy toward Israel and the Palestinians, fervently hoping that things remain somewhat quiet so that the issue can remain on the back burner. Perhaps the United States will be forced to adapt to a changing policy environment in which the two-state "peace process" paradigm is abandoned. Whichever of these options may unfold, US policy toward Israel and the Palestinians, by providing Israel with nearly unlimited military and diplomatic backing for its military occupation and apartheid policies toward Palestinians, is deeply flawed and in need of a fundamental reorientation.

However, it would be exceedingly foolhardy, and would reflect a misunderstanding of how the US political system works, to expect that one day US policymakers will wake up, realize the error of their ways and suddenly overhaul US policy toward Israel and the Palestinians to support human rights, international law and equality. It is true that there are US decision-makers, such as former representative Anthony Weiner, whose stunning ignorance about the Israeli-Palestinian conflict and glaring biases toward Israel help keep the US political system enthralled to a manifestly failed policy. However, there are more members of Congress, Capitol Hill staffers, administration officials and denizens of public policy think tanks who privately, and sometimes even publicly, understand that US policy toward Israel and the Palestinians is unbalanced, counter-productive and even immoral. The problem is not that decision-makers fail to see that US policy toward Israel and the Palestinians is perpetuating that conflict; the problem is that their political calculus militates against them changing this policy.

Obama, in his speech to the Muslim world in Cairo, Egypt, in June 2009, evinced a deeper level of empathy for and understanding of Palestinian plight than any previous sitting US president. Indeed, there is no reason to doubt Prime Minister Netanyahu's estimation that

Obama brought to the White House an "unbelievably informed" perspective on the Israeli-Palestinian conflict. The fact that Obama entered the White House with the personal experiences, knowledge and sympathies necessary to have guided a fundamental transformation of US policy toward Israel and the Palestinians only made the outcome of his policy choices that much more disappointing. But Obama's ratcheting up of military and diplomatic support of Israel to unprecedented levels also demonstrates that a president, no matter how well-intentioned, is subject to the pressures and constraints imposed by the well-oiled Israel lobby.

Instead of relying on politicians to do the right thing of their own volition, US civil society must continue to build upon the successes it has already achieved. It must educate fellow citizens about the negative repercussions of current US policy and challenge institutional support of Israel though campaigns of boycott, divestment and sanctions (BDS). In the case of the decades-long effort to end US support for apartheid South Africa, policy change, in the form of comprehensive sanctions against the apartheid regime, came about only after the tireless efforts of a largely grassroots movement had significantly shifted public opinion and the policies of institutions such as universities, labor unions and churches.

Undoubtedly, it will be more difficult to achieve this success in the case of Israel and the Palestinians due to the outsize influence of the Israel lobby and its significant head start in building support for Israel into the fabric of the US political system over the decades. However, the fact that the Israel lobby is mortally scared of the power and achievements of BDS campaigns in the United States is incontrovertible. Defenders of Israeli military occupation and apartheid toward Palestinians seldom try to confront their opponents on the merits of their case any longer. That battle cannot be won. Instead, they rely on a combination of moral and economic bribery, intimidation and censorship to try to keep the lid on the growing impatience and outrage felt by more and more Americans over their government's policies toward Israel and the Palestinians.

During his first run for the presidency, Barack Obama was asked at a campaign fund-raiser in Montclair, New Jersey, what he would do as president to bring about a just and lasting Israeli-Palestinian peace. Obama responded by recounting the story of President

Franklin Delano Roosevelt, who reportedly told labor organizers, "I agree with you, I want to do it, now make me do it." Whether or not this original incident was apocryphal, Obama cited this story to throw down his own challenge: "Make me do it."[16] Build a political constituency to challenge the Israel lobby and change US policy toward Israel and the Palestinians to support human rights, international law and equality, the candidate seemed to urge. During the Obama administration's first term, greater numbers of Americans picked up this gauntlet than ever before.

Obama was fond of an oft-used declaration of Dr. Martin Luther King, Jr., which the civil rights leader had himself paraphrased from the nineteenth-century abolitionist Theodore Parker. The president had this quote embroidered into a new Oval Office rug in August 2010. The quote read: "The arc of the moral universe is long, but it bends toward justice."[17] Ironically enough, the brand-new rug made one of its first public appearances in White House photos of Obama gathering together Mahmoud Abbas, Benjamin Netanyahu, Hosni Mubarak and Abdullah II on September 1, 2010 for the relaunching of direct Israeli-Palestinian negotiations. Despite the inspirational quote on the rug, however, Obama would not succeed through these negotiations in bringing about a just peace between Palestinians and Israelis.

However, King understood that the moral universe did not bend toward justice by itself. There were no foreordained victories because "human progress never rolls in on the wheels of inevitability," King told students at Southern Methodist University in March 1966. Rather, social change "comes through the tireless effort and the persistent work of dedicated individuals . . . We must have time and we must realize that the time is always right to do right."[18]

Palestinians deserve the freedom, justice and equality so long denied to them by Israel. Until Palestinians attain the totality of their individual and national human rights, a just and lasting Israeli-Palestinian peace will not take hold. The time is right to do right by working to end US support for Israeli military occupation and apartheid toward the Palestinian people.

Get Involved

The US Campaign to End the Israeli Occupation is a national coalition of more than 400 organizations working to end US support for Israeli military occupation and Israeli apartheid policies toward Palestinians. Visit our website endtheoccupation.org to get involved with our efforts at the national level. While you are there, find the link to a local group near you and join us as we work together to educate, organize and mobilize people to change US policy toward Israel and the Palestinians to support human rights, international law and equality.

Acknowledgments

This book would have not been possible without the support, encouragement and inspiration of so many people. To everyone who helped me in the process of writing this book, I want to profoundly thank you.

First, thank you to my wonderful wife, Mona, who was unflagging in her support and encouragement of this project. When I got stuck, she pressed me to continue. When I had my doubts, she erased them. Thank you, Mona, for the endless times I tried out my points on you and you provided me with valuable feedback that greatly helped me sharpen my arguments.

Also, thank you to my loving and supportive parents, Evie and Ralph, who encouraged me in this endeavor. Thanks for reminding me that I am following in the family footsteps by becoming an author. Thanks as well for getting me a new computer on which I wrote this book. I can't imagine writing it on my old, slow and tiny netbook!

Paul Karolyi, a recent graduate of George Washington University, deserves a huge amount of thanks for serving as my incredibly capable research assistant on this book. Paul read through probably thousands of documents and articles, unearthing a lot of the material I used in this book. Paul's strong writing and editing skills also improved the first draft of the manuscript immeasurably. I know that Paul's many talents will be of inestimable help to the Arab Association for Human Rights, a nongovernmental organization in Nazareth that does valuable work in advocating for civic equality for Palestinian citizens of Israel, where he is currently interning.

My thanks also go to Andrew Hsiao, senior editor at Verso Books, for believing in this book idea and for being willing to take a chance on this first-time author. Andrew expertly guided me through the book-writing process, patiently and knowledgeably answered all of my many questions, and provided exceptional encouragement and guidance at every step along the way.

Thanks also to a fantastic trio of mentors and venerable authors whose experience and expertise on book writing and the Israeli-Palestinian conflict proved invaluable in this project. First, thank you to Bill Fletcher, Jr., for inspiring and guiding me through the book proposal and writing process and for connecting me to people in the publishing world. Without Bill's support and expert direction at our monthly lunches at East Street Café in Union Station, this project would likely have remained just a vague dream. Thanks to Phyllis Bennis, who generously gave me as much of her time as needed to discuss the book as it evolved, and who several times calmed me down when I was on the verge of panic over not being able to write it. Thanks as well to Nadia Hijab, who despite the geographical and time zone distances, was always just a Skype call or email away from providing me with useful advice and feedback.

I would also like to thank US Campaign to End the Israeli Occupation interns Tom Stack and Robert Kirkpatrick for providing important assistance in transcribing interviews and tracking down obscure references. Also, thanks to Paola Wheeland for her helpful research assistance.

Thanks as well to all of the amazing people who agreed to be interviewed for this book, including Huwaida Arraf, Sue Dravis, Nancy Kricorian, Pat Minor, Richard Silverstein, Ann Wright and others who preferred to remain anonymous or provide me with information on background. The work that all of these activists are doing is so impressive and inspiring. A special thanks to Huwaida, one of the bravest and most strategic practitioners of nonviolent direct action I know, for reading and providing valuable feedback on the chapter discussing US policy toward Palestinian nonviolence.

I also owe tremendous thanks to Felicia Eaves and Peter Miller, co-chairs of the steering committee of the US Campaign to End the Israeli Occupation, for providing me the flexibility I needed to write this book and for believing that this project could help advance our organization's mission. It is an honor to work with them and all of the selfless and dedicated individuals on our steering committee.

Finally, thanks to my coworkers at the US Campaign to End the Israeli Occupation—Anna Baltzer, Mike Coogan, and Ramah Kudaimi—for patiently bearing with me through my idiosyncratic work hours while I was writing this book. I know that my frequent absences from the office added to their workload and I appreciate them for stepping in and picking up the slack. A special thanks to Ramah who provided me with valuable encouragement, feedback and suggestions for the book on our frequent commutes from the office in Washington to our homes in Virginia.

Needless to say, none of the individuals mentioned above bear any responsibility for the content of the book. Errors of omission or commission, faulty reasoning or lack of clarity are the sole responsibility of the author.

Notes

INTRODUCTION

1 "President Obama Delivers Remarks to State Department Employees," *CQ Transcriptions*, January 22, 2009, http://www.washingtonpost.com/wp-dyn/content/article/2009/01/22/AR2009012202550.html

2 "Obama Slams Bush, Former Pres. Clinton's Mideast Diplomacy," *Haaretz*, April 21, 2008, http://www.haaretz.com/news/obama-slams-bush-former-pres-clinton-s-mideast-diplomacy-1.244304

3 "Meeting Minutes: Saeb Erekat and General James Jones," October 21, 2009, The Palestine Papers, Al Jazeera, http://transparency.aljazeera.net/en/projects/thepalestinepapers/201218211130500198.html

4 "President Obama Delivers Remarks to State Department Employees."

5 "Remarks with Israeli Prime Minister Binyamin Netanyahu," Press Availability, Hillary Rodham Clinton, Secretary of State, Jerusalem, October 31, 2009, http://www.state.gov/secretary/rm/2009a/10/131145.htm

6 Aaron David Miller, "Israel's Lawyer," *Washington Post*, May 23, 2005, http://www.washingtonpost.com/wp-dyn/content/article/2005/05/22/AR2005052200883.html

7 Michael O'Brien, "Obama 'Disrespected' Israel, Threw It 'Under the Bus,' says Romney," *The Hill*, May 19, 2011, http://thehill.com/blogs/blog-briefing-room/news/162211-romney-obama-has-thrown-israel-under-the-bus

8 "Statement of General David H. Petraeus, US Army Commander, US Central Command, Before the Senate Armed Services Committee on the Posture of US Central Command," March 16, 2010, http://armed-services.senate.gov/statemnt/2010/03%20March/Petraeus%2003-16-10.pdf

CHAPTER 1: AN UNBELIEVABLY INFORMED PRESIDENT

1 "Codel [Congressional Delegation] Lieberman's Nov 16 Meeting with Prime Minister Netanyahu," Embassy Tel Aviv (Israel), November 20, 2009, 09TELAVIV2525, http://wikileaks.org/cable/2009/11/09TELA-VIV2525.html

2 Ali Abunimah, "How Barack Obama Learned to Love Israel," *Electronic Intifada*, March 4, 2007, http://electronicintifada.net/content/how-barack-obama-learned-love-israel/6786

3 Peter Wallsten, "Allies of Palestinians See a Friend in Barack Obama," April 10, 2008, *Los Angeles Times*, http://web.archive.org/web/20080415034859/http://www.latimes.com/news/politics/la-na-obama-mideast10apr10,0,5826085.story?page=2

4 Peter Wallsten, "Allies of Palestinians."

5 Peter Beinart, *The Crisis of Zionism*, New York: Times Books, 2012, pp. 82–83, 93.

6 CityPAC, http://www.citypac.org/home/?page_id=18 and Wallsten, "Allies of Palestinians."

7 "Illinois—109th Congress (2005-2006)," http://endtheoccupation.org/article.php?id=2263 and "Illinois—110th Congress (2007-2008)," http://endtheoccupation.org/article.php?id=2193.

8 Chuck Gowdie, "Obama Wraps up Middle East Trip," *Chicago ABC 7 News*, January 13, 2006, http://eot.us.archive.org/eot08/20080920005657/http://obama.senate.gov/news/060113-obama_wraps_up/

9 "Obama Meets Shalom, Offers Support for Israel," Associated Press, January 10, 2006, http://eot.us.archive.org/eot08/20080921092956/http://obama.senate.gov/news/060110-obama_meets_sha/print.php

10 Lynn Sweet, "Obama to Offer Pro-Israel Views at Chicago Gathering," *Chicago Sun-Times*, March 1, 2007, http://web.archive.org/web/20081007195142/http://www.barackobama.com/2007/03/01/obama_to_offer_proisrael_views.php

11 Senator Barack Obama, "AIPAC Policy Forum Remarks," March 2, 2007, Chicago, Illinois, http://eot.us.archive.org/eot08/20080920011755/http://obama.senate.gov/speech/070302-aipac_policy_fo/

12 "Obama Statement on Signing of New Memorandum of Understanding With Israel," August 16, 2007, Washington, DC, http://eot.us.archive.org/eot08/20080919222408/http://obama.senate.gov/press/070816-obama_statement_79/

13 "Welcome to Arab Americans for Obama" and "Welcome to Jewish

Americans for Obama," http://web.archive.org/web/20090121085541/
http://my.barackobama.com/page/content/aahome and http://web.
archive.org/web/20090118072559/http://my.barackobama.com/page/
content/jahome/

14 "Barack Obama and Joe Biden: A Strong Record of Supporting the Security, Peace, and Prosperity of Israel," http://web.archive.org/web
/20081201001512/http://obama.3cdn.net/34a7d4ce85c2cf1bc9_66m6b
5af8.pdf

15 Barack Obama, "At 60, Israel Has Much to Celebrate," *Yediot Ahronot*,
May 11, 2008, http://web.archive.org/web/20081128003031/http://www.
barackobama.com/2008/05/11/at_60_israel_has_much_to_celeb_2.php

16 Senator Barack Obama, AIPAC Policy Conference 2008, June 4, 2008,
http://aipac.org/~/media/Publications/Policy%20and%20Politics/
Speeches%20and%20Interviews/Speeches%20by%20Policymakers/2008
/06/PC_08_Obama.pdf

17 Glenn Kessler, "Obama Backs Away from Comment on Divided Jerusalem," *Washington Post*, June 6, 2008, http://www.washingtonpost.com/
wp-dyn/content/article/2008/06/05/AR2008060503510.html

18 "Obama's Speech in Sderot, Israel," *CQ Transcriptions*, July 23, 2008,
http://www.nytimes.com/2008/07/23/us/politics/23text-obama.html?_
r=1&ref=politics

19 Thomas Beaumont, "Mideast Response Shadows Obama," *Des Moines
Register*, May 3, 2007, and interview with Sue Dravis, June 9, 2012.

20 Interview with Pat Minor, June 6, 2012.

21 Yitzhak Benhorin,"Obama: Not Only Likudniks Can Be Pro-Israeli,"
Yediot Ahronot, February 26, 2008, http://www.ynetnews.com/articles
/0,7340,L-3511195,00.html

22 "Remarks by Vice President Biden: The Enduring Partnership between
the United States and Israel," March 11, 2010, http://www.whitehouse.
gov/the-press-office/remarks-vice-president-biden-enduring-partner-
ship-between-united-states-and-israel

23 "Vice President Joseph Biden Delivers Remarks to the Yeshiva Beth
Yehuda Anniversary Dinner," November 13, 2011, http://www.white-
house.gov/blog/2011/11/18/heart-motor-city-vice-president-biden-
addresses-yeshiva-beth-yehuda

24 "Remarks to the American Task Force on Palestine," Hillary Rodham
Clinton, Secretary of State, Washington, DC, October 20, 2010, http://
www.state.gov/secretary/rm/2010/10/149766.htm

25 Senator Hillary Clinton, AIPAC Policy Conference 2008, June 4, 2008,
http://aipac.org/~/media/Publications/Policy%20and%20Politics/

Speeches%20and%20Interviews/Speeches%20by%20Policymakers/2008
/06/PC_08_Clinton.pdf

26 "Remarks by Ambassador Susan E. Rice, US Permanent Representative to
the United Nations, at the AIPAC Synagogue Initiative Lunch," Susan E.
Rice, US Permanent Representative to the United Nations, US Mission to
the United Nations, Washington, DC, March 5, 2012, http://usun.state.
gov/briefing/statements/185239.htm

27 Rory McCarthy, "Gaza Truce Broken as Israeli Raid Kills Six Hamas
Gunmen," *The Guardian*, November 5, 2008, http://www.guardian.co.uk
/world/2008/nov/05/israelandthepalestinians

28 Barak Ravid, "Disinformation, Secrecy and Lies: How the Gaza Offensive
Came About," *Haaretz*, December 27, 2008, http://www.haaretz.com/
news/disinformation-secrecy-and-lies-how-the-gaza-offensive-came-
about-1.260347

29 "Operation Cast Lead: A Statistical Analysis," al-Haq, August 2009, http:
//www.alhaq.org/attachments/article/252/gaza-operation-cast-Lead-
statistical-analysis%20.pdf

30 "B'Tselem's Investigation of Fatalities in Operation Cast Lead," B'Tselem,
http://www.btselem.org/download/20090909_cast_lead_fatalities_eng.
pdf

31 "Report of the United Nations Fact-Finding Mission on the Gaza Conflict,"
Human Rights Council, A/HRC/12/48, September 25, 2009, p. 423, http://
www2.ohchr.org/english/bodies/hrcouncil/docs/12session/A-HRC-12-48.pdf

32 "Palestinian US College Grad Loses 2 Brothers in Israeli Shooting; Father
Watched Son Bleed to Death after Israeli Troops Bar Ambulances,"
Democracy Now!, January 21, 2009, http://www.democracynow.org/2009
/1/21/palestinian_us_college_grad_loses_2#transcript

33 "Report of the UN Fact-Finding Mission on the Gaza Conflict," pp. 177–179.

34 "The Israeli Arsenal Deployed against Gaza during Operation Cast Lead,"
Journal of Palestine Studies, Vol. XXXVIII, No. 3 (Spring 2009), pp.
175–191, http://www.palestine-studies.org/files/pdf/jps/10341.pdf

35 "Rain of Fire: Israel's Unlawful Use of White Phosphorus in Gaza,"
Human Rights Watch, March 2009, pp. 1, 10, 13, http://www.hrw.org/
sites/default/files/reports/iopt0309web.pdf

36 "Fuelling Conflict: Foreign Arms Supplies to Israel/Gaza," Amnesty
International, February 2009, pp. 31–32, 34, http://www.amnesty.org/en/
library/asset/MDE15/012/2009/en/278d5cfc-0b39-4409-bd68-
4c6f44d99a64/mde150122009en.pdf

37 United Nations Security Resolution 1860, January 8, 2009, http://daccess-
dds-ny.un.org/doc/UNDOC/GEN/N09/204/32/PDF/N0920432.pdf

38 *Congressional Record*, Volume 155, Number 3, January 8, 2009, pp. S181-183, http://www.gpo.gov/fdsys/pkg/CREC-2009-01-08/html/CREC2009-01-08-pt1-PgS181-8.htm

39 *Congressional Record*, Volume 155, Number 4, January 9, 2009, pp. H95-113, http://www.gpo.gov/fdsys/pkg/CREC-2009-01-09/html/CREC-2009-01-09-pt1-PgH95-3.htm

40 Michael D. Shear, "Obama's One President Philosophy Is Not One-Fit-All," *Washington Post*, December 31, 2008, http://www.washingtonpost.com/wp-dyn/content/article/2008/12/30/AR2008123003104.html

41 Interview with Ann Wright, June 11, 2012.

42 "Obama Breaks Silence on Gaza, Voices 'Deep Concern' over Civilian Deaths," *Haaretz*, January 6, 2009, http://www.haaretz.com/news/obama-breaks-silence-on-gaza-voices-deep-concern-over-civilian-deaths-1.267572

43 Richard Silverstein, "Israeli Diplomats Lobbied Obama on Behalf of Gaza War before Inauguration," *Tikun Olam*, April 30, 2009, http://www.richardsilverstein.com/tikun_olam/2009/04/30/israeli-diplomats-lobbied-obama-on-behalf-of-gaza-war-before-inauguration/

44 Seymour M. Hersh, "Syria Calling," *New Yorker*, April 6, 2009, http://www.newyorker.com/reporting/2009/04/06/090406fa_fact_hersh

CHAPTER 2: SETTLEMENTS HAVE TO BE STOPPED

1 George J. Mitchell, *Making Peace*, Berkeley: University of California Press, 1999, pp. 35–36.

2 Quartet Statement, January 30, 2006, quoted in Khaled Elgindy, "The Middle East Quartet: A Post-Mortem," The Saban Center for Middle East Policy at Brookings, Analysis Paper #25, February 2012, p. 19, http://www.brookings.edu/~/media/research/files/papers/2012/1/02%20middle%20east%20elgindy/02_middle_east_elgindy_b.pdf

3 Elgindy, "The Middle East Quartet," p. 20.

4 "Selected Experiences and Lessons: George Mitchell in Northern Ireland," The Palestine Papers, Al Jazeera, http://transparency.aljazeera.net/files/4617.pdf

5 "Secretary Clinton with Vice President Joe Biden Announce Appointment of Special Envoy for Middle East Peace George Mitchell and Special Representative for Afghanistan and Pakistan Richard Holbrooke," Washington, DC, January 22, 2009, http://www.state.gov/secretary/rm/2009a/01/115297.htm

6   "Sharm El-Sheikh Fact-Finding Committee," April 30, 2001, http://2001-2009.state.gov/p/nea/rls/rpt/3060.htm

7   "A Performance-Based Roadmap to a Permanent Two-State Solution to the Israeli-Palestinian Conflict," April 30, 2003, http://2001-2009.state.gov/r/pa/prs/ps/2003/20062.htm

8   Dennis Ross, *The Missing Peace: The Inside Story of the Fight for Middle East Peace*, New York: Farrar, Straus and Giroux, 2004, p. 55.

9   "Press Availability at the End of the Gaza Reconstruction Conference," Hillary Rodham Clinton, Secretary of State, Sharm el-Sheik [*sic*], Egypt, March 2, 2009, http://www.state.gov/secretary/rm/2009a/03/119929.htm

10 Barak Ravid and Natasha Mozgovaya, "Obama's Mideast Adviser Steps Down amid Stalled Peace Talks," *Haaretz*, November 10, 2011, http://www.haaretz.com/news/diplomacy-defense/obama-s-mideast-adviser-steps-down-amid-stalled-peace-talks-1.394861

11 Ben Smith, "US Foreign Policy: Who's in Charge?" *Politico*, January 22, 2009, http://www.politico.com/news/stories/0109/17811_Page2.html

12 "President Obama Delivers Remarks to State Department Employees," *CQ Transcriptions*, January 22, 2009, http://www.washingtonpost.com/wp-dyn/content/article/2009/01/22/AR2009012202550.html

13 "Memorandum of Understanding between Israel and the United States Regarding Prevention of the Supply of Arms and Related Materiel to Terrorist Groups," January 16, 2009, http://www.mfa.gov.il/MFA/Peace+Process/Reference+Documents/Israel-US_Memorandum_of_Understanding_16-Jan-2009.htm

14 "Egypt: Counter Smuggling Update," Embassy Cairo (Egypt), December 20, 2009, 09CAIRO2325, http://wikileaks.org/cable/2009/12/09CAIRO2325.html

15 "US Welcomes Agreement on Gaza Weapons Smuggling," Press Statement, Robert Wood, Acting Department Spokesman, Bureau of Public Affairs, Office of the Spokesman, Washington, DC, March 16, 2009, http://www.state.gov/r/pa/prs/ps/2009/03/120436.htm

16 "Israel/Occupied Palestinian Territories: Shipment Reaches Israel, President Obama Urged to Halt Further Exports," Press Release, Amnesty International, April 1, 2009 http://www.amnesty.org/en/for-media/press-releases israeloccupied-palestinian-territories-shipment-reaches-israel-president

17 "Israel May Be in Violation of Arms Export Control Act," Press Release, Congressman Dennis J. Kucinich, January 6, 2009, http://kucinich.house.gov/news/documentsingle.aspx?documentid=108151

18 "Gaza Sitrep [Situation Report], January 16, 1200," Embassy Tel Aviv (Israel), January 16, 2009, 09TELAVIV124, http://wikileaks.org/cable/2009/01/09TELAVIV124.html

19 "Some Additional Types of Goods Enter Gaza, Overall Access Remains Strictly Limited," Consulate Jerusalem (Israel), February 27, 2009, 09JERUSALEM360, http://wikileaks.org/cable/2009/02/09JERUSALEM360.html

20 "Humanitarian Aid Access to Gaza Remains Limited," Consulate Jerusalem (Israel), May 6, 2009, 09JERUSALEM749, http://wikileaks.org/cable/2009/05/09JERUSALEM749.html

21 "GOI [Government of Israel] Proposes International Mechanism for Funds to Gaza," Embassy Tel Aviv (Israel), March 11, 2009, 09TELAVIV600, http://wikileaks.org/cable/2009/03/09TELAVIV600.html

22 "Daily Press Briefing," Robert Wood, Acting Department Spokesman, US Department of State, February 25, 2009, http://www.state.gov/r/pa/prs/dpb/2009/02/119782.htm

23 "Intervention at the International Conference in Support of the Palestinian Economy for the Reconstruction of Gaza," Hillary Rodham Clinton, Secretary of State, Sharm el-Sheikh, Egypt, March 2, 2009, http://www.state.gov/secretary/rm/2009a/03/119900.htm

24 "The Ambassdor [sic] Briefs EU Ambassadors on the Secretary's Visit and the Sharm El-sheikh Donors Conference," Embassy Tel Aviv (Israel), March 12, 2009, 09TELAVIV601, http://wikileaks.org/cable/2009/03/09TELAVIV601.html

25 "United States Assistance to the Palestinians," Fact Sheet, Office of the Spokesman, US Department of State, Washington, DC, March 2, 2009, http://www.state.gov/r/pa/prs/ps/2009/03/119925.htm

26 "Gaza: Humanitarian Situation," BBC, January 30, 2009, http://news.bbc.co.uk/2/hi/middle_east/7845428.stm

27 "Kerry Statement at US-Muslim Relations Hearing," February 26, 2009, Washington, DC, http://www.kerry.senate.gov/press/speeches/speech/?id=62eb0ac0-1f11-4663-901d-db41be98dd12 and Elise Labott, "US officials: Hamas slipped note to Obama via senator," CNN, February 20, 2009, http://articles.cnn.com/2009-02-20/world/kerry.letter_1_fawzi-barhoum-consulate-palestinian-government?_s=PM:WORLD

28 "Hamas Letter to Obama," Institute for Public Accuracy, June 8, 2009, http://www.commondreams.org/newswire/2009/06/08-2

29 Howard Schneider, "Jimmy Carter Decries Israeli Restrictions on Gaza," Washington Post, June 17, 2009, http://www.washingtonpost.com/wp-dyn/content/article/2009/06/16/AR2009061603284.html

30 Peter Beinart, The Crisis of Zionism, New York: Times Books, 2012, p. 127.

31 "News Conference by the President," White House, Office of the Press Secretary, March 24, 2009, http://www.whitehouse.gov/the_press_office/News-Conference-by-the-President-3-24-2009

32 "Remarks by President Obama and Israeli Prime Minister Netanyahu of Israel in Press Availability," White House, Office of the Press Secretary, May 18, 2009, http://www.whitehouse.gov/the_press_office/Remarks-by-President-Obama-and-Israeli-Prime-Minister-Netanyahu-in-press-availability

33 "Press Availability with Egyptian Foreign Minister Ahmed Ali Aboul Gheit," Press Availability, Hillary Rodham Clinton, Secretary of State, Washington, DC, May 27, 2009, http://www.state.gov/secretary/rm/2009a/05/124009.htm

34 "Meeting Minutes: Dr. Saeb Erakat Meeting with the Negotiations Support Unit," June 2, 2009, The Palestine Papers, Al Jazeera, http://transparency.aljazeera.net/files/4625.pdf

35 Glenn Kessler, "1979 State Dept. Legal Opinion Raises New Questions about Israeli Settlements," *Washington Post*, June 17, 2009, http://www.washingtonpost.com/wp-dyn/content/article/2009/06/16/AR2009061603285.html

36 "Convention (IV) Relative to the Protection of Civilian Persons in Time of War," Geneva, Switzerland, August 12, 1949, International Committee of the Red Cross, http://www.icrc.org/ihl.nsf/full/380

37 "Comprehensive Settlement Population 1972–2010," Foundation for Middle East Peace, http://fmep.org/settlement_info/settlement-info-and-tables/stats-data/comprehensive-settlement-population-1972-2006

38 "Letter from Fayyad to Senator John F. Kerry," March 13, 2009, The Palestine Papers, Al Jazeera, http://transparency.aljazeera.net/files/4475.pdf

39 Nathan Guttman, "Key US Jews Wary of Netanyahu's Unbending Policy on Settlements," *Haaretz*, June 3, 2009, http://www.haaretz.com/jewish-world/2.209/key-u-s-jews-wary-of-netanyahu-s-unbending-policy-on-settlements-1.277227

40 "Lowey Discusses Peace Process and Iran with Foreign Minister Lieberman and Deputy Foreign Minister Ayalon," Embassy Tel Aviv (Israel), April 21, 2009, 09TELAVIV887, http://wikileaks.org/cable/2009/04/09TELAVIV887.html

41 "PM's [Prime Minister's] Speech at the Begin-Sadat Center at Bar-Ilan University," Prime Minister's Office, June 14, 2009, http://www.pmo.gov.il/PMOEng/Archive/Speeches/2009/06/speechbarilan140609.htm

42 "Remarks with Israeli Foreign Minister Avigdor Lieberman," Hillary Rodham Clinton, Secretary of State, Washington, DC, June 17, 2009, http://www.state.gov/secretary/rm/2009a/06/125044.htm

43 Daniel Kurtzer, "The Facts on Israel's Settlements," *Washington Post*, June

14, 2009, http://www.washingtonpost.com/wp-dyn/content/article/2009 /06/12/AR2009061203498.html

44   "PM's Speech at the Begin-Sadat Center at Bar-Ilan University."

45   "Leaked Israeli PM [Prime Minister] Netanyahu Video," *Channel 10* (Israel), Institute for Middle East Understanding Translation, July 21, 2010, http://imeu.net/news/article0019451.shtml

46   "Codel [Congressional delegation] Kyl's Meeting with Prime Minister Netanyahu: What Will the US Do about Iran?" Embassy Tel Aviv (Israel), April 28, 2009, 09TELAVIV936, http://wikileaks.org/cable/2009/04 /09TELAVIV936.html

47   "Statement from Press Secretary Robert Gibbs on Prime Minister Netanyahu's Speech," White House, Office of the Press Secretary, June 14, 2009, http://www.whitehouse.gov/the_press_office/Statement-from-Press-Secretary-Robert-Gibbs-on-Prime-Minister-Netanyahus-speech

48   "Briefing by Special Envoy for Middle East Peace George Mitchell on His Recent Travel to the Region and Efforts toward Achieving a Comprehensive Peace," Special Briefing, George Mitchell, Special Envoy for Middle East Peace, Washington, DC, June 16, 2009, http://www.state.gov/r/pa/ prs/ps/2009/06a/125011.htm

CHAPTER 3: NEGOTIATIONS MUST BEGIN SOON

1   Senator Christopher Dodd "Dear Colleague" Letter to President Barack Obama, May 18, 2009, http://www.endtheoccupation.org/downloads/ doddlettertoobama51909.pdf and Representatives Steny Hoyer and Eric Cantor "Dear Colleague" Letter to President Barack Obama, May 1, 2009, http://www.endtheoccupation.org/downloads/hoyerlettertoobama509. pdf

2   Laura Rozen, "Dennis Ross Move to NSC [National Security Council] Announced," The Cable, *Foreign Policy*, June 25, 2009, http://thecable. foreignpolicy.com/posts/2009/06/25/dennis_ross_move_to_nsc_ announced

3   "Letter to George Mitchell Regarding Settlement Freeze," August 10, 2009, The Palestine Papers, Al Jazeera, http://transparency.aljazeera.net/ files/4774.pdf

4   "Meeting Minutes: Saeb Erakat—David Hale," September 16, 2009, The Palestine Papers, Al Jazeera, http://transparency.aljazeera.net/files/4835. pdf

5   "Meeting Minutes: Saeb Erakat—David Hale," September 17, 2009, The Palestine Papers, Al Jazeera, http://transparency.aljazeera.net/files/4827.pdf

6   "Remarks by The President at Beginning of Trilateral Meeting With Israeli Prime Minister Netanyahu and Palestinian Authority President Abbas," White House, Office of the Press Secretary, New York, New York, September 22, 2009, http://www.whitehouse.gov/video/President-Obama-PM-Netanyahu-and-President-Abbas-Speak-to-the-Press#transcript

7   "Press Briefing by UN [sic] Special Envoy for Middle East Peace George Mitchell, on the President's Trilateral Meeting with Prime Minister Netanyahu of Israel and President Abbas of the Palestinian Authority," White House, Office of the Press Secretary, September 22, 2009, New York, New York, http://www.whitehouse.gov/the-press-office/briefing-us-special-envoy-middle-east-peace-george-mitchell

8   "Remarks with Israeli Prime Minister Binyamin Netanyahu," Press Availability, Hillary Rodham Clinton, Secretary of State, Jerusalem, October 31, 2009, http://www.state.gov/secretary/rm/2009a/10/131145.htm

9   "Remarks with Moroccan Foreign Minister Taieb Fassi-Fihri," Remarks, Hillary Rodham Clinton, Secretary of State, Marrakech, Morocco, November 2, 2009, http://www.state.gov/secretary/rm/2009a/11/131229.htm

10   Jimmy Carter, "For Israel, Land or Peace," *Washington Post*, November 26, 2000, http://www.cartercenter.org/news/documents/doc137.html

11   Thomas L. Friedman, "Baker Hails Israeli Freeze; Hints at Approval of Loan," *New York Times*, July 25, 1992, http://www.nytimes.com/1992/07/25/world/baker-hails-israeli-freeze-hints-at-approval-of-loan.html

12   Barak Ravid, "Netanyahu Declares 10-month Settlement Freeze 'to Restart Peace Talks'," *Haaretz*, November 25, 2009, http://www.haaretz.com/news/netanyahu-declares-10-month-settlement-freeze-to-restart-peace-talks-1.3435

13   "Briefing by Special Envoy for Middle East Peace George Mitchell," Special Briefing, George Mitchell, Special Envoy for Middle East Peace, Washington, DC, November 25, 2009, http://www.state.gov/r/pa/prs/ps/2009/nov/132447.htm

14   Lara Friedman, Director of Policy and Government Relations, Americans for Peace Now, and Hagit Ofran, Settlements Watch Director, Peace Now (Israel), "Top 6 Bogus Arguments for Opposing Extension of the Settlement Moratorium (or for Adding Loopholes)," *Settlements in Focus*, Volume 6, Number 5, July 29, 2010, http://peacenow.org/entries/bogus_arguments_for_opposing_extension_of_freeze

15   Friedman and Ofran, "The Settlements Moratorium—A Six-Month Accounting," *Settlements in Focus*, Volume 6, Issue 4, June 14, 2010,

http://peacenow.org/entries/settlements_moratorium_six-month_accounting

16 "US Non-Paper on Negotiations Framework," December 30, 2009, The Palestine Papers, Al Jazeera, http://transparency.aljazeera.net/files/4990.pdf

17 "NSU [Negotiations Support Unit] Comments to US Non-Paper on Negotiations Basis," The Palestine Papers, Al Jazeera, http://transparency.aljazeera.net/files/5009.pdf

18 "Meeting Minutes: Saeb Erekat and David Hale," January 15, 2010, The Palestine Papers, Al Jazeera, http://transparency.aljazeera.net/files/5012.pdf

19 "Palestinian Response to Senator Mitchell's Proposals," February 2010, The Palestine Papers, Al Jazeera, http://transparency.aljazeera.net/files/5043.pdf

20 Barak Ravid, Avi Issacharoff and Jonathan Lis, "Mideast Peace Talks Could Begin as Early as Sunday," *Haaretz*, March 4, 2010, http://www.haaretz.com/print-edition/news/mideast-peace-talks-could-begin-as-early-as-sunday-1.264098

21 "Statement by Special Envoy for Middle East Peace George Mitchell," Media Note, Office of the Spokesman, Washington, DC, March 8, 2010, http://www.state.gov/r/pa/prs/ps/2010/03/137916.htm

22 Yitzhak Benhorin, "AIPAC: US-Israel Tension Matter of Serious Concern," *Yediot Ahronot*, March 15, 2010, http://www.ynetnews.com/articles/0,7340,L-3862712,00.html

23 "Remarks by Vice President Biden and Prime Minister Netanyahu in a Joint Statement to the Press," White House, Office of the Vice President, March 9, 2010, http://www.whitehouse.gov/the-press-office/remarks-vice-president-biden-and-prime-minister-netanyahu-a-joint-statement-press

24 Ethan Bronner, "As Biden Visits, Israel Unveils Plan for New Settlements," *New York Times*, March 9, 2010, http://www.nytimes.com/2010/03/10/world/middleeast/10biden.html

25 "Statement by Vice President Joseph R. Biden, Jr.," White House, Office of the Vice President, March 9, 2010, http://www.whitehouse.gov/the-press-office/statement-vice-president-joseph-r-biden-jr

26 "Remarks by Vice President Biden and Palestinian Authority President Mahmoud Abbas," White House, Office of the Vice President, March 10, 2010, http://www.whitehouse.gov/the-press-office/remarks-vice-president-biden-and-palestinian-authority-president-mahmoud-abbas

27 "Daily Press Briefing," Philip J. Crowley, Assistant Secretary, Washington, DC, March 12, 2010, http://www.state.gov/r/pa/prs/dpb/2010/03/138304.htm

28 Glenn Kessler, "Clinton Rebukes Israel over East Jerusalem Plans, Cites Damage to Bilateral Ties," *Washington Post*, March 13, 2010, http://www.washingtonpost.com/wp-dyn/content/article/2010/03/12/AR2010031202615.html

29 Mark Landler and Ethan Bronner, "Israel Feeling Rising Anger from the US," *New York Times*, March 15, 2010, http://www.nytimes.com/2010/03/16/world/middleeast/16mideast.html

30 "Briefing by White House Press Secretary Robert Gibbs, 3/24/10," White House, Office of the Press Secretary, March 24, 2010, http://www.white-house.gov/the-press-office/briefing-white-house-press-secretary-robert-gibbs-32410

31 Giles Whittel, "Binyamin Netanyahu Humiliated after Barack Obama 'Dumped Him for Dinner,'" *Times of London*, March 26, 2010, quoted in "Reports: Netanyahu 'Humiliated' by Obama Snub," Fox News, http://www.foxnews.com/politics/2010/03/25/president-allegedly-dumps-israeli-prime-minister-dinner/

32 "Briefing by White House Press Secretary Robert Gibbs, 3/30/2010," White House, Office of the Press Secretary, March 30, 2010, http://www.whitehouse.gov/the-press-office/briefing-white-house-press-secretary-robert-gibbs-3302010

33 *Congressional Record*, Volume 156, Number 37, March 15, 2010, pp. H1414–1415, http://www.gpo.gov/fdsys/pkg/CREC-2010-03-15/html/CREC-2010-03-15-pt1-PgH1414-2.htm

34 *Congressional Record*, Volume 156, Number 37, March 15, 2010, pp. S1497–1499, http://www.gpo.gov/fdsys/pkg/CREC-2010-03-15/html/CREC-2010-03-15-pt1-PgS1497.htm

35 *Congressional Record*, Volume 156, Number 39, March 17, 2010, pp. H1522–1523, http://www.gpo.gov/fdsys/pkg/CREC-2010-03-17/html/CREC-2010-03-17-pt1-PgH1522-6.htm

36 *Congressional Record*, Volume 156, Number 57, April 21, 2010, pp. S2485–2486, http://www.gpo.gov/fdsys/pkg/CREC-2010-04-21/html/CREC-2010-04-21-pt1-PgS2485.htm

37 "Statement on Special Envoy George Mitchell's Trip," Press Statement, Washington, DC, May 9, 2010, http://www.state.gov/r/pa/prs/ps/2010/05/141637.htm

38 "Briefing on Middle East Peace Process," Special Briefing, Hillary Rodham Clinton, Secretary of State, George Mitchell, Special Envoy for Middle East Peace, Washington, DC, August 20, 2010, http://www.state.gov/secretary/rm/2010/08/146156.htm

CHAPTER 4: SETTLEMENTS ARE CORROSIVE TO ISRAEL'S FUTURE

1 "Press Briefing by Special Envoy for Middle East Peace Senator George Mitchell," White House, Office of the Press Secretary, August 31, 2010, http://www.whitehouse.gov/the-press-office/2010/08/31/press-briefing-special-envoy-middle-east-peace-senator-george-mitchell

2 "Remarks by President Obama, President Mubarak, His Majesty King Abdullah, Prime Minister Netanyahu and President Abbas before Working Dinner," White House, Office of the Press Secretary, September 1, 2010, http://www.whitehouse.gov/the-press-office/2010/09/01/remarks-president-obama-president-mubarak-his-majesty-king-abdullah-prim

3 "Briefing by Special Envoy for Middle East Peace George Mitchell on Middle East Peace Talks," Special Briefing, Washington, DC, September 2, 2010, http://www.state.gov/p/nea/rls/rm/146750.htm

4 "Briefing on Israeli-Palestinian Peace Talks," Special Briefing, George Mitchell, Special Envoy for Middle East Peace, Jerusalem, September 15, 2010, http://www.state.gov/p/nea/rls/rm/147206.htm

5 "Press Conference by President Obama," White House, Office of the Press Secretary, September 10, 2010, http://www.whitehouse.gov/the-press-office/2010/09/10/press-conference-president-obama

6 "Interview with Yaakov Eilon of Israel Channel 10," Interview, Hillary Rodham Clinton, Secretary of State, Jerusalem, September 16, 2010, http://www.state.gov/secretary/rm/2010/09/147440.htm

7 "Statement by the Quartet," Media Note, Office of the Spokesman, Washington, DC, September 21, 2010, http://www.state.gov/r/pa/prs/ps/2010/09/147514.htm

8 "Remarks by the President to the United Nations General Assembly," White House, Office of the Press Secretary, September 23, 2010, http://www.whitehouse.gov/the-press-office/2010/09/23/remarks-president-united-nations-general-assembly

9 Barak Ravid and Natasha Mozgovaya, "US Offers Israel Warplanes in Return for New Settlement Freeze," Haaretz, November 13, 2010, http://www.haaretz.com/news/diplomacy-defense/u-s-offers-israel-warplanes-in-return-for-new-settlement-freeze-1.324496

10 "Israel—F-35 Joint Strike Fighter Aircraft," News Release, Defense Security Cooperation Agency, Transmittal No. 08-83, September 29, 2008, http://www.dsca.mil/pressreleases/36-b/2008/Israel_08-83.pdf

11 Eli Berdenstein, "Obama's Letter: Incentives in Exchange for Lengthening

the Freeze," *Ma'ariv* (in Hebrew, author's translation), September 29, 2010, http://www.nrg.co.il/online/1/ART2/161/524.html?hp=1&cat=404

12 David Makovsky, "Dear Prime Minister: US Efforts to Keep the Peace Process on Track," Policy Watch #1707, Washington Institute for Near East Policy, September 29, 2010, http://www.washingtoninstitute.org/policy-analysis/view/dear-prime-minister-u.s.-efforts-to-keep-the-peace-process-on-track

13 Thomas L. Friedman, "Reality Check," *New York Times*, December 11, 2010, http://www.nytimes.com/2010/12/12/opinion/12friedman.html

14 Ian Black, "Arab League Urges US to Call Halt on Israeli Settlements," *The Guardian*, October 8, 2010, http://www.guardian.co.uk/world/2010/oct/09/arab-league-palestinian-israel

15 "Daily Press Briefing," Philip J. Crowley, Assistant Secretary, Washington, DC, December 8, 2010, http://www.state.gov/r/pa/prs/dpb/2010/12/152568.htm

16 "Remarks at the Brookings Institution's Saban Center for Middle East Policy Seventh Annual Forum," Hillary Rodham Clinton, Secretary of State, Washington, DC, December 10, 2010, http://www.state.gov/secretary/rm/2010/12/152664.htm

17 "Briefing by Special Envoy for Middle East Peace George Mitchell on His Recent Travel to the Region and Efforts toward Achieving a Comprehensive Peace," Special Briefing, George Mitchell, Special Envoy for Middle East Peace, Washington, DC, June 16, 2009, http://www.state.gov/r/pa/prs/ps/2009/06a/125011.htm

18 "Briefing on Middle East Peace Process," Special Briefing, Hillary Rodham Clinton, Secretary of State, George Mitchell, Special Envoy for Middle East Peace, Washington, DC, August 20, 2010, http://www.state.gov/secretary/rm/2010/08/146156.htm

19 "US-Soviet Letter of Invitation to Peace Talks in Madrid, 18 October 1991," *Journal of Palestine Studies*, Volume XXI, Number 2 (Winter 1992), p. 121, http://www.palestine-studies.org/files/pdf/jps/1551.pdf

20 "Declaration of Principles on Interim Self-Government Arrangements," September 13, 1993, http://www.mfa.gov.il/MFA/Peace+Process/Guide+to+the+Peace+Process/Declaration+of+Principles.htm

21 "Meeting Minutes: Saeb Erekat (SE)–Robert Serry (RS)," October 13, 2009, The Palestine Papers, Al Jazeera, http://transparency.aljazeera.net/files/4882.pdf

22 Khaled Elgindy, "The Middle East Quartet: A Post-Mortem," The Saban Center for Middle East Policy at Brookings, Analysis Paper #25, February 2012, p. 42, http://www.brookings.edu/~/media/research/files/papers/2012/1/02%20middle%20east%20elgindy/02_middle_east_elgindy_b.pdf

CHAPTER 5: MORE THAN 700 DAYS
OF FAILURE, NO SUCCESS

1 "Meeting Notes/Summary: Dr. Saeb Erekat Meeting with the Negotiation Support Unit & Heads of Committees," June 16, 2009, The Palestine Papers, Al Jazeera, http://transparency.aljazeera.net/files/4660.pdf

2 United Nations Security Council, S/2011/24, February 18, 2011, http://www.un.org/ga/search/view_doc.asp?symbol=S/2011/24

3 "Daily Press Briefing," Philip J. Crowley, Assistant Secretary, Washington, DC, January 13, 2011, http://www.state.gov/r/pa/prs/dpb/2011/01/154607.htm

4 Colum Lynch, "In Sharp Reversal, US Agrees to Rebuke Israel in Security Council," February 16, 2011, Turtle Bay: Reporting from Inside the United Nations, *Foreign Policy*, http://turtlebay.foreignpolicy.com/posts/2011/02/16/in_major_reversal_us_to_rebuke_israel_in_security_council and "Draft Presidential Statement," http://www.foreignpolicy.com/files/fp_uploaded_images/110216_statement.jpg

5 "Explanation of Vote by Ambassador Susan E. Rice, US Permanent Representative to the United Nations, on the Resolution on the Situation in the Middle East, including the question of Palestine, in the Security Council Chamber," Susan E. Rice, US Permanent Representative to the United Nations, US Mission to the United Nations, New York, New York, February 18, 2011, http://usun.state.gov/briefing/statements/2011/156816.htm

6 "President Bush Welcomes Prime Minister Abbas to White House," White House, Office of the Press Secretary, July 25, 2003, http://georgewbush-whitehouse.archives.gov/news/releases/2003/07/20030725-6.html

7 "Written Statement by the United States of America," January 30, 2004, p. 2, http://www.icj-cij.org/docket/files/131/1583.pdf

8 "Berman Counters Anti-Israel Billboards in San Fernando Valley, Reaffirms US-Israel Relationship and Commitment to Middle East Peace Process," June 25, 2012, http://www.house.gov/apps/list/press/ca28_berman/Berman_Counters_anti_Israel_Billboards.shtml

9 "Rep. Howard Berman Urges Administration to Veto Anti-Israel Resolution," February 17, 2011, http://democrats.foreignaffairs.house.gov/press_display.asp?id=802

10 "Ros-Lehtinen Comments on Reports that US Offered to Criticize Israel in UN Security Council Statement, Calls on Administration to Stand Publicly and Unequivocally with Israel at UN," February 17, 2011, http://foreignaffairs.house.gov/news/story/?1724

11 "Congressional Statements on the UN Security Council Settlements

Resolution," February 22, 2011, American Israel Public Affairs Committee, http://www.aipac.org/~/media/Publications/Policy%20and%20Politics/AIPAC%20Analyses/Issue%20Memos/2011/02/Statements_on_the_UN_Settlements_Resolution.pdf

12 Dan Ephron, "The Wrath of Abbas," *Newsweek*, April 24, 2011, http://www.thedailybeast.com/newsweek/2011/04/24/the-wrath-of-abbas.html

13 "The UK, France and Germany Are Seriously Concerned about the Current Stalemate in the Middle East Peace Process," February 22, 2011, United Kingdom Mission to the United Nations, http://ukun.fco.gov.uk/en/news/?id=553959782&view=News

14 "Letter from the Middle East Envoy George Mitchell to the President," White House, Office of the Press Secretary, May 13, 2011, http://www.whitehouse.gov/the-press-office/2011/05/13/letter-middle-east-envoy-george-mitchell-president

15 "Statement by the President on the Resignation of Middle East Envoy George Mitchell," White House, Office of the Press Secretary, May 13, 2011, http://www.whitehouse.gov/the-press-office/2011/05/13/statement-president-resignation-middle-east-envoy-george-mitchell

16 "Briefing on Middle East Peace Process," Special Briefing, Hillary Rodham Clinton, Secretary of State, George Mitchell, Special Envoy for Middle East Peace, Washington, DC, August 20, 2010, http://www.state.gov/secretary/rm/2010/08/146156.htm

17 Elliott Abrams, "The Resignation of George Mitchell," *Pressure Points*, Council on Foreign Relations, May 13, 2011, http://blogs.cfr.org/abrams/2011/05/13/the-resignation-of-george-mitchell/

18 "Remarks of President Barack Obama—As Prepared for Delivery—'A Moment of Opportunity,'" White House, Office of the Press Secretary, May 19, 2011, http://www.whitehouse.gov/the-press-office/2011/05/19/remarks-president-barack-obama-prepared-delivery-moment-opportunity

19 Mark Landler and Steven Lee Myers, "Obama Sees '67 Borders as Starting Point for Peace Deal," *New York Times*, May 19, 2011, http://www.nytimes.com/2011/05/20/world/middleeast/20speech.html?pagewanted=all

20 United Nations Security Council Resolution 242, November 22, 1967, http://unispal.un.org/unispal.nsf/0/7D35E1F729DF491C852 56EE700686136

21 "Remarks by President Obama and Prime Minister Netanyahu of Israel after Bilateral Meeting," White House, Office of the Press Secretary, May 20, 2011, http://www.whitehouse.gov/the-press-office/2011/05/20/remarks-president-obama-and-prime-minister-netanyahu-israel-after-bilate

22 "SWC [Simon Wiesenthal Center]: Israel Should Reject a Return to 1967 'Auschwitz' Borders," May 19, 2011, Simon Wiesenthal Center, http://www.wiesenthal.com/site/apps/nlnet/content2.aspx?c=lsKWLbPJLnF&b=4441467&ct=10711363

23 Lyndon B. Johnson, "Address at the State Department's Foreign Policy Conference for Educators," June 19, 1967, http://www.presidency.ucsb.edu/ws/index.php?pid=28308#ixzz1zDhslc4X

24 "Remarks by President Obama and Prime Minister Netanyahu of Israel after Bilateral Meeting."

25 Peter Beinart, *The Crisis of Zionism*, New York: Times Books, 2012, p. 152.

26 "Remarks by the President at the AIPAC Policy Conference 2011," White House, Office of the Press Secretary, May 22, 2011, http://www.white-house.gov/the-press-office/2011/05/22/remarks-president-aipac-policy-conference-2011

27 Jennifer Rubin, "Obama Double Downs at AIPAC," *Washington Post*, May 22, 2011, http://www.washingtonpost.com/blogs/right-turn/post/obama-double-downs-at-aipac/2011/03/29/AFhx9C9G_blog.html

28 "Speech by PM [Prime Minister] Netanyahu to a Joint Meeting of the US Congress," May 24, 2011, Prime Minister's Office, http://www.pmo.gov.il/PMOEng/Communication/PMSpeaks/speechcongress240511.htm

29 Jonathan Karl, "Israeli Prime Minister Gets 29 Standing Ovations in Congress, Sends Message to White House," *ABC News*, May 24, 2011, http://abcnews.go.com/blogs/politics/2011/05/israeli-prime-minister-gets-20-standing-ovations-in-congress-sends-message-to-white-house/

30 Beinart, *The Crisis of Zionism*, p. 154.

31 Rae Ablieah, "Why Did I Disrupt?" *Mondoweiss: The War of Ideas in the Middle East*, May 26, 2011, http://mondoweiss.net/2011/05/why-did-i-disrupt.html

32 Gwen Ackerman, "Netanyahu Said to Be Ready for Israel to Negotiate on Basis of 1967 Lines," *Bloomberg*, August 1, 2011, http://www.bloomberg.com/news/2011-08-02/netanyahu-said-to-be-ready-for-israel-to-negotiate-on-basis-of-1967-lines.html

CHAPTER 6: TIME FOR MY COURAGEOUS AND PROUD PEOPLE TO LIVE FREE

1 "Abbas: Settlements Are a Unilateral Step Taken by Israel," *Haaretz*, October 25, 2010, http://www.haaretz.com/news/diplomacy-defense/abbas-settlements-are-a-unilateral-step-taken-by-israel-1.321122

2   "Daily Press Briefing," Philip J. Crowley, Assistant Secretary, Washington, DC, October 26, 2010, http://www.state.gov/r/pa/prs/dpb/2010/10/150024.htm

3   John Quigley, *The Statehood of Palestine: International Law in the Middle East Conflict*, Cambridge: Cambridge University Press, 2010, pp. 153, 154.

4   Quigley, *The Statehood of Palestine*, p. 158.

5   "Ecuador Becomes Fifth Latin American Country to Recognize Palestinian State," *Haaretz*, December 25, 2010, http://www.haaretz.com/news/diplomacy-defense/ecuador-becomes-fifth-latin-american-country-to-recognize-palestinian-state-1.332845

6   "Daily Press Briefing," Philip J. Crowley, Assistant Secretary, Washington, DC, December 7, 2010, http://www.state.gov/r/pa/prs/dpb/2010/12/152489.htm

7   *Congressional Record*, Volume 156, Number 160, December 7, 2010, p. H8070, http://www.gpo.gov/fdsys/pkg/CREC-2010-12-07/html/CREC-2010-12-07-pt1-PgH8070-3.htm

8   H.Res.1765, December 15, 2010, 111th Congress, http://thomas.loc.gov/cgi-bin/query/z?c111:H.RES.1765:

9   *Congressional Record*, Volume 156, Number 166, December 15, 2010, pp. H8466-8471, http://www.gpo.gov/fdsys/pkg/CREC-2010-12-15/html/CREC-2010-12-15-pt1-PgH8466.htm

10 "Remarks of President Barack Obama—As Prepared for Delivery—'A Moment of Opportunity,'" White House, Office of the Press Secretary, May 19, 2011, http://www.whitehouse.gov/the-press-office/2011/05/19/remarks-president-barack-obama-prepared-delivery-moment-opportunity

11 "Remarks by the President at the AIPAC Policy Conference 2011," White House, Office of the Press Secretary, May 22, 2011, http://www.whitehouse.gov/the-press-office/2011/05/22/remarks-president-aipac-policy-conference-2011

12 Mahmoud Abbas, "The Long Overdue Palestinian State," *New York Times*, May 16, 2011, http://www.nytimes.com/2011/05/17/opinion/17abbas.html

13 "Recognizing the Palestinian State on the 1967 Border & Admission of Palestine as a Full Member of the United Nations," July 2011, PLO Negotiations Office, http://www.nad-plo.org/userfiles/file/fact%20sheet/who%20and%20why%20recognize%20Palestine%20Factsheet%20-%20english%20July%202011_pdf.pdf

14 S.Res.185, May 16, 2011, 112th Congress, http://thomas.loc.gov/cgi-bin/query/z?c112:S.RES.185:

15 *Congressional Record*, Volume 157, Number 95, June 29, 2011, p. S4195, http://www.gpo.gov/fdsys/pkg/CREC-2011-06-29/html/CREC-2011-06-29-pt1-PgS4181.htm

16 H.Res.268, July 7, 2011, 112th Congress, http://thomas.loc.gov/cgi-bin/query/z?c112:H.RES.268:

17 *Congressional Record*, Volume 157, Number 99, July 6, 2011, pp. H4625–4632, http://www.gpo.gov/fdsys/pkg/CREC-2011-07-06/html/CREC-2011-07-06-pt1-PgH4625-2.htm

18 "Remarks with French Foreign Minister Alain Juppe after Their Meeting," Hillary Rodham Clinton, Secretary of State, Washington, DC, June 6, 2011, http://www.state.gov/secretary/rm/2011/06/165158.htm

19 "Background Briefing on Quartet Working Dinner," Special Briefing, Senior Administration Official, July 11, 2011, http://www.state.gov/r/pa/prs/ps/2011/07/168030.htm

20 "Sen. John Kerry Holds a Hearing on the Nomination of Wendy Sherman to Be Undersecretary of State for Political Affairs," September 7, 2011, Political Transcript Wire, *Congressional Quarterly*, http://www.highbeam.com/doc/1P3-2444967371.html

21 "Daily Press Briefing," Victoria Nuland, Spokesperson, Washington, DC, September 8, 2011, http://www.state.gov/r/pa/prs/dpb/2011/09/171954.htm

22 "Daily Press Briefing," Victoria Nuland, Spokesperson, Washington, DC, September 6, 2011, http://www.state.gov/r/pa/prs/dpb/2011/09/171717.htm

23 "Sen. John Kerry Holds a Hearing," *Congressional Quarterly*.

24 Peter Beinart, *The Crisis of Zionism*, New York: Times Books, 2012, p. 156.

25 Abbas, "The Long Overdue Palestinian State," *New York Times*, May 16, 2011.

26 "Visit of the Minister of Justice of the Palestinian National Authority, Mr. Ali Khashan, to the ICC (22 January 2009)," International Criminal Court, February 6, 2009, http://www.icc-cpi.int/NR/rdonlyres/979C2995-9D3A-4E0D-8192-105395DC6F9A/280603/ICCOTP20090122Palestinerev1.pdf

27 *Congressional Record*, Volume 157, Number 141, September 21, 2011, pp. H6331–6337, http://www.gpo.gov/fdsys/pkg/CREC-2011-09-21/html/CREC-2011-09-21-pt1-PgH6331.htm

28 "Remarks by President Obama in Address to the United Nations General Assembly," White House, Office of the Press Secretary, New York, New York, September 21, 2011, http://www.whitehouse.gov/the-press-office

/2011/09/21/remarks-president-obama-address-united-nations-general-assembly

29 "Statement by H.E. [His Excellency] Mr. Mahmoud Abbas, President of the State of Palestine, Chairman of the Executive Committee of the Palestine Liberation Organization, President of the Palestinian National Authority before United Nations General Assembly, Sixty-sixth Session," New York, New York, September 23, 2011, http://gadebate.un.org/sites/default/files/gastatements/66/PS_en.pdf

30 Donald MacIntyre, "We Are the Victims of Collective Punishment, Say Palestinians," *The Independent*, October 1, 2011, http://www.independent.co.uk/news/world/middle-east/we-are-the-victims-of-collective-punishment-say-palestinians-2363998.html

31 Lara Friedman, "Congress Blocking Aid to the Palestinians: the Facts & What They Mean," Americans for Peace Now, October 3, 2011, http://peacenow.org/entries/congress_blocking_aid_to_the_palestinians_the_facts_what_they_mean

32 22 USC. § 287(e) (2011), http://www.gpo.gov/fdsys/pkg/USCODE-2011-title22/html/USCODE-2011-title22-chap7-subchapXVI-sec287e.htm

33 "US Statement in Explanation of Vote on Draft Resolution 9.1 Regarding Membership for Palestine in UNESCO," Statement as delivered by US Permanent Representative to UNESCO, Ambassador David T. Killion, United States Mission to UNESCO, October 31, 2011, http://unesco.usmission.gov/amb-statement-36gc-palestine.html

34 Steven Erlanger and Scott Sayare, "Unesco Accepts Palestinians as Full Members," *New York Times*, October 31, 2011, http://www.nytimes.com/2011/11/01/world/middleeast/unesco-approves-full-membership-for-palestinians.html?pagewanted=all

35 "Daily Press Briefing," Victoria Nuland, Spokesperson, Washington, DC, October 31, 2011, http://www.state.gov/r/pa/prs/dpb/2011/10/176434.htm

36 Steven Erlanger, "Palestinian Bid for Full Unesco Membership Imperils American Financing," *New York Times*, October 23, 2011, http://www.nytimes.com/2011/10/24/world/middleeast/palestinian-bid-to-join-unesco-could-imperil-us-funds.html?ref=middleeast

37 Timothy E. Wirth, "For the US, a Forced Withdrawal from UNESCO," *Los Angeles Times*, October 24, 2011, http://articles.latimes.com/2011/oct/24/opinion/la-oe-wirth-unesco-20111024

38 "WIPO [World Intellectual Property Organization] Briefing," Taken Question, Office of the Spokesperson, Washington, DC, October 31, 2011, http://www.state.gov/r/pa/prs/ps/2011/10/176417.htm

39 "Report of the Committee on the Admission of New Members Concerning the Application of Palestine for Admission to Membership in the United Nations," United Nations Security Council, S/2011/705, November 11, 2011, http://www.un.org/ga/search/view_doc.asp?symbol=S/2011/705

40 "Remarks by Ambassador Susan E. Rice, US Permanent Representative to the United Nations, at a meeting with the American Jewish Committee National Board of Governors," Susan E. Rice, US Permanent Representative to the United Nations, US Mission to the United Nations, New York, New York, January 23, 2012, http://usun.state.gov/briefing/statements/182371.htm

CHAPTER 7: REPEATED AND UNBALANCED CRITICISMS OF ISRAEL

1 "Report of the United Nations Fact-Finding Mission on the Gaza Conflict," United Nations General Assembly, Human Rights Council, Twelfth Session, Agenda item 7, A/HRC/12/48, September 25, 2009, pp. 159–166, http://www2.ohchr.org/english/bodies/hrcouncil/docs/12session/A-HRC-12-48.pdf

2 Ian Williams, "The NS [New Statesman] Interview: Richard Goldstone," *New Statesman*, December 30, 2009, http://www.newstatesman.com/middle-east/2010/01/interview-israel-law

3 "The Grave Violations of Human Rights in the Occupied Palestinian Territory Particularly Due to the Recent Israeli Military Attack against the Occupied Gaza Strip," United Nations General Assembly, A/HRC/S-9/L.1/Rev.2, January 12, 2009, http://unispal.un.org/UNISPAL.NSF/0/A8A783ACB5D0C6B88525753C0071F427

4 "Richard J. Goldstone Appointed to Lead Human Rights Council Fact-Finding Mission on Gaza Conflict," Human Rights Council, April 3, 2009, http://www.ohchr.org/EN/NewsEvents/Pages/DisplayNews.aspx?NewsID=8469&LangID=E

5 "US Posture toward the Durban Review Conference and Participation in the UN Human Rights Council," Press Statement, Robert Wood, Acting Department Spokesman, Office of the Spokesman, Washington, DC, February 27, 2009, http://www.state.gov/r/pa/prs/ps/2009/02/119892.htm

6 "US to Run for Election to the UN Human Rights Council," Press Statement, Gordon Duguid, Acting Deputy Department Spokesman, Bureau of Public Affairs, Office of the Spokesman, Washington, DC, March 31, 2009, http://www.state.gov/r/pa/prs/ps/2009/03/121049.htm

7 "GOI [Government of Israel] Rejects Cooperation With Goldstone Mission," Embassy Tel Aviv (Israel), May 11, 2009, 09TELAVIV1041, http://wikileaks.org/cable/2009/05/09TELAVIV1041.html

8 "Israel to Try New Tack on Goldstone Report, Upset with Pillay's Report," Mission Geneva (United Nations), August 19, 2009, 09GENEVA684, http://wikileaks.org/cable/2009/08/09GENEVA684.html

9 "The Ambassador's Meeting with Deputy Foreign Minister Ayalon," Embassy Tel Aviv (Israel), September 10, 2009, 09TELAVIV2004, http://wikileaks.org/cable/2009/09/09TELAVIV2004.html

10 "Daily Press Briefing," Ian Kelly, Department Spokesman, Washington, DC, September 15, 2009, http://www.state.gov/r/pa/prs/dpb/2009/sept/129224.htm

11 "Ambassador Rice's September 16 Meeting with Israeli Deputy Foreign Minister Ayalon and Secretary-general's Comments at Security Council Lunch on Goldstone Report," USUN New York (United Nations), September 17, 2009, 09USUNNEWYORK842, http://wikileaks.org/cable/2009/09/09USUNNEWYORK842.html

12 "Daily Press Briefing," Philip J. Crowley, Assistant Secretary, Washington, DC, September 17, 2009, http://www.state.gov/r/pa/prs/dpb/2009/sept/129322.htm

13 "Remarks to the Press," Ian Kelly, Department Spokesman, Washington, DC, September 18, 2009, http://www.state.gov/r/pa/prs/ps/2009/sept/129371.htm

14 Chaim Levinson, "Nearly 100% of All Military Court Cases in West Bank End in Conviction, Haaretz Learns," *Haaretz*, November 29, 2011, http://www.haaretz.com/print-edition/news/nearly-100-of-all-military-court-cases-in-west-bank-end-in-conviction-haaretz-learns-1.398369

15 "A Decade of Impunity for Harm to Civilians," Press Release, B'Tselem—The Israeli Information Center for Human Rights in the Occupied Territories, March 19, 2012, http://www.btselem.org/press-release/201203_decade_of_impunity

16 "Amnesty International's Updated Assessment of Israeli and Palestinian Investigations into the Gaza Conflict," Amnesty International, March 18, 2011, http://www.amnesty.org/en/library/asset/MDE15/018/2011/en/d7e260da-008a-461b-be03-85c223634a90/mde150182011en.html

17 "Israel Closes File on Gaza Family Killing," Al Jazeera, May 2, 2012, http://www.aljazeera.com/news/middleeast/2012/05/201251193818140881.html

18 "PA [Palestinian Authority] Health Minister Issues Press Release on Goldstone Report," Consulate Jerusalem (Israel), September 22, 2009, 09JERUSALEM1712, http://wikileaks.org/cable/2009/09/09JERUSALEM1712.html

19 "The Goldstone Report and the Human Rights Council," Embassy Tel Aviv (Israel), September 23, 2009, 09TELAVIV2102, http://wikileaks.org/cable/2009/09/09TELAVIV2102.html

20 "Action Request: Constructive Outcome from the Goldstone Report," Secretary of State (United States), September 23, 2009, 09STATE98567, http://wikileaks.org/cable/2009/09/09STATE98567.html

21 "US Response to the Report of the United Nations Fact-Finding Mission on the Gaza Conflict," Twelfth Session of the Human Rights Council, Statement by Michael Posner, United States Assistant Secretary of State for Democracy, Human Rights and Labor, Geneva, Switzerland, September 29, 2009, http://geneva.usmission.gov/2009/09/29/gaza-conflict/

22 "Abbas Defends Goldstone Vote Delay," Al Jazeera, October 11, 2009, http://www.aljazeera.com/news/middleeast/2009/10/20091011182856246590.html

23 "GOI [Government of Israel] Rejects Forming Gaza Investigatory Committee, Links Handling of Report to Peace Process," Embassy Tel Aviv (Israel), October 1, 2009, 09TELAVIV2167, http://wikileaks.org/cable/2009/10/09TELAVIV2167.html

24 Akiva Eldar, "Diskin to Abbas: Defer UN Vote on Goldstone or Face 'Second Gaza'," Haaretz, January 17, 2010, http://www.haaretz.com/print-edition/news/diskin-to-abbas-defer-un-vote-on-goldstone-or-face-second-gaza-1.261541

25 "The Human Rights Situation in the Occupied Palestinian Territory, including East Jerusalem," Human Rights Council, Twelfth Special Session, October 15-16, 2009, A/HRC/RES/S-12/1, http://daccess-dds-ny.un.org/doc/RESOLUTION/LTD/G09/168/07/PDF/G0916807.pdf?OpenElement

26 "Urgent Demarche Request on the Goldstone Report," Secretary of State (United States), October 14, 2009, 09STATE106423, http://wikileaks.org/cable/2009/10/09STATE106423.html

27 "EOV [Explanation of Vote]–Human Rights Situation in the Occupied Palestinian Territory including East Jerusalem," Douglas Griffiths, Charge d'Affaires, Mission of the United States, Geneva, Switzerland, October 16, 2009, http://geneva.usmission.gov/2009/10/16/eov-palestinianterritory/

28 "PA [Palestinian Authority] Presents Supporting Documentation for War Crimes Jurisdiction to the ICC [International Criminal Court]," October 21, 2009, Consulate Jerusalem (Israel), 09JERUSALEM1926, http://wikileaks.org/cable/2009/10/09JERUSALEM1926.html

29 "US Language on Bilateral Negotiations Track," undated, The Palestine Papers, Al Jazeera, http://ajtransparency.com/files/4845.pdf

30 "Meeting Minutes: Dr. Saeb Erekat–Sen. George Mitchell," October 2, 2009, The Palestine Papers, Al Jazeera, http://transparency.aljazeera.net/files/4844.pdf

31 "Meeting Minutes: Dr[.] Saeb Erekat–Sen[.] George Mitchell," October 21, 2009, The Palestine Papers, Al Jazeera, http://transparency.aljazeera.net/files/4899.pdf

32 "NSU [Negotiations Support Unit] Comments to US Non-Paper on Negotiations Basis," undated, The Palestine Papers, Al Jazeera, http://www.ajtransparency.com/en/projects/thepalestinepapers/20121821142109215.html

33 H.Res.867, 111th Congress (2009–2010), October 23, 2009, http://thomas.loc.gov/cgi-bin/bdquery/z?d111:h.res.00867:

34 Ron Kampeas, "Goldstone v. Ros-Lehtinen and Berman," *Jewish Telegraphic Agency*, October 30, 2009, http://blogs.jta.org/politics/article/2009/10/30/1008853/goldstone-v-ros-lehtinen-andberman

35 *Congressional Record*, Volume 155, Number 162, November 3, 2009, pp. H12232-12244, http://www.gpo.gov/fdsys/pkg/CREC-2009-11-03/html/CREC-2009-11-03-pt1-PgH12232-4.htm

36 "Follow-up to the Report of the United Nations Fact-Finding Mission on the Gaza Conflict," United Nations General Assembly, Sixty-fourth Session, Agenda item 64, A/RES/64/10, November 5, 2009, http://unispal.un.org/UNISPAL.NSF/0/9CC062414581D038852576C10055B066

37 "Explanation of Vote by Ambassador Alejandro D. Wolff, Deputy Permanent Representative, on a UN General Assembly Resolution on the UN Fact-Finding Mission on the Gaza Conflict, in the General Assembly," Alejandro Wolff, Deputy US Permanent Representative, US Mission to the United Nations, New York, New York, November 5, 2009, http://usun.state.gov/briefing/statements/2009/131448.htm

38 "Ambassador Rice,s [*sic*] October 21st Meeting with Israeli Foreign Minister Lieberman," Embassy Tel Aviv (Israel), October 27, 2009, 09TELAVIV2365, http://wikileaks.org/cable/2009/10/09TELAVIV2365.html

39 "Report of the International Fact-finding Mission to Investigate Violations of International Law, including International Humanitarian and Human Rights Law, Resulting from the Israeli Attacks on the Flotilla of Ships Carrying Humanitarian Assistance," United Nations General Assembly, Human Rights Council, Fifteenth session, Agenda item 1, A/HRC/15/21, September 27, 2010, pp. 37, 29, 30-31, 39-40, 13-14, 52, http://www2.ohchr.org/english/bodies/hrcouncil/docs/15session/A.HRC.15.21_en.pdf

40 "Opening Remarks to the Media at ICC Review Conference—Includes Statement on Gaza," Secretary-General Ban Ki-moon, Kampala, Uganda, May 31, 2010, http://www.un.org/apps/news/infocus/sgspeeches/search_full.asp?statID=828

41 "Remarks by Ambassador Alejandro Wolff, Deputy Permanent US Representative to the United Nations, at an Emergency Session of the Security Council," Alejandro Wolff, Deputy Permanent Representative to the United Nations, US Mission to the United Nations, New York, New York, May 31, 2010, http://usun.state.gov/briefing/statements/2010/142381.htm

42 "Statement by the President of the Security Council," United Nations Security Council, June 1, 2010, S/PRST/2010/9, http://daccess-dds-ny.un.org/doc/UNDOC/GEN/N10/382/79/PDF/N1038279.pdf?OpenElement

43 "Remarks by Ambassador Alejandro Wolff, Deputy Permanent Representative to the United Nations, at a Security Council Stakeout," Alejandro Wolff, Deputy Permanent Representative to the United Nations, US Mission to the United Nations, New York, New York, June 1, 2010, http://usun.state.gov/briefing/statements/2010/142435.htm

44 "Press Availability with Romanian Foreign Minister Teodor Baconschi after Their Meeting," Press Availability, Hillary Rodham Clinton, Secretary of State, Washington, DC, June 1, 2010, http://www.state.gov/secretary/rm/2010/06/142460.htm

45 "The Grave Attacks by Israeli Forces against the Humanitarian Boat Convoy," United Nations General Assembly, Human Rights Council, Fourteenth Session, Agenda item 1, June 2, 2010, A/HRC/RES/14/1, http://daccess-dds-ny.un.org/doc/UNDOC/GEN/G10/145/34/PDF/G1014534.pdf?OpenElement

46 "Explanation of Vote: Human Rights Council Resolution on Free Gaza Flotilla," Ambassador Eileen Chamberlain Donahoe, Human Rights Council, 14th Session, Geneva, June 2, 2010, http://geneva.usmission.gov/2010/06/02/hrc-resolution/

47 "Follow-up to the Report of the Independent International Fact-finding Mission on the Incident of the Humanitarian Flotilla," United Nations General Assembly, Human Rights Council, Fifteenth Session, Agenda item 1, September 29, 2010, A/HRC/RES/15/1, http://daccess-dds-ny.un.org/doc/UNDOC/GEN/G10/166/05/PDF/G1016605.pdf?OpenElement

48 "Explanation of US Vote on HRC Resolution Related to the Report of the Fact-Finding Mission Pursuant to Resolution 14/1," Ambassador Eileen

Chamberlain Donahoe, UN Human Rights Council, Fifteenth Session, Geneva, September 29, 2010, http://geneva.usmission.gov/2010/10/01/explanation-resolution-141-2/

49 "Statement by Ambassador Susan E. Rice, US Permanent Representative to the United Nations, on Secretary General Ban's Panel Concerning the May 31 Flotilla Incident," Susan E. Rice, US Permanent Representative to the United Nations, US Mission to the United Nations, New York, New York, August 2, 2010, http://usun.state.gov/briefing/statements/2010/145549.htm

50 José Antonio Gutiérrez and David Landy, "Uribe's Appointment to Flotilla Probe Guarantees Its Failure," *Electronic Intifada*, August, 6, 2010, http://electronicintifada.net/content/uribes-appointment-flotilla-probe-guarantees-its-failure/8968

51 "Report of the Secretary-General's Panel of Inquiry on the 31 May 2010 Flotilla Incident," September 2011, pp. 7–10, 3–6, http://www.un.org/News/dh/infocus/middle_east/Gaza_Flotilla_Panel_Report.pdf

CHAPTER 8: A BROADER, DEEPER, MORE INTENSE MILITARY RELATIONSHIP WITH ISRAEL THAN EVER

1 Connie Bruck, "The Influencer," *New Yorker*, May 10, 2010, http://www.newyorker.com/reporting/2010/05/10/100510fa_fact_bruck?currentPage=all

2 "The Obama Administration's Approach to US-Israel Security Cooperation: Preserving Israel's Qualitative Military Edge," Remarks, Andrew J. Shapiro, Assistant Secretary, Political-Military Affairs, Remarks at the Brookings Saban Center for Middle East Policy, Washington, DC, July 16, 2010, http://www.state.gov/t/pm/rls/rm/144753.htm

3 "Remarks by the President at AIPAC Policy Conference," White House, Office of the Press Secretary, March 4, 2012, http://www.whitehouse.gov/the-press-office/2012/03/04/remarks-president-aipac-policy-conference-0

4 "Vice President Joseph Biden Delivers Remarks to the Yeshiva Beth Yehuda Anniversary Dinner," November 13, 2011, Detroit, Michigan, http://www.whitehouse.gov/blog/2011/11/18/heart-motor-city-vice-president-biden-addresses-yeshiva-beth-yehuda

5 "Address by PM [Prime Minister] Netanyahu at the AIPAC Policy Conference 2011," May 23, 2011, http://www.pmo.gov.il/PMOEng/Communication/PMSpeaks/speechaipac230511.htm

6 "Naval Vessel Transfer Authority," P.L. 110-429, 110th Congress, p. 122,

Stat.   4842,   http://www.gpo.gov/fdsys/pkg/PLAW-110publ429/html/ PLAW-110publ429.htm

7 "Assistant Secretary Of Defense Vershbow Meets with Senior Israeli Defense Officials," Embassy Tel Aviv (Israel), November 16, 2009, 09TELA-VIV2482, http://wikileaks.org/cable/2009/11/09TELAVIV2482.html

8 Lyndon B. Johnson, "Address at the State Department's Foreign Policy Conference for Educators," June 19, 1967, The American Presidency Project, http://www.presidency.ucsb.edu/ws/index.php?pid=28308

9 Josh Ruebner, "US Military Aid to Israel: Policy Implications & Options," US Campaign to End the Israeli Occupation, March 2012, pp. 10–11, 18-19, 8-9, http://www.aidtoisrael.org/policypaper

10 Shapiro, "The Obama Administration's Approach to US-Israel Security Cooperation."

11 H.Con.Res.270, 111th Congress, 2nd Session, April 28, 2009, http:// thomas.loc.gov/cgi-bin/query/z?c111:H.CON.RES.270:

12 Ruebner, "US Military Aid to Israel," pp. 12–13, "Case Study #1: Tear Gas."

13 "Remarks by the President and the Vice President at Town Hall Meeting in Tampa, Florida," White House, Office of the Press Secretary, January 28, 2010,   http://www.whitehouse.gov/the-press-office/remarks-president-and-vice-president-town-hall-meeting-tampa-florida

14 Jeremy Sharp, Specialist in Middle East Affairs, "US Foreign Aid to Israel," RL33222, Congressional Research Service, March 12, 2012, "Table 1. Defense Budget Appropriations for US-Israeli Missile Defense: FY2006-FY2012," p. 15, http://assets.opencrs.com/rptsRL33222_20120312. pdf and "Consolidated and Further Continuing Appropriations Act, 2013," H.R.933, 113th Congress, 1st Session, Section 8070, p. 117, http://www. gpo.gov/fdsys/pkg/BILLS-113hr933enr/pdf/BILLS-113hr933enr.pdf

15 Yaakov Katz and Yaakov Lappin, "Iron Dome Ups Its Interception Rate to over 90%," *Jerusalem Post*, March 10, 2012, http://www.jpost.com/ Defense/Article.aspx?id=261257

16 "Weekly Report on Israeli Human Rights Violations in the Occupied Palestinian Territory (08 – 14 March 2012)," Palestinian Centre for Human Rights, March 15, 2012, http://www.pchrgaza.org/portal/en/ index.php?option=com_content&view=article&id=8259:weekly-report-on-israeli-human-rights-violations-in-the-occupied-palestinian-territory-08-14-march-2012&catid=84:weekly-2009&Itemid=183

17 "Deputy Assistant Secretary Rose in Israel on Missile Defense," Remarks by Frank A. Rose, Deputy Assistant Secretary, Bureau of Arms Control, Verification and Compliance, 2nd Annual Israel Multinational Missile Defense Conference, Tel Aviv, Israel, July 25, 2011, http://translations.

state.gov/st/english/texttrans/2011/07/20110725124844su0.9719158. html

18 "Remarks by Dennis Ross, Special Assistant to the President and Senior Director for the Central Region, AIPAC National Summit," White House, Office of the Press Secretary, Hollywood, Florida, October 25, 2010, http: //www.whitehouse.gov/the-press-office/2010/10/25/remarks-dennis-ross-special-assistant-president-and-senior-director-cent

19 "Speech as Delivered by Secretary of Defense Leon E. Panetta," AIPAC Policy Conference, Washington, DC, March 6, 2012, http://www.defense. gov/speeches/speech.aspx?speechid=1659

20 "Dempsey: US-Israel Drill to Take Place in Fall," *Jerusalem Post*, June 30, 2012, http://www.jpost.com/Defense/Article.aspx?id=275764

21 "Vice President Joseph Biden Delivers Remarks to the Yeshiva Beth Yehuda Anniversary Dinner."

22 Jim Zanotti, Specialist in Middle Eastern Affairs, "US Foreign Aid to the Palestinians," Congressional Research Service, RS22967, June 15, 2012, "Table 3. US Bilateral Assistance to the Palestinians, FY2005-FY2013," p. 11, and "Table 4. Historical US Government Contributions to UNRWA," p. 18, http://www.fas.org/sgp/crs/mideast/RS22967.pdf and "Making Supplemental Appropriations for the Fiscal Year Ending September 30, 2009, and for Other Purposes," Conference Report 111-151, 111th Congress, 1st Session, pp. 129,131,133, http://www.gpo.gov/fdsys/pkg/ CRPT-111hrpt151/pdf/CRPT-111hrpt151.pdf

23 "Our Work: West Bank and Gaza," US Agency for International Development, http://www.usaid.gov/where-we-work/middle-east/west-bank-and-gaza/our-work

24 "The Economic Costs of the Israeli Occupation for the Occupied Palestinian Territory," Palestinian Ministry of National Economy in cooperation with the Applied Research Institute-Jerusalem (ARIJ), September 2011, p. ii, http: //www.mne.gov.ps/pdf/EconomiccostsofoccupationforPalestine.pdf

25 "About Us," US Agency for International Development, West Bank/Gaza, http://transition.usaid.gov/wbg/aboutUs.html

26 "Making Emergency Supplemental Appropriations for Fiscal Year Ending September 30, 2005, and for Other Purposes," Conference Report 109-72, 109th Congress, 1st Session, p. 132, http://www.gpo.gov/fdsys/pkg/ CRPT-109hrpt72/pdf/CRPT-109hrpt72.pdf

27 "Israeli Assistance Steps and Humanitarian Measures towards the Palestinians following the Palestinian Elections and the Sharm el-Sheikh Summit," Israel Ministry of Foreign Affairs, Division for the United Nations and International Organizations, May 26, 2005, http://www.mfa.

gov.il/MFA/MFAArchive/2000_2009/2005/Israeli+assistance+and+hum anitarian+measures+towards+the+Palestinians+-+May+2005.htm

28 "Legal Consequences of the Construction of a Wall in the Occupied Palestinian Territory," International Court of Justice, Advisory Opinion, July 9, 2004, p. 64, http://www.icj-cij.org/docket/files/131/1671.pdf

29 "Fact Sheet: Trade Facilitation Project (TFP)," US Agency for International Development, West Bank/Gaza, January 2011, http://transition. usaid.gov/wbg/misc/ECO/PEO%20TFP%20fact%20sheet.pdf

30 "The Economic Costs of the Israeli Occupation for the Occupied Palestinian Territory," p. iv.

31 "Fact Sheet: Infrastructure Needs Program (INP)," US Agency for International Development, West Bank/Gaza, January 2011, http://transition. usaid.gov/wbg/misc/WRI/INP%20fact%20sheet.pdf

32 "Fragmented Lives: Humanitarian Overview 2011," United Nations, Office for the Coordination of Humanitarian Affairs, Occupied Palestinian Territory, "Limited Availability of Water in West Bank," http://www. ochaopt.org/annual/

33 "Separate and Unequal: Israel's Discriminatory Treatment of Palestinians in the Occupied Palestinian Territories," Human Rights Watch, December 2010, pp. 1, 14, http://www.hrw.org/sites/default/files/reports/iopt-1210webwcover_0.pdf

34 Nadia Hijab and Jesse Rosenfeld, "Palestinian Roads: Cementing Statehood, or Israeli Annexation?" *The Nation*, April 30, 2010, http://www. thenation.com/article/palestinian-roads-cementing-statehood-or-israeli-annexation#

35 Zanotti, "US Foreign Aid to the Palestinians," pp. 13–14.

36 "Press Conference with Palestinian Authority Prime Minister Salam Fayyad," Press Conference, Hillary Rodham Clinton, Secretary of State, Washington, DC, July 24, 2009, http://www.state.gov/secretary/rm/2009a /july/126444.htm

37 "Performance Evaluation of Palestinian Authority Security Forces Infrastructure Construction Projects in the West Bank," US Department of State and the Broadcasting Board of Governors, Office of Inspector General, Report Number MERO-I-11-03, March 2011, pp. 5, 13, 16, http: //oig.state.gov/documents/organization/162557.pdf

38 "Training and Logistical Support for Palestinian Authority Security Forces: Performance Evaluation," US Department of State and the Broadcasting Board of Governors, Office of Inspector General, Report Number MERO-I-11-09, July 2011, pp. 4, 6, 8, 11, http://oig.state.gov/documents/organization/171993.pdf

39 "United States Security Coordinator for Israel and the Palestinian Authority (USSC)," US Department of State, http://www.state.gov/s/ussc/index.htm

40 Lieutenant General Keith Dayton, US Security Coordinator, Israel and the Palestinian Authority, Program of the Soref Symposium, Michael Stein Address on US Middle East Policy, Washington Institute for Near East Policy, May 7, 2009, http://www.washingtoninstitute.org/html/pdf/DaytonKeynote.pdf

41 Mark Perry, "Dayton's Mission: A Reader's Guide," January 25, 2011, The Palestine Papers, Al Jazeera, http://www.aljazeera.com/palestinepapers/2011/01/2011125145732219555.html

42 Steven White and P.J. Dermer, "How Obama Missed an Opportunity for Middle East Peace," *Foreign Policy*, May 18, 2012, http://www.foreignpolicy.com/articles/2012/05/18/how_obama_missed_an_opportunity_for_middle_east_peace

43 "Meeting Summary: Dr. Saeb Erekat – LTG [Lieutenant General] Keith Dayton, NAD [Negotiations Affairs Department]," Ramallah, June 24, 2009, The Palestine Papers, Al Jazeera, http://transparency.aljazeera.net/files/4676.pdf

44 "Promoting Peace? Reexamining US Aid to the Palestinian Authority, Part II," Hearing before the Committee on Foreign Affairs, House of Representatives, 112th Congress, 1st Session, September 14, 2011, Serial No. 112–68, p. 32, http://foreignaffairs.house.gov/112/68296.pdf

45 Ethan Bronner, "Israel's West Bank General Warns against Radicals," *New York Times*, October 11, 2011, http://www.nytimes.com/2011/10/12/world/middleeast/israels-west-bank-general-warns-against-radicals.html

46 "Consolidated Appropriations Act, 2012," H.R.2055, 112th Congress, 1st Session, Sections 7036-7040, 7086, pp. 433–437, 479–480, http://www.gpo.gov/fdsys/pkg/BILLS-112hr2055enr/pdf/BILLS-112hr2055enr.pdf

47 Josh Rogin, "Senate Fight Today over Palestinian 'Refugees,' " The Cable, *Foreign Policy*, May 24, 2012, http://thecable.foreignpolicy.com/posts/2012/05/24/senate_fight_today_over_palestinian_refugees

48 Thomas R. Nides, Deputy Secretary of State, letter to Senator Patrick Leahy, Chairman, Subcommittee on State, Foreign Operations, and Related Programs, Committee on Appropriations, United States Senate, May 24, 2012, http://www.scribd.com/doc/94703915/DepSec-State-Opposes-Kirk-Amdt

CHAPTER 9: ANTI-AMERICAN SENTIMENT FOMENTED BY US FAVORITISM FOR ISRAEL

1 "Report of the Committee on Armed Services, House of Representatives, on H.R.4310, National Defense Authorization Act for Fiscal Year 2013," 112th Congress, 2nd Session, Report 112–479, p. 111, http://www.gpo. gov/fdsys/pkg/CRPT-112hrpt479/pdf/CRPT-112hrpt479.pdf

2 *Congressional Record*, Volume 156, Number 76, May 19, 2010, pp. H3617–3620, http://www.gpo.gov/fdsys/pkg/CREC-2010-05-19/html/CREC-2010-05-19-pt1-PgH3617.htm

3 "Final Vote Results for Roll Call 284," H.R. 5327, May 20, 2010, http:// clerk.house.gov/evs/2010/roll284.xml

4 "Remarks by National Security Advisor James L. Jones at the Washington Institute for Near East Policy," Michael Stein Address, Soref Symposium, 25th Anniversary Soref Gala, White House, Office of the Press Secretary, April 21, 2010, http://www.whitehouse.gov/the-press-office/ remarks-national-security-advisor-james-l-jones-washington-institute-near-east-poli

5 "The Obama Administration's Approach to US-Israel Security Cooperation: Preserving Israel's Qualitative Military Edge," Remarks, Andrew J. Shapiro, Assistant Secretary, Political-Military Affairs, Remarks at the Brookings Saban Center for Middle East Policy, Washington, DC, July 16, 2010, http://www.state.gov/t/pm/rls/rm/144753.htm

6 "About US Central Command (CENTCOM)," United States Central Command, http://www.centcom.mil/about-u-s-central-command-centcom

7 Mark Perry, "The Petraeus Briefing: Biden's Embarrassment Is Not the Whole Story," The Middle East Channel, *Foreign Policy*, March 13, 2010, http://mideast.foreignpolicy.com/posts/2010/03/14/the_petraeus_briefing_biden_s_embarrassment_is_not_the_whole_story

8 Interview with former US diplomat, July 26, 2012.

9 Laura Rozen, "What Biden told Netanyahu Behind Closed Doors: 'This Is Starting to Get Dangerous for Us,'" *Politico*, March 11, 2010, http://www. politico.com/blogs/laurarozen/0310/What_Biden_told_Netanyahu_ behind_closed_doors_This_is_starting_to_get_dangerous_for_us.html

10 "Statement of General David H. Petraeus, US Army, Commander, US Central Command, before the Senate Armed Services Committee, on the Posture of US Central Command," March 16, 2010, http://www. armed-services.senate.gov/statemnt/2010/03%20March/Petraeus%20 03-16-10.pdf

11 Interview with former US diplomat, July 26, 2012.

12 "Press Conference by the President at the Nuclear Security Summit," White House, Office of the Press Secretary, April 13, 2010, http://www. whitehouse.gov/the-press-office/press-conference-president-nuclear-security-summit

13 Mark Landler and Helene Cooper, "Obama Speech Signals a US Shift on Middle East," *New York Times*, April 14, 2010, http://www.nytimes.com /2010/04/15/world/middleeast/15mideast.html

14 "Remarks by Secretary of Defense Leon E. Panetta at the Saban Center," Secretary of Defense Leon E. Panetta, US Department of Defense, December 2, 2011, http://www.defense.gov/transcripts/transcript aspx?transcriptid=4937

15 "The Islamic Response to the Government's Nine Accusations," *United States of America v. Khalid Sheikh Mohammed, Walid Muhammad Salih Mubarak Bin 'Attash, Ramzi Bin Al Shibh, Ali Abdul-Aziz Ali, Mustafa Ahmed Adam Al Hawsawi*, D-101, http://www.defense.gov/news/ Order%20Regarding%20Pro%20Se%20Filing%20to%20Islamic%20 Resp%20to%20Gov%209%20Accusations.pdf

16 "DoD [Department of Defense] News Briefing with Press Secretary Geoff Morrell from the Pentagon," Pentagon Press Secretary Geoff Morrell, US Department of Defense, October 14, 2009, http://www.defense.gov/tran-scripts/transcript.aspx?transcriptid=4498

17 "Daily Press Briefing," Philip J. Crowley, Assistant Secretary, US Depart-ment of State, Washington, DC, January 26, 2011, http://www.state.gov/r /pa/prs/dpb/2011/01/155391.htm

18 "Erdoğan: Turkish Navy to Protect Gaza Aid," Al Jazeera, September 9, 2011, http://www.aljazeera.com/news/europe/2011/09/201198225646614806. html

19 "The North Atlantic Treaty," Washington, DC, April 4, 1949, http://www. nato.int/cps/en/natolive/official_texts_17120.htm

20 "Daily Press Briefing," Victoria Nuland, Spokesperson, US Department of State, Washington, DC, September 9, 2011, http://www.state.gov/r/pa/ prs/dpb/2011/09/172061.htm

21 Serkan Demirta, "Turkey Blocks Israel from NATO Summit," *Hurriyet Daily News*, April 23, 2012, http://www.hurriyetdailynews.com/turkey-blocks-israel-from-nato-summit.aspx?pageID=238&nID=19033&News CatID=338

22 "Daily Press Briefing," Victoria Nuland, Spokesperson, US Department of State, Washington, DC, April 23, 2012, http://www.state.gov/r/pa/prs/ dpb/2012/04/188322.htm

23 Ran Dagoni, "US Excludes Israel from Anti-terror Forum Because of

Turkey," *Globes*, June 10, 2012, http://www.globes.co.il/serveen/globes/docview.asp?did=1000755761

24 "Daily Press Briefing," Patrick Ventrell, Director, Press Office, US Department of State, Washington, DC, July 10, 2012, http://www.state.gov/r/pa/prs/dpb/2012/07/194830.htm

25 "State's Brimmer in Miami on US-Israel Multilateral Cooperation," Remarks by Esther Brimmer, Assistant Secretary, Bureau of International Organization Affairs, US Department of State, Miami, Florida, April 24, 2012, http://translations.state.gov/st/english/texttrans/2012/05/201205014843.html

26 "Remarks of President Barack Obama—As Prepared for Delivery—'A Moment of Opportunity,'" White House, Office of the Press Secretary, May 19, 2011, http://www.whitehouse.gov/the-press-office/2011/05/19/remarks-president-barack-obama-prepared-delivery-moment-opportunity

27 "Remarks by the President at the AIPAC Policy Conference 2011," White House, Office of the Press Secretary, May 22, 2011, http://www.whitehouse.gov/the-press-office/2011/05/22/remarks-president-aipac-policy-conference-2011

28 "Egypt to Open Rafah Border Permanently," Al Jazeera, May 25, 2011, http://www.aljazeera.com/news/middleeast/2011/05/2011525174117897741.html

29 Brian Whitaker, "Sharon Likens Arafat to Bin Laden," *The Guardian*, September 14, 2011, http://www.guardian.co.uk/world/2001/sep/14/israel.september11

30 Ellen Nakashima and Joby Warrick, "Stuxnet Was Work of US and Israeli Experts, Officials Say," *Washington Post*, June 1, 2012, http://www.washingtonpost.com/world/national-security/stuxnet-was-work-of-us-and-israeli-experts-officials-say/2012/06/01/gJQAInEy6U_story.html

31 Jeffrey Goldberg, "Obama to Iran and Israel: 'As President of the United States, I Don't Bluff,'" *Atlantic*, March 2, 2012, http://www.theatlantic.com/international/archive/2012/03/obama-to-iran-and-israel-as-president-of-the-united-states-i-dont-bluff/253875/

32 "Israel says Iran's Nuclear Program Soon Will Be Strike-proof," *USA Today*, March 19, 2010, http://www.usatoday.com/news/world/story/2012-03-19/israel-iran-threats/53654670/1

33 "Remarks by the President at AIPAC Policy Conference," White House, Office of the Press Secretary, March 4, 2012, http://www.whitehouse.gov/the-press-office/2012/03/04/remarks-president-aipac-policy-conference-0

34 "Israeli Prime Minister Benjamin Netanyahu," AIPAC Policy Conference, March 5, 2012, http://aipac.org/get-involved/attend-policy-conference/follow-pc/monday-gala-plenary/prime-minister-benjamin-netanyahu

35 "United States–Israel Enhanced Security Cooperation Act of 2012," S.2165, 112th Congress, 2nd Session, http://www.gpo.gov/fdsys/pkg/BILLS-112s2165enr/pdf/BILLS-112s2165enr.pdf

36 Ben Smith, "On a Hot Mic (or Not), No Love for Bibi," *Politico*, November 7, 2011, http://www.politico.com/blogs/bensmith/1111/On_a_hot_mic_or_not_no_love_for_Bibi.html

37 Haim Malka, "Crossroads: The Future of the US-Israel Strategic Partnership," Center for Strategic and International Studies, 2011, p. xiii, http://csis.org/files/publication/110908_Malka_CrossroadsUSIsrael_Web.pdf

CHAPTER 10: WE DON'T DO GANDHI VERY WELL

1 "IDF [Israel Defense Forces] Plans Harsher Methods with West Bank Demonstrations," Embassy Tel Aviv (Israel), February 16, 2010, 10TELAVIV344, http://wikileaks.org/cable/2010/02/10TELAVIV344.html

2 "Remarks by the President on a New Beginning," White House, Office of the Press Secretary, Cairo University, Cairo, Egypt, June 4, 2009, http://www.whitehouse.gov/the-press-office/remarks-president-cairo-university-6-04-09

3 Mazin B. Qumsiyeh, *Popular Resistance in Palestine: A History of Hope and Empowerment*, London: Pluto Press, 2011.

4 Mary Elizabeth King, *A Quiet Revolution: The First Palestinian Intifada and Nonviolent Resistance*, New York: Nation Books, 2007.

5 "Remarks of President Barack Obama—As Prepared for Delivery—'A Moment of Opportunity,'" White House, Office of the Press Secretary, May 19, 2011, http://www.whitehouse.gov/the-press-office/2011/05/19/remarks-president-barack-obama-prepared-delivery-moment-opportunity

6 Martin Luther King, Jr., *I Have a Dream: Writings and Speeches that Changed the World*, edited by James M. Washington, San Francisco: Harper San Francisco, 1992, "Letter from a Birmingham Jail," p. 91.

7 Interview with Huwaida Arraf, July 30, 2012.

8 "Israeli Military Orders Relevant to the Arrest, Detention and Prosecution of Palestinians," Addameer: Prisoner Support and Human Rights Association, http://www.addameer.org/etemplate.php?id=292

9 "The Universal Declaration of Human Rights," http://www.un.org/en/documents/udhr/

10 Ahmet Doğan, "A Father Speaks for His Son," *Albany Times Union*, February 24, 2011, http://www.timesunion.com/opinion/article/A-father-speaks-for-his-son-1027970.php

11 "Remarks with Indian Minister of External Affairs S.M. Krishna after Their Meeting," Remarks, Hillary Rodham Clinton, Secretary of State, Washington, DC, June 3, 2010, http://www.state.gov/secretary/rm/2010/06/142642.htm

12 "Daily Press Briefing," Philip J. Crowley, Assistant Secretary, Washington, DC, June 3, 2010, http://www.state.gov/r/pa/prs/dpb/2010/06/142651.htm

13 " 'Furkan Had a Huge Heart': Ahmet Doğan on His Son, Killed One Year Ago in Gaza Flotilla Raid," *Democracy Now!*, May 31, 2011, http://www.democracynow.org/blog/2011/5/31/furkan_had_a_huge_heart_ahmet_dogan_on_the_life_and_death_of_his_19_year_old_son_killed_one_year_ago_in_the_israeli_attack_on_a_gaza_bound_aid

14 "Department of State, Foreign Operations, and Related Programs Appropriations Bill, 2011," 111th Congress, 2nd Session, Senate Report 111-237, p. 57, http://www.gpo.gov/fdsys/pkg/CRPT-111srpt237/pdf/CRPT-111srpt237.pdf

15 Daniel Edelson, "Bilin Resident Charged with Displaying Used Bullets," *Yediot Ahronot*, December 23, 2009, http://www.ynetnews.com/articles/0,7340,L-3824423,00.html

16 "Abdallah Abu Rahmah's Letter from Ofer Prison," Addameer: Prisoners' Support and Human Rights Association, January 1, 2010, http://addameer.info/?p=1496

17 "Israeli Military Court Extends Jail Term for Palestinian Anti-wall Activist," Amnesty International, January 11, 2011, http://www.amnesty.org/en/news-and-updates/israeli-military-court-extends-jail-term-palestinian-anti-wall-activist-2011-01-11

18 Majida Abu Rahmah, "My Husband: Jailed for Protesting Israel's Wall," *Huffington Post*, January 4, 2010, http://www.huffingtonpost.com/majda-abu-rahmah/my-husband-jailed-for-pro_b_410613.html

19 "Remarks at Townhall on Human Rights Day," Remarks, Michael H. Posner, Assistant Secretary, Bureau of Democracy, Human Rights, and Labor, Harold Hongju Koh, Legal Advisor, US Department of State, Philip J. Crowley, Assistant Secretary, Bureau of Public Affairs, Washington, DC, December 10, 2010, http://www.state.gov/j/drl/rls/rm/2010/153655.htm

20 "Daily Press Briefing," Philip J. Crowley, Assistant Secretary, Washington, DC, December 10, 2010, http://www.state.gov/r/pa/prs/dpb/2010/12/152652.htm

21 "Daily Press Briefing," Philip J. Crowley, Assistant Secretary, Washington, DC, December 15, 2010, http://www.state.gov/r/pa/prs/dpb/2010/12/152930.htm

22 Harriet Sherwood, "Thirteen Killed as Israeli Troops Open Fire on Nakba Day Border Protests," *Guardian*, May 15, 2011, http://www.guardian.co.uk/world/2011/may/15/israeli-troops-kill-eight-nakba-protests

23 "The Universal Declaration of Human Rights."

24 "Daily Press Briefing," Mark C. Toner, Acting Deputy Department Spokesman, Washington, DC, May 16, 2011, http://www.state.gov/r/pa/prs/dpb/2011/05/163509.htm

25 "Gaza 'Anniversary' Flotilla," Press Statement, Victoria Nuland, Department Spokesperson, Office of the Spokesperson, Washington, DC, June 24, 2011, http://www.state.gov/r/pa/prs/ps/2011/06/166967.htm

26 Interview with Huwaida Arraf, July 30, 2012.

27 "Daily Press Briefing," Victoria Nuland, Spokesperson, Washington, DC, July 8, 2011, http://www.state.gov/r/pa/prs/dpb/2011/07/167942.htm

28 Sandra Tamari, "Deportation Shows Israel's Intolerance," *Belleville* (Illinois) *News-Democrat*, June 19, 2012, http://www.bnd.com/2012/06/19/2217610/deportation-show-israels-intolerance.html

29 "Daily Press Briefing," Mark C. Toner, Deputy Spokesperson, Washington, DC, June 6, 2012, http://www.state.gov/r/pa/prs/dpb/2012/06/191900.htm

30 "American Citizen Denied Entry into Israel (Taken Question)," Taken Question, Office of the Spokesperson, Washington, DC, June 6, 2012, http://www.state.gov/r/pa/prs/ps/2012/06/191899.htm

31 "Country Reports on Human Rights Practices for 2011: Israel and the Occupied Territories," Bureau of Democracy, Human Rights and Labor, US Department of State, http://www.state.gov/j/drl/rls/hrrpt/humanrightsreport/index.htm?dlid=186429

32 "Universal Declaration of Human Rights."

33 "Hunger-striking Prisoner Not Backing Down," Ma'an News Agency, February 11, 2012, http://www.maannews.net/eng/ViewDetails.aspx?ID=459445

34 "Addameer Calls for Continued Solidarity with Palestinian Prisoners as Mass Hunger Strike is Launched," Addameer: Prisoner Support and Human Rights Association, Ramallah, April 18, 2012, http://www.addameer.org/etemplate.php?id=461

35 "Hunger Strike Ends for Akram Rikhawi after 102 days," Addameer: Prisoner Support and Human Rights Association, Ramallah, July 23, 2012, http://www.addameer.org/etemplate.php?id=498

36 "Update: Situation of Long-Term Hunger Strikers Becomes Increas-

ingly Urgent," Addameer: Prisoner Support and Human Rights Association, Ramallah, May 10, 2012, http://www.addameer.org/etemplate. php?id=478

37 "Daily Press Briefing," Victoria Nuland, Spokesperson, Washington, DC, May 11, 2012, http://www.state.gov/r/pa/prs/dpb/2012/05/189753.htm

CHAPTER 11: AN ORDINARY POLITICAL DISCOURSE

1 Howard Kohr, AIPAC Policy Conference 2009, May 3, 2009, http://www. aipac.org/~/media/Publications/Policy%20and%20Politics/ Speeches%20and%20Interviews/Speeches%20by%20AIPAC%20Leadership/2009/05/HowardKohr.pdf

2 "Palestinian Civil Society Calls for Boycott, Divestment and Sanctions against Israel until It Complies with International Law and Universal Principles of Human Rights," July 9, 2005, Palestinian BDS National Committee (BNC), http://www.bdsmovement.net/call

3 Omar Barghouti, *BDS: Boycott, Divestment, Sanctions—The Global Struggle for Palestinian Rights*, Chicago: Haymarket Books, 2011, pp. 58, 61.

4 Jacob Berkman, "Federations, JCPA Teaming to Fight Delegitimization of Israel," *Jewish Telegraphic Agency*, October 25, 2010, http://www.jta.org/ news/article/2010/10/24/2741418/jfna-and-jcpa-create-6-million-network-to-fight-delegitimization-of-israel

5 *Congressional Record*, Volume 156, Number 86, June 9, 2010, pp. H4302– 4303, http://www.gpo.gov/fdsys/pkg/CREC-2010-06-09/html/CREC-2010-06-09-pt1-PgH4302-5.htm

6 "Remarks by the President at AIPAC Policy Conference," White House, Office of the Press Secretary, March 4, 2012, http://www.whitehouse. gov/the-press-office/2012/03/04/remarks-president-aipac-policy-conference-0

7 Gal Beckerman, "Palestinian-Led Movement to Boycott Israel Is Gaining Support," *Jewish Daily Forward*, September 16, 2009, http://forward.com /articles/114212/palestinian-led-movement-to-boycott-israel-is-gain/

8 "In Major Boycott Movement Success, Africa Israel Says No Plans to Build More Settlements," Press Release, Adalah-NY: The New York Campaign for the Boycott of Israel, November 3, 2010, http://adalahny. org/press-release/423/major-boycott-movement-success-africa-israel-says-no-plans-build-more-settlements

9 Interview with Nancy Kricorian, Stolen Beauty Campaign Manager, August 2, 2012.

10 Nancy Kricorian, "Stolen Beauty Victory: Costco Feels the Love," *Pink*

Tank, January 18, 2010, http://codepink4peace.org/blog/2010/01/stolen-beauty-victory-costco-feels-the-love/

11 Amira Hass, "Disney Family Member Renounces Her Investments in Israel's Ahava Cosmetics," *Haaretz*, July 16, 2012, http://www.haaretz.com/news/diplomacy-defense/disney-family-member-renounces-her-investments-in-israel-s-ahava-cosmetics-1.451506

12 "PACBI Guidelines for the International Cultural Boycott of Israel (Revised October 2010)," Palestinian Campaign for the Academic and Cultural Boycott of Israel (PACBI), July 20, 2009, http://www.pacbi.org/etemplate.php?id=1047

13 "BDS at 7!–Celebrating, Reflecting and Further Mainstreaming," Palestinian BDS National Committee, July 9, 2012, http://www.bdsmovement.net/2012/bds-at-7-9206

14 Alice Walker, "Supporting Boycotts, Divestment and Sanctions against Israel," *Huffington Post*, June 7, 2010, http://www.huffingtonpost.com/alice-walker/supporting-bds-boycott-di_b_603840.html

15 Victoria Colliver and David R. Baker, "Hundreds in Oakland Protest Gaza Blockade," *San Francisco Chronicle*, June 21, 2010, http://www.sfgate.com/bayarea/article/Hundreds-in-Oakland-protest-Gaza-blockade-3260772.php

16 Natasha Mozgovaya, "Food Co-op in Rachel Corrie's Hometown Boycotts Israeli Goods," *Haaretz*, July 20, 2010, http://www.haaretz.com/blogs/focus-u-s-a/food-co-op-in-rachel-corrie-s-hometown-boycotts-israeli-goods-1.302980

17 Phan Nguyen, "Who's Who behind the Olympia Food Co-op Lawsuit," *Mondoweiss: The War of Ideas in the Middle East*, February 22, 2012, http://mondoweiss.net/2012/02/whos-who-behind-the-olympia-food-co-op-lawsuit-2.html

18 "Judge Dismisses Lawsuit Filed over Boycott of Israeli Goods," Press Release, Center for Constitutional Rights, February 27, 2012, http://www.ccrjustice.org/newsroom/press-releases/judge-dismisses-lawsuit-filed-over-boycott-of-israeli-goods

19 Jeremy Pawloski, "5 Olympia Food Co-op Members Who Sued to End Israeli Boycott Must Pay $160K," *Olympian*, July 12, 2012, http://www.theolympian.com/2012/07/12/2171566/olympia-food-co-op-defendants.html

20 "Hampshire College First in US to Divest from Israel," Students for Justice in Palestine (Hampshire College), *Electronic Intifada*, February 12, 2009, http://www.electronicintifada.net/content/hampshire-college-first-us-divest-israel/932

21 "Student Organizations Resolve to Organize Nationally for Palestine," Students for Justice in Palestine National Conference, October 18, 2011, http://www.sjpnational.org/2011/10/18/student-organizations-resolve-organize-nationally-palestine/

22 Anna Baltzer, "BDS Scorecard: Methodists Recommend Sanctions and Boycotts; Reject Divestment," *Mondoweiss: The War of Ideas in the Middle East*, May 5, 2012, http://www.mondoweiss.net/2012/05/bds-scorecard-methodists-recommend-sanctions-reject-divestment.html

23 "Quakers Divest from Caterpillar!," US Campaign to End the Israeli Occupation, May 17, 2012, http://www.endtheoccupation.org/article.php?id=3210

24 Toby Tabachnick, "Boycott Measure Passes," *The Jewish Chronicle*, July 12, 2012, http://www.thejewishchronicle.net/view/full_story/19288908/article-Boycott-measure-passes

25 Anna Baltzer, "The Pendulum Swings & A New Era Has Begun: Presbyterian Church (USA) Endorses Boycott, Splits on Divestment," *Jadaliyya*, July 12, 2012, http://www.jadaliyya.com/pages/index/6420/the-pendulum-swings-and-a-new-era-has-begun_presby

26 "About Us," MSCI, http://www.msci.com

27 Naomi Zeveloff, "Israel Was 'Key' Issue in Caterpillar Dump," *Jewish Daily Forward*, June 25, 2012, http://www.forward.com/articles/158433/israel-was-key-issue-in-caterpillar-dump/

28 "Caterpillar Removed from TIAA-CREF's Social Choice Funds," We Divest Campaign, June 21, 2012, http://www.wedivest.org/2012/06/catremovedpressrelease/

29 "Ackerman Blasts NYU Israel-Divestment Push," October 12, 2011, http://www.ackerman.house.gov/index.cfm?sectionid=254&itemid=1758

30 Patrick O'Connor, "Israeli and Palestinian Voices on the US Op-ed Pages," *Electronic Intifada*, March 13, 2006, http://www.electronicintifada.net/content/israeli-and-palestinian-voices-us-op-ed-pages/5895

31 Arthur S. Brisbane, "Tangled Relationships in Jerusalem," *New York Times*, September 24, 2011, http://www.nytimes.com/2011/09/25/opinion/sunday/tangled-relationships-in-jerusalem.html

32 Interview with media activist, August 3, 2012.

33 George Bisharat, "Israel and Palestine: A True One-state Solution," *Washington Post*, September 3, 2010, http://www.washingtonpost.com/wp-dyn/content/article/2010/09/02/AR2010090204665.html

34 Rashid Khalidi, "Palestinians Need an Honest Broker," *USA Today*,

September 22, 2011, http://www.usatoday.com/news/opinion/story/2011-09-22/Palestnian-statehood-bid-Palestine/50519368/1

35 Yousef Munayyer, "Not All Israeli Citizens Are Equal," *New York Times*, May 23, 2012, http://www.nytimes.com/2012/05/24/opinion/not-all-israeli-citizens-are-equal.html

36 Walter Pincus, "United States Needs to Reevaluate Its Assistance to Israel," *Washington Post*, October 17, 2011, http://www.washingtonpost.com/world/national-security/united-states-needs-to-reevaluate-its-assistance-to-israel/2011/10/15/gIQAK5XksL_story.html

37 Walter Pincus, "Is US Going Above and Beyond for Israel?," *Washington Post*, May 16, 2012, http://www.washingtonpost.com/world/national-security/2012/05/16/gIQAJhikUU_story.html

38 "Christians of the Holy Land," *60 Minutes*, April 22, 2012, http://www.cbsnews.com/8301-18560_162-57417408/christians-of-the-holy-land/

39 Lynn Sweet, "Tina Fey as Sarah Palin Nails It Again on 'Saturday Night Live' Debate Skit," *Chicago Sun-Times*, October 4, 2008, http://www.blogs.suntimes.com/sweet/2008/10/tina_fey_as_sarah_palin_nails.html

40 "*The Simpsons* Episode: 'The Greatest Story Ever D'ohed,'" March 28, 2010, http://www.tvguide.com/tvshows/the-simpsons-2010/episode-16-season-21/the-greatest-story-ever-dohed/100521

41 Maureen Clare Murphy, "Daily Show Takes on US Punishment of UNESCO over Palestine Membership," *Electronic Intifada*, March 16, 2012, http://www.electronicintifada.net/blogs/maureen-clare-murphy/daily-show-takes-us-punishment-unesco-over-palestine-membership

CHAPTER 12: THROWING ISRAEL UNDER THE BUS

1 Gal Beckerman, "Congressmen Spark More Heat Than Light in Goldstone Report Debate," *Jewish Daily Forward*, March 7, 2011, http://www.forward.com/articles/135921/congressmen-spark-more-heat-than-light-in-goldston/

2 David Freedlander, "David Weprin Calls Obama's Israel Policy 'Outrageous,'" *Politicker*, July 14, 2011, http://www.politicker.com/2011/07/david-weprin-calls-obamas-israel-policy-outrageous/

3 Reid Pillifant, "On Israel and Entitlements, Ed Koch for Bob Turner," *Politicker*, July 25, 2011, http://www.politicker.com/2011/07/on-israel-and-entitlements-ed-koch-for-bob-turner/

4 Ashley Parker, "Weiner's Exit Sets Off a Race to Be Israel's Better Friend," *New York Times*, July 26, 2011, http://www.nytimes.com/2011/07/27/nyregion/race-to-replace-weiner-in-house-may-turn-on-israel-policy.html

5 "Congressional Report Cards," US Campaign to End the Israeli Occupation, http://www.endtheoccupation.org/article.php?list=type&type=202

6 Azi Paybarah, "Ackerman Rebuffs Koch's Call to Make Weprin Race a Proxy for Obama's Israel Policy," *Politicker*, July 12, 2011, http://www.politicker.com/2011/07/ackerman-rebuffs-kochs-call-to-make-weprin-race-a-proxy-for-obamas-israel-policy/

7 "Peace and Security for Israel: Remarks as Prepared by Antony Blinken, Deputy Assistant to the President and National Security Advisor to the Vice President," J Street Conference, Washington, DC, March 26, 2012, http://www.whitehouse.gov/blog/2012/03/26/remarks-antony-blinken-j-street-conference

8 Haim Malka, "Crossroads: The Future of the US-Israel Strategic Partnership," Center for Strategic and International Studies, 2011, p. 51, http://www.csis.org/files/publication/110908_Malka_CrossroadsUSIsrael_Web.pdf

9 "National Pledge for Unity on Israel," American Jewish Committee and Anti-Defamation League, http://www.adl.org/unitypledge/

10 Adam Kredo, "Should Israel Be a Partisan Issue in American Politics?," *Washington Jewish Week*, November 2, 2011, http://www.washingtonjewishweek.com/Main.asp?SectionID=4&SubSectionID=4&ArticleID=15988

11 Jeremy Ben-Ami, "What 'Pro-Israel' Should Mean," *Washington Post*, December 15, 2011, http://www.washingtonpost.com/opinions/what-pro-israel-should-mean/2011/12/15/gIQAlbaCzO_story.html

12 "Pro-Israel: Top Contributors to Federal Candidates, Parties, and Outside Groups," and "Pro-Israel: Top Recipients," Center for Responsive Politics, accessed August 9, 2012, http://www.opensecrets.org/industries/contrib.php?cycle=2012&ind=Q05 and http://www.opensecrets.org/industries/recips.php?cycle=2012&ind=Q05

13 "2012 Super PACs: How Many Donors Give?," Center for Responsive Politics, accessed August 9, 2012, http://www.opensecrets.org/outside-spending/donor_stats.php

14 "2012 Top Donors to Outside Spending Groups," Center for Responsive Politics, accessed August 9, 2012, http://www.opensecrets.org/outside-spending/summ.php?cycle=2012&disp=D&type=V

15 Steven Bertoni, "Exclusive: Adelson's Pro-Romney Donations Will Be 'Limitless,' Could Top $100M," *Forbes*, June 13, 2012, http://www.forbes.com/sites/stevenbertoni/2012/06/13/exclusive-adelsons-pro-romney-donations-will-be-limitless-could-top-100m/

16 Mike McIntire and Michael Luo, "The Man behind Gingrich's Money," *New York Times*, January 28, 2012, http://www.nytimes.com/2012/01/29/us/politics/the-man-behind-gingrichs-money.html?pagewanted=all

17 Gary Rosenblatt, "Billionaire Adelson Defends Gingrich," *New York Jewish Week*, May 17, 2011, http://www.thejewishweek.com/blogs/gary_rosenblatt/billionaire_adelson_defends_gingrich

18 Michael Isikoff, "Gingrich Funder Isn't Trying to 'Buy' the Presidency, Aide says," *NBC News*, January 27, 2012, http://www.firstread.nbcnews.com/_news/2012/01/27/10249298-gingrich-funder-isnt-trying-to-buy-the-presidency-aide-says

19 "2012 Top Donors to Outside Spending Groups," Center for Responsive Politics.

20 Chris McGreal, "Gambling with Peace: How US Bingo Dollars Are Funding Israeli Settlements," *The Guardian*, July 19, 2009, http://www.guardian.co.uk/world/2009/jul/19/us-bingo-funding-israeli-settlements

21 Robert P. Jones and Daniel Cox, "Chosen for What? Jewish Values in 2012: Findings from the 2012 Jewish Values Survey," Public Religion Research Institute, April 3, 2012, p. 11, http://www.publicreligion.org/site/wp-content/uploads/2012/04/Jewish-Values-Report.pdf

22 Farid Senzai, "Engaging American Muslims: Political Trends and Attitudes," Institute for Social Policy and Understanding, April 2012, p. 45, http://www.ispu.org/pdfs/ISPU%20Report_Political%20Participation_Senzai_WEB.pdf

23 Lucy Madison, "Mitt Romney Accuses Obama of Throwing Israel 'Under the Bus,'" *CBS News*, May 19, 2011, http://www.cbsnews.com/8301-503544_162-20064466-503544.html

24 Mark Halperin, "TRANSCRIPT: Remarks by Rick Perry at Republican Jewish Coalition Forum," *Time*, December 7, 2011, http://www.thepage.time.com/2011/12/07/transcript-remarks-by-rick-perry-at-republican-jewish-coalition-forum/

25 Mark Halperin, "TRANSCRIPT: Michele Bachmann Delivers Remarks at Republican Jewish Coalition Forum," *Time*, December 7, 2011, http://www.thepage.time.com/2011/12/07/transcript-michele-bachmann-delivers-remarks-at-republican-jewish-coalition-forum/

26 Benedict Anderson, *Imagined Communities: Reflections on the Origin and Spread of Nationalism*, London: Verso, 1983, p. 15.

27 Kim Geiger, "Newt Gingrich Defends Calling Palestinians 'an Invented' People," *Los Angeles Times*, December 10, 2011, http://www.articles.latimes.com/2011/dec/10/news/la-pn-gingrich-palestinians-20111210

28 "Full Transcript: ABC News Iowa Republican Debate," *ABC News*,

December 11, 2011, p. 21, http://abcnews.go.com/Politics/full-transcript-abc-news-iowa-republican-debate/story?id=15134849&page=21

29 Josh Ruebner, "The Phony War over Which US Party Loves Israel Most," *Electronic Intifada*, January 10, 2012, http://electronicintifada.net/content/phony-war-over-which-us-party-loves-israel-most/10794

30 "Full Transcript: ABC News Iowa Republican Debate," p. 22.

31 Natasha Mozgovaya, "On Israel, Romney Promises to Do 'the Opposite of Obama,'" *Haaretz*, June 16, 2012, http://www.haaretz.com/news/u-s-elections-2012/on-israel-romney-promises-to-do-the-opposite-of-obama.premium-1.436784

32 Zeke Miller, "Debbie Wasserman Schultz: Only Candidate Playing Politics with Israel Is Romney," *Buzz Feed*, July 23, 2012, http://www.buzzfeed.com/zekejmiller/debbie-wasserman-schultz-only-candidate-playing-p

33 "Mitt Romney Delivers Remarks in Jerusalem," Press Release, July 29, 2012, http://www.mittromney.com/news/press/2012/07/mitt-romney-delivers-remarks-jerusalem

34 Jaime Novogrod and Domenico Montanaro, "McCain: Israeli-Palestinian Differences Have 'Nothing to Do with Cultures,'" *NBC News*, July 30, 2012, http://firstread.nbcnews.com/_news/2012/07/30/13034595-mccain-israeli-palestinian-differences-have-nothing-to-do-with-cultures?lite

CONCLUSION

1 "Remarks at the US-Islamic World Forum," Remarks, Hillary Rodham Clinton, Secretary of State, Doha, Qatar, February 14, 2010, http://www.state.gov/secretary/rm/2010/02/136678.htm

2 "Remarks by President Obama in Address to the United Nations General Assembly," White House, Office of the Press Secretary, September 21, 2011, http://www.whitehouse.gov/the-press-office/2011/09/21/remarks-president-obama-address-united-nations-general-assembly

3 "Remarks by President Obama in Address to the United Nations General Assembly," September 21, 2011.

4 Scott Wilson, "Where Obama Failed on Forging Peace in the Middle East," *Washington Post*, July 14, 2012, http://www.washingtonpost.com/politics/obama-searches-for-middle-east-peace/2012/07/14/gJQAQQiKlW_story.html

5 "Growing Majority of Americans Oppose Israel Building Settlements," World Public Opinion: Global Public Opinion on International Affairs, April 29, 2009, http://www.worldpublicopinion.org/pipa/articles/brunitedstatescanadara/604.php

6 Mancur Olson, *The Logic of Collective Action: Public Goods and the Theory of Groups*, Cambridge: Harvard University Press, 1965, p. 35.

7 Scott Wilson, "Where Obama Failed on Forging Peace in the Middle East."

8 "Daily Press Briefing," Victoria Nuland, Spokesperson, Washington, DC, August 11, 2011, http://www.state.gov/r/pa/prs/dpb/2011/08/170420.htm

9 David A. Nichols, *Eisenhower 1956: The President's Year of Crisis: Suez and the Brink of War*, New York: Simon & Schuster, 2011, pp. 225–226.

10 Steven L. Spiegel, *The Other Arab-Israeli Conflict: Making America's Middle East Policy, from Truman to Reagan*, Chicago: University of Chicago Press, 1985, p. 77.

11 "George Mitchell, US Special Envoy to the Middle East," *Charlie Rose Show*, January 6, 2010, http://www.charlierose.com/download/transcript/10796

12 "Remarks by the President at the AIPAC Policy Conference 2011," White House, Office of the Press Secretary, May 22, 2011, http://www.whitehouse.gov/the-press-office/2011/05/22/remarks-president-aipac-policy-conference-2011

13 "Conclusions and Recommendations," The Commission to Examine the Status of Building in Judea and Samaria, unofficial translation http://unispal.un.org/UNISPAL.NSF/0/D9D07DCF58E-781C585257A3A005956A6

14 "Report on the Status of Construction in the Judea and Samaria Region," author's translation, June 21, 2012, http://www.pmo.gov.il/Documents/doch090712.pdf

15 Alistair Horne, *A Savage War of Peace: Algeria 1954–1962*, New York: New York Review of Books, 2011, p. 422.

16 Amy Goodman, "Make Obama Keep His Promises," *Seattle Post-Intelligencer*, January 21, 2009, http://www.seattlepi.com/local/opinion/article/Goodman-Make-Obama-keep-his-promises-1298087.php

17 Jamie Stiehm, "Oval Office Rug Gets History Wrong," *Washington Post*, September 4, 2010, http://www.washingtonpost.com/wp-dyn/content/article/2010/09/03/AR2010090305100.html

18 "Martin Luther King Jr. Visited SMU [Southern Methodist University] in 1966," Southern Methodist University, http://www.smu.edu/newsinfo/stories/mlk-speech-excerpts-1966.asp

Index